INCLUDES TWO VOLUMES

Starting, building, managing and protecting
YOUR NEW BUSINESS

BUSINESS *with a* PURPOSE

"In my over 30 years of experience in starting my own businesses, as well as counseling others in starting theirs, I would have relished having this book."
–Ron Blue, President, Kingdom Advisors
Chairman, Crown Financial Ministries Board of Directors

INCLUDES TWO VOLUMES

Starting, building, managing and protecting
YOUR NEW BUSINESS

BUSINESS *with a* PURPOSE

"In my over 30 years of experience in starting my own businesses, as well as counseling others in starting theirs, I would have relished having this book."
–Ron Blue, President, Kingdom Advisors
Chairman, Crown Financial Ministries Board of Directors

DARRELL GRIFFIN

Outskirts Press, Inc.
Denver, Colorado

Legal Notice

This book is sold with the understanding that the author and the publisher is not engaged in rendering legal, accounting or other professional services. Questions relevant to the specific tax, business, legal and/or accounting needs of the reader should be addressed to practicing members of those professions.

The information and suggestions contained herein have been developed from sources deemed reliable, but cannot be guaranteed as to how they apply to your specific application. Moreover, due to the fact that tax laws are never static but ever changing, the assistance of a competent professional skilled in taxation is recommended before implementation of any material contained herein.

The author and publisher specifically disclaims any liability, loss or risk, personal or otherwise, incurred as a consequence, directly or indirectly, of the use and application of any of the techniques of the contents of this book.

Comments from people who have read the advance manuscript of *Business with a Purpose*.

Ron Blue
President, Kingdom Advisors
Chairman, Crown Financial Ministries Board of Directors

"In my over 30 years of experience in starting my own businesses, as well as counseling others in starting theirs, I would have relished having this book. **Business with a Purpose** would have been a reference book, helping me to answer so many questions about where to go and what to do. This is an extremely useful, practical book for about every entrepreneur who desires to start a business that honors God. I recommend and endorse with much enthusiasm."

One of the most highly respected and widely published Christian writers today.

Dudley Rutherford
Senior Pastor
Shepherd of the Hills
Porter Ranch, CA

Business with a Purpose is, in essence, a business bible. And what I mean by that is that it is an extensive, detailed blueprint for starting, running, and owning a successful business based on biblical principles. It will help you avoid costly mistakes—your time and your resources—of having to go through the learning curve of building a business on your own. The reader will benefit exponentially from the wisdom that can be gleaned from this book!

Dudley Rutherford is the senior pastor of Shepherd of the Hills, a 10,000-member church in Porter Ranch, California , which has four daughter churches and five satellite campuses. He has been blessed with the ability to convey God's truth dynamically, passionately, and clearly. He is also the founder of CallOnJesus.com. Dudley 's published works are *Proverbs in a Haystack*, *Romancing Royalty*, and *Keeping a Smile on Your Faith*.

Rick Kasel
Pastor, Stewardship & Estate Planning
Shepherd Of the Hills
Porter Ranch, Ca

"I have had the privilege of seeing this book develop from concept to reality, having read it several times in the process. This book reflects a wealth of Darrell's experience in business and provides real hands on tools for the readers use, based upon that experience. *Business With A Purpose* uniquely addresses and connects the role of creativity in small business with the Creator as the resource, and our relationship as Christians with that Creator.

In a very practical way, Darrell invites us to call on that relationship in the actual formation of our business. In effect he provides a way for the Christian to not only dedicate their business to God, but to actually invite Him in as a full partner! I believe this book is truly inspired for such a time as this."

Ernest Tamayo, Jr.
Real Estate Investing, Property Management, and Development
Houston, Texas

"After reading this very comprehensive and principled book, I find myself quoting Darrell Griffin on a daily basis, as I conduct my business. Mr. Griffin's principles are based on good Christian values, and sound business practices. In addition, the book is packed with innovative strategies to help you succeed in business... and in life!"

Ernest Tamayo, Jr. has successful invested in residential multi-unit buildings over the last ten years in the Houston, Texas area. His successful businesses have allowed him to pursue his first love, metal sculpting on a full time basis.

M. Shawn Walden
Pastor
Shepherd of the Hills
Porter Ranch, California

"… I thought the chapter on small businesses was very inspiring statistically. It seemed to me that it would encourage someone who is wavering on whether to step out in faith and attempt to start their own business or maybe encourage those who already have to hang in there that have already started one…This work will be a regular resource that I refer people to who are wrestling with running or starting their own business. It would prove especially helpful to those who need wise counsel on evaluating where they are in their business plan. It would also prove helpful to those who might be tempted to shortcut the path to success by compromising their ethics or integrity."

Shepherd of the Hills is a Bible based non-denominational church. It has been blessed with tremendous growth over the last several years and has an average Sunday attendance of 10,000 worshippers.

Sue Jesse
Vice President of Operations and Co-founder
Smart Post Sound
Burbank, California

"I have to say I was really impressed when I read your book… while reading through the manuscript the word comprehensive continually came to mind. Six of us started a small business and thankfully, while we didn't have the advantage of having this book for guidance, we did fit much of the startup criteria you outlined…I would think anyone would be foolish not to read this cover to cover if they were considering start their own business. The thoroughness and attention to every detail of starting a successful business is astounding. The information is priceless. I found myself checking our procedures against your guidelines and taking note of where we could improve our company. The Biblical verses outlining Christian principals are what each of us should live by both in the business world and our everyday life."

Smart Post Sound is the oldest and youngest sound companies in the entertainment industry. Their previous incarnation as Echo Sound Services changed the way post production sound was delivered to the creative community. Home to the top sound designers and re-recording mixers in the business, Smart Post Sound has earned 13 Emmys, 32 Golden Reels, and more industry recognition for quality and service than any other sound company.

Richard and Debbie Barchard
Barchard Cleaning and Handyman
Stockton, California

""If you want to walk on water you have to get out of the boat," "You have to deploy your time, talent and treasure properly to reap the rewards" are a couple of thoughts expressed in "Business with a Purpose" that stand out in my mind. I wasn't really sure where our business was going. We started it to generate a little extra money and it just got out of hand. We basically have to get our business going in the right way. We will use your book to help us organize more. We didn't buy a business, we just started up with no money. *Business with a Purpose* can be helpful to any business, startup or established, f you use your time, talent and treasure with the right purpose in life.

Richard and Debbie started their business with no capital in 2008. It has grown incredibly fast to the point where they are now hiring employees. They originally started cleaning homes for real estate agents after tenants moved out. They have now expanded into small repairs and maintenance for individuals, realtors and property management companies.

Steve Tristan
Owner
JT Blinds
Parish member at Saint Ferdinand's Catholic Church, San Fernando, CA

"*Business with a Purpose* is an awesome detailed planning tool for people who want to start their own small business while simultaneously keeping their Christian values. Starting a business from scratch with no working capital is not easy. I looked for guidance everywhere. Talking to friends and family about it gave me mixed results, and research on the net usually meant costly membership fees. I found better results talking to my ex-employer, other small business owners, our parish priest, and many books including our bible. I had always wanted to have my own business and be in charge of my own destiny. It took months of research for me to come to a decision to start our new venture and years of further research to realize that our company is not in my hands but with God. I appreciate this book because if offers many years of Mr. Griffin's professional experience as an accountant and business person with the guidance of faith and scripture. If I had this book when I first started my business, it would have saved me a lot of money and many hours of research time."

JT Blinds is a Window Coverings & Screens manufacturer & contractor, supplying the multi-family housing, construction, interior design, & commercial industries.

JT Blinds
Sylmar, CA 91342

JT Blinds Company Mission Statement
To honor and serve God in everything we do.
Develop everlasting relationships with our customers, employees, associates, suppliers, and their families.
Provide quality products to the marketplace quickly and affordably while growing profitably.

Elizabeth Wozniak
Manager
Praises Bookstore, Shepherd of the Hills, California

…From what I have seen, it looks like this would be a valuable resource for those looking to start a Christian business…

Acknowledgments

Profound thanks to Kim, my loving wife, my best friend and the center of my universe. She has stood beside me through the bad times and the good times. She was always the one with the full-time job, while I pursued my dreams. Without her encouragement and support this book would not exist. I would also like to thank my children Rene, Darrell, Jr., Sommer, Christian, Alexis and Jordan for putting up with my long hours and late nights while working on this book.

I would like to thank Rick Kasel, a pastor at Shepherd of the Hills Church in Porter Ranch, California. He has been my mentor on this project from its inception.

I would also like to thank Babsi Arn, Sue Jesse, Carie McCarter J.R. Tamayo and Ann Norda. Each of them reviewed Business with a Purpose in its infancy, and provided valuable review notes and insight from their unique perspective.

Finally I would like to thank Bridgett Horstmann, my Author Representative at OutSkirt Press, Inc. who always kept the project on track.

Business with a Purpose

Business with a Purpose
Volume I – Starting and Operating
Your New Business

Introduction

Everyone, at one time or another, dreams of starting his or her own business. There is a certain romance surrounding the thought of "being the master of your own fate." Many people dream the entrepreneurial dream and never act upon it, choosing instead to continue working in the same job for thirty years and get the gold watch, the rocking chair, and a membership in AARP. Some people are thrown into starting a new business by personal circumstances or a changing economy. During 2009, Microsoft had its first-ever mass dismissal, laying off 5,000 workers; Sprint Nextel announced it will lay off 8,000 employees; Home Depot laid off 7,000 employees.

Dudley C. Rutherford, Senior Pastor at Shepherd of the Hills Church in Porter Ranch, California, recently gave a sermon entitled "Time to Dream." In his sermon, he gave four reasons we fail to dream: we become contented with what we have and where we are in life; we get tired; as we get older, we get settled in our existing life; and finally, we are afraid of change. These points were mentioned as reasons churches stop growing. The overriding cause is because of their members' inability to dream. I recognized them as the reasons many of us are hindered in our overall ability to dream.

As is the practice at Shepherd of the Hills, several of the sermon series have CD-video support materials prepared for the meetings of the small life groups (groups of approximately ten members designed to help keep them connected to the church). The video prepared for this particular sermon featured Tim Winters, the Shepherd of the Hills Executive Pastor. In the video, he talks about the benefits of dreams. Dreams give us direction (If you aim at nothing in particular, you will hit it every time), dreams increase our potential, dreams help us prioritize, dreams add value to our work, and dreams help us predict our future.

Throughout your reading of this book, please keep in mind one of my favorite passages in the Bible, distilled down to one simple sentence:

You can't walk on water unless you get out of the boat.

This distillation was taken from the New International Version of the Bible.

It is important for us, as Christian businessmen, to be *in* this world but not *of* this world. We can continue using a boat for an analogy of this principle. "A boat belongs in the water, but water does not belong in the boat."

^{25}During the fourth watch of the night, Jesus went out to them, walking on the lake. ^{26}When the disciples saw him walking on the lake, they were terrified. "It's a ghost," they said, and cried out in fear. ^{27}But Jesus immediately said to them: "Take courage! It is I. Don't be afraid." ^{28}"Lord, if it's you," Peter replied, "tell me to come to you on the water." ^{29}"Come," he said. Then Peter got down out of the boat, walked on the water and came toward Jesus. ^{30}But when he saw the wind, he was afraid and, beginning to sink, cried out, "Lord, save me!" ^{31}Immediately Jesus reached out his hand and caught him. "You of little faith," he said, "why did you doubt?" ^{32}And when they climbed into the boat, the wind died down. ^{33}Then those who were in the boat worshiped him, saying, "Truly you are the Son of God."
Matthew 14:25-33

I personally take two distinct messages from these verses:
Get out of your comfort zone if you want to accomplish great things.
Keep your faith in Jesus, and you will be able to walk on water during calm times or stormy times.
And talking about FAITH, here is another one of my favorite scriptures:
"Faith is being sure of what we hope for and certain of what we do not see."
Hebrews 11:1

People are often afraid to start their own business thinking that it is impossible to "go up against the big boys."
Apple Computer started out in a garage and grew to be a billion dollar business.

Steve Jobs and Steve Wozniak, along with Ronald G. Wayne, formed the Apple Computer Company on April Fools' Day, 1976. Six months after Apple began, Jobs and Wozniak were splitting a monthly salary of $250. Apple's first formal business plan set a goal for sales to grow to $500 million in ten years. As it turns out, the company passed that mark in half the time.

Steve Wozniak (26) and Steve Jobs (21) finished their work on a preassembled computer circuit board. The first prototype had taken about six months to design and 40 hours to build. It had no keyboard, case, sound, or graphics. They called it the Apple I. The Apple I debuted at the Homebrew Computer Club in Palo Alto, California. The Byte Shop computer store ordered 50 Apple I boards. Jobs sold his VW van and Wozniak sold his Hewlett-Packard programmable calculator, raising $1,350 to finance production.

For their fiscal year ending in 2007, Apple (in January of 2007, they dropped the word "Computer" from their name to reflect the fact that they are expanding outside of the computer market) reported more than $32 billion in sales. Not bad for a couple of garage hobbyists who thought they could make a little money with their product back in 1976: two men who were not afraid to dream.

The major principles of success of this book are:

- **Have the right partner in business – God.**
- **Failing to plan is planning to fail.**
- **Manage your God-given resources (Time, Talent, and Treasures) properly.**
- **Take a risk and get out of the boat—remember you have God on your side.**
- **There are things that big business will never do as well as small business.**
- **Creativity is the major competitive tool of the small and new business.**
- **Christians can think more creatively than non-Christians.**

This book is written blending my experiences gained in starting successful businesses, personal experiences of other successful entrepreneurs, and some MBA theory that has real-life application. This is then wrapped up in Godly principles of the proper management of the three "Ts" that God has loaned to us—Time, Talent, and Treasures.

"He" is used throughout this book. It is meant to reflect both male and female where appropriate.

Overview Of Small Business In America

The United States government defines a small business as a business employing fewer than 500 people. A lot of people never realize how important small businesses are to the U.S. economy. According to the Small Business Administration in a recent report called "Small Business by the Numbers," small business represents 99.7% of all employers. If this is not impressive, I don't know what is. Here are some equally relevant statistics from the booklet:

- Small businesses employs more than 50% of all employees.
- Small business represents more than 44.5% of all U.S. payrolls.
- Small business generates 60% to 80% of all new jobs.
- Small businesses produce 13 to 14 times more patents per employee than large patenting firms.
- Small businesses are employers of more than 39% of high technology employees such as engineers, scientists, and computer workers.
- Small businesses make up more than 97% of all registered exporters.
- There are approximately 22.9 million small businesses in America.

The bottom line is that small business is the foundation of the American economy.
The president's report on Small Business of 2003 stated that small business continues to be the primary method by which women, minorities, and immigrants enter the business world in the United States. According to this report, the number of African American

businesses increased over 26% in the last 5 years, and the number of Hispanic businesses rose over 30% for the same period. This tells us that the large corporate environments have not presented equal opportunities to these groups, and so a large number of these groups took matters into their own hands (the American way) and started their own businesses.

Finally, why are small businesses so important to the U.S. economy? Where do you think big businesses are birthed from? Of course, from small businesses. Did General Motors start as a big business? Of course not. Did Proctor and Gamble (two guys that had a fascination with being clean and making candles) start as a big business? No. P&G started as a small business in 1837. That year, the Proctor and Gamble Company began as a small, family-operated soap and candle making company. Early on, as electricity came into wide use, they had to rethink their company and move away from one of their primary products—the candle. Today, P&G markets almost 300 products to more than five billion consumers in 140 countries. Today, P&G has more than 98,000 employees generating more than $40 billion in annual revenues. Not bad for a little partnership started by two brothers-in-law.

"All companies with zero to 500 employees" is a pretty broad definition of "small business." Let's take a closer look at "small business" according to the U.S. Census Bureau.[1]

According to this U.S. Census report, nearly three-quarters of all U.S. business firms have no payroll. Most are self-employed persons operating unincorporated businesses and may or may not be the owner's principal source of income. Because non-employers account for only about 3% of business receipts, they are not included in most business statistics, including most reports from the Economic Census.

Here are some interesting statistics from the U.S. Census Bureau:

Firms with no employees	9.94%
1 to 4 employees	38.11%
5 to 9 employees	14.57%
10 to 19 employees	9.17%
20 to 99 employees	9.45%
100 to 499 employees	4.45%
500 or more employees	14.31%

These statistics tell us that almost 63% of small businesses in America have fewer than 10 employees.

---

1   U.S. Census Bureau, *Statistics about Business Size (including Small Business) from the U.S. Census Bureau*, 2002.

We often hear from various sources that only one in ten start-up businesses survive past the first year. New firms are believed to have high closure rates, and these closures are believed to be failures; but two U.S. Census Bureau data sources illustrate that these assumptions may not be justified. The Business Information Tracking Series (BITS) study showed that about half of new employer firms survive beyond four years, and the Characteristics of Business Owners (CBO) showed that about a third of closed businesses were successful at closure. These two studies encompassed about 5.5 million employer firms. The BITS Study showed that 66% of new employers survive two years or more, and 40% survive six years or more.

This same study uncovered some more traits that appear, at least in the report, to be important factors in successful businesses during the start-up period. The report showed that the factors that best explained the likelihood of survival were:

- Being an employer firm (a firm with employees).
- Having start-up capital greater than $50,000.
- Having a college degree.
- Starting a business for personal reasons.

It is believed that starting a business for personal reasons gives the owner increased motivation to keep a business going. So even if the business is barely afloat, better business opportunities are available, or job offers arise, the owner who has started a business for personal reasons probably gains satisfaction from the lifestyle and therefore does what it takes to keep the business going.

Three other factors—previously owning another business, having multiple owners, and being home-based at start-up—also seem to increase survivability. The first two factors indicate more resources, but the third, being home-based at start-up, would seem to signal fewer, not more resources. However, since businesses that are home-based also keep costs low, odds of survival are increased. The home-based business owner probably enjoys the work-from-home lifestyle, so he or she would be more likely to continue a struggling business. Being home-based at start-up was not a factor in the CBO study that looked at businesses that closed but were successful. The factor of being home-based was primarily a factor of success during start-up and not over the long term of the business.

On the negative side, relatively young owners who tended to be in service or retail trades, did not have start-up capital, and were located in urban or suburban areas were more likely to close their businesses. Young owners and individuals in urban and suburban areas may have better job opportunities. Owning a business comes at a higher opportunity cost for them, and they may therefore be more likely to close their businesses. The sum of these variables shows a tendency to have a venture that is small, easy to start, and easy to close.

Overall, the results of the CBO report tended to support the idea that having "significant start-up funds" and the motivation to continue in the business in the face of adversity increase the odds of survival of the business.

There is an interesting finding in the report concerning funding of the start-up business. Start-up companies with capital of either zero or $50,000 or more have higher rates of success than companies that were somewhere in between. One possible explanation for this is that the start-ups with no capital have lower initial expectations and perform labor-intensive activities, while start-ups with a small amount of capital may not have enough capital to achieve the minimum efficient scale for their chosen industry.

An article in *Inc.* magazine, "Charging Ahead," states "Americans are often said to be addicted to plastic, and that's especially true for entrepreneurs. About half of all small businesses finance their formation or expansion with credit cards, according to a survey by the National Small Business Association and Arthur Andersen. The same survey shows that only 6% were financed with an SBA loan, and just 2% received venture capital funding." I would never recommend financing your business with a credit card, since it's an expensive source of capital and credit card spending can quickly get away from you.

The retail-trade-related start-ups had the lowest level of success, while services had the highest level of success. The basic reason put forth by the CBO study was that retail start-ups are easier to copy and breed competition. Service firms often have a "secret sauce," a specialized skill contributed by the owner that is more difficult to duplicate.

The CBO study showed that about half of new businesses remained open for a reasonable time period of 3 years or more and further showed that about a third of all closed businesses closed while successful. **Contrary to popular belief, not all closures are failures**. Only 33% of new businesses closed under circumstances that owners considered unsuccessful.

The factors leading to business survival were similar to those outlined in a number of other studies. Size and resource indicators such as having employees, a good amount of starting capital, and an educated owner correlated with survival.

The bottom line is that potential entrepreneurs, particularly those planning small ventures, have less to fear than what is commonly believed.

Some Basic Christian Principles For Business

OVERVIEW ▬▬▬▬▬▬▬▬▬▬▬▬▬▬▬▬▬▬▬▬▬▬▬▬▬▬▬▬▬▬▬

There are some Christians who feel it is impossible to be a good businessman and a good Christian. There is ample text in the Bible that supports Christians going into business for themselves. You should always operate by the simple rule that "Christian values always take precedence over the 'bottom line.'" This should always help you keep things in check. There will always be some conflict between being a "success" in business and keeping your Christian values. But you, as a Christian, already face conflict making decisions in your everyday life. There is a great book entitled *Believers in Business* by Laura L. Nash, PhD that deals with resolving the tensions between Christian faith, business ethics, competition, and our definitions of success. Through extensive interviews, Dr. Nash has organized these recurring themes into seven basic tension points:

- The love of God and the pursuit of profits.
- Love and the competitive drive.
- People's needs and the profit obligations.
- Humility and the ego of success.
- Family and work.
- Charity and wealth.
- Faithful witness and in the secular city.

The first part of each "tension" describes an important Christian theme, while the second half describes some basic components of business enterprise.[2]   Dr. Nash's interviews were conducted with successful CEOs across the country. The bottom line is that there will always be some conflict between Christian principles and profit motives, but they can be minimized as long as you put God first. There is the popular phrase "What would Jesus do (WWJD)? By asking yourself this question whenever there is a potential conflict you will find it quickly dissolves. Some examples of putting God first using the WWJD? tool are:

- Fairness and truthfulness in your advertisements – WWJD?
- Closing your business on the Sabbath (Sunday) to allow your employees a Biblical day of rest – WWJD?.
- Reviewing a situation where you can charge a premium on your products that is short supply – WWJD?
- You have an opportunity to grind a supplier down to the point he is not making any profit because you are his biggest client – WWJD?

As we mentioned, there is ample support in the Bible encouraging believers to go into business for themselves. Here are just a few examples:

"Then Isaac sowed in that land, and received in the same year an hundredfold: and the Lord blessed him. And the man waxed great, and went forward, and grew until he became very great: (you can probably substitute "rich" for "great" in this verse). For he had possession of flocks, and possession of flocks, and possession of herds, and great store of servants: and the Philistines envied him."
Genesis 26:12-14

"Beloved, I wish above all things that thou mayest prosper and be in health, even as thy soul Prospereth."
3 John 1:2

"If ye be willing and obedient, ye shall eat the good of the land."
Isaiah 1:19

"So the Lord blessed the latter end of Job more than his beginning: for he had fourteen thousand sheep, and six thousand camels, and a thousand yoke of oxen, and a thousand donkeys."
Job 42:12

---

2   Laura L. Nash, PhD, *Believers in Business*, Atlanta: Thomas Nelson Publishers, 1994, pg. 37.

"Then Isaac sowed in that land, and received in the same year an hundredfold; and the Lord blessed him."
Genesis 26:12

"And thou shalt not glean thy vineyard, neither shalt thou gather every grape of thy vineyard; thou shalt leave them for the poor and stranger; I am the Lord your God."

(Get your just rewards for being a good businessman, but don't be a pig about it; remember those who do not have your resources.)
Leviticus 19:10

"And Abram was very rich in cattle, in silver, and in gold."

(It's not a sin to be rich, but it is a sin to be greedy.)
Genesis 13:2

"He becometh poor that dealeth with a slack hand: but the hand of the diligent maketh rich."

(God is telling us that we should work hard and use our resources wisely.)
Proverbs 10:4

Starting a business founded on Christian principles is really the only way to start a business. God gives us, or loans to us, Time, Talent, and Treasures. We are expected to manage these resources wisely and to the best of our abilities. The Bible is without question the greatest book of all time. It also is an incredible guide to doing business as shown above and throughout this book. It should be an active part of your business-book reference library alongside your accounting manual and marketing books (and of course this book). Below is a small sample of scriptures from the Bible that are useful in relationship to being in business. The "Book" is full of thousands of similar scriptures. I have selected these. You may want to select your own favorite scriptures.

DEALING WITH OTHERS IN BUSINESS

Treat your employees, your vendors, and your customers with respect, and never lose control of your temper. This is pretty straightforward and logical advice, but we tend to forget it all too often.

"Since an overseer is entrusted with God's work, he must be blameless—not overbearing, not quick-tempered, not given to drunkenness, not violent, not pursuing dishonest gain. Rather he must be hospitable, one who loves what is good, who is self-controlled, upright, holy and disciplined."
Titus 1:7

GOOD NAME

"A good name is more desirable than great riches."
Proverbs 22:1

"A good name is better than fine perfume."
Ecclesiastes 7:1

(Samuels's farewell speech) "Here I stand. Testify against me in the presence of the Lord and his anointed. Whose ox have I taken? Whose donkey have I taken? Whom have I cheated? Whom have I oppressed? From whose hand have I accepted a bribe to make me shut my eyes? If I have done any of these, I will make them right." "You have not cheated or oppressed us," they replied. "You have not taken anything from anyone's hand."
1 Samuel 12:3-4

HUMILITY

Okay, so all of a sudden, the business starts doing well, and the local Chamber of Commerce asks you to speak on the topic of "Building the Successful Business." Put on the brakes for a minute and remember who REALLY built the business. Be sure to give GOD the credit he deserves when you deliver your speech to the Chamber of Commerce.

We should be humble with the knowledge that God owns every thing and he has given us our Time, Talent, and Treasures.

"For this is what the high and lofty One says—he who lives forever, whose name is holy: I live in a high and holy place, but also with him who is contrite and lowly in spirit, to revive the spirit of the lowly and to revive the heart of the contrite."
Isaiah 57:15

"When pride comes, then comes disgrace, but with humility comes wisdom."
Proverbs 11:2

"Do nothing out of selfish ambition or vain conceit, but in humility consider others better than yourselves. [4] Each of you should look not only to your own interests, but also to the interests of others."
Philippians 2:3-4

INTEGRITY IN BUSINESS

There is no question that God expects nothing less than 100% honesty by Christians in business.

"Do not have two differing weights in your bag—one heavy, one light. [14] Do not have two differing measures in your house—one large, one small. [15] You must have accurate and honest weights and measures, so that you may live long in the land the LORD your God is giving you. [16] For the LORD your God detests anyone who does these things, anyone who deals dishonesty."
Deuteronomy 25:13-16

"The LORD abhors dishonest scales, but accurate weights are his delight."
Proverbs 11:1

PLANNING

You will often hear from some Christians "Why plan, it is all in Gods hands." Not the right attitude when it comes to managing what God gave you.

"The plans of the diligent lead to profit as surely as haste leads to poverty."
Proverbs 21:5

SEEK WISE COUNSEL

I have often heard the saying "A fool seeks his own counsel." It is always best to learn from others' mistakes and successes. It is much less expensive and much less painful.

The ancient King Rehoboam learned a valuable lesson in seeking wise counsel when he took the advice of friends over the elders.

The whole assembly of Israel went to Rehoboam and said to him, "Your father put a heavy yoke on us, but now lighten the harsh labor and the heavy yoke he put on us and we will serve you." Rehoboam answered, "Go away for three days and then come back to me." So the people went away. Then King Rehoboam consulted the elders who had served his father Solomon during his lifetime. "How would you advise me to answer these people?" he asked. They replied, "If today you will be a servant to these people and serve them and give them a favorable answer, they will always be your servants."

But Rehoboam rejected the advice the elders gave him and consulted the young men who had grown up with him and were serving him. His young friends said to tell the people, "I will make it even heavier. My father scourged you with whips; I will scourge you with scorpions."

Rehoboam had to escape in his chariot to Jerusalem.

1 Kings 12:1-20 (paraphrased)

RESPONSIBILITY ━━━━━━━━━━━━━━━━━━━━━━━━━━━━━━

The Time, Talent, and Treasures that God gave us should be managed as if our (eternal) life depends on it—because it does.

"Timothy, guard what has been entrusted to your care. Turn away from godless chatter and opposing ideas of what is falsely called knowledge, which some have professed and in so doing have wandered from the faith. Grace be with you."

1 Timothy 6:20

"We have different gifts, according to the grace given us. If a man's gift is prophesying, let him use it in proportion to his faith. If it is serving, let him serve; if it is teaching, let him teach; if it is encouraging, let him encourage; if it is contributing to the needs of others, let him give generously; if it is leadership, let him govern diligently; if it is showing mercy, let him do it cheerfully."

Romans 12:6-8

TAXES, PAYMENT THEREOF━━━━━━━━━━━━━━━━━━━━━━━

No one likes paying taxes, but it is logical that the services that we receive from our government (roads, police protection, fire protection, etc.) have to be paid for somehow. This does not mean that we should pay more taxes than we absolutely have to pay.

Then Jesus said to them, "Give to Caesar what is Caesar's and to God what is God's."

And they were amazed at him.

Mark 12:17

Then the Pharisees went out and laid plans to trap him in his words.[16] They sent their disciples to him along with the Herodians. "Teacher," they said, "we know you are a man of integrity and that you teach the way of God in accordance with the truth. You aren't swayed by men, because you pay no attention to who they are.[17] Tell us then, what is your opinion? Is it right to pay taxes to Caesar or not?" [18] But Jesus, knowing their evil intent, said, "You hypocrites, why are you trying to trap me? [19] Show me the coin used

for paying the tax." They brought him a denarius, [20] and he asked them, "Whose portrait is this? And whose inscription?" [21] "Caesar's," they replied. Then he said to them, "Give to Caesar what is Caesar's, and to God what is God's." [22] When they heard this, they were amazed. So they left him and went away.
Matthew 22:15-22

TITHING

I have included a number of passages about tithing, as I feel that this is one of the most important reasons for success for a Christian business—giving back to the Lord.

"Then Melchizedek king of Salem brought out bread and wine. He was priest of God Most High, [19] and he blessed Abram, saying, "Blessed be Abram by God Most High,

Creator of heaven and earth. And blessed be God Most High, who delivered your enemies into your hand." Then Abram gave him a tenth of everything.
Genesis 14:18-20

"I give to the Levites all the tithes in Israel as their inheritance in return for the work they do while serving at the Tent of Meeting."
Numbers 18:21

"Instead, I give to the Levites as their inheritance the tithes that the Israelites present as an offering to the LORD. That is why I said concerning them: 'They will have no inheritance among the Israelites.' "
Numbers 18:24

"In this way you also will present an offering to the LORD from all the tithes you receive from the Israelites. From these tithes you must give the LORD's portion to Aaron the priest."
Numbers 18:28

"Bring your burnt offerings and sacrifices, your tithes and special gifts, what you have vowed to give and your freewill offerings, and the firstborn of your herds and flocks."
Deuteronomy 12:6

"Then to the place the LORD your God will choose as a dwelling for his Name-there you are to bring everything I command you: your burnt offerings and sacrifices, your tithes and special gifts, and all the choice possessions you have vowed to the LORD."
Deuteronomy 12:11

"Be sure to set aside a tenth of all that your fields produce each year."
Deuteronomy 14:22

"At the end of every three years, bring all the tithes of that year's produce and store it in your towns."
Deuteronomy 14:28

"When you have entered the land the LORD your God is giving you as an inheritance and have taken possession of it and settled in it."
Deuteronomy 26:1

"Then they faithfully brought in the contributions, tithes and dedicated gifts. Conaniah, a Levite, was in charge of these things, and his brother Shimei was next in rank."
2 Chronicles 31:12

"Moreover, we will bring to the storerooms of the house of our God, to the priests, the first of our ground meal, of our grain offerings, of the fruit of all our trees and of our new wine and oil. And we will bring a tithe of our crops to the Levites, for it is the Levites who collect the tithes in all the towns where we work."
Nehemiah 10:37

"A priest descended from Aaron is to accompany the Levites when they receive the tithes, and the Levites are to bring a tenth of the tithes up to the house of our God, to the storerooms of the treasury."
Nehemiah 10:38

"At that time men were appointed to be in charge of the storerooms for the contributions, first fruits and tithes. From the fields around the towns they were to bring into the storerooms the portions required by the Law for the priests and the Levites, for Judah was pleased with the ministering priests and Levites."
Nehemiah 12:44

"[A]nd he had provided him with a large room formerly used to store the grain offerings and incense and temple articles, and also the tithes of grain, new wine and oil prescribed for the Levites, singers and gatekeepers, as well as the contributions for the priests."
Nehemiah 13:5

"All Judah brought the tithes of grain, new wine and oil into the storerooms."
Nehemiah 13:12

"Go to Bethel and sin; go to Gilgal and sin yet more. Bring your sacrifices every morning, your tithes every three years."
Amos 4:4

"Will a man rob God? Yet you rob me. But you ask, 'How do we rob you?' In tithes and offerings."
Malachi 3:8

OBEDIENCE

This principle is not all that hard to understand. He is the master and we are his servants.

"But seek first his kingdom and his righteousness, and all these things will be given to you as well."
Matthew 6:33

FOLLOWING GOD'S WORD

It is great to have a big business reference library. I do, but the most referred-to book in your library should be your Bible. If not, go back to square one and start over.

"Do not let this Book of the Law depart from your mouth; meditate on it day and night, so that you may be careful to do everything written in it. Then you will be prosperous and successful."
Joshua 1:8

CAUSE AND EFFECT

Now this is very easy to understand. You reap what you sow. Be mean and nasty in business, and guess what you will get back in return. Cheat your customers, and guess what you will get back in return. On the other hand, be ethical, honest, and fair, always look for the win-win situation, and you will be amazed by the positive results.

"A man reaps what he sows."
Galatians 6:7

"Whoever sows sparingly will also reap sparingly.
Whoever sows generously will also reap generously."
II Corinthians 9:6

GOD'S LAWS OF MULTIPLICATION

You cannot "out-give" God. Give to God what you are supposed to, and it will be multiplied back to you. This is one of those laws that cannot be refuted. There are a number of such laws, such as "Don't spit in the wind" and "If you jump off a building, you will fall." "You cannot out-give God" is one of those laws that are irrefutable. You can plant one third of a bushel of corn, and it will yield 30 bushels of corn. This is part of God's law of multiplication.

"Give and it will be given to you. A good measure, pressed down, shaken together and running over, will be poured into your lap. For with the measure you use, it will be measured to you."
Luke 6:38

"Bring the whole tithe into the storehouse, that there may be food in my house. Test me in this," says the Lord Almighty, "and see if I will not throw open the floodgates of heaven and pour out so much blessing that you will not have room enough for it."
Malachi 3:10

STEWARDSHIP ━━━━━━━━━━━━━━━━━━━━━━━━━━━━━

God has allowed you to manage some of his resources while you are here on this earth. According to Dictionary.com, the definition of a steward is "One who manages another's property, finances, or other affairs." There are scores of references in the Bible about who owns the resources that we have at our disposal here on planet earth. Here are a few references:

"In the beginning God created the heaven and the earth."
Genesis 1:1

"The earth is the Lord's, and the fullness thereof; the world, and they that dwell therein."
Psalm 24:1

"The earth is the Lord's, and everything in it, the world, and all who live in it; for every animal of the forest is mine, and the cattle on a thousand hills. The silver is mine and the gold is mine, declares the Lord Almighty."
Matthew 25:14-30

"But thou shalt remember the Lord God: for it is he that giveth thee power to get wealth, that he may establish his covenant which he swore unto thy fathers, as it is this day."
Deuteronomy 8:18

Some Relevant Thoughts From Great Minds

This author is a 100% dyed-in-the-wool Christian, but here is a news flash— "CHRISTIANS DO NOT HAVE A MONOPOLY ON WISDOM AND INTELLIGENCE IN THE BUSINESS WORLD." If I find a good idea about business, I don't care if the originator is a Christian or not, I will use his idea and learn from his experiences as long as his ideas do not run contrary to God's principles. All goodness and good come from Christ regardless of their earthly source. So on that note, here are some gems of wisdom from assorted great minds of the world, be they Christians, questionable Christians, or outright pagans. I separate these from the wisdom of the Bible above because they are from man, and I did not feel it appropriate to mingle them with the wisdom of God.

DEALING WITH OTHERS IN BUSINESS (partners, employees, government, competitors)

"Anger makes dull men witty, but it keeps them poor."
Francis Bacon

"A superior man is modest in his speech but exceeds in his actions."
Confucius

"The superior man understands what is right; the inferior man understands what will sell."
Confucius

"Anger is never without an argument, but seldom with a good one."
Indira Gandhi

"You cannot shake hands with a clenched fist."
Indira Gandhi

"He is happy whom circumstances suit his temper; but he is more excellent who suits his temper to any circumstances."
David Hume

"Always recognize that human individuals are ends, and do not use them as means to your end."
Immanuel Kant

"Once you label me, you negate me."
Soren Kierkegaard

"I have always thought the actions of men the best interpreters of their thoughts."
John Locke

"Go on, get out. Last words are for fools who haven't said enough."
Karl Marx

"The best weapon against an enemy is another enemy."
Friedrich Nietzsche

"Those that are most slow in making a promise are the most faithful in the performance of it."
Jean Jacques Rousseau

"Only the guy who isn't rowing has time to rock the boat."
Jean-Paul Sartre

"Treat people as if they were what they ought to be and you help them to become what they are capable of being."
Johann Wolfgang von Goethe

"I praise loudly; I blame softly."
Queen Catherine II

"Great people are those who make others feel that they, too, can become great."
Mark Twain

HUMILITY

"Money is like manure, not good except it be spread."
Francis Bacon

"The good man is the man who, no matter how morally unworthy he has been, is moving to become better."
John Dewey

"Nothing is enough for the man to whom enough is too little."
Epicurus
"The art of being wise is the art of knowing what to overlook."
William James

RESEARCH

"Observe your enemies, for they first find out your faults."
Antisthenes
"Some books are to be tasted, others to be swallowed, and some few to be chewed and digested."
Francis Bacon
"Who questions much, shall learn much, and retain much."
Francis Bacon
"It is of great use to the sailor to know the length of his line, though he cannot with it fathom all the depths of the ocean."
John Locke

SEEK WISE COUNSEL

"To see and listen to the wicked is already the beginning of wickedness."
Confucius
"You cannot open a book without learning something."
Confucius
"No man's knowledge here can go beyond his experience."
John Locke
"To prejudge other men's notions before we have looked into them is not to show their darkness but to put out our own eyes."
John Locke

SIZE

"A great city is not to be confounded with a populous one."
Aristotle
"I would rather be first in a little Iberian village than second in Rome."
Epicurus

"The least movement is of importance to all nature. The entire ocean is affected by a pebble."
Blaise Pascal

P.M.A. (POSITIVE MENTAL ATTITUDE) ━━━━━━━━━━━━━━━

"The sun is new each day."
Heraclitus

"That man is a success who has lived well, laughed often, and loved much."
Robert Louis Stevenson

"Life is a mirror; if you frown at it, it frowns back: if you smile, it returns the greeting."
William Makepeace Thackeray

PLANNING ━━━━━━━━━━━━━━━━━━━━━━━━━━━━━

"Do what you have always done and you will get what you have always got."
Author unknown

"Well begun is half done."
Aristotle

"And remember, no matter where you go, there you are."
Confucius

"It does not matter how slowly you go, so long as you do not stop."
Confucius

"Life is really simple, but we insist on making it complicated."
Confucius

"When it is obvious that the goals can not be reached, don't adjust the goals, adjust the action steps."
Confucius

"Arriving at one goal is the starting point to another."
John Dewey

"Have a bias toward action—let's see something happen now. You can break that big plan into small steps and take the first step right away."
Indira Gandhi

"Change alone is unchanging."
Heraclitus
"If you do not expect the unexpected, you will not find it, for it is not to be reached by search or trail."
Heraclitus
"No man ever steps in the same river twice, for it's not the same river and he's not the same man."
Heraclitus
"It seems essential, in relationships and all tasks, that we concentrate only on what is most significant and important."
Soren Kierkegaard
"Patience is necessary, and one cannot reap immediately where one has sown"
Soren Kierkegaard
"In the long run, we only hit what we aim at."
Henry David Thoreau
"We cannot do everything at once, but we can do something at once."
Calvin Coolidge

KNOW YOUR CUSTOMER

"Different men seek after happiness in different ways and by different means, and so make for themselves different modes of life and forms of government."
Aristotle
"Man is by nature a political animal."
Aristotle

ENTREPRENEURIAL SPIRIT

"Hope is a waking dream."
Aristotle
"Nature does nothing uselessly."
Aristotle
"There is no great genius without a mixture of madness."
Aristotle

"You will never do anything in this world without courage. It is the greatest quality of the mind next to honor."
Aristotle

"A man must make his opportunity, as oft as find it."
Francis Bacon

"In order for the light to shine so brightly, the darkness must be present."
Francis Bacon

"Choose a job you love, and you will never have to work a day in your life."
Confucius

"Our greatest glory is not in never falling, but in rising every time we fall."
Confucius

"Failure is instructive. The person who really thinks learns quite as much from his failures as from his successes."
John Dewey

"To me, faith is not worrying."
John Dewey

"Skillful pilots gain their reputation from storms and tempests."
Epicurus

"The greater the difficulty, the more the glory in surmounting it."
Epicurus

"Big results require big ambitions."
Heraclitus

"To dare is to lose one's footing momentarily. Not to dare is to lose oneself."
Soren Kierkegaard

"That which does not kill us makes us stronger."
Friedrich Nietzche

"The struggle alone pleases us, not the victory."
Blaise Pascal

"A lost battle is a battle one thinks one has lost."
Jean-Paul Sartre

"Courage is the mastery of fear—not absence of it."
Mark Twain

RESOURCEFULNESS

"If one way is better than another, that, you may be sure, is nature's way."
Aristotle

CREATIVITY (INVENTIVENESS) ━━━━━━━━━━━━━━━

"It is not once nor twice but times without number that the same ideas make their appearances in the world."
Aristotle

"Acorns were good until bread was found."
Francis Bacon

"As the births of living creatures are at first ill-shapen, so are all innovations, which are the births of time."
Francis Bacon

"Cure the disease and kill the patient."
Francis Bacon

"He that will not apply new remedies must expect new evils, for time is the greatest innovator."
Francis Bacon

"Write down the thoughts of the moment. Those that come unsought for are commonly the most valuable."
Francis Bacon

"No man was ever great by imitation."
Samuel Johnson

"They are ill discoverers that think there is no land, when they can see nothing but sea."
Francis Bacon

Do You Really Want To Be An Entrepreneur?

REASONS FOR STARTING A BUSINESS ━━━━━━━━━━━━━

There are a number of different reasons that people have for starting a business. I started a business because I was a lousy employee. Whatever your reasons, make absolutely sure that your decision is also based on your having a solid relationship with God. Make sure you have spent adequate time on your knees seeking God's counsel. I did not like being an employee for many of the reasons listed below. Here are some of the reasons I most often hear from people eager to start their own business:

FREEDOM FROM THE 9 TO 5 DAILY WORK ROUTINE

This is a double-edged sword. The 9 to 5 routine is more often than not traded in for a 7 to 7 routine. When this author first started his business, he used to joke with his wife that he was only working half a day each day—literally.

FLEXIBILITY

Closely related to the freedom in #1 above is the idea of flexibility. Say you want to go watch your ten-year-old daughter's midday Tae Kwon Do class. Can you imagine asking your current boss for the time off to do this? But although there is more flexibility being self-employed, the work still has to get done. So when you drop you daughter off at home, you might find yourself at the office until midnight getting caught up.

THE "THRILL OF THE KILL"

The excitement of taking risks. There are those people who enjoy the thrill of competition, winning, completing something. This can be extremely exciting and can also be ulcer generating. When you work for someone else, you leave work, you go home and have fun or do whatever you want. Most of the responsibilities are left with your employer. When you have started your business, the risks that you have taken during the day may follow you home. Your employees will be able to shut off the day's business activity as you used to do, but your daily risks taken may find their way into your mind long after you have closed and locked the front door to the office. Here is a personal example:

At Easy Brain Labs, Inc., we were considering offers from Hasbro and Mattel for a product that we had developed. The Mattel deal was substantially better than the Hasbro deal. We had started dealing with Mattel months before Hasbro came into the picture, but Mattel still hadn't closed the deal and seemed to be stalling indefinitely. Hasbro went from original discussions to final contract offer within a couple of months. Our dilemma: should we take the less attractive Hasbro deal or hold out for the Mattel deal? If we waited on Mattel, we risked losing the Hasbro deal in the process. Needless to say, the thought process for this situation did not shut off when I locked the office door each evening. My daily prayer for this situation went something like this:

A. God, give me the wisdom to make the right decision.
B. God, let me be able to shut off my business thoughts so that I don't short-change my family.
C. Your will be done.
D. Thank you for allowing me to be in the position of having to make this decision.
E. Thank you for your love, thank you for the family you have given to me, thank you for the , Time, Talents, Treasures you have given to me.

CREATIVITY

You feel that you can do "so much more" than you are currently able to do in your current job. You have developed a cool new product or service, and you think it can be a major moneymaker. You want to see a direct relationship between your creativeness and the potential rewards.

BEING YOUR OWN BOSS

Controlling your own present and future. You will experience a more direct relationship between what you do and what you earn when you run your own business. You decide what paper to use, what pencils to use, the color of the paint on the office walls. All of this seems great, but realize that along with the creative things that you like to do at work, you will also have to do all of the boring but essential administrative work. Easy Brain Labs, Inc., my toy design company, is a fun business, but it generates a lot of administrative work that has to be done on a daily basis. For example, there are tasks such as billing customers, reconciling bank accounts, reviewing contracts, paying bills, ordering supplies, discussing insurance requirements, reviewing financial statements with my accountant, and the list goes on.

IMPROVING YOUR STANDARD OF LIVING

Sometimes the thought of the next "cost of living" increase of 2% serves as a de-motivator rather than a motivator. It is difficult to get rich in a normal 9 to 5 job. Richness comes in a number of different ways. I find richness in spending more time with my family, making a difference in the world, and, of course, in earning a greater income.

BOREDOM WITH YOUR PRESENT JOB

Sometimes it becomes harder to get up in the morning and get ready to go to the same routine job you have had for over 10 years. Same job, same daily grind, different day. Many people have started their own companies and earned less pay but have been much happier being the captains of their own ship.

MAKING MONEY WHILE YOU SLEEP

This is an interesting phenomenon. Unless you are in retail where you have to be there every minute the door is open, your company can make money while you sleep. Easy Brain Labs, Inc. is a company started by the author and two partners. Easy Brain Labs develops toys and partners with major toy companies such as Mattel and Hasbro. Their toy designs are sold around the world, and the royalties are generated around the clock. It's kind of a nice thought that when you lay your head down on your pillow at night, the money machine is still cranking out royalties to you.

YOU HAVE BEEN LAID OFF OR FIRED

With today's uncertain economic climate, you may be forced into starting your own business to support your family.

CHARACTERISTICS OF AN ENTREPRENEUR ━━━━━━

There are a lot more people who desire to go into business than have what it takes to be a success in business. After you have determined that you really would like to go into business for yourself, you then need to take a serious look at your qualifications. Do you have what it takes?

Take the Entrepreneurial Checklist test. Answer each question Yes or No. Divide your number of Yes answers by 20 to assess your percentage. Are you an entrepreneur?

Certain skills and experience are critical to the success of a business. Since it is unlikely that you possess all the skills and experience necessary, you'll need to hire personnel to supply those you lack. There are some basic and special skills you will need for your particular business.

		Yes/No
1.	Do you like to make your own decisions?	y
2.	Do you enjoy competition?	y
3.	Do you have will power and self-discipline?	y
4.	Do you like people and get along well with them?	y
5.	Do you have good health?	
6.	Are you a good leader?	y
7.	Do you get things done on time?	y
8.	Can you live without taking money from the business for the first year?	y
9.	Do you adapt well to change?	y
10.	Are you confident?	y
11.	Are you aware that running your own business may require 12–16 hours a day, 6–7 days per week?	y
12.	Do you stick with a project until it is completed?	y
13.	Do you have the physical stamina to handle the workload and schedule?	y

14.	Do you have the emotional strength to withstand strain?	X
15.	Are you prepared to lose your savings?	
16.	Is your family prepared to lower their standard of living until your business is firmly established?	
17.	Do you have work experience in the type of business you are considering?	
18.	Do you have any business training?	
19.	Can you set limits?	
20.	Can you juggle multiple tasks/obligations well?	
Total		

This checklist was developed by the Clatsop County, Oregon Biz Center, a nonprofit business consulting center. The Biz Center is physically located in Seaside, Oregon but serves all of Clatsop County and western Columbia County and responds to online inquiries. The checklist and other business reference aids can be obtained at the following Web address:

http://www.clatsopcc.edu/bizcenter/Resources/Entreprenchecklist.htm

The above checklist is a good way to help you be more objective about your qualifications, but it is only an aid, not an absolute answer. It is pretty difficult to determine the level of your internal desire to start a business with a checklist.

Let's say that you got a decent score on the above checklist of 70% or more. Here are three important questions that you should ask yourself that are more important than any question on the checklist:

- Do you have an unshakable inner sense that God has called you to start a business?
- Do you feel that you can be the best servant for the Lord by starting a business?
- Will your new business venture get in the way of your walk with God?

<u>Do being a Christian and being successful in business go hand-in-hand?</u>

Many in the Christian Business world call this the theory of "prosperity gospel." In the book written by Dr. Laura L. Nash, PhD entitled *Believers in Business*, she quotes

Elmer Johnson, former executive vice president of General Motors, from comments he made to a group of evangelical CEOs:

> I am rather repelled, as I am sure you are, by the sight of pious, so-called Christian business leaders who like to crow about the vital connection between their faith or virtue and their business success. I am not so sure that there is much of a connection. If anything, the distribution of sainthood may be inversely related to the distribution of wealth and income. A faith that is viewed as utilitarian is not worth bothering about. Second, I have seen too many effective business leaders who share our human and social values, but who do not share our Christian faith, for me to think that you and I have any monopoly on wisdom just because we are Christians.[3]

Being a Christian will not guarantee success in business, no more than going to church makes you a Christian, but you can't have a better partner than God. As Christians, we normally have a priority list that we live by. Normally, we put God first, then family, then our jobs. One of the challenges that Christian businessmen have is to always be on guard that our priorities stay in the correct order. It is so easy, once the business starts moving forward, to let our newly formed companies start cutting into our other priorities.

Say that you have started a new business, and in addition to selling your product during the week, you find that your accounting is not up-to-date enough to allow you and your employees to make proper decisions for next week's selling efforts. Your wife wakes up on Sunday morning, reaches over to your side of the bed and you are not there. She goes downstairs and you are at the kitchen table pouring over your accounting records. She tells you that it is time to starting getting ready for church. You say that you can't go because you have to get the accounting up-to-date. This is the third week in a row that you have done this. Not a good situation.

Being a good businessman will never make you a good Christian, and being a good Christian will never make you a good businessman.

Jesus Christ was very specific when He said, "No servant can serve two masters. Either he will hate the one, and love the other, or he will be devoted to the one and despise the other. You cannot serve God and money." (Luke 16:13)

---

3 Laura L. Nash, PhD, *Believers in Business,* Atlanta: Thomas Nelson Publishers, 1994, pg. 62.

PROS AND CONS OF STARTING A BUSINESS ━━━━━━━━

There are a number of good reasons to start a business, and many equally good reasons to not start a business. The following checklist was taken from the Business Owner's Toolkit at http://www.toolkit.com.[4]

Pros:

- You have the chance to make a lot more money than you can make working for someone else.
- You'll be your own boss and make the decisions that are crucial to your business's success or failure.
- You may be the boss of other people.
- You'll have job security—no one can fire you.
- You'll have the chance to put your ideas into practice.
- You may participate in every aspect of running a business.
- You'll learn more about every aspect of a business and gain experience in a variety of disciplines.
- You'll have the chance to work directly with your customers.
- You'll be able to benefit the local economy, such as by hiring other people to work for you.
- You'll have the personal satisfaction of creating and running a successful business.
- You'll be able to work in a field or area that you really enjoy.
- You'll have the chance to build real retirement value (for example, by selling the business when you retire).
- You'll have the chance to put down roots in a community and to provide a sense of belonging and stability for your family.

Cons:

- You may have to take a large financial risk.
- You will probably have to work long hours and may have fewer opportunities to take vacations.
- You may end up spending a lot of your time attending to the details of running a business and less time doing the things you really enjoy.

---

4   *Pros and Cons of Owning a Business* http://www.toolkit.com/small_business_guide/sbg.aspx?nid=P01_0150, 2010.

- You may find that your income is not steady and that there are times when you don't have much income at all.
- You may have to undertake tasks you find unpleasant, such as firing someone or refusing to hire a friend or relative.
- You may have to learn many new disciplines, such as filing and bookkeeping, inventory control, production planning, advertising and promotion, market research, and general management.

Special pros and cons of the home-based business:

- Your start-up costs will be lower.
- Your operating costs will be lower than they would be if you were renting space and paying utilities.
- Your commute will be shorter.
- If your location is unimportant to your business, you can theoretically live anywhere and still operate your business.
- You may be more flexible in your schedule if your business can be conducted at your convenience or outside "normal" weekday business hours.
- On the other hand, you're much more vulnerable to interruptions from family members, neighbors, and door-to-door salespeople.
- You may have trouble attracting qualified employees.
- You may be less accessible to suppliers.
- You may have an image problem, although with the growing popularity of home businesses, that's less common.
- You may run out of space at home if your business grows.

Do I Buy A Business, Buy A Franchise Or Start My Own?

The three primary ways to get into business are to start your own business, buy an existing business, or buy a franchise. There are pros and cons to each approach. If you have $500 burning a hole in your pocket and you want to start a business, you probably will not think too long or hard about buying an existing business or buying a franchise. There is a certain sense of satisfaction about "bootstrapping" a business from the ground up. Many of you reading this book will not have the cash to take the franchise route or the "buying a business" route. We will spend a little time discussing the options of buying and existing business or buying a franchise. The rest of this book is dedicated to the individual that decides to start his own business although a lot of the information in "Business with a Purpose can be applied to purchasing a going business or franchise.

Each year, thousands of people make the decision to go into business for themselves. Because of the risk and work involved in starting a new business, many new entrepreneurs may choose to buy an existing business through a business broker or may choose franchising as an alternative to starting a new business from scratch.

BUY AN EXISTING BUSINESS

A way to get into a business fast is to buy an existing business. Be sure to read the section below entitled "Forms, Contracts, and Agreements for a Business Purchase," as some of the forms should be completed at the start of your business search. Glenn Cooper, CEO of Maine Business Brokers' Network, lists a number of reasons in one of his recent newsletters:[5]

5   Glenn Cooper, CBA, BVAL, CBI, 7 Reasons to Buy a Going Business, Business Buying and Selling, the monthly newsletter of Maine Business Brokers' Network, Glen@MainBusinessBrokers.com, 2010.

- You get an established customer base.

  Customers and/or clients have loyalties to locations and businesses that remain even after the owner sells the business. Customer acquisition through advertising is expensive.

- You get experienced employees.

  Experienced, skilled, and predictable employees are a valued asset of a going concern. They're not on the balance sheet, and you, as the buyer, do not pay for them directly. They often know the business operations quite well, and they can be reenergized by new ownership.

- You get a recognized market position.

  A going business has a market position measured by its sales level and profitability.

- Your business operating systems are in place.

  Also minimizing the chances for failure are the business's established systems. Sales and marketing, accounting, inventory tracking, employee payroll, and production systems are all in place.

- You often get the best combination of seller, bank, or vendor financing.

  Because of the first four advantages—customers, employees, market position, and established systems—more-favorable financing terms are available to the buyer of an established business. Seller, bank, and even vendor financing is often readily available.

- You have immediate cash flow.

  A buyer of a going concern often has immediate cash flow. In fact, that's what the financing partners (the seller, the banker, and the vendors) want to see.

- You have a reduced risk of business failure.

  Existing businesses, on the other hand, are much less likely to fail than start-ups. The risk is lower because the customers, employees, and the market position are known, the financing is more favorable, and the cash flow is immediate.

Let's assume that you have the cash flow (including funds supplied by your lenders and/or investors), and you have made the decision to buy an existing business. You now have to find a business to buy, evaluate it, determine the proper selling price, and negotiate a deal.

FINDING A BUSINESS TO BUY

There are a number of ways to find a business to buy. Before you start the process of finding a business, you should have your acquisition team in place—your accountant and your attorney. I would not recommend buying a business without the services of your accountant and your attorney. You first need to determine what type of business you want to buy. The business that you buy will be part of your life for a long time, so make sure that it is the right business. You should not just buy a business because it makes money; make sure it is an endeavor that you can enjoy. Part of this process should include research into the industry in which you are contemplating buying a business. You will want to perform a PEST (political, economic, social, and technology) analysis for the type of business you are contemplating. See the CREATIVE THINKING IN BUSINESS chapter of this book for a discussion of PEST analysis.

Although the business will be a functioning entity when you purchase it, your chance of success is greater if you have some prior experience in that particular industry. It would be wise to take some basic business classes to familiarize yourself with fundamental accounting, marketing, and business management.

So you have chosen the type of business you'd like to buy. Where do you find acquisition candidates? I happen to be a fan of business brokers, but here are some other avenues you could pursue:

– Industry associations

   Almost all businesses have associations. Most phone books have sections for associations. Your public library has the Encyclopedia of Associations. Call and ask the particular associations whom to talk to about buying a business in their industry.

– People at church

Church is an integral part of life, and there are people at church who may not directly know of a business for sale, but they may know people whom you can call. My church has an average attendance on Sunday of over 6,000 people. These people represent a broad cross section of the community. Our church also has smaller "life groups," where people get together outside of church to stay connected. Most of the life group members are involved in other areas of the church and other life groups. If you have a similar setup at church, let your life group know that you are looking for a particular type of business to purchase. Don't forget the church bulletin board.

– Product suppliers

If you are interested in buying a small paint store, call the various suppliers of paint. Talk to some painters. Product suppliers are always interested in keeping their retail outlets open and will tell you if they know if any businesses for sale.

– Cold call current owners

If you are driving down the street and see a small business that fits the profile of the business that you are interested in buying, talk to the owner. If his business is not for sale, ask him if he knows of any competitors that are thinking about selling. He probably will not give you the name of a close competitor, but he might know someone outside of his competitive area. The one big advantage of finding a business this way is that you may be the only person who knows the business is for sale. On the other hand, the business has probably not been prepared for sale, and you have a better than even chance of connecting with an unreasonable seller.

– Magazines

There are some really useful magazines that are a good source of business acquisition opportunities. Probably the best magazine out there is *Entrepreneur Magazine*. Its name says it all.

– Newspaper classified ads

The newspapers in the United States have always been a good source for commerce. I happen to get the *Los Angeles Times* delivered to my house. It has a good list of businesses for sale. There will also be a lot of garbage in this section of the newspaper. You will have to sift through the clutter of multilevel marketing schemes and the useless "work-from-home" schemes. These often sound way too good to be true, and they almost always are too good to be true. Don't waste your time with these "opportunities."

– Internet search

The Internet is a "shotgun" approach to conducting your search for a business unless you know where to go. Unfortunately, there is more garbage on the Internet than in your local newspapers. The real challenge is filtering through the garbage. A good place to start is www.bizbuysell.com. It has some really useful tools to get you started in the right direction.

– Local chamber of commerce

Your local chamber of commerce should have its finger on the business pulse of your community and know of businesses that may be for sale. They typically will not have a database of businesses for sale, as selling businesses is not part of their core mission statement or core competencies.

– Your attorney and accountant

Your accountant or attorney may be able to help you find a good business for sale. If he has a client that is thinking about selling his business, you may find out about it before its availability is made public. The one problem you will have is determining whom they will represent in negotiating the buy-sell transaction: you or the seller?

– Your insurance broker

Your insurance broker can be a good source for prospective business acquisitions. Insurance brokers build their businesses based on their ability to network in the business community. They will typically know of the health and retirement prospects of various clients who are business owners.

— Your banker

Banking has become somewhat of an impersonal business, unlike in the old days when your banker knew you by name. But all businesses still have checking accounts at their local bank. It is worth a call to your banker to ask him if he knows of any businesses that may be for sale in your area of interest.

— Place ads in trade journals and other business publications.

You will probably get overwhelmed with responses when you do this. The problem is that most of them will be useless responses from people trying to sell you useless things. You should make sure that you put a blind ad in the publication so that you have anonymity in your search.

— Business broker

A business broker is in the business of buying and selling businesses. Although this is a valuable way of finding and buying a business, brokers account for only 10% of all businesses sold. They typically work off of a commission from the seller, so they will normally try to get the highest price possible. They will obviously not be representing your best interest as the buyer. According to Glen Cooper, CEO of Maine Business Brokers' Network, the average business broker will have about 20 listings that will meet your specifications. Cooper further states that there are probably about 200 to 300 businesses for sale per million people in any given area. This means that you will normally have to approach at least a dozen brokers to get a complete picture of the opportunities in your area. Business brokers do not have a multiple listing service as do real estate brokers.

Ask the business broker to introduce you to prospective business owners, and then have these business owners share their confidential information with you. In order to do this, you must give the broker information that shows the seller that you are a legitimate buyer. This normally includes your tax returns, resume, and financial statements.

Since business brokers are in the business of selling businesses, they know what information needs to be prepared and how to present it to potential buyers. This can help make your review process go a lot quicker and smoother. But keep in mind, as previously stated, they represent the buyer, not you. This means that you absolutely need to have your accountant and attorney involved early in the process.

You will probably look at dozens of businesses before you start the process of requesting documents for your review. So that you do not waste anyone's time, you should have some general guidelines on what you want:
- The amount of cash that you plan to invest
- The amount of debt you are willing to assume
- The total price you are willing to pay
- The type of business you want to buy
- The location where you want to have your business

Once you have your candidate business, you then need to evaluate it.

EVALUATE YOUR ACQUISITION CANDIDATE

The process of evaluating the business you are considering buying is called a "due diligence review of your prospective acquisition candidate. This is normally accomplished using a due diligence checklist. Since this review is time-consuming, you will only do it after you have selected your final candidate business for acquisition. As stated above, when you buy an existing business, you are buying certain advantages over starting a business from scratch. You want to make sure that the "advantages" you are buying really exist and at their perceived value:

- You get an established customer base.
- You get experienced employees.
- Your business operating systems are in place.
- You often get the best combination of seller, bank, or vendor financing.

- You have immediate cash flow.
- You have a reduced risk of business failure.

Your accountant will gather certain documents and perform tests based on a due diligence checklist. The PEST analysis mentioned and the SWOT (strengths, weaknesses, opportunities, and threats) analysis should also be part of your total evaluation package. The PEST analysis and the SWOT analysis are both discussed in the chapter of this book entitled CREATIVE THINKING IN BUSINESS.

Taking care of the resources that God has given you and common sense dictate that you do a comprehensive review of your candidate business. Your accountant will probably be conducting his due diligence review assuming that there are probably "skeletons in the closet." The auditing experience (and thus built-in suspicion) of most accountants comes into play while conducting a due diligence review. But keep in mind that a "due diligence review" is not an audit. Skeletons that sometimes pop out of the closet are:

- Unrecorded liabilities (bills that are owed but are not in the accounting records)
- Assets that should have been recorded as expenses. When an expense is erroneously recorded as an asset, it makes both the profit and loss statement and the balance sheet look better than they really are. Creative entrepreneurs have been known to record travel, employee wages, and other expenses as balance sheet assets.
- Credit problems with vendors
- Inflated sales by recording a sale when it possibly should be recorded as a deferred sale, which is a liability. This can happen when a customer has given the company funds but the company has not yet performed the services for the customer or delivered goods to the customer.
- Personal affairs of the seller that could preclude him from selling the business, such as divorce, judgments, or litigation.
- Impending change in a zoning law or other city ordinance
- Rapidly developing technology that may render products obsolete
- Undisclosed owners of the business
- Pending increase in workers' compensation
- Inability to get insurance coverage because of excess claims
- Major increases anticipated for needed insurance coverage

- Downward business trends for the business.
- A big-box store coming into the area or other competition
- Major governmental regulations being passed
- Major increases in rent coming up
- Major clients not renewing contracts
- Obsolete inventory
- Major equipment near end of life cycle
- Non-compete agreements expiring
- Union contracts up for renewal
- Leases that are not assignable
- Key employees leaving or retiring
- Expiring patents
- Expiring licenses
- Expiring franchise agreements
- Undisclosed litigation
- Increasing difficulty in getting raw materials
- Increasing prices of raw materials
- Obsolete machinery
- Deterioration of the neighborhood and increasing security concerns
- Unpaid taxes
- Nonperformance on key contracts
- Threats of eminent domain from a governmental entity

Your due diligence package will normally cover the following areas:

- Discussions as to why the seller is selling his business
- Review of assets and liabilities
- Profit and loss review
- SWOT analysis
- PEST analysis

REASON FOR SELLING BUSINESS

As you would when buying a used car, you would want to know why the seller is selling his business. If it's for any reason other than retirement or death of the owner, you need to be suspicious. There may be reasons that are not normally uncovered in a due diligence review. Even after the seller gives you his reasons for selling, continue to keep this question in mind as you perform your due diligence review. Maybe the seller has inside knowledge that a major competitor is moving into the area, or an undesirable tenant business is moving in next door, or maybe there has been a significant increase in crime in the area.

ASSETS AND LIABILITIES (Review Of The Balance Sheet)

As you learn from the chapter in this book entitled KEEPING TRACK OF YOUR BUSINESS (ACCOUNTING AND OTHER FUN THINGS), your balance sheet is the financial statement that summarizes your financial records showing your assets, liabilities, and the owner's equity. Your assets will equal your liabilities plus the owner's equity. Your accountant will want to make sure that all of the assets listed are indeed real and that all liabilities are properly recorded.

You will want to inspect the business premises and check for worn-looking, nonfunctioning, or out-of-date equipment. You will want to make sure that all equipment, furniture, and fixtures on the balance sheet physically exist.

There will be certain assets used in the business that don't appear on the balance sheet. For these assets, there will normally be lease agreements that should be reviewed. You should make sure that these documents can be transferred to the new owner without penalty. Also, make sure that they are not near expiring and do have ongoing terms that are favorable. Other assets that may not be reflected on the balance sheet or may not have a physical presence are patents, trademarks, copyrights, mailing lists, vendor lists, customer lists, and others. Inspect the integrity of these assets, as they will be vital to the success of your business.

If you are assuming responsibility for accounts receivable, then you should make sure that they are real and collectible. Your accountant may advise you not to buy the accounts receivable, instead letting the seller keep them and collect and deduct the amount of the accounts receivable from the selling price of the business. This way, you don't have to worry about collecting them. You still need to review them, since poor quality in accounts receivable could indicate sales, collections, and cash flow issues that you will have to live with after you take over the business.

Your accountant will help you validate that liabilities are properly recorded on the balance sheet. A buyer may delay recording liabilities on the balance sheet to make it look more attractive. You will want to agree to accept only the liabilities recorded in a detailed list of liabilities. Anything not on that list will remain the seller's responsibility. Certain "hidden" liabilities that may pop up are:

– Unpaid bills

Your accountant will review an aging of accounts payable, looking for old accounts payable. I would probably perform what is called a "subsequent payment test. This would enable me to see if there were bills paid immediately following the date of the accounts payable aging report. It would show any bills paid that were not on the aging report.

– Employee benefits

Small businesses often overlook recording of employee benefits such as pension contributions, vacation accruals, promised bonuses, and other employee benefits. Another area that is often overlooked by employers is the proper accrual of payroll tax liabilities.

– Unrecorded lease obligations

According to generally accepted accounting principles, certain leases are operating leases, and others are capital leases. Capital leases need to be recorded in the accounting records as an asset with the future lease payments recorded as a liability. Your accountant will know the difference.

REVENUES AND EXPENSES (Review Of Profit And Loss Statement) ━━━━━━━

When you and your accountant review the profit and loss statements of your prospective business, you will be looking for the following:

– Trends

You will want to see if there are changes in revenues and expenses by comparing the profit and loss statements to one another over a period of time. Five years would be ideal. You will want to see if there are changes in select ratios such as the percentage of wages and cost of sales when compared to sales.

– The Business Story

After you have met with the seller and key employees, you want to see if the seller's profit and loss statement reflects the business as discussed.

PERSONNEL

There will possibly be key employees who are an integral part of the success of the business you are thinking about buying. You will want to talk to these key people to determine how they feel about your purchase of the business. You want to make sure that they will be there when you own the business.

You will want to gauge how much of the "competitive edge" of the business is in the seller's head. When the seller goes, what holes are left in the business? You may want to make sure that the seller stays on with the business for a specified period of time or will be a consultant for a specified period of time. You will want to make sure that the personnel files of the employees are complete with the proper confidentiality forms and that there are no employee grievances that can turn into litigation.

CUSTOMERS

Although your accountant will have reviewed the accounts receivable, you need to get a listing of all customers from the seller. You should contact these customers (especially the key customers) and make sure that they will continue to do business with you as the new owner. If the business has few key customers that make up the bulk of the sales of the business, this is a big red flag and adds tremendous risk to the business. If the loss of one or two key customers would hurt the viability of the business, I would possibly consider a different business. I have also seen situations where the customers of the business being purchased were companies that were owned by the seller or close family members or friends of the seller.

LOCATION

You know what they say in real estate: "location, location, location." If you buy a business that depends on location for its success, you need to closely examine all aspects of its location. Does the area seem to be growing, or is it shrinking? Is it crime-ridden? Is gentrification happening? *Gentrification* is defined by Dictionary.com as "the restoration and upgrading of deteriorated urban property by middle-class or affluent people."

DETERMINING THE RIGHT BUYING PRICE OF YOUR PROSPECTIVE BUSINESS

Ideally, the right buying price is the price agreed to between the seller and the buyer after comprehensive due diligence procedures have been performed.

Accurately valuing a small business is one of the most difficult aspects of buying a business. There are dozens of variables to consider. The valuation of a business is not a precise science but more of an art. The valuation that you and your accountant develop will no doubt differ substantially from the value in the seller's mind. Sellers are emotionally attached to their businesses, and they expect to be compensated for the years of hard work that they put into their businesses. The businesses are their "babies." Whatever price you develop and offer, you have to make sure that you can pay this valuation and turn a profit from the business.

According to Ken Schultz of Schultz Partners, Ptd, Ltd.[6], there are a number of different methods used to value businesses in today's marketplace, depending upon the size, profitability and nature of the business being valued.

Ultimately, valuations attempt to value the future maintainable profits of an enterprise. Generally the market accepts the latest year's profit as a basis for valuing small to medium-sized businesses, whereas for larger businesses, the average of the last two or three years profit together with a detailed and realistic operating budget may be preferred.

ASSET VALUATION METHOD ━━━━━━━━━━━━━━━━━━

Under-performing businesses (where the profit derived from the business is not commensurate with the capital invested in the business by way of plant and stock) are valued according to the Asset Valuation Method.

There is no goodwill component and the value of the business is derived solely from the value of the plant and equipment (usually at current market value) and stock.

This method is used when other valuation methods give a value that is less than the net tangible assets of a business. This is based on the concept that a business owner

---

6   Ken Schultz, *Business Valuation Methods,* http://www.schultzpartners.com.au/valuations.html, 2008.

is highly unlikely to sell his business for less than he can receive by way of an orderly disposal of the business assets.

Stock is valued at invoice cost, but may be discounted depending upon the amount of slow-moving or dead stock.

Plant & equipment is usually valued by an independent valuation expert.

DISCOUNTED CASH FLOW METHOD (DCF)

This method is favored by the large accounting firms, although it is generally not applicable to small and medium businesses. In theory it is one of the best valuation methods. It attempts to put a value, in today's terms, on future cash flows in an enterprise.

A DCF valuation is based on the concept that the value of a business depends on the future net cash flow of the business discounted back to present value at an appropriate discount rate.

Future cash flows consist of two elements:

1. The net cash amounts generated each year

2. The net cash expected from the ultimate sale of the business at a point in the future

This method is useful where future cash flows can be predicted with reasonable accuracy, such as mining companies or large, stable companies.

It could also be applied where a small or medium company has long term contracts for the supply of goods and services or where the company has a history of regular cash flows.

Unfortunately, it is generally not suitable for valuing most other small to medium companies because of the difficulty of estimating cash flows some years into the future, the difficulty of estimating the sale price of the business in the future and the difficulty of assessing a suitable discount rate.

RETURN ON INVESTMENT (R.O.I.) METHOD

This is the most common method used to value businesses worth up to about $2 million. It should more correctly be called the Return to an Owner/Operator Method (R.O.O.) as it is based on a return to an owner before he draws a wage. It reflects the percentage returns to an owner on his capital investment in the business. The net profit used in the calculation is not the same as shown on the Profit & Loss Statement. A number of adjustments and "add-backs" are made to the P&L Statement to reflect the return to an owner and to add back non-business expenses and one-off expenses.

This is calculated as:

Return on Investment (R.O.I)	=	Net Profit / Purchase Price	x	100 / 1

R.O.I.'s for specific industries are based on sales evidence from previous business sales

Given the R.O.I. for a specific industry (and making adjustment for special features of a particular business), the valuation is arrived at by transposing the above formula.

Purchase Price	=	Net Profit / R.O.I.	x	100 / 1

See the panel on the right for an example.

This figure is the total price of the business, including plant, stock and goodwill. The goodwill is derived by subtracting the value of plant and stock from the calculated purchase price.

For businesses in this price range the net profit or operating profit is defined as the return to an owner-operator before interest, tax, depreciation and owners' salary. Hence a number of add-backs are made to the net profit as shown on the tax return.

For businesses in this price range, usually only the business assets are valued and sold. Assets include plant & equipment, stock, work-in-progress, trading names, goodwill and intellectual property.

Debtors are not included. These are retained by the vendor, who also pays out the creditors at settlement.

PRICE TO EARNING (P/E) METHOD AND THE EBIT METHOD

The EBIT Method

This is the most common method of valuing private businesses worth around $2 million and above. Relatively few add-backs are made to the book profit when valuing a large business. Interest is added back and depreciation in some cases. Owners' wages are not added back (but may be adjusted to bring them in line with commercial rates) as these businesses are valued as running under management.

There are two related profit figures:

EBIT – earnings before interest and tax.

EBITDA – earnings before interest, tax, depreciation and amortization.

The EBIT figure is usually used in valuation calculations, although the EBITDA can be used.

The EBIT method of valuation is simply calculated by the following formula:

Value of business
= Profit x EBIT Multiple

For example, if the EBIT is $2.5 million and the multiple is four, the value is $10 million. This is the value of the business assets comprising stock, plant & equipment and goodwill. Debtors and creditors are not usually included.

It is becoming increasingly common for the purchaser to buy the entire company by way of purchase of the shares in the company. In this case the final price is adjusted to reflect the other items on the balance sheet, including debtors, creditors, accruals for staff entitlements and perhaps company debt.

The EBIT multiple to be applied to value a business can vary from around two up to around six, and sometimes higher, depending upon a number of factors, including:

- The total EBIT figure (a business earning an EBIT of $10 million will attract a higher multiple than one earning $1 million)
- The quality of the management team
- Stability of sales and profits
- The type of industry
- Barriers to entry
- The ability of the business to generate profits without the owner's involvement
- Growth potential
- Market dominance.

Price to Earnings (P/E) Method

This is the method used to value public companies. It can also be used to value private companies. The P/E method is essentially the same as the EBIT method except that the after-tax profit is used in the calculation and a different ratio is used to compensate for this.

The P/E ratio to be used in the calculations is extracted from sales evidence. It can also be extracted from published public company information. This method requires locating a few public companies similar to the one being valued. The average P/E of the public companies is derived. This figure is then discounted anywhere from fifty to eighty per cent to reflect the generally smaller size of the business and the lack of share liquidity compared to public companies.

Some private company owners get carried away when they see P/E's of 12 to 15 for public companies similar to theirs. They need to bear in mind two factors:

- The discount factor mentioned above.
- The fact that a P/E is equivalent to about 1.3 times an EBIT because of the after-tax nature of P/E. That is, a P/E of 10 is approximately equivalent to an EBIT of 7.

Rule-of-Thumb Method

This once-popular method simply values a business as multiple of its gross income, with each industry having its own multiple. It has fallen out of favour because the overheads required to earn the same income can vary significantly from one business to the next, even within the same industry. It is now used only to value accounting practices and real estate rent rolls. Virtually all other businesses are valued by using one of the methods above.

Although these are the primary methods to value businesses there are others. The bottom line is the method used to value a business will be the one agreed to by the buyer and seller.

The final price will be what the seller will accept and what the buyer will agree to pay.

DEAL STRUCTURE

So you have found a business, completed all your due diligence, and have decided on a price. Now, it is time to structure a deal. **Price negotiation must stop once you move into the deal structure stage, or the deal is likely to start unraveling.**

You definitely need to involve your accountant and attorney at this state of the business acquisition process. There are a number of different ways to structure the acquisition of a business. Some of them have extreme tax implications for you as the buyer.

- Asset vs. Stock Transaction

  Purchasing the assets of a business rather than the stock offers the buyer some tax advantages as well as the benefit of acquiring only the assets that he wants and none of the liabilities. One negative element to structuring your deal as an asset purchase rather than a stock purchase is that some contracts may not be assignable to the new owners of the "asset only" purchased entity. Most sellers of businesses prefer to sell their company via a stock sell, since they can often obtain tax-favored capital gains treatment on the sale.

- Leveraged Buy-Out

  This approach to structuring a deal uses the assets of the acquired company as collateral for the purchase of the business. The buyer puts in very little money. Instead of a down payment from you as the buyer with the owner financing the rest, a loan is secured with the assets serving as collateral. This approach will normally only work if the business has a large physical asset base. The downside is that the company then becomes burdened with the associated debt.

- Stock Exchange or Merger

  This approach to structuring a deal sounds complicated, and it is complicated. But the benefits can make it a worthwhile way to structure your deal. For example, the seller can receive stock in another company and not have to pay immediate tax on the sale of his company.

- Installment Sale

  Almost no businesses are purchased with all cash. In most cases, you, the buyer, provide for a down payment, and the rest is financed by the seller through a promissory note secured by the assets of the business.

According the Small Business Administration, your agreement of sales or letter of intent should include the following elements:

- Total purchase price offered
- Breakdown of the elements of the price (down payment, owner-financed portion)
- Listing of the assets and/or liabilities being purchased and their estimated values
- Operating condition of all equipment at the time of sales
- Right to offset undisclosed liabilities against future payments
- A provision calling for compliance with the Bulk Transfer provisions of the Uniform Commercial Code
- Warranties for clear and marketable title, validity, and assumability of existing contracts, tax and legal liability limitations, and any other appropriate warranties
- A provision to make the sale conditional on lease agreements, financial verification, transfer of licenses, and ability to obtain financing
- Provision for prorating of rent, utilities, wages, and prepaid expenses
- A non-compete agreement from the seller
- Allocation of purchase price
- Restrictions on how the business should be operated until settlement
- Date of the settlement

In structuring your deal, remember that most deals include the provision that the seller will finance a major portion of the acquisition price. I would personally never enter into a deal to buy a business that required me to pay for 100% of the business up front. There are pros and cons to pay the full price of a business up front:

Pros

- You may be able to negotiate a deep discount
- Easy to transact
- The deal is completed and you will not have to interact with the seller anymore

Cons

- Assets may not be described by seller, but your recourse will be difficult because he will have all of your money. Some examples would by the client list was inflated, patents were not at as strong has presented in selling documents, worthless inventory co-mingled with the good inventory.

- May deplete you cash and take away your used for operations of your new business.
- No incentive for the seller to help you be successful as he will have all of his money.

FORMS, CONTRACTS, AND AGREEMENTS FOR A BUSINESS PURCHASE

There are some important documents that will be required throughout the business acquisition process. It is critical that you document your business acquisition process completely. Proper documentation serves as evidence of your process, keeps you organized and will keep you more organized in your review process.

- Letter of Intent

    Most business acquisition processes will begin with the Letter of Intent. It can be binding or nonbinding. I would typically include access to due diligence information, confidentiality provisions, and a provision that the buyer cannot shop your offer.

- Confidentiality Agreement

    The Confidentiality Agreement is an agreement between the buyer and the seller in which they agree, prior to exchanging information, that any proprietary or confidential information exchanged shall be held in confidence. The basic elements to the Confidentiality Agreement are:
    1. Scope of information covered
    2. Exceptions to confidentiality
    3. Limitations to whom you can disclose the subject information to
    4. Term of the agreement
    5. Non-solicitation of employees

- Due Diligence

    You will disclose to the buyer the information that you wish him to supply to you for your due diligence review.

- Definitive Agreement

    This agreement is the BIG agreement. It sets out all of the terms and conditions of the buy-sell agreement, including the conditions of closing. I will typically include the following provisions:

- Exact description of the business being bought
- Terms of the deal
- Representations and warranties
- Pre-closing covenants
- Conditions of closing
- Closing mechanics
- Indemnifications
- State of controlling law
- Post-closing covenants and/or agreements

— Settlement Sheet

The Settlement Sheet shows costs and/or adjustments to be made at time of settlement.

— Escrow Agreement

The Escrow Agreement identifies the conditions for escrow and the amount.

— Bill of Sale

The Bill of Sale identifies the assets purchased, their individual purchase prices, and their total price.

— Promissory Note

Most business purchase transactions include the seller's financing a portion of the purchase. If the owner finances any part of the purchase price, the Promissory Note specifies the amount of the note and terms for payment.

— Non-compete Agreement

This is a very important document that is often overlooked. It protects the buyer from immediate competition from the seller for a specific number of years. A non-compete agreement may also be in terms of geography (distance), territory, product line restriction and other areas of restriction. It must be for a reasonable period of time to be enforceable.

— Employee or Consulting Agreement

In many business acquisitions, the seller will stay on with the business during a transition period. He will normally be compensated for his services during this time period above and beyond the buy-sell agreement that you signed with him.

Once you sign all of the proper agreements and you have bought your new business, the fun begins. You are now a business owner.

BUYING A FRANCHISE

A franchise typically enables you, the investor or "franchisee," to operate a business on an almost immediate basis. A franchise will have a greater chance of success than a business you start from scratch. Some studies indicate that the failure rate of franchised businesses is less than 5%. A recent study by Dr. Timothy Bates, a professor at Wayne State University in Detroit, found the franchise failure rate to actually exceed 30% and that the franchises made lower profits than independent entrepreneurs. Still, the failure rate is less for franchisees than the failure rate for businesses that started from scratch. Franchisors are closely regulated by the Federal Trade Commission, which should give you a little more comfort. Much of the information for this section BUYING A FRANCHISE comes from various publications issued by the Federal Trade Commission. Franchising has been a popular way of starting a business for decades. Here are some quick facts about franchises:[7]

- An estimated 1,500 different franchisors (franchise companies) operate in the United States.
- The franchise industry accounts for 40% of all retail sales in the U.S.
- A new franchise opens every 8 minutes of every day.
- Approximately 1 out of every 12 businesses in the U.S. is a franchise business.

7   *Quick Franchise Facts, Franchising Industry Statistics,* AZfranchises.com, www.azfranchises.com/franchisefacts.htm, 2010.

- More than 75 different industries use franchising as a means to offer goods and services.

- Most franchise companies have fewer than 100 units.

- The top franchise industry is fast food.

- The top franchise company is McDonald's.

Franchiseseek, an international franchise and global investment opportunities website[8] recently reported that franchising is responsible for 760,000 businesses, 18 million jobs, 14% of the private sector employment, and over $500 billion in payroll.

According to Sellfranchise[9], people that buy franchises are generally happy with their purposes. According to their report "Buying an Existing Franchise Business the overall satisfaction in owning a franchise was high among the more than 1,0000 franchise owners polled. ""Nine out of 10 respondents' expectations were either exceeded (18%), mostly met (48% or somewhat met (24%).

The initial franchise fee may be a barrier for you to buy a franchise.

8   Franchise Statistics, http://www.franchiseek.com/USA/Franchise_USA_Statistics.htm, 2010
9   Buying an Existing Franchise Business, http://www.sellfranchise.com/buying/franchisefacts.html, 2010

BOND'S FRANCHISE GUIDE DETAILED INDUSTRY STATISTICS	Average Franchise Fee	Average Total Investment	Average Royalty %
Automotive Products & Services	$23,000	$199,900	5.70%
Auto / Truck / Trailer Rental	$31,500	$232,300	8.60%
Building & Remodeling/Furniture/Appliance Repair	$20,500	$67,700	5.60%
Business: Financial Services	$21,500	$76,300	8.90%
Business: Advertising & Promotion	$18,000	$48,700	5.50%
Business: Internet/Telecommunications/Misc.	$22,700	$74,400	20.90%
Child Development / Education / Products	$21,300	$144,100	15.90%
Education / Personal Development / Training	$30,300	$128,400	8.20%
Employment & Personnel	$25,500	$104,400	7.20%
Food: Donuts / Cookies / Bagels	$25,400	$231,900	5.30%
Food: Coffee	$20,700	$218,200	6.00%
Food: Ice Cream / Yogurt	$22,700	$185,700	5.40%
Food: Quick Service / Take-out	$21,200	$337,300	4.90%
Food: Restaurant / Family-Style	$33,400	$375,800	4.50%
Food: Specialty Foods	$22,300	$230,800	5.30%
Hairstyling Salons	$17,100	$102,600	5.60%
Health / Fitness / Beauty	$19,100	$194,300	6.50%
Laundry & Dry Cleaning	$19,200	$224,300	6.60%
Lawn and Garden	$34,000	$80,000	6.90%
Lodging	$31,700	$362,100	4.80%
Maid Service & Home Cleaning	$13,100	$49,300	5.40%
Maintenance / Cleaning / Sanitation	$19,300	$63,500	9.90%
Medical / Optical / Dental A52Products & Services	$27,400	$214,700	5.00%
Packaging & Mailing	$25,300	$93,000	5.70%
Printing & Graphics	$25,700	$271,300	5.60%
Publications	$12,000	$21,400	8.10%
Real Estate Inspection Services	$20,400	$29,300	7.10%
Real Estate Services	$13,600	$99,100	5.80%
Recreation & Entertainment	$20,600	$371,900	8.50%
Rental Services	$16,400	$208,800	5.30%
Retail: Art. Art Supplies and Framing	$28,200	$127,600	5.50%
Retail: Athletic Wear / Sporting Goods	$31,400	$256,000	11.30%
Retail: Clothing / Shoes / Accessories	$21,700	$104,500	5.70%
Retail: Convenience Stores / Supermarkets / Drugs	$22,700	$353,200	4.30%
Retail: Home Furnishings	$21,100	$163,500	4.10%
Retail: Home Improvement & Hardware	$30,200	$303,500	4.70%
Retail: Pet Products & Services	$17,600	$149,300	5.40%
Retail: Photographic Products & Services	$20,200	$132,200	6.00%
Retail: Specialty	$25,100	$193,600	5.30%
Retail: Video / Audio / Electronics	$20,000	$95,300	4.00%
Retail: Miscellaneous	$24,200	$139,800	4.30%
Security & Safety Systems	$26,100	$317,100	6.80%
Signs	$23,700	$114,800	5.90%
Travel	$20,000	$52,200	2.30%

Fig. 1 – Bond Franchise Report

This listing is from the 19th Edition of *Bond's Franchise Guide* published by Source Book Publications (www.sourcebookpublications.com). The most current guide available, as of this writing, is for 2008. It shows the average franchise fee by industry category.

As you can see, the franchise fee is a small portion of the start-up capital that you will need to start up your own franchise. The average total investment is just to get things started. It does not include the money necessary to continue funding your company until it becomes profitable. It could take a year or more for your franchise to become profitable. As with any business, if you borrow funds to get it started, you may become profitable long before you have a positive cash flow. Debt service (paying off your business loan) will not show as an expense on your profit and loss statement but will be counted as a cash outflow.

Most franchises will require that you pay a monthly royalty based on gross sales. The "Average Royalty" column reflects the average royalty by industry category.

	Average Franchise Fee	Average Total Investment	Average Royalty %
Categories with Lowest Avg. Franchise Fee:			
Publications	$12,000	$21,400	8.10%
Maid Service & Home Cleaning	$13,100	$49,300	5.40%
Real Estate Services	$13,600	$99,100	5.80%
Categories with Lowest Avg. Total Investment:			
Publications	$12,000	$21,400	8.10%
Real Estate Inspection Services	$20,400	$29,300	7.10%
Business: Advertising & Promotion	$18,000	$48,700	5.50%
Categories with Lowest Avg. Royalty Fee:			
Travel	$20,000	$52,200	2.30%
Retail: Video / Audio / Electronics	$20,000	$95,300	4.00%
Retail: Home Furnishings	$21,100	$163,500	4.10%

Fig.2 – Bond Franchise Report_2

This table, taken from *Bond's Franchise Guide*, shows that the company categories with the lowest initial franchise fees are publication, maid service, and real estate franchises. Keep in mind that these are average franchise fees. As an example, a McDonald's franchise fee may be several hundred thousand dollars.

By paying a franchise fee that may cost several thousand dollars, you are given a format or system developed by the company ("franchisor"), the right to use the franchisor's name for a limited time, and assistance. For example, the franchisor may help you find a location for your outlet or require you to locate in a certain area, provide initial training and an operating manual, and advise you on management, marketing, or personnel. Some franchisors offer ongoing support such as monthly newsletters, a toll-free 800 telephone number for technical assistance, and periodic workshops or seminars.

A franchise is a legal and commercial relationship between the owner of a trademark, service mark, trade name, or advertising symbol and an individual or group wishing to use that identification in a business. The franchise agreement governs the method of conducting business between the two parties. Generally, a franchisee sells goods or services that are either supplied by the franchisor or that meet the franchisor's quality standards.

Franchising is based on mutual trust between the franchisor and franchisee. Because this relationship is based on trust, it is critical, if you are considering franchising as a way to start a business, that you thoroughly investigate the franchise. The franchise agreement will only be as good as the people behind it. Check out the franchisor executives thoroughly. Get to know current franchisees. Make sure they are happy with their decision to become franchisees. As the saying goes, "The proof is in the pudding."

There are primarily two forms of franchising:

1. Product and/or trade name franchising
2. Business format franchising

In the simplest form, a franchisor owns the right to the name or trademark and sells that right to a franchisee. This is known as "product and/or trade name franchising." The more complex form, "business format franchising," involves a broader, ongoing relationship between the two parties. Business format franchises often provide a full range of services, including site selection, training, product supply, marketing plans, and even assistance in obtaining financing.

THE TYPICAL FRANCHISE SYSTEM

The Cost of Buying a Franchise

In exchange for obtaining the right to use the franchisor's name and its assistance, you may pay some or all of the following fees and expenses:

Initial Franchise Fee And Other Expenses

Your initial franchise fee, which may be nonrefundable, may cost several thousand to several hundred thousand dollars. You may also incur significant costs to rent, build, and equip an outlet and to purchase initial inventory. Other costs include operating licenses and insurance. You also may be required to pay a "grand opening" fee to the franchisor to promote your new outlet. The average total investment as listed in the *Bond's Franchise Guide* does not include the operating capital that you will need to keep your business going until you start generating a profit

> Pro: You are buying proven expertise, experience, and the public's perception (hopefully positive) of the name of the franchise. Hopefully, when you open your doors, people will walk in because they have had a positive experience at other locations that are part of your franchise.
> Con: A cash outlay that you may not be able to afford.

Continuing Royalty Payments

You may have to pay the franchisor royalties based on a percentage of your weekly or monthly gross income. You often must pay royalties even if your outlet has not earned significant income during that time. In addition, royalties are usually paid for the right to use the franchisor's name. So even if the franchisor fails to provide promised support services, you still may have to pay royalties for the duration of your franchise agreement. You will have to deal with the franchisor "non-performance" separately from your required royalty payments.

> Pro: You are buying a continuing "built-in consultant." Your continuing franchise fee will be used to keep your corporate franchise strong and growing.
> Con You pay these fees even if you are not happy with the franchisor's "services." You will be paying these franchise fees for as long as you own the franchise. They are payable to your franchisor whether you are profitable or not.

Advertising Fees

You may have to pay into an advertising fund. Some portion of the advertising fees may go for national advertising or to attract new franchise owners, but not to target your particular outlet. In this particular scenario, your advertising budget will include fees that will not generate any direct business for your new company.

> Pro: You are building the public's recognition of your franchise.

Con: These are not advertising dollars that directly benefit your company.   The
dollars that you spend may be used for non-customer-generating purposes.
As noted above, some of these dollars will go to attract other franchisees to
your franchise.   This obviously does not generate direct business for you.

OTHER IMPORTANT CONSIDERATIONS WHEN CONSIDERING A FRANCHISE

Controls

To ensure uniformity, franchisors typically control how franchisees conduct business. These
controls may significantly restrict your ability to exercise your own business judgment.

Pro: Customers feel confident that they can get consistent goods and services
whenever they go to a franchise location.

Con: Innovation is not encouraged. You will do things their way only. You will not
be developing any patents or specialized operating procedures if you are a
franchisee.

Site Approval

Many franchisors must pre-approve sites for outlets. This may increase the likelihood
that your outlet will attract customers. The franchisor has normally proven that it knows
how to select locations. The selection of a retail location involves complex analysis.
There are dozens of variables to consider in your selection process. Your franchisor
will hopefully be very knowledgeable about this process. The franchisor, using its own
"success formula," may not approve a site you select.

Pro: Your franchisor has probably located scores of successful franchisee units,
and you get the benefit of their experience.

Con: Whatever location they choose will be your location. You are subject to your
franchisor's decision. You may have some other location in mind, but it is
irrelevant if your franchisor does not approve.

Design or Appearance Standards

Franchisors may impose design or appearance standards to ensure customers
receive the same quality of goods and services in each outlet. Some franchisors require
periodic renovations or seasonal design changes. Make absolutely sure that you have
computed these initial costs into your acquisition budget. If your franchisor requires

periodic remodeling, make sure that you have these estimates keyed in to your capital improvements budget. Complying with these standards may increase your costs.

> Pro: Your franchisor has years of experience to benefit from.
> Cons: You will have to spend money on the initial design and subsequent design changes. The design changes may not make sense for you or even seem necessary, but you may have to make them anyway.

Restrictions on Goods and Services Offered for Sale

Franchisors may restrict the goods and services offered for sale. For example, as a restaurant franchise owner, you may not be able to add to your menu popular items or delete items that are unpopular. This brings up a memory of a recipe for my grandmother's "Cream Tacos." It was a meal that no one could get enough of. If you decide to start your business by buying into a franchise, forget your grandmother's cream tacos. They would not be part of the franchisor's uniform menu. Similarly, as an automobile transmission repair franchise owner, you might not be able to perform other types of automotive work, such as brake or electrical system repairs.

> Pro: You do not have to think about, research, or source the products you are selling in your business. You have an experienced, educated, and proven buying staff with your franchisor.
> Con: You can dream about the success of the "pet rock" and the "wall walker" that made millions, but if they are not part of your franchisor's list of acceptable products, you will not be allowed to sell them at your store.

Restrictions on Methods of Operation

Franchisors may require you to operate in a particular manner. The franchisor might require you to operate during certain hours, use only preapproved signs, employee uniforms, and advertisements, or abide by certain accounting or bookkeeping procedures. These restrictions may impede you from operating your outlet as you deem best. This is an area that may make the hair stand up on the back of the neck of true entrepreneurs. If you have a true entrepreneurial spirit, you may not want to sign on the dotted line of a franchise agreement. Keep in mind that you do not get to make all of the operating decisions. A lot of them will be made for you. You are starting a business, and your franchisor has perfected the operation of your particular type of business. On the positive side, your franchisor will have spent a lot of money and resources developing standard operating policies and procedures. On the other hand, it will serve to restrict your ability to innovate. The franchisor also may require you to purchase supplies only from an approved supplier, even if you can buy similar goods elsewhere at a lower cost.

Pro: The operation of your company will be organized around your "franchise operating" manual. Owning a franchise is somewhere between being an entrepreneur and being employed in a "9 to 5" position with a big company. As an entrepreneur, a lot of your time will be spent experimenting with different ways to run your business. As a franchisee, you don't have to spend your time in this area.

Con: Being a franchisee is not about the entrepreneurial spirit. It is about safety with a proven way of doing business. Do what you are told by your franchisor, and you should realize the profit margins that they promised you. But don't expect to create the next phenomenon.

Restrictions of Sales Area

Franchisors may limit your business to a specific territory. While these territorial restrictions may ensure that other franchisees will not compete with you for the same customers, they could impede your ability to open additional outlets or move to a more profitable location.

Pro: Fellow franchise owners will not encroach on your territory. You have a well-defined area in which to grow your business.

Con: You can only expand in your current territory. To be able to expand outside of your territory, you normally have to buy another franchise. If economic conditions degrade in your assigned territory, you will not have the diversity of geography to help you overcome localized degradation of economic conditions.

Terminations and Renewal

You can lose the right to your franchise if you breach the franchise contract. In addition, the franchise contract is designed for a limited time; there is no guarantee that you will be able to renew it. You need to be familiar with federal and state laws concerning the nonrenewal provisions found in most franchise agreements. In most cases, your franchisor wants you to renew your agreement.

Pro: This provision normally keeps renegade franchisees in line.

Con: This is a big one. Your franchisor does not have to renew your contract. You are at their mercy. If they do not renew your franchise agreement, you are basically out of business. This is something to keep in mind.

Franchise Terminations

A franchisor can end your franchise agreement if, for example, you fail to pay royalties or abide by performance standards and sales restrictions. If your franchise is terminated, you may lose your investment.

Pro: This provision keeps your fellow franchisees in line. The fear of termination helps keep the standards of the franchisor in place and enforced.

Con: Nonconformance can cause you to lose your entire investment.

Renewals

Franchise agreements typically run for 15 to 20 years. After that time, the franchisor may decline to renew your contract. Also, be aware that renewals need not provide the original terms and conditions. The franchisor may raise the royalty payments or impose new design standards and sales restrictions. Your previous territory may be reduced, possibly resulting in more competition from company-owned outlets or other franchisees.

Pro: Most franchisors provide for renewal terms identical to the original terms. You don't have to sign an agreement that has one-sided renewal. A purchase of a franchise is a decision that is probably a lifetime decision.

Con: Loosely drafted renewal terms in your franchise agreement will leave your financial future uncertain. Don't sign an agreement unless it contains fair renewal terms.

Like any other investment, purchasing a franchise is a risk. When selecting a franchise, carefully consider a number of factors, such as the demand for the products or services, likely competition, the franchisor's background, and the level of support you will receive. In addition to the subjects discussed below, be sure to go through your SWOT (strengths, weaknesses, opportunities, and threats) analysis and PEST (politics, economics, social, and technology) analysis found in the CREATIVE THINKING IN BUSINESS chapter of this book.

Demand

Is there a demand for the franchisor's products or services in your community? Has the demand continued to grow, or is it a fad? Is the demand seasonal? For example, lawn and garden care or swimming pool maintenance may be profitable only in the spring or summer. Is there likely to be a continuing demand for the products or services in the future? Is the demand likely to be temporary, such as selling a fad food item? Do the products or services generate repeat business? Can your products or services be sold by others?

Competition

What is the level of competition, in your authorized territory, nationally, and in your community? How many franchised and company-owned outlets does the franchisor have in your area? How many competing companies sell the same or similar products or services? Are these competing companies well established, with wide name recognition in your community? Do they offer the same goods and services at the same or a lower price?

Your Ability to Operate the Business

Sometimes, franchisors fail. Will you be able to operate your outlet even if the franchisor goes out of business? Will you need the franchisor's ongoing training, advertising, or other assistance to succeed? Will you have access to the same or similar suppliers? Could you conduct the business alone if you must lay off personnel to cut costs?

Name Recognition

A primary reason for purchasing a franchise is the right to associate with the company's name. The more widely recognized the name, the more likely it will draw customers who know its products or services. Therefore, before purchasing a franchise, consider:

- The company's name and how widely recognized it is—does it have a registered trademark?
- How long has the franchisor been in operation?
- Does the company have a reputation for quality products or services?
- Have consumers filed complaints against the franchise with the Better Business Bureau or a local consumer protection agency?

Training and Support Services

Another reason for purchasing a franchise is to obtain support from the franchisor. What training and ongoing support does the franchisor provide? How does their training compare with the training for typical workers in the industry? Could you compete with others who have more formal training? What backgrounds do the current franchise owners have? Do they have prior technical backgrounds or special training that helps them succeed? Do you have a similar background? What will the franchisor's training cost? The training costs will include hotel, travel, time away from your business, and the cost of the training.

Franchisor's Experience

Many franchisors operate well-established companies with years of experience both in selling goods or services and in managing a franchise system. Some franchisors started by operating their own business. There is no guarantee, however, that a successful entrepreneur can successfully manage a franchise system.

Carefully consider how long the franchisor has managed a franchise system. Do you feel comfortable with the franchisor's expertise? If franchisors have little experience in managing a chain of franchises, their promises of guidance, training, and other support may be unreliable or of insufficient value.

Growth

A growing franchise system increases the franchisor's name recognition and may enable you to attract customers. Growth alone does not ensure successful franchisees; a company that grows too quickly may not be able to support its franchisees with all the promised support services. Make sure the franchisor has sufficient financial assets and staff to support the franchisees. This is where your accountant can come in handy. He will evaluate the liquidity of the franchisor and do a trend analysis to see if there have been positive financial trends over a period of years.

Get Substantiation for Any Earnings Representations

Some franchisors may tell you how much you can earn if you invest in their franchise system or how current franchisees in their system are performing. Be careful. The FTC (Federal Trade Commission requires that franchisors making such claims provide you with written substantiation. This is explained in more detail in the section "Investigating Franchise Offers." Make sure you ask for and obtain written substantiation for any income projections, or income or profit claims. If the franchisor does not have the required substantiation, or refuses to provide it to you, consider its claims to be suspect and walk away from this "opportunity."

Study Franchisor's Offering

Do not sign any contract or make any payment until you have the opportunity to investigate the franchisor's offering thoroughly. As will be explained further in the next section, the FTC's Franchise Rule requires the franchisor to provide you with a disclosure document containing important information about the franchise system. Study the disclosure document carefully. Take time to speak with current and former franchisees about their experiences. Because investing in a franchise can entail a significant investment, you should have an attorney review the disclosure document and franchise contract, and have an accountant review the company's financial disclosures.

Investigating Franchise Offerings

Before investing in any franchise system, be sure to get a copy of the franchisor's disclosure document. Sometimes this document is called a Franchise Offering Circular. Under the FTC's Franchise Rule, you must receive the document at least 10 business days before you are asked to sign any contract or pay any money to the franchisor. You should read the entire disclosure document. Make sure you understand all of the provisions. The following outline will help you to understand key provisions of typical disclosure documents. It also will help you ask questions about the disclosures. Get clarifications or answers to your concerns before you invest.

Business Background

The disclosure document identifies the executives of the franchise system and describes their prior experience. Consider not only their general business background but their experience in managing a franchise system. Also, consider how long they have been with the company. Investing with an inexperienced franchisor will be riskier than investing with an experienced one.

Litigation History

The disclosure document helps you assess the background of the franchisor and its executives by requiring the disclosure of prior litigation. The disclosure document tells you if the franchisor or any of its executive officers have been convicted of felonies involving, for example, fraud, any violation of franchise law, or unfair or deceptive practices law or are subject to any state or federal injunctions involving similar misconduct. It also will tell you if the franchisor or any of its executives have been held liable in or settled a civil action involving the franchise relationship. A number of claims against the franchisor may indicate that it has not performed according to its agreements or, at the very least, that franchisees have been dissatisfied with the franchisor's performance. Be aware that some franchisors may try to conceal an executive's litigation history by removing the individual's name from their disclosure documents. I would recommend having your attorney review this document thoroughly, especially the litigation history.

Bankruptcy

The disclosure document tells you if the franchisor or any of its executives have recently been involved in a bankruptcy. This will help you to assess the franchisor's financial stability and general business acumen and to predict if the company is financially capable of delivering promised support services.

Costs

The disclosure document tells you the costs of starting one of the company's franchises. It will describe any initial deposit or franchise fee, which may be nonrefundable, and costs for initial inventory, signs, equipment, leases, or rentals. Be aware that there may be other undisclosed costs. The following checklist will help you ask about the potential costs of a franchisee:

- Continuing royalty payments
- Advertising payments, both to local and national advertising funds
- Grand opening or other initial business promotions
- Business or operating licenses
- Product or service supply costs
- Real estate and leasehold improvements
- Discretionary equipment such as a computer system or business alarm system
- Training
- Legal fees
- Financial and accounting advice
- Insurance
- Compliance with local ordinances, such as zoning, waste removal, and fire, and other safety codes

- Health insurance
- Employee salaries and benefits

It may take several months or longer to get your business started. Include in your total cost estimate all operating expenses for the first year and your personal living expenses for up to two years. Compare your estimates with the costs of other franchisees as well as with competing franchise systems. Perhaps you can get a better deal with another franchisor. Have your accountant help you do a complete analysis of the cost of starting a franchise. Most people grossly underestimate the cost associated with starting a business.

Training and Other Assistance

The disclosure document will explain the franchisor's training and assistance program. Make sure you understand the level of training offered. The following checklist will help you ask the right questions:

- How many employees are eligible for training?
- Can new employees receive training, and if so, is there any additional cost?
- How long are the training sessions?
- How much time is spent on technical training, business management training, and marketing?
- Who teaches the training courses and what are their qualifications?
- What type of ongoing training does the company offer and at what cost?
- Whom can you speak to if problems arise?
- How many support personnel are assigned to your area?
- How many franchisees will the support personnel service?
- Will someone be available to come to your franchised outlet to provide more-individual assistance?

The level of training you need depends on your own business experience and knowledge of the franchisor's goods and services. Keep in mind that primary reasons for investing in a franchise, as opposed to starting your own business, are training and assistance. If you have doubts that the training might be insufficient to handle day-to-day business operations, consider another franchise opportunity more suited to your background.

Advertising

As mentioned above you often must contribute a percentage of your income to an advertising fund even if you disagree with how these funds are used. The disclosure document provides information on advertising costs. The following checklist will help you assess whether the franchisor's advertising will benefit you:

- How much of the advertising fund is spent on administrative costs?
- Are there other expenses paid from the advertising fund?
- Do franchisees have any control over how the advertising dollars are spent?
- What advertising promotions has the company already engaged in?
- How successful did those promotions seem to be?
- What advertising developments are expected in the near future?
- How much of the fund is spent on national advertising?
- How much of the fund is spent on advertising in your area?
- How much of the fund is spent on selling more franchises?
- Do all franchisees contribute equally to the advertising fund?
- Do you need the franchisor's consent to conduct your own advertising?
- Are there rebates or advertising contribution discounts if you conduct your own advertising?
- Does the franchisor receive any commissions or rebates when it places advertisements? Do franchisees benefit from such commissions or rebates, or does the franchisor profit from them?

Current and Former Franchisees

The disclosure document provides important information about current and former franchisees. Determine how many franchises are currently operating. A large number of franchisees in your area may mean significant competition. Pay attention to the number of terminated franchises. A large number of terminated, cancelled, or non-renewed franchises may indicate problems. Be aware that some companies may try to conceal the number of failed franchises by repurchasing failed outlets and then listing them as company-owned outlets.

If you buy an existing outlet, ask the franchisor how many owners operated that outlet and over what period of time. A number of different owners over a short period of time may indicate that the location is not a profitable one, or that the franchisor has not supported that outlet with promised services.

The disclosure document gives you the names and addresses of current franchisees and franchisees that have left the system within the last year. Speaking with current and former franchisees is probably the most reliable way to verify the franchisor's claims. Visit or phone as many of the current and former franchisees as possible. Ask them about their experiences. See for yourself the volume and type of business being done.

The following checklist will help you ask current and former franchisees valuable questions:

- How long has the franchisee operated the franchise?
- Where is the franchise located?
- What was their total investment?
- Were there any hidden or unexpected costs?
- How long did it take them to cover operating costs and earn a reasonable income?
- Are they satisfied with the cost, delivery, and quality of the goods or services sold?
- What were their backgrounds prior to becoming a franchisee?
- Was the franchisor's training program and continuing training adequate?
- What ongoing assistance does the franchisor provide?
- Is that assistance consistently adequate?
- Are they satisfied with the franchisor's advertising program?
- Does the franchisor fulfill its contractual obligations?
- Would the franchisee invest in another outlet from the franchisor?
- Would the franchisee recommend the investment to someone with your goals, income requirements, and background?

Be aware that some franchisors may give you a separate reference list of selected franchisees to contact. Be careful. Those on the list may be individuals who are paid by the franchisor to give a good opinion of the company.

Earnings Potential

You may want to know how much money you can make if you invest in a particular franchise system. Be careful. Earnings projections can be misleading. Insist upon written substantiation for any earnings projections or suggestions about your potential income or sales.

Franchisors are not required to make earnings claims, but if they do, the FTC's Franchise Rule requires franchisors to have a reasonable basis for these claims and to provide you with a document that substantiates them. This substantiation includes the bases and assumptions upon which these claims are made. Make sure you get and review the earnings claims document. Consider the following in reviewing any earnings claims:

Sample Size. A franchisor may claim that franchisees in its system earned, for example, $50,000 on average last year. This claim may be deceptive, however, if only a few franchisees earned that income and it does not represent the typical earnings of franchisees. Ask how many franchisees were included in the number and what the total number of franchisees is.

Average Incomes. A franchisor may claim that the franchisees in its system earn an average income of, for example, $75,000 a year. Average figures like this tell you very little about how each individual franchisee performs. Remember, a few, very successful franchisees can inflate the average. An average figure may make the overall franchise system look more successful than it actually is.

Gross Sales. Some franchisors provide figures for the gross sales revenues of their franchisees. These figures, however, do not tell you anything about the franchisees' actual costs or profits. An outlet with high gross sales revenue on paper actually may be losing money because of high overhead, rent, and other expenses.

Net Profits. Franchisors often do not have data on net profits of their franchisees. If you do receive net profit statements, ask whether they provide information about company-owned outlets. Company-owned outlets might have lower costs because they can buy equipment, inventory, and other items in larger quantities or may own, rather than lease their property.

Geographic Relevance. Earnings may vary in different parts of the country. An ice cream store franchise in a southern state, such as Florida, may expect to earn more income than a similar franchise in a northern state, such as Minnesota. If you hear that a franchisee earned a particular income, ask where that franchisee is located.

Franchisee's Background. Keep in mind that franchisees have varying levels of skills and educational backgrounds. Franchisees with advanced technical or business backgrounds can succeed in instances where more typical franchisees cannot. The success of some franchisees is no guarantee that you will be equally successful.

Financial History

The disclosure document provides you with important information about the company's financial status, including audited financial statements. Be aware that investing in a financially unstable franchisor is a significant risk: the company may go out of business or into bankruptcy after you have invested your money.

Hire a lawyer or an accountant to review the franchisor's financial statements. Do not attempt to extract this important information from the disclosure document unless you have considerable background in these matters. Your lawyer or accountant can help you understand the following:

- Does the franchisor have steady growth?
- Does the franchisor have a growth plan?
- Does the franchisor make most of its income from the sale of franchises or from continuing royalties?
- Does the franchisor devote sufficient funds to support its franchise system?

Additional Sources of Information

Before you invest in a franchise system, investigate the franchisor thoroughly. In addition to reading the company's disclosure document and speaking with current and former franchisees, you should speak with the following:

Your Lawyer and Accountant

Investing in a franchise is costly. Your accountant can help you understand the company's financial statements, develop a business plan, and assess any earnings projections and the assumptions upon which they are based. Your accountant can help you pick a franchise system that is best suited to your investment resources and your goals.

Franchise contracts are usually long and complex. A contract problem that arises after you have signed the contract may be impossible or very expensive to fix. Your lawyer will help you to understand your obligations under the contract so that you will not be surprised later. Make sure your lawyer is experienced in franchise matters. It is best to rely upon your own lawyer or accountant rather than those of the franchisor because of possible conflict of interest.

Banks and Other Financial Institutions

These organizations may provide an unbiased view of the franchise opportunity you are considering. Your banker should be able to get a Dun & Bradstreet report or similar reports on the franchisor.

Better Business Bureau

Check with the local Better Business Bureau (BBB) . Ask if any consumers have complained about the company's products, services, or personnel.

Government Departments

Several states regulate the sale of franchises. Check with your state Division of Securities or Office of Attorney General for more information about your rights as a franchise owner in your state.

Federal Trade Commission (FTC)

The FTC publishes information that may be of interest to you, including business guides like Getting Business Credit and Buying by Phone.

Whether you start your business from scratch, buy an existing business, or buy a franchise, the rest of this book should help guide you around the speed bumps of entrepreneurship on your road to business success. Let God come with you for the ride and help you navigate around the many potholes and road hazards that you will, no doubt, encounter on your journey.

STARTING YOUR OWN BUSINESS

You may know that you want to start a business, but you don't know exactly what business you want to start. If you haven't read chapter DO YOU REALLY WANT TO BE AN ENTREPRENEUR? you might want to read it before reading this section. You might also want to read chapter CREATIVE THINKING IN BUSINESS. The entrepreneur is a rare breed of person, and you should make sure that you are ready for the pleasures and rigors of starting your own business.

IDEAS FOR NEW BUSINESSES

Business ideas are all around you. They are lurking in your garage, in your basement, in your kitchen, and in your children's room. You'll find them in magazine ads, at your neighbor's house, and at work. They are right there in the vegetables you brought in from the yard . . . in the stack of papers next to your laser printer . . . in the back of your truck . . . and at the back of your mind.

Here is a sample list of businesses that you can start for under $1,000, many taken from www.businesstown.com. This Website took the information from Adams – Businesses You Can Start Almanac. A great source of new business ideas. It is good idea to purchase the latest edition as they are always adding new businesses.

Businesses You Can Start With Little or No Money. You can start many of these businesses for under $1,000

Airbrush Artist
Apartment Cleaning and Prep Service
Art Show Promoter
Auction Website
Auto Paint Touch-Up Professional
Automobile Broker
Back-Hoe Operator
Band Manager
Baked Goods – general
Baked Goods – specialized
Barter Online Systems
Blade-Sharpening Service
Block Party Organizer
Bicycle Customizing
Bicycle Maintenance
Boardinghouse Operator
Book Indexer
Book Outliner
Bookkeeping Service – general
Bookkeeping Service – specialized
Bounty Hunter
Brush Hauling and Yard Cleanup
Cabinet Cleaning/ Resurfacing
Cake Decorator
Calligrapher
Candle Maker

Canned Goods
Car Detailing
Car Headlight/Taillight Installer
Car Washing, Waxing, on-site
Car Wheel Cleaner
Carpet Cleaner
Caterer –Specialized Food
Child Care Referral Service
Childbirth Instructor
Chimney Cleaner
Chrome Cleaner
Circular/ Advertising Distributor (door-to-door)
City Bicycle Tour Organizer/Guide
College Application Consultant
College Dorm Room Cleaning
Commercial Plant Watering Service
Computer Repair
Computer Installation
Computer Software Consultant
Crafts Fair Promoter
Curb Painter
Curtain Maker
Delivery, Local
DMV Runner and Line Holder
Dog Sitter

Dog Trainer

Dog Walker

Doll Repair Service

Door Installer

Driveway Cleaning and Repair

Driveway Degreasing

eBay Consolidator

Email Marketer, Specialized Merchandise

Etiquette Adviser

Faux Brick Repairs and Installer

Fence Repair and Installer

First Aid/CPR Instructor

Furniture Maker, Custom

Garage Sale Consultant

Genealogical Service (Family History Writer)

Gerontology Consultant

Grocery Delivery Contractor

Gutter Cleaner

Hair Braider

Handbill Distributor

Handyman Network

Home Schooling Teacher

Horse Trainer

Hospitality Service

Ice Sculpting

In-Home Mail Service

In-Home Daycare Incorporation Service for Businesses

Information Publisher (online, booklets, etc.)

Ironing/Laundry Service

Jewelry Designer

Knitting/Crocheting Instructor

Karate Studio

Key Making

Law Library Management

Lawn Care Service

Legal Document Prep/Filing Service

Literary/ Publishing Agent

Loan Broker

Magician

Makeup Artist

Merchandise Demonstrator

Model Builder

Mobile Book/Magazine Distributor

Mortgage Loan Broker

Motor Vehicle Transportation

Movie Site Scout

Multilevel Marketing

Mural Painter

Mystery Shopper

Newsletter Publisher, specialized

Notary Public

Nutrition Consultant

Packing/Unpacking Service

Parapsychologist

Party Planner

Personal Instructor/Fitness Trainer

Personal Menu Service

Personal Shopper

Pet Groomer

Pet Psychologist

Pet Sitter

Pet Walking

Photographer, Freelance
Plant Sitter
Plant (Indoor) Watering and Maintenance
Private Tutor
Professional Organizer
Real Estate Agent/Home Researcher
Recycler
Reminder Service
Roommate Referral Service
Scanning Service
School Child Escort
Shoe Repair
Shopping Promotion
Sidewalk Musician for Businesses
Sign Painter
Silk Flower Arranger
Sprinkler (PVC) Installer and Repairman
Stationary Designer
Storyteller
Stress Management Counselor
Tailor

Taste Tester for Food Companies
Toy Assembler
Toy Cleaning Service
Toy Designer
Toy Exchange/Trade Service
Toy Repair Service
Traveling Secretary
Tree Topper
Tutor
Vacation Rentals Broker
Wall Paneling Installer
Wallpaper Installer
Wallpaper Stripper
Web-based Store, specialized merchandise)
Writer
Wellness Instructor
Window Cleaner – residential
Window Cleaner – commercial
Yard Decoration Installation
Yard Decoration Planner

Other sources of ideas for businesses to start:

The Yellow Pages

If you don't know what type of business you'd like to start, but you definitely want to be in business for yourself, try this little game. Open the Yellow Pages to any page randomly. Then open the Yellow Pages a second time randomly to another page. See of you can develop a business from the two different pages. As an example, let's say your first random page was car washes, and your second was printers. Maybe you can offer printer services to car washes in your area. As people come into the car wash office, you can offer them quick printing services. You can offer everything from basic photocopying to a full-service printing service at heavy traffic car washes.

The business you are already working for

This does not necessarily mean going into direct competition with your company. This author was working years ago for a film production company as their accountant. I mentioned to the CEO that I wanted to quit to start my own accounting and consulting company. They became my first client.

Local chamber of commerce

The typical chamber of commerce is so conservative and old-fashioned that you have to put a mirror under their noses to make sure that they are still alive. Don't expect them to be innovative. But, they are a wealth of information when it comes to statistics and historical information. They love to see new businesses come into their territories. It is probably not a bad idea to join the local chamber of commerce so that you can display the cute little plastic plaque they give you. You can display it prominently next to your city business license and the traditional framed first dollar bill that you take into your business.

Small Business Administration

I personally have not had much luck in getting anything from this independent governmental agency other than a few ten-year-old publications extolling the benefits of starting a business selling eight-track tapes. They tend to be a little behind the times and can only help you if you don't need their help. But they may be good for a random idea for a business to start. If nothing else, you can exchange ideas with the other 20 people waiting in line for their services.

Bureau of Labor Statistics

These guys have a really cool Website if you have a thirst for statistics in the extreme. They have more statistics (see their Website at http://stats.bls.gov) than you will ever be able to use. Look at their table of contents:

Inflation & Consumer Spending

Consumer Price Index • Inflation Calculator • Contract Escalation • Producer Price Indexes • Import/Export Price Indexes • Consumer Expenditures • Price Index Research

Wages, Earnings & Benefits

Wages by Area and Occupation • Earnings by Industry • Employee Benefits • Employment Costs • State and County Wages • National Compensation Data • Collective Bargaining

Productivity

Productivity and Costs • Multifactor Productivity • International Comparisons

Safety & Health

Injuries and Illnesses • Fatalities

International

Import/Export Price Indexes • Foreign Labor Statistics • International Technical Cooperation

Occupations

Occupational Outlook Handbook • Occupational Outlook Quarterly • Employment • Wages by Area and Occupation • Injuries, Illnesses, and Fatalities • Employment Projections • Standard Occupational Classification (SOC)

Demographics

Demographic Characteristics of the Labor Force • Geographic Profile of Employment and Unemployment • Consumer Expenditures • Injuries, Illnesses, and Fatalities • Longitudinal Studies • Time Use

Other Statistical Sites

FEDSTATS • Census Bureau • Bureau of Economic Analysis • More »

BLS Information Offices

New England (Boston, MA) • New York-New Jersey (New York, NY) • Mid-Atlantic (Philadelphia, PA) • Southeast (Atlanta, GA) • Midwest (Chicago, IL) • Southwest (Dallas, TX) • Mountain-Plains (Kansas City, MO) • Western (San Francisco, CA)

Is this impressive or what? You can jump into this Website and find yourself in statistics and numbers up to your eyeballs. But, take a walk through this Website as a generator of ideas. Try to ignore most of the mundane stats and use the site to generate ideas for new businesses.

Entrepreneur magazine

An incredible source of ideas for businesses. This magazine is absolutely geared to the small business person. You should spend the $60 a year to get this magazine monthly. Not only is this a "must have" magazine but they have some of the best books available on entrepreneurship available in their bookstore.

Local junior colleges and universities

Most junior colleges and universities have extension courses in various business subjects. This is also a great source of consultants. Many instructors in extension programs are also working professionals with real jobs in their chosen fields. Most colleges have also found out about the Internet and have Websites that fully explain their offerings.

Guides to franchises (sold in most bookstores)

There are many good franchising guides to be found in any bookstore of any size. I am not promoting buying a franchise, but the guides are excellent resources to generate ideas for businesses.

Newspapers

Almost every section of your daily or weekly newspaper is a good source for business ideas. As an example, the *Los Angeles Times* for March 7, 2010 generated the following ideas for me:

A. Front page, "From sickbed, Garfield legend is still delivering." "...Nearly three decades later, James Escalante finds himself far from Garfield High School in East Los Angeles, the place that made him internationally famous for turning a generation of low-income students in calculus whizzes." At the time of reading this article the Los Angeles School District is considering laying off thousands of teachers to close one of the largest budget gaps in school district history. This is a sad time in school district's across America. I have talked to a couple of teachers that have started their own consulting businesses in anticipation of their getting laid off. One is an English teacher who has started giving classes to small and medium sized companies on reporting writing. Our family utilizes the services of an incredible pre-calculus teacher to privately tutor our daughter at $65.00 an hour. We must always schedule our daughter's time with him a week in advance because of his busy schedule. In addition to tutoring our daughter through pre-calculus he makes himself available via phone to offer help on any questions she may have concerning her daily homework. His services have improved our daughters grades substantially, while at the same time enhancing his lifestyle and personal finances.

B. California section, "A food fight for leviathans – Scientists revise their view of great white sharks as studies suggest the mysterious creatures migrate long distances to feast on giant squids in deep ocean waters." I read this story Sunday morning after my drive home from a trip to the YMCA to workout. I passed by a bus sitting in a field of weeds. The bus was sitting up on blocks with the tall grass growing up through where it's headlights had been. I started thinking after reading the article in the L.A. Times that it would be fun to organize weekend tours of local restaurants on a brightly painted school bus, with live entertainment on the bus oriented toward the type of food being toured that day. If I were doing this I would select restaurants that would allow the customers to tour the kitchen and watch the food being prepared.

C. Business section, "Hunting for cheap flats."– Graffiti cleanup service, touch-up painting service, service that gets houses ready for sale, lease or rent. Not a particularly glamorous business but it can be a hearty business. My cousin Richard Barchard and his wife Debbie, in Stockton, California found it harder and hard to make ends meet in this difficult economy. They approached a property management company to clean their properties when tenants move out. They got a couple of assignments from the property management company and now they are on their way to building a good business.

You get the general idea. Any section of the newspaper can generate business ideas.

Internet

"Google it" has become a standard American term for "search for it on the Internet." Just go to your Google (or any other search engine) site and type in "business ideas" or "start a business," and you will generate such a long list of Websites with business ideas that you'll never have time to read them all.

Friends

Just tell your circle of friends that you are going to start a business, and watch the advice begin to gush from them. It will begin to occupy all of your conversations with them. You'll be amazed how many ideas (some good, many bad) they will generate. Use this idea generation source carefully.

Department of Labor

The Department of Labor is a rich source of ideas for starting a business. They have an online publication called *Occupational Outlook Handbook*. One of the occupation categories included in the online handbook is Bookkeeping, Accounting, and Auditing Clerks.[10]

BOOKKEEPING, ACCOUNTING, AND AUDITING CLERKS

NATURE OF THE WORK

Bookkeeping, Accounting, and Auditing Clerks

Bookkeeping, accounting, and auditing clerks are an organization's financial record keepers. They update and maintain one or more accounting records, including those that tabulate expenditures, receipts, accounts payable and receivable, and profit and loss. They have a wide range of skills and knowledge from full-charge bookkeepers who can maintain an entire company's books to accounting clerks who handle specific accounts. All of these clerks make numerous computations each day and, increasingly, must be comfortable using computers to calculate and record data.

In small establishments, *bookkeeping clerks* handle all financial transactions and record keeping. They record all transactions, post

---

10   U.S. Department of Labor, *Occupational Outlook Handbook, 2010-2011 Edition* (online at http://stats.bls.gov/oco/home.htm), 2010.

debits and credits, produce financial statements, and prepare reports and summaries for supervisors and managers. Bookkeepers also prepare bank deposits by compiling data from cashiers, verifying and balancing receipts, and sending cash, checks, and other forms of payment to the bank. They also may handle payroll, make purchases, prepare invoices, and keep track of overdue accounts.

In large offices and accounting departments, *accounting clerks* have more specialized tasks. Their titles often reflect the type of accounting they do, such as accounts payable clerk or accounts receivable clerk. In addition, their responsibilities vary by level of experience. Entry-level accounting clerks post details of transactions, total accounts, and compute interest charges. They also may monitor loans and accounts to ensure that payments are up to date.

More advanced accounting clerks may total, balance, and reconcile billing vouchers; ensure completeness and accuracy of data; and code documents according to company procedures. These workers post transactions in journals and on computer files and update the files when needed. Senior clerks also review computer printouts against manually maintained journals and make necessary corrections. They may review invoices and statements to ensure that all the information appearing on them is accurate and complete, and they may reconcile computer reports with operating reports.

Auditing clerks verify records of transactions posted by other workers. They check figures, postings, and documents to ensure that they are correct, mathematically accurate, and properly coded. They also correct or note errors for accountants or other workers to adjust.

As organizations continue to computerize their financial records, many bookkeeping, accounting, and auditing clerks are using specialized accounting software on personal computers. With manual posting to general ledgers becoming obsolete, these clerks increasingly are posting charges to accounts on computer spreadsheets and databases. They now enter information from receipts or bills into computers, and the information is then stored electronically, as computer printouts, or both. The widespread use of computers also has enabled bookkeeping, accounting, and auditing clerks to take on additional responsibilities, such as payroll, procurement, and billing. Many of these functions require these clerks to write letters, make phone calls to customers or clients, and interact with colleagues. Therefore, good communication skills are becoming increasingly important in the occupation.

EMPLOYMENT

Bookkeeping, accounting, and auditing clerks held about 2.1 million jobs in 2008. They work in nearly all industries and at all levels of government. State and local government, educational services, healthcare, and the accounting, tax preparation, bookkeeping, and payroll services industries are among the individual industries employing the largest numbers of these clerks.

Job Outlook About this section

Job growth is projected to be <u>about as fast as the average</u>. The large size of this occupation ensures plentiful job opportunities, as many bookkeeping, accounting, and auditing clerks are expected to retire or transfer to other occupations.

Employment change. Employment of bookkeeping, accounting, and auditing clerks is projected to grow by 10 percent during the 2008–2018 decade, which is about as fast as the average for all occupations. This occupation is one of the largest growth occupations in the economy, with about 212,400 new jobs expected over the projections decade.

A growing economy will result in more financial transactions and other activities that require recordkeeping by these workers. Additionally, an increased emphasis on accuracy, accountability, and transparency in the reporting of financial data for public companies will increase the demand for these workers. Also, new regulations and reporting methods, including the use of International Financial Reporting Standards, should result in additional demand for clerks involved in accounting and auditing. However, growth will be limited by improvements in accounting software and document-scanning technology that make it easier to record, track, audit, and file financial information, including transactions and reports. Moreover, companies will continue to outsource their bookkeeping, accounting, and, in some cases, auditing functions to third party contractors located both domestically and abroad.

Job prospects. While many job openings are expected to result from job growth, even more openings will stem from the need to replace existing workers who leave. Each year, numerous jobs will become available, as clerks transfer to other occupations or leave the labor force. The large size of this occupation ensures plentiful job openings, including many opportunities for temporary and part-time work.

Clerks who can carry out a wider range of bookkeeping and accounting activities will be in greater demand than specialized clerks. For example, demand for full-charge bookkeepers is expected to increase, because they can perform a wider variety of financial transactions, including payroll and billing. Certified Bookkeepers (CBs) and those with several years of accounting or bookkeeping experience who have demonstrated that they can handle a range of tasks will have the best job prospects.

The Department of Labor listing of job outlooks is divided into the following categories:

- Management
- Professional and Related
- Service
- Sales
- Administrative Support
- Farming and Related
- Construction
- Installation and Related
- Production
- Transportation
- Job Opportunities in the Armed Forces
- Tomorrow's Jobs
- OOH (Occupational Outlook) Reprints
- Other OOH Info
- Order

California EDD (Employment Development Department) and other state employment development departments

The California Employment Development Department has a great Web site at www.caljobs.ca.gov. This Web site is rich with jobs in all industries. As you are going through this Web site, look for those areas where there are a lot of openings and see if there is a need you can fill with a new company.

Your own evaluation of businesses needed in your community

The other day, I was asked to clean out the garage and put up some new storage shelves. What if someone opened a business that specialized in diagnosing storage issues at home and then either cleaned out the garage for the person or built them new shelves? Maybe you could diagnose the problems and then serve as the project manager and farm the various tasks out to other small contractors.

Here is a little business that I stumbled onto the other day. I wear blue jeans (Levi's only) all the time. After a few years, the buttonholes on the fly wear out and won't stay fastened. There is a store down the street from my house that does only two things: repair worn and torn Levi's (don't try to take in a pair of any denims except for Levi's) and sell used Levi's.

Each summer, I find a number of wasp nests under the eaves of my house. I don't really like the job of getting rid of these pests, so I would like to see a business that did just that.

Services or goods that you have received but have not been happy with.

I hate the paint on my house. Every once in a while, my house could use a touch-up, and this would make the original paint job last a lot longer. It is impossible to get a painter to come by and do a touch-up job on my house. This seems like an easy business to start. Just drive down a street and take down the addresses of houses needing paint touch-up. Also, keep track of the paint numbers and brands for follow-up business the next year.

Observe trends starting to develop. As an example, every major electronics company is starting to manufacture MP3 players. As a small start-up, you might be able to manufacture an MP3 player. Here are some ways you could benefit from this new trend:

Produce accessories for MP3 players such as leather covers. I have friends that started producing thin plastic "skins" for cell phones. They got this idea from seeing many kiosks in the malls selling "skins" that actually violated the phone manufacturer's warranties by requiring the removal of the covers of the phones. They came up with the idea of a super thin cover that merely slips over the existing cover, thus not violating any phone manufacturer's warranties. They started their company with only a few thousand dollars. They don't own any manufacturing plants or retail stores. They came up with the idea and contracted with an OEM (original equipment manufacturer) company that manufactured the covers for them on a contract basis. They then contracted with a distribution company to sell the product to retailers.

Since MP3s are the latest craze and will probably be here for a while and morph into the PVP (personal video player) market, there will be a market for peripherals such as headphones, memory devices, extended batteries, and other devices that enhance the utility of the players. Maybe sell these peripherals from small kiosks in a few malls.

Business brokers

There are some very reputable business brokers that put buyers and sellers together much the same way that real estate agents connect buyers and sellers. Remember that a broker will normally be representing the seller, so be sure to get your attorney involved in the transaction.

Your accountant

Your accountant would like nothing better than to see you start a new business so that you would need more of his services. Your accountant is not just a number cruncher. If he is, then you are being charged for services that are really only bookkeeping services. Use your accountant to help you generate ideas for a company AND to independently evaluate your ideas. Also, keep in mind that attorneys are not by nature risk takers. Remember, the overall premise of this book is "You can't walk on water unless you get out of the boat."

Your attorney

Most attorneys will usually take the safe approach to business ideas. You may be lucky enough to have an attorney who has not been trained to think only inside the box. Attorneys, unfortunately, spend years of training and education learning what they "should not do."

Your children

This may, at first, seem like an odd source of new business ideas. But think about it for a minute. We spend time in college learning to work within the box by the rules of acceptable business practices. This is useful, but it begs the saying "Do what you have always done, and you will always get what you always got." Kids have not been corrupted by the idea of "standard operating procedures." They think outside the box because they have not had the years of indoctrination of our education system—they still have some original thinking and creativity left.

DETERMINING IF YOUR PROPOSED BUSINESS IS A GOOD IDEA

Entrepreneurs come in all shapes, sizes, and ages. Ryan Allis, now just 23, is a remarkable success story. I have used his method of business opportunity analysis in this book. It's been a good example of teaching an old dog new tricks. Use his approach in conjunction with the PEST and SWOT methods discussed in the CREATIVE THINKING IN BUSINESS chapter of this book.

Ryan Allis, author of *Zero to One Million*, is a young serial entrepreneur and an international speaker, author, and syndicated columnist on the topics of entrepreneurship, personal development, and Web marketing. At the age of 17, he helped build a company from zero to one million in sales over the course of fourteen months. At the age of 18, he wrote and published a book entitled *Zero to One Million: How to Build a Company to $1 Million in Sales*. Today, at the age of 19, he has been a keynote speaker and panel participant at conferences from Chicago to Nigeria. As a student and successful entrepreneur, he is able to deliver a unique message that connects with young audiences and aspiring entrepreneurs alike. As a team leader with the Lead America Business

& Entrepreneurship Conference, Ryan has traveled the United States helping to teach entrepreneurship to high school students. As a patron of the Youth Development and Entrepreneurship Foundation, he traveled across Nigeria in August 2004 to inspire over 5,500 youths and launched his book on the African continent.

In order to successfully analyze your business ideas, you must pass them through specific tests to determine if they truly are valid opportunities. The imagined business must have a demonstrated need, ready market, and ability to provide a solid return on investment.

Is the idea feasible in the marketplace? Is there demand? Can it be done? Are you able to pull together the persons and resources to pull it off before the window of opportunity closes? These questions must be considered and answered.

Opportunity-focused entrepreneurs start with the customer and the market in mind. They analyze the market to determine industry issues, market structure, market size, growth rate, market capacity, attainable market share, cost structure, the core economics, exit strategy issues, time to breakeven, opportunity costs, and barriers to entry. Below is a model that entrepreneurs can use to evaluate their business ideas and plans.

To evaluate opportunities, entrepreneurs ask the following questions:[11]

- What is the need you fill or problem you solve? (Value Proposition)
- Whom are you selling to? (Target Market)
- How would you make money? (Revenue Model)
- How will you differentiate your company from what is already out there? (Unique Selling Proposition)
- What are the barriers to entry?
- How many competitors do you have and of what quality are they? (Competitive Analysis)
- How big is your market in dollars? (Market Size)
- How fast is the market growing or shrinking? (Market Growth)
- What percentage of the market do you believe you could gain? (Market Share)
- What type of company would this be? (Lifestyle or High Potential, Sole Proprietorship or Corporation)
- How much would it cost to get started? (Start-up Costs)
- Do you plan to use debt capital or raise investment? If so, how much and what type? (Investment Needs)
- Do you plan to sell your company or go public (list the company on the stock markets) one day? (Exit Strategy)

---

11   Ryan Allis, *Business Idea and Opportunity Evaluation,* www.zeromillion.com, 2004.

- If you take on investment, how much money do you think your investors will get back in return? (Return on Investment)

Let's take these fourteen questions and turn them into an easy model that you can use to evaluate your business ideas. This is called the RAMP model.

THE RAMP MODEL

Let's start with the first letter, R, which stands for Return. Return really is return on investment.

R	Discuss Exit Strategy (acquisition or IPO (initial public offering)).
R	Is it profitable? Will your revenues be higher than your expenses?
R	Time to Break Even. How long before cash flow is positive? How long until the company begins to have an aggregate net income?
R	Investment Needed. How much money will it take to start up this venture? Will it be $20,000, $200,000, or $2,000,000?

When you look at the investment needed, make sure that you do a cash flow analysis. Cash flow can and will often be different than the amounts that appear on your profit and loss statement. You may make a sale but not collect the cash for it for a month or more. Generally accepted accounting principles require that the income be recorded once the customer has received his goods or services.

As discussed in the chapter entitled KEEPING TRACK OF YOUR BUSINESS (ACCOUNTING AND OTHER FUN THINGS), not all expenditures are considered expenses. If you need a large piece of machinery for your business, it will be a cash outlay, but its cost will be amortized over a period of years.

It seems like everyone who invests in a new business finds that it takes twice as long to make the business profitable than originally planned. Because of this, it is important to include your living expenses in your cash flow planning. Most banks, credit card companies, grocery stores, and kids' private schools like to be paid in cash, check, credit card, or money order and not in promises. You should include a contingency amount in your cash flow projections and have a fallback position. We hear lots of stories about people who had a winning idea for a business and ran up their credit card balances in that pursuit. Some day those credit card balances have to be paid.

Now let's look at A. A stands for Advantages.

A	Look at Cost Structure (suppliers, what each element will cost to source or manufacture)
A	Barriers to Entry (large competitors, regulations, patents, large capital requirements). If there are many barriers to entry, it will be difficult to enter a market. It will also be difficult for competitors to enter your market.
A	Intellectual Property. Do you have a proprietary advantage such as a patent or exclusive license on your product or service?
A	Distribution Channel. How will you be selling your product? Will you sell it direct to the consumer via the Internet, sell it to wholesalers, sell it to businesses, or sell it to retail stores? If you can develop a unique distribution channel, you will surely have an advantage.

There are lots advantages to being a small business. Many big businesses rely heavily on small businesses for their survival. One asset that big business cannot corner the market on is creativity. It is often difficult for creativity to live and thrive in large companies because of the typical dynamics of that environment. Many big companies say that they are nimble, have open door policies, and are quick decision makers. Of course, these quick decisions often come after double-blind studies, focus groups, and numerous committee meetings. I am sure all of us have seen the poster that is often given away free at print shops that shows a camel designed by a big-company committee—it's a picture of a donkey.

Howard Shultz, Chairman and CEO of Starbucks and author of *Pour Your Heart Into It*, talks at length in his book about the great number of companies that lose their creativity as they grow. Mr. Shultz writes about the issues that a growing company faces in the chapter "You Can Grow Big and Stay Small." He states, "The danger is that the bigger the company gets, the less personal it feels, to both partners [employees] and customers."[12] Howard, so far, has done a marvelous job of keeping the small company spirit alive at Starbucks. His company is one of the rare examples of a big company with that small company charm. Many of the innovations that Starbucks experienced during its growth were from partners (employees). I, for one, can't get by a week without at least a few Starbucks trips. I used to say, "Let's get a coffee"; now I say, "Let's get a Starbucks." The bottom line moral to this story is "Stay small as you get big."

---

12   Howard Schultz, *Pour Your Heart Into It*, New York: Hyperion, pg. 275, 1997.

Now let's look at M. M stands for Market.

M	The Need. Is there a big need for this product or service? Try to avoid ideas that sound cool but fulfill no real need. Make sure your product or service fills a need or solves a problem.
M	Analyze Target Market. Who are you selling to? Businesses? Consumers? What demographics?
M	Pricing (what you charge, the price; will there be a high enough markup?).
M	Analyze Market Size.

A few years ago, there was a fad called "The Pet Rock." It was a sensation, for a minute, and then it faded. The Pet Rock was a fad, not a business. There was not a need for this product, but it was fun, for a minute. As to pricing, don't build your business on being price competitive because the big boys can eat your lunch on this one. Take Starbucks as an example. A cup of coffee at Starbucks is more than a cup of coffee at Denny's. So why is Starbucks so successful? They are not selling a cup of coffee, but an experience. So what is an experience worth?

Your chances of success are increased dramatically if you have a big market. You also have to consider who the competitors are. Say that you have a new yo-yo design that you want to introduce to the market. Immediately, you are going to go up against Duncan. I personally would rather have a Duncan yo-yo than a brand WYZ yo-yo. Market size is a critical thing to look at, but also look at the major players in the market. It is difficult to slay Goliath—BUT NOT IMPOSSIBLE!

Finally, let's look at P. P stands for Potential.

P	Risk vs. Reward. How risky is the opportunity? If it is very risky, is there a chance for the business to do very well? Will there be a high reward for the founders and investors if the company succeeds?
P	The Team. Is the team right for the business? Do they have knowledge in this area?
P	Timing. Is the market ready for your product? You may have a great idea for flying cars, but if consumers are not ready for your product, you may not be able to turn your idea into a successful business.
P	Goal Fit. Does the business concept fit the goals of the team to create a high potential or lifestyle business?

Risk analysis is a vital element of your decision process in deciding what business to go into. If the business is a low-risk business, it will probably have the following attributes:

- A large number of people willing, able, and ready to jump into the arena with you. Get the visual image of you and twenty of your closest friends in a bathtub.
- Low returns
- Low profits
- Ease of entry by just about everyone who has a couple of dollars and frustration with their current state in life.

The bottom line in risk analysis is this: make sure you do not put yourself and your family on the street if your business does not work. On the other hand, don't bother getting into a business that has no risk, because it probably is not real or at least seven of your ten neighbors are in the same business, and you can all have a barbeque and discuss how glad you are that you didn't quit your full-time jobs.

By using the RAMP model and the fourteen questions above, you should be able to thoroughly analyze your business ideas and any opportunities presented to you.

The Business Plan And Operating Your Business

This chapter is called "THE BUSINESS PLAN AND OPERATING YOUR BUSINESS," because it is this author's opinion that to properly operate your business, you need to have a plan. By plan, I do not mean a document that is prepared once and then placed in a drawer or put on a shelf to collect dust. Your business plan should be an integral part of the overall management of your business. Even if you are not going to seek funding using your business plan, you should complete it and place it in a three-ring binder, divided by major topic, and refer to it often. This way, you can file notes and other pieces of useful information as you come across them. Periodically, you should update your business plan and incorporate the new information that you have collected in your business plan binder.

WHAT IS A BUSINESS PLAN? ──────────────────────

A business plan is a written document that synthesizes all of the essential aspects and information about your business, whether it's an existing business or one that you are intending to start. It is a plan that details the type of business you are in or want to be in, what resources are needed, and how you intend to use those resources to capitalize on your particular business opportunity. Your business plan must be a flexible document that can easily be tailored for a variety of people who may be reviewing it. The typical business plan will concisely describe the opportunity, the environment in which it exists, and how to exploit it. Your plan should be drafted so that it can easily be modified for the different audiences who will be studying it and making decisions based on it. You will also want to have a comprehensive version and an overview for

each of these. And your business plan should be based on Godly principles.
A business plan is a selling tool and a management tool.

WHY PLAN FOR YOUR BUSINESS AND PREPARE A BUSINESS PLAN? ──────

PLANNING OR CHAOS?

Failing to plan is planning to fail, and how can you know where you are going unless you know where you want to go? There is a saying "If you don't know where you are going, any plan will get you there!" This is why you should prepare an annual business plan in the broad sense. Also, as we have discussed in the chapter of this book entitled SOME BASIC CHRISTIAN PRINCIPLES FOR BUSINESS, we must properly plan for and manage the Time, Talent, and Treasures that God has loaned to us during our time on this planet. It simply makes all the difference between organized activity and unplanned chaos. It forces some degree of thought-out structure onto what otherwise might be a series of randomized events that you call your business or prospective business. Whether you are seeking funds for your business or not, you need to prepare a business plan for your prospective or existing business.

There is a lot of evidence that shows that people who write plans are more successful than those who do not. Plans aren't always followed, but people who create a plan are better off.

GET THE FINANCING TO MAKE IT HAPPEN

If you are seeking seed capital or other financing to start your company, then it is absolutely necessary to have a business plan. If you don't have a business plan, you probably should not be asking anyone for funds. You business plan will be your primary selling tool.

GETTING TO KNOW YOUR BUSINESS BETTER

Many people will only prepare a business plan when they start the business or when they are seeking financing. The process of creating a business plan is well worth the exercise. You have heard the saying "A great trip is not determined solely by the destination, but also by the journey itself"; so it is with a business plan. As you go through the process of preparing your business plan, you will get to know your business much better and will be able to look at it more objectively.   The result will be a blueprint of your business. It combines a strategic vision of the company with the data that will turn the business plan into a performance-enhancing tool by means of planning, measuring, and improving. With these attributes, your business plan will be an excellent selling tool and an excellent operating tool.

A BUSINESS PLAN IS A LIVING, BREATHING, DYNAMIC TOOL, NOT A STATIC DOCUMENT TO GATHER DUST ON A BOOKSHELF

For already-existing businesses, the necessity of a business plan may appear at various stages: when applying for a loan, for example, or at a difficult moment when readjustment of some parameters is necessary, or when you have to rethink essential business directions. Many of these issues can be avoided if you make it a habit to prepare a business plan on an annual basis. Once the business plan is drafted, it is much easier to update it each year. Many more businesses, start-ups and existing businesses alike, would be more successful if their owners were more knowledgeable about their business's internal strengths and weaknesses and the threats and opportunities with which they operate. The annual preparation of a business plan forces you to know your business.

CREATING YOUR BUSINESS PLAN ━━━━━━━━━━━━━━━━━━━━

GETTING STARTED

The most difficult part of any task is getting started. It is no different with a business plan. The way to start is "Just Do It!" The blank page on your computer screen (I hope that you are writing this on a computer, as it will be infinitely easier) can be very intimidating. To start the process, take the business plan outline in this chapter and use it as the skeleton for your own business plan. Don't reinvent the wheel. As I have said in a number of places throughout this book, use most of the information in this book as guidelines, not as rules. Look over the proposed outline and start filling in the sections that you feel most comfortable with at the moment. As you begin to fill in these sections, you will get more comfortable so that the sections that seemed problematic to you at first will not seem insurmountable. As you are writing, you will also have thoughts, ideas, and questions. This is when it's good to use bullet points and notes for the sections you are ready to write but haven't fully fleshed out yet. Again, this is the beauty of writing with a computer. A good practice is to mark each of these potential ideas for future work with a "***" before and another "***" after the note to let you know that you need to go back and turn these little "helpers" into complete thoughts. As a matter of fact, I stopped working this section last night, and I placed the "***" before and after my last thought so that I would know where I left off.

Although you can start writing your business plan anywhere in the outline provided, I suggest starting by writing the Executive Summary.

WRITING FOR YOUR READER ━━━━━━━━━━━━━━━━━━━━━

Different readers of business plans will be looking for different "hot buttons" when they review your business plan.

Debt Financiers

If you intend to give your business plan to an investor that is a debt financier (including a bank), you will want to stress the factors that are in place to give the investor a feeling of certainty that the investment will be repaid. There are pluses and minuses to having debt financing investors involved in your entity. The good news is that they do not invest in the upside of your business. They are not your partners; they are your creditors. As your business grows, they do not share in this growth. Once they are repaid, they have nothing to do with your business. A downside is that they do expect to be repaid, and with interest. The interest is where they get their profits. They will also typically have what is called a "perfected" interest in your business. This means that if you do not pay back their "investment" as promised, they can take your assets and/or your entire business to satisfy the amounts you owe them.

Sometimes a debt financier will not invest in your entire entity but finance a particular type of equipment and use the equipment as security for his investment in your company.

All debt financiers will want to see in your business plan assurances of how they will get their loan repaid.

Equity Investors

If the potential investor is an equity investor, he will want to see that there is a potential huge upside to investing in your venture; otherwise, he will possibly opt for the security of putting the money into a certificate of deposit with a bank. He will also want to know his options for exiting his investment in your venture. If an investor puts money into your venture, he will normally be looking for a way to capitalize on the growth in worth of your venture. Normally, the only way your investor can realize a profit on his investment is to sell his interest in the company. This is very difficult, in most cases, for anyone investing in a private enterprise. As a matter of fact, your lawyers will normally draft a clause stating that the investor cannot transfer his interest to a third party without your written permission. Imagine having your investor sell his interest in your business to one of your competitors. Although you will not talk hard dollars in terms of exit strategy in your business plan, you still need to be ready to articulate potential exit strategies.

Friends and Family

This is a popular term in the venture capital world. When you go to a venture capitalist, he will often ask you for a list of possible investors in your business for your initial round of financing that they normally call the "friends and family" round. These venture capitalists may not be able to get you financing, but they have been able to add some new names to their list of potential investors with your friends and family list. When you are writing a business plan for your friends and family, you should write it with the same degree of integrity that you would for outside investors and probably even more so. The friends and family that you submit your business plan to will probably not be very sophisticated financially and will need more basic explanations than a professional investor would. Also, make sure that they are not betting their grocery money or their kids' college funds on your new venture. You would not want to lose family relationships at the same time you lose your business if it does not work. Pray and think long and hard before soliciting "friends and family" money for your new or existing business venture.

A Business Plan Written for Internal Purposes

If you are writing the business plan as part of your management process, there are certain areas that will be given less attention than if you were writing the sections for presentation to outsiders. You might want to skip or write very little for the general background sections or the sections on the industry. But it could be a very good idea to update these areas each year. In doing so, you will generate new ideas and probably uncover some areas where your company needs improvement. The exercise in researching and writing these sections and the information that you uncover will serve to help keep you pointed in the right direction. I have found that going through this process annually keeps my corporate mission clearly defined.

WRITING FOR DIFFERENT METHODS OF PRESENTATION.

We have already discussed that different business plans will be written for different types of investors. They will also be written for different methods of delivery:

TO SUPPORT A FACE-TO-FACE MEETING ━━━━━━━━━━━━━━━

If your business plan is being prepared for face-to-face meetings, your business plan will probably need to be integrated into some type of visual presentation. These visual presentations are normally in the form of either slide shows or Microsoft PowerPoint® presentations. If this is the case, the business plan will normally be used as a "leave behind" tool for your investors to review. Your visual presentation should be reviewed for internal consistency with your business plan. You must remember to revise your visual presentation materials every time you revise your business plan.

SENDING THROUGH THE MAIL ━━━━━━━━━━━━━━━━━━━━━

A business plan that is sent through the mail is possibly the only thing your prospective investor will see to make his decision about investing in your proposed business. You probably will not see him face-to-face before he decides when and if to move forward with your proposal. I recommend sending a business plan only if it is absolutely necessary, because the investor demands it or the geography demands it. In this scenario, your plan will probably be one of scores of business plans in a pile on your potential investor's desk. Most likely, some MBA nonpaid intern will review your plan, trying to apply his newly learned skills from his university classes to analyze your business plan. If you know or suspect this is the case with your business plan, you have to find ways to rise above the clutter of the other business plans and get your business plan noticed. This is without tainting it by flying in the face of what investors traditionally like business plans to look like on the inside and the outside. As you see from the section below entitled THE COVER OF YOUR BUSINESS PLAN, there is a certain tradition to business plan cover design that you don't want to violate. But, with this being said, there are other ways to get your business plan noticed and read.

Here are just a few somewhat creative ways get your business plan noticed without violating the basic traditions of business plan cover design:

If appropriate, send it with a sample of your product. If you are a toy designer and you know that your client has young kids, by all means, send a number of sample toys in the box with your business plan.

Find out something about the intended recipient of your business plan. If he collects tee shirts (which a surprising number of high-powered investors do), by all means, send a few along with your business plan. A couple of points are worth mentioning here: 1) Never give out just one business card when meeting people, and never give out just one tee shirt. These are really cheap ways of advertising, so give them away generously. 2) Don't send a shirt he can't or possibly won't want to wear. Don't send it if it isn't first quality. This may sound a little dumb, but don't send it if it has one of those collars that loses its shape on the first washing.

If you haven't yet manufactured your product, send along something related to your business. As an example, one of my businesses was a company that formatted films for pocket PCs and palm pilots. We sent our business plan to our potential investor along with a PDA and several reformatted films. We got the investment.

VIEWING ONLINE ━━━━━━━━━━━━━━━━━━━━━━━━━━━━━━━━

With today's technology, some venture capitalists require you to send your business plan via a PDF or Word document via email. There are pros and cons to this required approach.

Pros

It is quick—the business plan gets to your investor in seconds rather than days.

It is easy to modify your business plan specifically for your target investor.

The average new entrepreneur seeking investment is typically not very sophisticated in the area of computers and the Internet, and thus it's easy to "shine" in this area with a little expertise (yours or acquired from someone else).

You can easily have multiple business plans tailored to specific investors.

You have a record of business plans sent out via email. This way, you can easily track which business plan was sent to which investor. You can also easily track follow-up correspondence sent via email. Sending out your business plan is similar to sending out your resume when you look for a job. You will probably send out a hundred business plans to a qualified list of investors to get 10 people interested in reading it, and finally, you will possibly get one serious investor.

Cons

Your investor looks at a lot more business plans when they are submitted online, which increases the competing business plan clutter that you have to cut through. Getting your business plan noticed, picked up, and read becomes more difficult.

Business plans submitted online somehow lose their individuality—you cannot use better paper, it does not have a presence on your investor's desk. It is, instead, locked in his computer with thousands of pieces of other data.

BUSINESS PLAN WEB SITE ━━━━━━━━━━

It is very easy to develop a simple Web site where investors can go to learn about your business and gain access to your business plan. For only a few dollars a month, most search engine companies, such as Yahoo, will host a very inexpensive Website for you. Yahoo will even give you simple, yet powerful, tools for building a truly professional-looking and functional Website.

Pros

Easy and immediate access for your potential investors.

You can structure the Website so that you can tailor the elements of your business plan to each particular investor.

Video and audio elements can be included in your business plan.

Investors' access to your business plan elements can be timed so that potential investors can be locked out after a specified period of time.

The business world is getting used to the idea of online tools.

It is easy to amend your Web site-based business plan.

With a Web site-based business plan, you can "stretch" the rules of traditional business plans pertaining to length and content.

When an investor goes to your Web site, he can download the elements he wants to review or review them online.

Your business plan can be dynamic, and you can make changes based on select events.

Cons

The Internet is a cluttered medium.

A written business plan will lie on a potential investor's desk, easy to spot; whereas, the Web site-based business plan may be out-of-sight, out-of-mind.

A Web site-based business plan tends to be a little less personal than a hardcopy business plan.

Some older investors will favor the traditional written business plan and will not look favorably on "high tech" approaches to business plans.

ELEVATOR PITCHES

These plans are called "elevator pitches" because you normally only have 2 to 3 minutes to introduce yourself and your business plan to the investor.

PITCHES AT INVESTOR CONFERENCES

There are numerous investment banking conferences given each year. Many of them are in the "cattle call" format in which you are given 3 to 5 minutes to pitch your plan. At the conference, you will want to have, in addition to your elevator pitch, an abbreviated elevator pitch, formatted business plan to leave behind with the people you actually get to pitch to.

STRATEGY IN YOUR BUSINESS PLAN

When investors put money into your new or existing venture, they are not investing in hard assets, they are investing in your "vision." They are buying into your hopes and dreams based on your business plan. They are also looking for a sound business strategy. They want to know the customer needs you are planning to fill and how you propose to do it. The first part of your business plan is mainly outlining strategy. The next part describes how you plan to execute your strategy. Strategy, as defined by William R. Glueck and Lawrence R. Jauch:

> Strategy is a unified, comprehensive, and integrated plan that relates the strategic advantages of the firm to the challenges of the environment and is designed to ensure that the basic objectives of the enterprise are achieved through proper execution by the organization.[13]

This definition is over 25 years old but no one has yet given a better definition. The Bible is over two thousand years old and will never be replaced as the infallible word

---

13 William R. Glueck and Lawrence R. Jauch, *Business Policy and Strategic Management,* New York: McGraw-Hill, pg. 8, 1984.

of God. In business, you will normally set goals that can be tested against your overall corporate strategy. Your strategy will help you achieve these goals. Your business plan will also describe the tactics you plan to use to achieve your goals as well as your overall corporate strategy. In other words, your strategy is what your tactics are wrapped in to achieve your business goals.

A BUSINESS PLAN IS ALL ABOUT COMPETITION

Business is about competition. What will you do better than your competition? What will be your USP (unique selling proposition)? If there is nothing that you do differently than your competition, then don't bother writing a business plan and don't bother starting your own business. There will naturally be some things you do similar to your competitors. If so, reflect in your business plan how you intend to do them better. Will you be operating cheaper, more efficiently, more effectively? Can you find a particular market niche to focus on? Can you find a unique strategy? Can you position your products differently? Can you use different sales or marketing vehicles?

THE BUSINESS PLAN SHOULD NOT BE THE LENGTH OF A NOVEL

Business plans are not terribly exciting to read. You need to "get in, say what you need to say, and get out" as one of my college professors used to say. The successful business plan is typically 10–30 pages in length, including graphs and charts. Don't put your investor to sleep. A lot of investors will actually weigh business plans in their hands and read the "lighter" ones first. Be as brief as possible but say everything you need to say in your plan. Try not to get tossed into the "heavy" business plan stack. Each of us has sat in front of a preacher who loved to hear himself talk and gave a ninety-minute sermon that could have been comfortably wrapped up in thirty minutes. The unfortunate part about using too many words (in a sermon or business plan) is that the extra unneeded words dilute the message and discount the really important words. Don't let your business plan drown in a sea of repetitive, unnecessary words.

Minor details distract from your main selling points. Even worse, adding a minor detail that an investor dislikes may lead to rejection. Remember the old adage, K.I.S.S. or "keep it simple, stupid." Or if you are a more polite person, K.I.S.S. stands for "keep it simple, smarty."

AVOID HYPE

Most investors can see right through hype. Stick to the facts. Having a business plan filled with hype wastes your time and the investor's time. As already mentioned, you will have to perform to the expectations created by your business plan. An overhyped business plan would not be a good reflection on your Christian walk.

BUSINESS PLANS ARE NEVER REALLY FINISHED

Business plans are living, breathing documents that should be allowed to constantly evolve and change. Business plans are always "works in progress," just like you are as a Christian. A static business plan will quickly become outdated. This is where the computer has made preparing business plans so much easier. Since your business plan will be constantly evolving and refined, it's a good idea to have different versions on your computer ready for printing. It often makes sense to have a separate file for each major section so that you can mix and match sections depending on your needs. You should always print out an extra copy of each business plan that you send out to investors. Put the extra copy in a folder under the investor's name. This way, you will always know which version you sent to each investor. Also, you will have it handy to answer any questions he may have. Keep in mind, also, that if you do get questions, it's a good sign that there is interest in your proposed business.

ALWAYS REVEAL YOUR WEAKNESSES AND RISKS IN YOUR PLANS

As a Christian businessman, you never want to mislead a potential investor. It is important that any investor know that all businesses, including yours, have certain risks and weaknesses associated with them. The risk of being sued for misleading investors is less when you have properly reflected your potential investor's risk in the business plan. With all of this being said, don't lead with your weaknesses. Put them at the back of your business plan. Always lead with your strengths.

DON'T TELL YOUR INVESTOR WHAT HE WILL BE GETTING FOR HIS INVESTMENT IN THE BUSINESS PLAN.

Your business plan will be an information document, a disclosure document, and a sales document. Listing your investor's return for his investment in the document will put you at a disadvantage:

- You will have already disclosed a starting point of negotiation for your potential investor. His position can only go up from your disclosed "deal."
- You may be selling yourself short. He might have been willing and able to give you a better deal.

- You may turn investors off if you have listed a deal structure that does not make sense for that particular investor. I have seen many people talk themselves out of a deal before the negotiation even started by disclosing deal structures up front before finding out what the investor was looking for.

SELL BENEFITS, NOT FEATURES

All good salesmen know that you always sell more when you sell your customers on benefits and not features. If you sell fire alarms, go ahead and tell your potential buyer that the fire alarm is made of the finest steel available, but also tell him that it might one day save his family.

USE AUTHORITATIVE SOURCES AS SUPPORT IN YOUR BUSINESS PLAN

If there are certain elements in your business plan that lend themselves to using authoritative support, by all means include it in your business plan. As an example, if your company will be producing and selling accessories for Game Boy handheld toys, a good piece of authoritative information would be a quote from *Gamer Magazine* stating that there are over 20 million Game Boy owners in the United States today.

YOU ARE RESPONSIBLE TO PEOPLE AND TO GOD FOR WHAT YOU PUT INTO YOUR BUSINESS PLAN.

As a Christian, you have extra added responsibility in the preparation of a business plan. Although a selling document must be truthful and be a fair representation of what you are proposing as a business investment opportunity, you will also be held accountable for its contents by those potential investors reviewing it and by God.

> "Since an overseer is entrusted with God's work, he must be blameless—not overbearing, not quick-tempered, not given to drunkenness, not violent, not pursuing dishonest gain. Rather he must be hospitable, one who loves what is good, who is self-controlled, upright, holy and disciplined."

Titus 1:7

> "Do not have two differing weights in your bag—one heavy, one light. 14 Do not have two differing measures in your house—one large, one small. 15 You must have accurate and honest weights and measures, so that you may live long in the land the LORD your God is giving you. 16 For the LORD your God detests anyone who does these things, anyone who deals dishonesty."

Deuteronomy 25:13

> "The LORD abhors dishonest scales, but accurate weights are his delight."

Proverbs 11:1

This verse could not make it any clearer as to how God feels about dishonesty in business. The good news for Christians in business is that God is standing beside you. But, this also means he is watching you and how you conduct yourself in business. Be as accurate as possible when preparing a business plan, because you will have to either meet or exceed the expectations that you set forth. If you do not honestly follow your own business plan, you will have to do a substantial amount of explaining. God will not sue you, but your investors will.

WRITING YOUR BUSINESS PLAN

PHYSICAL FORMAT

The saying "There's no second chance to make a good first impression," is highly appropriate when it comes to the opening sections of your business plan and its overall appearance. With computer programs like Word for Windows and Excel, business plans look more professional than in the past. I hate to wear business suits, preferring to go to the office each day in a tee shirt and Levis; but for presentations, it's Brooks Brothers suits—look professional, and you are halfway there.

Binding

The contents of your business plan must be superbly written, but that is not enough. It must also look professional and be visually appealing. It should be printed on high-quality paper and be properly bound. Most business plans are bound with wire binding, plastic comb binding, or Velobind® (sometimes called *perfect bind*), or put in three-ring binders. Your business plan should look good and be usable.

	Advantages	Disadvantages
Wire Binding	sturdy, lies flat for reading	costly, wires get bent when stacked

Fig.3 – Wire binding

Plastic Comb   lies flat, inexpensivenot sturdy

Fig.4 – Comb binding

Velobind® very sturdy, great for shipping   will not lie flat

Fig.5 – Velobind

Ring Binder Easy to update, lies flat   not good for shipping, expensive

Fig.6 – 3 Ring Binder

Three-ring binders have been used for years but are bulky and expensive and, hence, have fallen out of favor over the last three years. Plastic comb binding is the most widely used now.

Page layout

Make sure the layout of each page is balanced and visually pleasing, with a lot of open space—paragraphs, lines, and characters should not be too closely spaced. With the publishing tools now available, there is always the temptation to frequently change fonts, box text, and use lots of graphics. Use these features judiciously, or your business plan will start to look too "cute." The text is generally easier to read if you use a font with serifs, such as New Times Roman, Charter, or Garamond, and the margins are justified. For a professional quality, use a sans-serif font, such as Arial, Modern, or Verdana for titles, tables, and outlines. Choose one of each, and stay consistent throughout your business plan.

Tabs and Titles

Each subject, with titled heading, should have its own section (in the full business report, not in the executive summary) and be separated with tabbed index dividers keyed to the table of contents. Tabbed index dividers make it easier for your reader to locate information. It is best to use printed tabs if you can. Avery and other label manufacturers sell labeling packages that can produce computer-printed labels.

Color

Stay away from bright, fancy colors. You should use white, high-quality paper. The cover should be clear (with your professional-looking cover page showing through) or a very light color, dark blue or black.

Graphics

Charts, pictures, illustrations, and graphs are normally acceptable if appropriate to the business plan subject. Don't just throw charts and graphs in your business plan to "spice it up." A good general rule is that if a good graphic can convey a message better than the same amount of space used by text, then by all means use the graphic.

Always use color, when appropriate. If you are going to use extensive colored graphics, choose a theme of three or four rich colors and use them consistently throughout your business plan.

Mailing Labels And Packaging

Again, don't get real cute with the mailing labels and packaging. Make sure your package is professional. One thing that investors hate is opening a package and finding a lot of packaging material to discard. Stay away from the packaging foam "peanuts" if at all possible. Before packaging your business plan for mailing, visualize the investor opening the package and having to get down on his hands and knees to scoop up all of the packaging supplies that spilled to the ground.

Internal Consistency

I have seen so many business plans that are NOT internally consistent. I have seen summary financial projections in the executive summary section that do not agree with the detailed projections in the main body of the business plan. A good way to avoid this problem is to structure your Excel spreadsheets so that the summary financial projections come from the same data as the detailed projections. Also, it is a good idea to import both the summary projections and the detailed projections directly into your business plan to avoid typing mistakes.

Always double- and triple-check your financial numbers so that they add up properly. If an investor finds numbers that do not add up properly or he finds internal inconsistencies, he will probably file it immediately—right in the "round file."

BUSINESS PLAN OUTLINE ━━━━━━━━━━━━━━━

At this point, you may just want to review the list of the typical parts of a business plan below. Or for a more in depth discussion of each part, go to the next section, entitled "THE PARTS OF YOUR BUSINESS PLAN."

Cover Page

Executive Summary

Table of Contents

Description of the Business

      Summary Description of the Business
           Mission
           Business Model
           Objectives and Strategy
           Strengths, Weaknesses, Opportunities, and Threats Analysis
           Products and Services
           Intellectual Property
           Location
           Legal Structure
           Management
           Personnel
           Accounting and Legal

      Marketing Plan
           Overview of Goals of Your Marketing Plan
           Market Analysis
           Your Marketing Demographics and Psychographics
           Competition
           Marketing Strategy
           Your Unique Selling Proposition
           Sales and Distribution
           Packaging
           Pricing
           Branding

Advertising Strategy
Public Relations
Customer Service
Implementation of Marketing Strategy

Financial Documents
Use of Funds
Performa (projected forward for a number of periods) Cash Flow
Three-Year Income Statement Projections
Three Year Projected Balance Sheets
Breakeven Analysis
Key Ratio Analysis

If an Existing Business
Profit and Loss Statements—3 years of actual performance
Balance Sheet—3 years, Actual
Financial Statement Analysis

Optional Supporting Documents
Personal Resume
Owner's Personal Financial Statements
Credit Reports
Leases, Etc.
Patent Summaries
Letters of Reference
Contracts
Other Legal Documents

THE PARTS OF YOUR BUSINESS PLAN

The parts of your business plan listed below are RECOMMENDATIONS, and naturally, every business plan will be written a little differently. Most business plans would not have all of these parts. Use these sections as guidelines in building your own business plans.

The Cover

Don't decorate the cover of your business plan. As glamorous as Hollywood appears to be, successful screenwriters learned long ago you never, never decorate the front of a film script. A good screenwriter may get a little wild and use a Times Roman font instead of Pica but knows that is where his creative latitude ends. The same tradition pertains to business plans. The cover and the contents should be simple and straightforward. Most business plan readers begin to wonder about the substance of your business plan if it looks too slick.

Your plan may be the only plan that he is looking at, BUT, your business plan will be competing with hundreds of other distractions such as phone calls, spreadsheets, newspapers lying on his desk, magazines, financial statements from his existing businesses or investments, and a hundred other distractions. Realistically, your business plan will also be competing for attention with a number of other business plans.

There are a number of things that you should consider for the cover of your business plan to increase its chance of getting read.

Headline

Start your cover page with an appropriate headline that will interrupt and engage your prospective investors. Use the headline to tell them something newsworthy about your venture, but don't get cute—keep it professional.

Company Name

Believe it or not, I have seen business plans without the name of the business or proposed business on the front cover. Seeing a business plan without the name of the company on the front is like starting to watch a film without the beginning title credits. The name may not tell your prospective investor what type of business he will be reading about or what you are asking for, but he has to have a way of referring to it. As an example, say you have a business plan for a toy design company and you have decided to call it Easy Brain Labs. Do you think it better for him to ask his secretary for the "Easy Brain Labs" business plan or for "that business plan from that toy designer"?

Whatever you decide to call your company, remember that you will have to live with it for a long time. You will be building up "goodwill" for your company as people begin to recognize your company name.

Many people have a really tough time developing a name for their company. If you are in this boat, you're not alone. A name is one of the most important decisions you can make. See the chapter in this book entitled FORMING YOUR BUSINESS.

Contact Information

Wouldn't it be awful to have an investor fall in love with a business plan and not know whom to contact about it? So, yes, contact information is really important.

Be sure to include the following information:

Your first and last names
Address (avoid using a post office box)
City, state, zip code
Phone number
Fax number
Email address (avoid those cute little personal-sounding email addresses)

Number of the Business Plan

You need to control the number of business plans you have out to investors and thus must include a business plan number in each one. There is an obvious side benefit to putting a control number on each business plan distributed. This is a subtle way of letting your investors know that there are a number of business plans out to other investors.

Executive Summary

The Executive Summary is probably the most important part of your business plan. If you don't grab your investor here, you will not grab him at all. Also, this is the only part that some investors will read before they turn the business plan over to their investment advisors (e.g., accountants, attorneys) for a more comprehensive review. It is difficult to distill your entire business down to 1 or 2 pages. In school, we are trained that "more is better" when it comes to writing reports. Don't be swayed by the temptation to impress your potential investors with volume. Keep it short and sweet.

The Executive Summary Must Stand On Its Own. There will be a situation where you may be asked by certain investors to submit only a summary; so, in these cases, make sure that it tells the entire story of your investment opportunity in a summarized format.

As odd as it seems, it's best to write the Executive Summary before you write the actual business plan. Whenever I say this, the first question I get is "How do I write the Executive Summary when I haven't written the business plan and, thus, have nothing to summarize?" The Executive Summary will actually help you write the business plan. The process will help you crystallize your thoughts.

What Your Executive Summary Is Not:
- an abstract of the business plan.
- an introduction to your business plan.
- a preface to the business plan.
- a random collection of business plan highlights.

What Your Executive Summary Is:
- a miniature version of your business plan.
- 3 to 5 minute read of a condensed version of your business plan.
- a brief document.

Your Executive Summary Will Serve Several Purposes:

Crystallize Your Thoughts

Your executive summary is your business plan in miniature. It contains your business plan's highlights and key points. To write an executive summary, focus on the issues that are most important to your business's success—past and future—and set aside those matters that are tangential.

Provide The Foundation For Your Full Business Plan

There is nothing worse than sitting and staring at a blank piece of paper and knowing that you are going to be creating a document that is 10 to 30 pages in length. The idea of creating a 1 to 2 page document is much less daunting. But once you have the draft of your Executive Summary completed, you will have written material (no blank page to stare at) to use as your outline. The process of "adding meat to the bones of your Executive Summary" to generate your complete business plan will be much easier.

Set Priorities

The Executive Summary, like the business plan, should be organized according to the items' order of importance. Writing the Executive Summary forces you to choose and prioritize the many points you want to make in the business plan. Prioritizing these elements is critical to making your business plan as effective as possible.

Make Readers Want To Read More

Your Executive Summary must quickly capture your potential investor's interest and imagination and compel him to read more.

What to Specifically Include in Your Executive Summary

Stage of Business—In ten words or fewer, state the industry you are in and the stage of your business or proposed business. This would be start-up, first-round financing, development-phase financing, etc.

Business Summary—A brief paragraph describing what your business does or what you propose to do. Describe the industry you are in and what product/service you plan to sell into your chosen industry. Describe your market's geography, demographics, etc. If you have developed a great new cream sauce for tacos, don't just say you are in the food industry. Spend a few extra words and tell them you are in the Mexican food business.

Products and/or Service—Briefly describe your product and/or service and how you will get it to market. Will you be making it, buying it wholesale, or importing it? State whether your product is readily available or if you have a prototype to present. If you only have a prototype, tell the investor the resources (i.e., Time, Talent, and Treasures) that it will take to get the prototype ready for manufacturing. If you don't have a prototype, you need to have some way to convey your product idea to your potential investor, and you have to be able to prove to him that you can make the product or deliver your service. If it's not possible to have a working prototype, then have a "works-like, looks-like" built.

There was a company that designed a small adapter for Game Boy® handheld game units that allowed their owners to watch DVDs on them. The company could not afford to build a prototype because it was composed of some rather exotic electronic circuitry. What they did instead was get a Game Boy game cartridge and load a movie sample onto it. They then had a plastic manufacturer put together a "model" of the final device. The cost of the look-alike model was approximately $1,000, while an actual prototype would have cost over $100,000 to build. A lot of investors will tell you it is okay if you present your idea on the back of a napkin. They will say this as they quietly put your plan in the "reject" pile.

If you can't put together a prototype or a works-like, looks-like, then spend a few hundred dollars and have an artist draw a few representations of the final product. You can find lot of out-of-work graphic artists at guru.com or craigslist.org.

Strategies and Goals—Give a brief couple of sentences describing how you will utilize your products/services to gain advantage in the marketplace.

Management—Keep it brief. Only list the top two or three executives. A good investor will invest his money in a proposed business based on a good idea and a good business team. The business team must be relevant. They should have some type of relevant experience and/or relevant academic background.

Competitive Advantage—List some other similar or competing companies (and their products and/or services) that are currently out in the market. Briefly explain your competitive advantages. If you can't briefly explain your competitive advantages, you might be in the wrong business. Some examples of competitive advantages are:

- Cheaper
- More readily available
- Higher quality
- Advantageous supplier agreements
- Updated, state of the art
- New technology
- Does more things
- Does its tasks quicker, with fewer steps
- Move convenient
- Open more hours
- Lasts longer
- More attractive
- Available in more colors
- More compact
- More accessories available
- Lower consumption of consumables
- Works better with other devices on the market
- Exclusivity
- Easier to maintain
- More portable
- Easier to store
- Better warrantee or guarantee

Funds Needed—Briefly state the amount of funds you are asking for and in what form (equity or debt) and how you will be spending the funds. Most investors want to see that the funds requested are being deployed into assets that will build the company. They typically do not want to see all of the money going to salaries and wages (to you) while you create a product or service.

Financial data—Provide a snapshot of where you have been (if an existing business), where you want to go, and how you propose to get there.

Provide a summary schedule outlining how you'll use the proceeds you raise. Keep it at a high level; you'll have the details in the plan itself.

Provide a columnar summary of key historical financial figures like sales, net income, assets, liabilities, and net worth. If there are some negative aspects to this schedule, give brief explanations to negative figures. Many times, the funds you are asking for will remedy these troubled areas.

Provide a columnar schedule of key projected financial figures for three years out similar to those listed in your history. You will want to list the top two or three financial assumptions you are basing your projections on. In the body of your plan, you will normally give more detailed line item assumptions.

Exit strategy—I don't normally include exit strategy in a business plan. But you should be ready to articulate this element of your plan when you get someone interested. Discussion of exit strategy should tell HOW your investor can get return on his investment, but don't paint yourself into a box by telling him HOW MUCH he gets for his investment. For example, you might merge with a larger company, go public in five years, sell the business to a financial or a strategic buyer, spin off stand-alone new businesses from segments of your business, or sell off select intellectual property or developed assets.

Table Of Contents

This seems obvious for any document that is more than a few pages long, but many people fail to include a table of contents in a business plan. A well-written business plan will not send an investor stumbling through it to find information. Don't turn your business plan into an index; just include the major topics on a consistent basis.

Summary Description Of The Business

Mission Statement

In a paragraph or two, give a broad overview of the nature of your business, telling when and why the company was formed or will be formed. This is most often referred to as the Mission Statement of the company. Include God in your Mission Statement, as this short couple of sentences and/or paragraphs will guide your business. If you don't know where you are going, how will you know when you are lost? In a small company, you will normally have a good sense of the direction, principles, and goals of the company; but unless you have a crystal clear sense of direction, you will find yourself wandering in the forest. Your investors want to know that you have a clearly defined purpose for your business, that you know where you are going, and that you won't easily get off course.

The best organizational mission statement clearly describes a company's guiding philosophies. It's an important tool to bring everyone in the company together and moving in the same direction.

Mission Statements Answer These Specific Questions:

Why does this business exist?
What is your unique selling proposition?
What are we committed to providing to our customers?
What promise are we making to our clients?
What wants, needs, desires, pain, or problems do our product/services solve?

Some general questions will help define your commitment in several areas of your business.

Clients/Customers: Are you committed to providing high-quality service? Are you Godly fair, honest, courteous, and professional in your business dealings? Are you sensitive to your clients'/customers' needs and dedicated to their satisfaction?

Team Members: Do you recognize the importance of each individual and his or her active role in the success of the entire company? Do you provide your people opportunities to grow and feel motivated in their accomplishments? Do you encourage the flow of communication and exchange of ideas through all levels of the company? Give this area some thought even if you do not have any employees. It will encompass not just employees but all people whom you come into contact with in your business to serve the needs of your clients/customers.

Industry: Are you committed to engaging in honest, lawful, and professional business practices within your industry? Do you respect the related industries that contribute to your success? Are you committed to providing growth to your industry? How do you distinguish yourself from your competitors?

Community: Are you committed to the enhancement of the community of which you are a part? Do you contribute to its economic vitality and consider the environmental impact of your growth? Are you a symbol of leadership and active participation in community affairs? Do you give glory to God? Do you present a good Christian image to everyone whom you have dealings with?

How to Write a Mission Statement

Keep it short. McDonald's mission statement is only four words: "quality, consistency, cleanliness, service." Make it only long enough to cover the intended purpose of your company, but don't waste words.

Make it "memorizable." Don't use "quarter" words when "nickel" words will do. People can remember the nickel words better than the quarter words.

Make it easy to say, understand, and hear. When you are on the phone, make sure that the person at the other end can hear it and understand it.

It should look good on a tee shirt. There are some good mission statements that are a few paragraphs long, but if it can fit on a tee shirt, it will be remembered.

Make it a "becoming" statement. Look forward to what you want your company to become. Don't just state what your company is; tell us how you will reach your goals.

Make it unique. Show how your company is different from other companies.

Good mission statements describe why your company or business unit exists. Good mission statements go a step farther in that they are short and memorable, communicating in just a few words the company's focus. Great mission statements always reflect the benefit your customers receive and answer the question, Why does your company exist?

Ultimately, mission statements are not about money but about meeting the customer's needs. Businesses must produce a profit, but the enterprise must be balanced in terms of both customer and corporate needs. Unbalanced businesses will almost always fail.

Often, some of the best mission statements are an integral part of a company's branding strategy that compels customers to buy. But at the same time, most mission statements can and do direct and influence all significant management decisions.

A mission statement is part of your overall business plan.

Samples of Company Mission Statements

IBM

Our goal is simply stated. We want to be the best service organization in the world.

Wal-Mart

To give ordinary folk the chance to buy the same things as rich people.

Ben & Jerry's

Our mission consists of three interrelated parts:

Product Mission: To make, distribute, and sell the finest quality, all-natural ice cream and related products in a wide variety of innovative flavors made from Vermont dairy products.

Social Mission: To operate the company in a way that actively recognizes the central role that business plays in the structure of society by initiating innovative ways to improve the quality of life in a broad community: local, national, and international.

Economic Mission: To operate the company on a sound financial basis of profitable growth.

Southwest Airlines

The mission of Southwest Airlines is dedication to the highest quality of Customer Service delivered with a sense of warmth, friendliness, individual pride, and Company Spirit.

Nightingale-Conant

To be the preeminent publisher and provider of self-improvement resources that inspires and empowers individuals to lead the lives they most desire.

Nike

To bring inspiration and innovation to every athlete in the world.

Microsoft

To enable people and businesses throughout the world to realize their full potential.

Amazon.com

Amazon.com seeks to be the world's most customer-centric company, where customers can find and discover anything they may want to buy online at a great price.

Don't forget your real mission for your life and your business. You should have as part of your mission a statement that the primary purpose of your business is to glorify God. But, there are a number of ways to glorify our God. You want to manage the resources that God has given you to start your business and make them grow so that you can give more to God. You, your company, and the way you conduct your business should be a testament to the world for God. Being in business gives you the opportunity to witness to customers, vendors, and employees. You may have some employees that would object to your outright witnessing to them. You can witness by the way you do business. There are also other ways you can witness to the world, including your employees.

Each transaction of your business (e.g., checks you write, invoices you bill) should glorify God.

Business Model

Describe your company's model and why it is unique to your industry. Here is where you give a brief introduction to your company. Give a quick couple of lines about your "secret sauce," why you are different. This is where you elaborate on the Competitive Advantage outlined in your Executive Summary. An example is "Other toy inventor companies will present concepts—we will present completed prototypes."

Objectives and Strategy

Here, you tell your investor (remember your business plan is not just for investors) what your specific objectives are and how you plan to achieve them. You will concentrate on giving an overview of your strategy, focusing on short- and® long-term objectives. Key words that might be found in this section are:

Objective samples	Strategy samples
Increase sales 100%	Adding two new milling machines
Improve gross margin20%	Utilize existing excess capacity
Launch our innovative new product	Capture an untapped market
Sustain competitive advantage	Strategic alliances with world's biggest supplier

Fill a niche that has been overlooked	Focus on the sale of cut flowers
Achieve 200X sales of $1.1 million.	Expand into silk flowers
Open gift shop in Stockton, CA at Third Street Public Market with a five-year lease	Locate our gift shops close to anchor stores that will maximize foot traffic to our stores
For 200X, expand into direct mail catalogs	Start by using cooperative mail service packs
Maintain gross margin of 25%	Buying raw materials by truckloads
Establish annual growth rate of 25%	Capture major share of growing community sales
Expand product family by adding 10 different kinds of flowers and flower center arrangements in 200X	Work with other merchants in my shopping

It is sometimes a lot easier to convey your objectives and strategies in a table. The table would outline each objective and how (strategy) you plan to achieve it.

In this section, it is really important to describe your key strategic relationships. Remember your investor is investing in "people," and strategic relationships are a key component of success. Here are some examples of key relationships:

Suppliers
Lawyers
Business advisors
Celebrities
Manufacturers
Board members
Existing investors
High-level recognized executives
Artisans
Elected officials
Retired elected officials
Bankers
Accountants with expertise in your chosen area

SWOT Analysis

Here, you discuss your Strengths, Weaknesses, Opportunities, and Threats. This is NOT where you discuss your risks. In this area, threats can be turned into marketing advantages. As an example, let's say you have been providing bookkeeping services to small companies. Inexpensive computer software has become a threat to your business. No longer do your clients need you to "do their books." But they now need help setting up their systems, interpreting their financial statements, reconciling, and analyzing their financial results. You are now no longer a $20 an hour bookkeeper, but a $100 an hour consultant. SWOT analysis is covered in the chapter entitled CREATIVE THINKING IN BUSINESS in this book.

PEST Analysis

PEST analysis stands for "Political, Economic, Social, and Technological analysis" and describes a framework of macro-environmental factors used in business environmental review and analysis.

PEST analysis along with the SWOT analysis (above) can be used as a basis for the analysis of business and environmental factors. PEST analysis is a useful strategic tool for understanding business position, market growth or decline, potential and direction for the operations of your business, or potential new business.

It is a part of the external analysis when doing market research and gives a certain overview of the different macro-environmental factors that you have to take into account when deciding on going into business for yourself. It is also an important part of your ongoing planning once you have started your business. Political factors include areas such as federal, state, and local tax policy; employment laws; environmental regulations; trade restrictions and tariffs; and political stability. Economic factors are the economic growth, interest rates, exchange rates, changes in money supply, stock market fluctuations, and inflation rate. Social factors look at the cultural aspects and include pop culture, health consciousness, population growth rate, aging of demographic groups, impact of society's attitude changes, career attitudes, and emphasis on safety. The technological factors also include ecological and environmental factors, such as R&D activity, automation, technology incentives, and the rate of technological change.

The PEST factors combined with external micro-environmental factors can be classified as opportunities and threats in a SWOT analysis.

Products and Services

Give your potential investor an overview of the process so that he feels informed about your business. With this understanding, he is now "on your side" and can participate more intelligently in conversation with you and ask more-appropriate questions. You will naturally emphasize your competitive advantages. Always talk about your channels of distribution for your goods and services. This does not just mean the physical distribution of your products and services. It means how the sale is made. As an example, you might never actually take possession of the product. Instead, you might drop-ship it directly from the supplier. This would be an important factor to mention, as you have no inventory risk with drop-shipping.

If you are the manufacturer and/or wholesale distributor of a product:

Describe your products. Tell briefly about your manufacturing process. Include information on suppliers and availability of materials.

If you are a retailer:

Describe the products you sell. Include information about your sources and handling of inventory and fulfillment. As mentioned above, discuss your channels of distribution. As an example, if you already have inventory in storage, it might make sense to be on the Internet with a selling Website or be on Amazon.com or eBay.com.

If you provide a service:

Describe your service and how you deliver it. How is your service unique? Do you deliver it in a special way, at a special price? How do you plan to expand your current offering of service? Do you plan to offer your service on the Internet? List future products or services you plan to provide.

Intellectual Property

All investors like intellectual property. It tells them that you might have something unique, something that can be protected and is possibly worth investing in. It also tells them that you have enough confidence in your product, process, or service to protect it. Give a listing of patent, copyright, and trademark applications and those that have been granted. A brief statement about them would be appropriate. Be ready to produce copies of the filed documents for your investor's review.

Location

You know what they say in the real estate business: "Location, location, location." Yes, your location is important. If you are currently in business, your investor will want to know that you have your locations secured with a good lease and that you have room for growth. You will need to be able to project the cost of your current or proposed location. This would include lease payments, utilities, maintenance, property taxes, mortgage payments, etc. If your location looks good and is a selling point, by all means include pictures. Be able to produce legal documents supporting your location. The review of these types of legal agreements will almost always be part of an investor's due diligence review.

Legal Structure

Even if you are a sole proprietor, you should probably be incorporated. In today's litigious society, you need the protection of incorporation. If you are a corporation with a number of partners and/or investors, mention this fact in this section. If you have subsidiaries, mention this fact here. If a major company has a minority ownership in your company, be sure to mention it here. If you are seeking funds to start a new business, discuss the corporate structure you will establish once you have secured funding. Always try to keep your company ownership as simple and uncomplicated as possible. A complex equity structure tends to scare investors.

List All Major Owners ━━━━━━━━━━━

Management

Savvy investors know that they are investing in people when they invest in companies. The management of your company must be appropriate for the challenge. You have, no doubt, heard the stories of entrepreneurs that start "hot" new companies and are replaced because their board of directors feels that the executive does not have the skills to take the company to the next level. Remember when Steve Jobs was replaced at Apple Computer? The point here is that existing or proposed management must be appropriate to the challenge. Don't list Uncle Eddie as an executive just because he invested a few dollars or because he came up with the idea.

List the people who are (or will be) running the business. Include a paragraph about them and their special qualifications. Describe their responsibilities and abilities.

Have their complete resumes available for examination. And make sure that you have researched them completely. Nothing is more damaging to your business plan than to have resumes that are "inflated" and not factual.

People

List key personnel and give brief backgrounds if you already have people identified. Be able to show why you will need certain numbers and types of people in your new or existing venture. If you can justify your personnel count objective, do it. As an example, if you are opening a car wash, you know how many shifts you will be operating, how many cars your system can process in an hour, and thus, how many people you will need. If you are currently in the car wash business, you will have records telling you the average number of cars that you have historically processed for each day of the week. If you are new to the business, you will be able to develop a model showing how many cars are owned in your area, how often the average person washes his car, etc.

Accounting and Legal

Discuss any accounting needs that are particular to your business and industry. Tell your business plan readers what bookkeeping systems you will be using and what types of reports you will be issuing. You may have developed a particularly easy to use and simple accounting system. Tell about it in your business plan. Tell about the outside accountant you are currently using, and talk about any special skills he or his firm might possess. The same goes for your attorney. Your potential investors will want to make sure that they get R.A.T. (relevant, accurate, and timely) financial and operational reports should they become investors in your company.

The Marketing Plan

What is a marketing plan? The Marketing Plan defines all of the components of your marketing strategy. You will address the details of your market analysis, sales, advertising, and public relations campaigns. The plan should also integrate traditional (offline) programs with new media (online) strategies. Don't forget the Internet, email campaigns, and a good Web page with an easy-to-use shopping cart. Refer to the GROWING YOUR BUSINESS chapter of this book for a discussion of how to formulate the amount you should spend on your marketing. Your marketing plan will often be an integral part of your business plan.

Overview of the Goals of Your Marketing Plan

Give your reader a brief overview of your marketing plan goals. You should not be open-ended or too broad here. Don't say something like "We want to grow really big and make lots of money." Your goals might include something like one of these statements:

Nonfinancial Goals

1. To grow steadily in market share each year from our current 10% to 30% over the next two years.
2. To introduce our new line of products and thus increase sales by 20%.
3. To leverage our database advantages and increase annual sales to existing customers by 20%.
4. To move into a new geographical area and deploy our already successful retail store plan and bring these new stores to breakeven within 18 months.
5. To grow the percentage of sales from our store's Web site from 5% to 30% over two years.
6. Using cultural and language translations of our Web site, open up markets for our line of ethnic seasonings in Europe and South America, and achieve breakeven in these markets within 12 months.
7. To introduce our ethnic seasoning line in the four major western US grocery store chains, two of the chains in the first 18 months, increasing retail unit sales by 15%.
8. To increase monthly traffic to our Web site store from 6,000 to 12,000 per month over the next year.
9. To reduce churn in our customer base from 50% to 15% over the next 12 months. (Churn is the customers you lose. As an example, if you have a growth of 45% and your churn is 25%, your real net growth is only 20%. This is important, because customers are normally a lot harder to retain than to acquire.)
10. Ad e-commerce capability to our business.

Financial goals:

1. To grow initial annual sales to $2 million in 20XX, to $4 million by 20XX, and to $6 million by 20XX.
2. To diversify our product line so that no one product accounts for over 10% of our total revenues.
3. To increase our average order size from $50.00 to $75.00 by the end of the year.

Market Analysis

Your Market Demographics and Psychographics

This is where you identify your target market with soundly researched statistics, such as demographics and psychographics, and discuss special niches within your chosen market. Dictionary.com defines demographics as "the characteristics of human populations and population segments, especially when used to identify consumer markets: *The demographics of the Southwest indicate a growing population of older consumers.*"

Demographical information is vitally important information about your market. You need to know whom you are trying to sell your product or services to in order to effectively utilize your God-given 3 Ts (Time, Talent, and Treasures). But, you also need to know WHY they are buying your goods and/or services. Psychographics is the use of demographics to study and measure attitudes, values, lifestyles, and opinions for marketing purposes. See the chapter entitled *GROWING YOUR BUSINESS* for a more complete discussion on market segmentation and your target market.

Competition

Discuss your major competitors within your industry and those that might not be direct competitors but nevertheless make take some of your business. There are competitors that can offer alternative solutions to the problems you are solving for consumers. As an example, say that you are starting a company that installs computers for home users. Your competition is other people who provide this service AND computer manufacturers that have now begun to build "plug 'n' play" computers that you can run directly out of the box.

The barriers to entry concept (how easy it is for others to jump into the business if they see you are doing well) is normally an important element to include in your business plan. If it is easy for a person to enter into your industry and take some of your business, an investor will want to see you address this issue. He does not want to help you build your company (with his funds) only to see someone "piggyback" on your success. He does not want to see you build a solid road and have someone else use it without paying a toll.

Is your industry concentrated, or is it fragmented? Are there only a few large competitors, or are there a lot of smaller players? Discuss the major players in your industry. Discuss their strengths and weaknesses.

Discuss where your market is now and where it is likely to be in the future. As part of this discussion, talk about the major factors that will influence your market. This will be easier after you have completed a detailed PEST and SWOT analysis as discussed in the "CREATIVE THINKING IN BUSINESS" chapter of this book.

P.E.S.T. is an acronym for the Political, Economic, Social, and Technological factors of the external environment, and SWOT is an acronym for Strengths, Weaknesses, Opportunities, and Threats.

Marketing Strategy

What about strategy associated with marketing? Let's settle on a definition of marketing strategy as follows:

> Marketing Strategy is a set of specific ideas and actions that outline and guide decisions on the best way to create, distribute, promote, and price a product or service (manage the marketing-mix variables).

Your Unique Selling Proposition

You can't really talk effectively about marketing strategy without discussing your Unique Selling Proposition (USP). What is your Unique Selling Proposition? It's what sets you apart from your competitors, what makes your customers want to do business with you rather than your competitors.

There are a couple of major benefits in thinking about, developing, and documenting your USP. First, it clearly differentiates your business in the eyes of your current and potential customers or clients. Second, it focuses your company on delivering the promise of the USP.

It can be a detailed set of performance standards, or it can be a short, catchy phrase or a memorable slogan. Your USP should be tested to ensure that it addresses a need that is truly important to your buyer. But, a memorable slogan that conveys your USP is well… memorable.

Sales and Distribution

How are you going to distribute your products or services? There are so many ways to distribute your products or services that you should consider them all. You have gone through the trouble of inventing, buying, licensing, and partnering on a new product or service concept that you need to make sure you get your product to customers any way you can that is profitable, ethical, and honest. The smart entrepreneur will always be on the lookout for new ways to distribute his products. See the chapter GROWING YOUR

BUSINESS for some ideas for distribution of your product.

Packaging

Why is your packaging better than the competition's? Do you offer packaging that will appeal to the retailer and to the purchaser? This is not always easy to do. A retailer will want every square foot of his retail shelves to generate as much money as possible each day. If he can sell a $4 product 100 times a month or a $40 product 100 times a month from the same shelf space, guess which one he will want to sell? The consumer may want packaging that spreads out and shows everything he is getting, but the retailer will want a nice, compact package design. Retailers have different concerns than consumers.

Consumers want to see the product in action on the package. They want to see what they are getting. Packaging is a science unto itself. There are a number of good books that deal with the subject of successful packaging; so be sure to buy one or more. There are certain colors, shapes, and other elements to packaging that can substantially increase your sales. But keep in mind that you must first sell to the retailer placing your product on their valuable shelf "real estate." Retailers want packaging that can hang on a rack, sit on a shelf, or move off the shelf or rack quickly.

Pricing (price strategy and competitive position)

Pricing your product or service is one of the toughest decisions that you will make for your business. If you are a small retailer, you don't have to go into panic mode when one of the big-box stores such as Wal-Mart moves into your neighborhood. Although they present a challenge to you, it doesn't have to spell doom. Wal-Mart can probably beat you in pricing, but there are other tools in your arsenal that Wal-Mart does not have:

- Your ability to move quickly. You don't have to fill out a request form in triplicate, get committee approval, or put your decisions up for a vote.
- Your creative thinking skills (see the chapter "CREATIVE THINKING IN BUSINESS" in this book). As this chapter on creative thinking will tell you, big corporations often smother creativity with their corporate rules, committees, and approval processes and procedures.
- Ability to get products that Wal-Mart does not stock. If you have a really "hot" product that Wal-Mart does not stock, it will take them months or even years to start stocking it, especially if it's a local favorite.

- Better service. As a small retailer, you can always give better service than the big-box stores.
- Your product knowledge. Most stores, even big-box stores, do not train their people adequately in the areas of product knowledge. You will know your products much better than the clerks at the big-box stores.
- You are local and you know the local needs, wants, and desires.
- Convenience. How many times have you wanted to just "dash" into a store for a quick purchase? Try "dashing" into a Wal-Mart.
- You can configure your products more conveniently than Wal-Mart. Your customers might not want to buy 48 rolls of toilet paper when there is only one person living at home.

There is a place in the retail landscape for the big-box stores and for small local stores. An ideal situation is to take advantage of the heavy consumer traffic created by a big-box store. This will be easier if you have products with truly strong USPs (unique selling propositions).

Branding

A brand can be a company, product, or service that has been given a distinct identity and that has been consistently promoted. A well-developed brand can be the most valuable asset that you have. Everyone knows Coke, Band-Aid, Kleenex, etc. A brand is more than a name: it's what the product looks like, what colors consumers associate with it, and the benefits of using the product. Basically, branding is everything that makes consumers recognize your product. Your entire company can find itself wrapped around its brand. When your brand becomes better known than your company, you have a definite strategic advantage.

Advertising Strategies

This element of marketing strategy is concerned with how you are going to get your message out to your existing and potential customers. There is a wide range of methods for getting your message out to the world. It's important to be able to measure the effectiveness of your advertising. It's tempting for the new business owner to advertise only because he wants to see his company and products in print. Advertising has to be effective, and its effectiveness has to be measurable.

Traditional advertising is somewhat difficult to measure. Direct response advertising is a little easier to measure, because every direct response ad dollar spent will result in direct orders and/or sales of your product. Direct response advertising is where you have a response mechanism built into your ads. An example is an infomercial. You will normally have an 800 number with a call to action in the infomercial directing viewers to "call the 800 number on the screen and order the product now!"

There are ways to measure the effectiveness of traditional advertising. Here are some ways from *Start Your Own Business* by Rieva Lesonsky and the staff of *Entrepreneur* Magazine:[14]

1. Run the same ad in two different publications with a different identification mark on each.
2. Ask customers to clip the ad and bring it in for a discount.
3. If you sell via the Internet, mail, or other direct response channel, media code each advertisement so that you can tell which ads came from them.
4. If you are advertising in more than one magazine, offer slightly different prices in each one so that you can distinguish where the sales are coming from.
5. Isolate your ad in one magazine only so that you know the sales came from that particular ad.
6. Stop running an ad that you normally run to see if there is a drop-off in sales.

It's not enough to say you have an advertising strategy. You have to demonstrate that you have some way to measure its effectiveness.

According to Rieva Lesonsky, one study showed that an ad from a new company has to be noticed by a prospect a total of three times before that prospect becomes a customer. Never show in your advertising strategy that you are going to have an advertising campaign. Almost all advertising campaigns need to have continuity to be effective. Most types of advertising are measured in terms of reach and frequency. Reach involves how many people will see your ads, and frequency is a measure of how many times your intended viewers will see your ads.

Does this sound familiar? How many times does God have to send the message of salvation before we will listen?

Public Relations

When you mention "public relations" (PR), most people think about certain channels

14   Rieva Lesonsky, *Start Your Own Business*, Irvine, California: Entrepreneur Press, pg. 506 and 508, 2007.

of communication, particularly editorial publicity, sponsorships, and 'launch events' for new products. However, there is much more to consider with PR.

Take a look at the definition by the Public Relations Institute of Australia[15]:

> Public relations is the deliberate, planned and sustained effort to establish and maintain mutual understanding between an organization (or individual) and its (or their) publics. It's key to effective communication in all sectors of business, government, academic and not-for-profit.

> Public relations is not limited to certain media, and it is not about promoting products or services.

Public relations can and should use any media, including TV and print advertising, to establish and maintain goodwill and mutual understanding between an organization and its publics.

Good public relations helps to support your advertising message, making your ad dollars work a lot harder and more effectively for you. Public relations includes the following elements:

- Your online presence
- Press releases when events happen at your company
- Interviews with the press
- Getting listed in important journals
- Getting important people to say good things about your company, products, and services

Customer Service

What is customer service? According to Jamier L. Scott "Customer service is a series of activities designed to enhance the level of customer satisfaction – that is, the feeling that a product or service has met the customer expectation.".[16] Good customer service makes the customer feel that he matters before, during, and after the sale. Customer service is a critical element of the relationship between your business and your customer. Oftentimes, especially if you sell primarily over the Internet, Customer service is the only contact your customers will have with a live person representing your company. Here are some interesting statistics from Sideroad.com. The author did a

---

15   Public Relations Institute of Australia (http://pria.com.au/), 2010.
16   Turban, Efraim, *Electronic Commerce: A Managerial Perspective*, New Jersey:Prentice Hall, 2002

brief informal survey to see if these statistics were still relevant today (2010) and yes they are still relevant.[17]

- It can cost up to five times as much to attract a new customer than to retain an existing one.
- The average business never hears from 96% of its unhappy customers.
- For every complaint received, the average company, in fact, has 26 customers with problems, 6 of which are serious in nature.
- Surprisingly, of the people who have problems, complainers are more likely than non-complainers to do business again with a company that upset them, even if the problem isn't satisfactorily resolved.
- Of customers who register a complaint, between 54% and 70% will do business again with the organization if their complaint is resolved. That figure goes up to an impressive 95% if the customer feels that the complaint was resolved quickly.
- The average customer who has a problem with an organization tells 9 or 10 people about it; 13% of the people who have a problem with an organization recount the incident to more than 20 people.
- Customers who have complained to an organization and had their complaints satisfactorily resolved tell an average of 5 people about the treatment they received.

In this section of the business plan, point out what special approaches you have to customer service.

Implementation of Marketing Strategy

As a new company, many of your marketing responsibilities will be outsourced to professionals. When doing this, be sure to check the companies out completely. Marketing and public relations companies are in the business of convincing companies, especially small companies to spend money on marketing and public relations. Many ad agencies and public relations agencies will try to get you to spend beyond your budget. After carefully selecting your marketing and public relations companies, watch them closely. At first, you will probably do many of your marketing and public relations functions in-house.

As part of this section of your business plan, you should try to put a timeline to

---

17   Dr. John T. Self, *Customer Service Facts and Figures,* www.sideroad.com, 1998.

your marketing strategy. Naturally, your timeline will experience many revisions as circumstances change.

Financial Statements

Financial Statements are the quantitative interpretation of everything you stated in the organizational and marketing plans. Do not do this part of your plan until you have finished those two sections. There is a language of accounting called Generally Accepted Accounting Principles (referred to as *GAAP*). Your projections and actual financial statements should always be prepared in conformity with GAAP.

Financial Statements are the records used to show past, current, and projected finances. The following are the major documents you will want to include in your business plan. The work is much easier if they are done in the order presented, because they build on each other, utilizing information from the ones previously developed.

Summary Of Financial Needs

This is an outline giving the following information:
- Why you are applying for financing
- How much capital you need
- How the funds will be used

You will want to be relatively precise here. If you can't demonstrate clearly what you need funds for, you are going to make any potential investor more than a little nervous. Remember that there are always hidden costs or costs that you may have not considered that are associated with your funding needs. Say you have a printing company and you want to buy a new printing press. You look in a printer supply catalog and find just the right printer. You include this in your business plan. But here are some things you forgot:

- Cost of transporting the printing press from Hong Kong to Denver— hundreds of dollars.

- After measuring the doorway into your printing press room, you find that you have to knock out part of the wall and make a bigger door.

- You find that your current wiring will not accommodate the increased power requirements of your new printing press.

- Your city has environmental compliance laws that require that you hire an engineer to evaluate your new printing press and its impact on the local water and sewer systems.

- You forgot to include the cost of disposing of your old printing press.

As ridiculous as this example seems, this author has seen business plans leave out important elements, like the above items, from their funding needs. It is also important to include a contingency of 5% to 10% because, no matter how careful you are in developing your funding needs number, you will, more often than not, leave something out. You definitely won't want to go back to your investor and ask for more funds.

Pro Forma Cash Flow Statement

This document projects what your business plan means in terms of net dollars generated from operations. It shows cash inflow and outflow over a period of time and is used for internal planning. It is of prime interest to your lender and shows how you intend to repay your loan if you are borrowing funds. Investors want to know that you will have sufficient cash flow to operate your business according to your stated plans.

There are certain items on your financial statements that do not require an outlay of cash and vice versa. As an example, you will have depreciation in your profit and loss statement, but it will not require a cash outlay. You may show a positive net income in your income statement, but it will not show the cash you paid on a loan, because it is not an expense on your profit and loss statement. Cash flow statements show both how much and when cash must flow in and out of your business.

Three-Year Income Projection

A Pro Forma Profit & Loss (Income) Statement, known as a *P&L*, should show projections for your company for the next three years. The utility of your projected Profit and Loss Statement will be substantially enhanced if you include a list of line item assumptions. Each line on your P&L should have a stated assumption of how the number was developed.

Here is an example of a line item assumption for sales:

There are 25 million Game Boy® owners in the world. Of these owners, we assume that we can sell our Game Boy® DVD adapter to 5% of Game Boy® owners, which means we can sell 1,250,000 million units of our adapters for the first year. We will have the adapter in 20,000 of the 50,000 stores that carry this type of product worldwide. This means that we will sell an average of 62 units per store over the stated 12-month period. This is an average of a little over 5 units per store, per month.

Some of your expense assumptions will depend on your revenue projection numbers.

Projected Balance Sheet

Projection of Assets, Liabilities, and Net Worth of your company at the end of the three years for which you have presented Profit and Loss Statements. You can't complete the projected balance sheets without first completing the projected profit and loss Statements. There are certain items that will not flow from your profit and loss statements into your projected balance sheets. An example would be if you must borrow funds from time to time to even out your cash flow. This will only be a balance sheet transaction increasing liabilities and increasing assets (cash).

Breakeven Analysis

The break-even point is the point at which a company's expenses exactly match the sales or service volume. It can be expressed in total dollars or revenue exactly offset by total expenses, total units of sales, or production. This analysis can be done either mathematically or graphically. In a new business, potential investors will be interested in the length of time that your business will take to reach breakeven. See the chapter entitled KEEPING TRACK OF YOUR BUSINESS (ACCOUNTING AND OTHER FUN THINGS) and specifically the section in the chapter entitled "Operations Reporting and Financial Analysis."

Note: The following are actual performance (Historical) statements. They reflect the activity of your business in the past.

If your business is new and has not yet begun operations, the financial section will end here, and you will possibly add a personal financial history statement. If yours is an established business, you will include the following actual performance statements:

Profit And Loss Statement (Income Statement)

Your Profit and Loss Statement shows your business's financial activity over a period of time, typically for three years, presented one year at a time. It is a picture showing how your business has actually performed and is an excellent tool for assessing your business. Your ledger is closed and balanced, and both the revenue and expense totals are transferred to this statement. See the chapter entitled "KEEPING TRACK OF YOUR BUSINESS (ACCOUNTING AND OTHER FUN THINGS)."

Any unusual transactions need to be fully explained so that your readers get a true picture of your operations.

Balance Sheet

Your Balance Sheet shows the condition of the business as of a fixed date. It is a snapshot of your company's financial condition at a particular point in time. It is usually done at the close of an accounting period and contains the following major sections: Assets, Liabilities, and Net Worth (often referred to as *equity*).

Financial Statement Analysis

In this section, you will use your income statements and balance sheets to develop an analysis of relationships and comparisons of items in a single year's financial statement, comparative financial statements for a period of time, and/or your statements with those of other businesses. Your measurements are expressed as ratios or percentages that can be used to compare your business with industry standards.

If you are seeking a lender or investor, ratio analysis as compared to industry standards will be especially critical in determining whether or not the loan or venture funds are justified.

- Here are some important terms to understand:
    - Liquidity Analysis (net working capital, current ratio, quick ratio)
    - Profitability Analysis (gross profit margin, operating profit margin, net profit margin)
    - Debt Ratios (debt to assets, debt to equity)
    - Measures of Investment (return on investment)
    - Vertical financial statement analysis (shows relationship of components in a single financial statement)
    - Horizontal financial statement analysis (percentage analysis of the increases and decreases in the items on comparative financial statement)

Exit Strategy

Although I don't recommend putting an Exit Strategy section in the business plan, it is a good idea to have it ready for discussion purposes or for insertion into your business plan should it be requested. I don't normally include it, because it doesn't make sense to start talking about exiting before the investor comes on board. Get him hooked and then discuss exit strategy.

Investors greatly desire and are motivated by a clear picture of a company's exit strategy. They will want to know the timing and method through which they can "cash in" on their investment. This picture best comes into focus when the key valuation and liquidity drivers of the company are clearly delineated. An excellent method to accomplish this is through descriptions of comparable firms that have had successful liquidity events, either through acquisition, merger, or an initial public offering (IPO). As said above don't include exit strategy information with your business plan.

In most cases, investors only make money when the business reaches a successful exit event. As such, it is critical that you are ready to explain the expected exit, detail why this exit was chosen, and validate a realistic exit price.

Risk Analysis

All investors know that there are substantial risks associated with businesses, especially with start-up businesses. No investor expects a risk-free plan. Angel investors and venture capitialists (VCs) know start-ups are incredibly risky. An angel investor is normally someone who is affluent and provides the capital for a startup business. This id normally done in exchange for a substantial ownership position. If they don't understand this, don't take their money—they don't know what they're doing, and as a Christian, you will not want to take advantage of them! Most projects fail for reasons that could have been (and sometimes were) predicted far in advance. Since entrepreneurs are optimistic by nature, they tend to brush off predictions of doom and charge ahead anyway, assuming they will find a way to overcome identified risks. One of the best reasons for completing this section of your business plan is that it will make you stop and analyze your potential areas of risk.

If properly stated, your risk analysis will show your potential investors that you have properly planned for potential risk. Address the risk in your plan so that your investor does not develop his own risk analysis without the benefit of seeing your strategy for addressing his risk concerns.

The risk analysis in your plan demonstrates that you've thought through potential risks, that you know how to plan for them, and that your plan can survive when things go wrong.

Your plan can address several kinds of risk. You don't need to address every imaginable risk, but doing a SWOT (Strengths, Weaknesses, Opportunities, Threats) analysis will reveal risks that you should disclose. You do not have to disclose remote or unlikely risks, only those that could seriously impact the viability of your business.

If you show your investors that you are prepared to address these risks, they will be much more confident about investing in your business.

The key is acknowledging that things can go wrong and demonstrating some creativity in finding a solution. You certainly needn't respond to every risk imaginable. Your goal is to provide evidence that you have thought out strategies to deal with the most onerous potential risks.

Supporting Documents

This section of your plan will contain all of the records that back up the information you have given in the main parts of your business plan. I would be selective in including these supporting documents with your business plan. There is always the possibility of including too much information. The most common supporting documents are:

Personal Resumes

Include resumes for owners and management. They shouldn't be more than one page each. It should include the following information relevant to your business plan:

> Work history
> Accomplishments
> Education
> Special certifications

Personal Financial Statements

This will be a standard personal financial statement prepared showing your Assets, Liabilities, and Net Worth.

Credit Reports and Financial Letters of Reference

This includes business and personal letters of reference from suppliers, wholesalers, credit bureaus, and banks. If you have personal or business relationships with people you do not necessarily do direct business with but who can attest to your business ethics and reliability, you might want to include them here.

Copies of Leases, Mortgages, Purchase Agreements, and Contracts

All agreements currently in force between you, your company and a leasing agency, mortgage company or other agency. This would include important equipment leases, supplier agreements, and other relevant contracts and agreements.

Other Legal Agreements

All legal papers pertaining to your legal structure (e.g., partnership agreements, incorporation documents), proprietary rights, insurance, etc.

Miscellaneous Documents

This category includes all other documents that have been referred to, but not included, in the main body of the plan (e.g., examples, location plans, demographics, competition analysis, advertising rate sheets, cost analysis).

Forming Your Business

NAMING YOUR BUSINESS AND YOUR PRODUCTS

The name you give your business can be one of the most important decisions that you ever make in starting your business. According to the Bible, "A good name is more to be desired than great riches." (Matthew 16:26)

Coming up with a meaningful name for your business is no easy task. You will want to give your name a lot of thought. You will be building goodwill (hopefully) surrounding your business name, and you will have to live with it for a long time; so give it careful consideration. Be sure to refer to the chapter in this book called "CREATIVE THINKING IN BUSINESS" for ideas to get the creative juices flowing.

20 STRATEGIES FOR NAMING YOUR BUSINESS

1. A name can make your company seem big (but do keep it honest).

Global Building Maintenance, Inc.	vs.	Frankie's Janitorial
International Gift, Inc.	vs.	Bric-a-Brac Store
Sonic Automotive Engineering	vs.	Burt's Auto Repair
Jon's Supermarket	vs.	Jon's Groceries

2. Associate your company with something meaningful.

    Animals

    Dove Soap
    Eagle Press
    Fox Publishing

Game Shark
Gorilla Glue
Lions Share Distribution
Lynx Software
Rabbit Messenger Service
Tiger Electronics

Places

Atlas Van and Storage
Cisco (short for "San Francisco")
Dessert Inn
Global Supplies
Great Plains Software
Great Western Digital
Jet Blue (as in blue skies)
L. A. Gear
Outback Steakhouse
Paris Furs
San Francisco Bakery
Seattle's Best
Universal Studios

Quality

Best Buy
Certified Grocers
Convenience
Easy's Deli
Excel Consulting
EZ Deli
Fast Friend Dry Cleaners
Good Guys
Great Beginnings
Great Expectations
Handy Car Wash
Midas Muffler
Minute Man Press

Network Solutions
One-Stop Shopping
Pro-Sporting Goods
Quality Markets
Quick-Stop Auto
Super Cuts
Superior Roofing
Top Auto
Tuneup Masters
U-Sell Realty

Historical/Famous Figures

Alexander Granite
Ben Franklin Stoves
Columbus Adventures
Edison Electric
Lincoln Insurance
Starbucks (character in Herman Melville's Moby Dick)
Washington Savings

Precious Metals, Gems, Wonders of the World, Other Objects

Apple (favorite fruit of Steve Jobs)
Diamond Floors
Glacier Water Company
Golden Restaurant
Lava Soap Company
Niagara Dry Cleaning
Nike (Greek goddess of Victory)
Pepsi (from pepsin, an enzyme in the stomach)
Pyramid Publishing
Rain Forest Shampoo
Rainbow Bakery
Ruby Press
Silver Spur Coffee
Target

      Royalty

      Burger King
      King's Ransom Get-a-ways
      Monarch Paint
      Princess Cruises

3.   Combine common words.

      Best Buy
      BuyRite
      Chemclean
      Electrolux
      GoodYear
      Microsoft
      RiteAid
      Safeway Foods

4.   Create a new word.

      Accenture (Accent on the Future)
      Adecco
      Amoco (American Oil Co)
      BenQ (BringEnjoymentQuality)
      Compaq (computer and pack)
      Exxon
      LEGGO ("leg godt" – "play well" in Danish)
      Nextel
      Nolo Press
      Nortel (Northern Telecom)
      Qantas (Queensland And Northern Territory Aerial Services)
      RAND (Research and Development)
      SEGA (Service Games of Japan)
      Toshiba (merger of Tokyo Electric Co and SHIBAura Engineering works)
      Unisys
      Wal-Mart
      Yahoo! (an acronym for Yet Another Hierarchical Officious Oracle and a word made up from the book Gulliver's Travels)

5. Use initials creatively.

> AMD (Adv Micro Devices)
> BASF (initials of first products)
> BEA (initials of first owners)
> Hotmail (creative use of HTML)
> Intel (integrated electronics)
> KFC (Kentucky Fried Chicken)
> LG (combination of Lucky brand and Goldstar brand in Korea)
> Nabisco (National Biscuit Company)
> RCA (Radio Corporation of America)
> SAP (Systems, Applications, Products in Data Processing)

6. Use foreign words with appropriate meanings.

> Audi (listen in English)
> Daewoo ("Great Universe" in Korean)
> Nintendo (three Japanese characters that mean "Heaven blessed hard work")
> Pixar (action [verb] of making pixels in Spanish)
> Sanyo (three oceans in Chinese)
> Sony (from the Latin word "sonus" meaning sound)
> Veritas (Latin for "truth")
> Volvo (Latin for "I roll")
> Xerox (the Greek root "Xer" means "dry" as in dry copying)

7. Use combinations of the owner's names or initials.

> Adidas (Adolf Dassler)
> Ahold (Albert Holding)
> Casio (Kashio Tadao)
> Hasbro (Hassenfeld Brothers)
> IKEA (Ingvar Kamprad)
> Mattel ("Matt" and "Elliot")
> Taco Bell (founder Glen Bell)

8. Include benefits of your Company in your name.

> 24 Hour Fitness

AccuPay
Caring Hands Daycare
Endless Games
Federal Express
Green Clean
LA Fitness
Network Solutions
Office Max
QuickBooks
Safe Lock and Key
Safe Storage
Save Mart
Supercuts
University Games

9. Say Something About Your Products

AirFlow Air Conditioning and Heating
ChemLawn
Digital Equipment
Doggie Daycare
Game Stop
Healthy Discounts
Learning Annex
Protect Patrol
Safe Lock and Key
Sparkle Car Wash
Toys R Us

10. Use Alliteration

Delicious Dogs
Excellent Electronics
Fun Feet
Gemini Gardeners
Good Grocers
Griffin Golf

Happy Hamburgers
Stop N' Shop

11. Use Initials that are easy to remember

ABC
AMD
AT&T
BBC
CBS
HP
IBM
KFC
LG
NBC
PAX
RCA
SEC

12. Target Your Name to Your Customers

Bass Pro Sports
Big 5 Sports
Big and Tall
Kids Korner
Outfitters
Weight Watchers

13. Play on Words (but don't get too cute).

4 Eyes (eyeglasses)
Come Hear (Here) Music
CYI (Can you Imagine toys)
FunRise Toys
Gazillion Bubbles
IM Here (Instant Messaging)
Shear Pleasure Hair Salon

14. Use Your Own Name in an Inventive Way

> Brown Color Tiles (we have other colors also!)
> Erickson Travel
> Green's Lawn Care
> Griffin Investments ("Griffin" actually means "guardian of the treasury")
> Little Day Care
> Shepherd Dog Grooming (all breeds)
> Stone Counter Tops (we have other types of tops also)
> Top's Roofing
> Wells Plumbing

15. Look through the phone book and other directories for ideas

> Classifieds in the newspaper
> Mall directories
> Random searches on the Internet
> University course catalogs
> Yellow Pages

16. Keep your business name short.

I once worked for a certified public accounting firm that had the following name: Bowman, Fong, McKnight, Hubbard, Anderson and Murphy. This name was printed on every business card. Do you think this was as easy to remember as Arthur Andersen? At the time, Arthur Andersen was one of the largest accounting firms in the world

17. Don't Be Too Exclusive.

Let's say that you start your landscaping service in Van Nuys, California (Southern California) and call it Van Nuys Landscaping. Let's also say that your business is going really well and you are thinking about opening another office in Stockton, California (Northern California), and maybe even franchising it. The Van Nuys Landscaping name will be limiting.

18. Use a name that is available as a URL (Internet Web address). This is not absolutely necessary, but it can be a big benefit. Check with the Web site servers to see availability. Don't base your name solely on the fact that you

can get its URL. If you business name is not available as a URL modify a URL by adding, subtracting or changing the order of key words.

19. Stay away from controversial names. Any name that would upset any large group of people is just not good for business. It never hurts to make sure that your name is family-friendly.

20. K.I.S.S. (Keep It Simple, Smarty). With a name, the K.I.S.S. concept is incredibly important.

Keeping the above strategies in mind, do the following to get the ball rolling in creating your company name:

- List 10 synonyms associated with your proposed business.
- List your products and services (up to 10).
- List 10 adjectives that describe the business you are contemplating.
- List 10 special features of your proposed business.
- List 10 benefits associated with your proposed business.
- Combine two to three of the words to form candidates for business names.

Try your name ideas out on various family members and friends. Once you have a couple of candidates that you like, see about getting them protected with a trademark. See the chapter entitled RISK MANAGEMENT (MORE THAN INSURANCE).

LEGAL FORM OF YOUR BUSINESS

There are many forms of business by which you can operate your company. The most common forms are sole proprietorship, partnership, "C" corporation, and limited liability company (LLC). Under most circumstances, this author recommends either a C Corporation or an LLC. The reasons will become obvious in the discussion below. The decision that you make about the form of doing business will have lasting, financial, tax, operational, and legal implications. I do recommend that you consult a certified public accountant and/or attorney when forming your company. This discussion of business formation is for your informational purposes only.

When forming a business, you have the following business options:

- Sole proprietorship

- Partnership
- Limited partnership
- Limited liability company
- Incorporating as a subchapter S corporation (closely held corporation)
- Incorporating as a C corporation (C Corp)

SOLE PROPRIETORSHIPS

Sole proprietorship is the simplest form of business ownership. You are a sole proprietor if you are the sole owner of your business. A sole proprietorship does not require any filing with the state to start operating the business. However, there are some serious drawbacks to this form of business ownership.

The most significant drawback to operating as a sole proprietorship is that it affords you the least protection for your assets, both personal and business. Anything you do as a sole proprietor may expose your personal assets to garnishment or liens based on the debts or actions of the business enterprise. There are other forms of doing business, such as a corporation or limited liability company, which will protect your personal assets.

Pros
- Absolute authority in decision making
- Total flexibility in management of the company
- No bosses (such as stockholders) to issue orders
- Ease of formation
- Easy to get out of business
- Low start-up costs
- Possible taxation benefits since your sole proprietor income is personal income and can be offset against your other personal income on your personal tax return. No "double taxation" as is the case with corporations.
- Less government control and intervention
- The income you generate is yours (less the part that you have to give to God and Uncle Sam). Do not forget to pay tithes on your next income.

Cons
- Exposure of personal assets to business losses and lawsuits. If your business fails and the business assets are not enough to cover the obligations of the business, then the business debtors may look to your personal assets for recovery.
- Difficulty in obtaining long-term financing from loans and outside investments

- Certain types of expenses are not available to sole proprietors. These include such things as workers' compensation and personal health insurance on the sole proprietor. Selling your business becomes difficult if you are a sole proprietor.
- You will probably have to make quarterly estimated tax payments to the IRS and your state (if your state has a state income tax).

PARTNERSHIPS

A partnership may expose you to even more risk than the sole proprietorship form of conducting your business. A partnership is formed when there are two or more owners of a business. Again, this form of business also does not require any filing with the state. If you start a business with a partner without completing any forms or agreements, you would be considered a partnership. All partners are directly liable for the obligations of the partnership. I never recommend the partnership form of doing business for this reason as well as others. Imagine if your partner dies and you find yourself in business with his surviving children or his wife. Partnerships are great breeding grounds for future conflict. There are agreements that you can put into place to deal with the death of a partner, but there are still many reasons that the partnership form of doing business is not generally recommended.

Pros

- Same as for sole proprietorship form of business
- You may not have all of the talents that are needed to start a business on your own, so a partnership makes it easy to bring in those talents you don't have (along with numerous headaches)
- Moral support. Sometimes it is easier to travel down the road of owning a business with someone.
- Most investors will be more comfortable with a "team" rather than a sole proprietor. This form of doing business may make it easier to raise funds.
- A partnership is more flexible than a corporation, but less flexible than a sole proprietorship.
- When more than one person starts a business, there are typically greater assets put into the business.
- The risk associated with a partnership is normally less than for a sole proprietorship. There is often someone to cover for you if you get sick or have to be out of the office for an extended time.

Cons
- Same as for sole proprietorship and then some
- Complex partnership agreements should be drafted covering areas such as:
  - Objectives of the partnership
  - Division of profits and losses
  - Amount of each partner's investments
  - What happens if one partner is no longer able to function?
  - What happens if one partner creates personal debts that affect the business?
  - Date of commencement of operations
  - Duties and responsibilities of each partner
  - How decisions will be made
  - Address any special conditions that are out of the scope of normal business operations.
  - Any special consideration given to a particular partner
  - Dissolving the partnership
- Difficulty in finding the right partner
- The partnership cannot be sold without the consent of all partners
- Eventually all partnerships will come to the point where partners feel that they are not being fairly compensated for the resources (e.g., Time, Talent, Treasures) they are contributing to the business.

LIMITED PARTNERSHIPS

A Limited Partnership (LP) is an association of individuals who get involved in running the business on a day-to-day basis and other individuals who are only passively involved. "Passively involved" typically means their involvement only includes investing money or other assets into the business. There are some important differences between a general partnership and a limited partnership. A limited partnership is normally required to register with its state government. Another important difference is that interests in an LP cannot be freely transferred or sold without filing additional documents with the state.

Probably the most important feature of an LP is that limited partners are not personally responsible for the debts of the business. This is called "limited liability." A limited partner is one that is not actively involved in the operations of the business. General partners, the ones actually running the business on a day-to-day basis, do risk their personal assets for the company's debts and negligent acts.

Pros
- Limited liability to the limited partners
- Can attract large sums of investment cash
- Can attract talent
- Can spread risk over a large number of investors and partners

Cons

- Must file with the state in which the limited partnership is doing business
- Not easy to transfer or sell interests, and you are required inform your state in filings
- Oftentimes you must deal with people you do not know when they become limited partners
- General partners are liable for negligent acts and debts of the LP

LIMITED LIABILITY COMPANY

A limited liability company ("LLC") affords its members the same protection as a corporation when it comes to sheltering them from liability. Another great thing about LLCs is that through operation agreements, the control of the company can be separated from the ownership of the company. As an example, a member who only owns 25% of the company could have control of company operations through written operation agreements.

Pros
- Limited liability for members
- Avoidance of the double taxation of "C" corporations
- Flexibility in operating control and ownership structure
- Any business losses may be written off by the individual members, and income is reported on the individual members' tax returns
- No restriction on the number of members
- Less-complicated reporting for federal and state reporting, which is required for "C" corporations (no requirement for board of directors and regular board of directors meetings)

Cons

- More-complicated reporting than for sole a proprietorship and partnership
- Not regarded a "real" corporation by some investors
- Not able to use the company as separate entity from the owners for tax planning purposes

CORPORATIONS

For legal and tax purposes, a corporation is a separate entity from its owners, an entity that can enter into contracts, make purchases, must pay taxes, and can sue and be sued on its own behalf. Once created, a corporation becomes a "living, breathing" entity, separate from its creators and owners.

There are two types of corporations, the "C" corporation and the subchapter "S" corporation. A "C" corporation is publicly held, and the "S" corporation is referred to as a "closely held corporation." There are certain qualifications that must be met if a company wants to be recognized as an "S" corporation:

- Must have only one class of stock
- Must not have more than 35 shareholders
- Must not be part of an affiliated group of corporations
- Must be a domestic (not foreign) corporation
- Must have only shareholders who are individuals, a decedent's estate, or one of a special class of trust (not corporations or partnerships)
- Must not have any shareholders who are nonresident aliens

After a business has incorporated, all shareholders must consent to subchapter S treatment. The election to be treated as a Subchapter S corporation must be filed with the Internal Revenue Service in a timely manner. The profits and losses of a subchapter S are passed on to shareholders and are not subject to double taxation that characterizes the C corporation. Double taxation means that the when income is recorded in your corporation books, it will be taxed at corporate rates. When you take money out of your corporation in the form of officers' salaries, you will be taxed again on the amount you take out as compensation.

Pros
- Survivability—its existence does not depend on who owns it at any given time
- Owners enjoy limited liability
- Easier to raise money than for other forms of doing business
- Easy to transfer units of ownership
- A corporation can establish its own credit rating
- A corporation seems "more real" to outside investors
- A corporation has value separate from that of the owners

Cons
- Owner may have to cosign or guarantee debt of new corporation
- To maintain limited liability status, a corporation must follow substantial corporate formalities.
- Double taxation of C corporations

In today's litigious business environment where there is an overabundance of hungry attorneys, I recommend, under most circumstances, that you form your company as a Limited Liability Company (LLC) or a corporation. You need to protect your family (personal) assets from the world when you jump into a new business, and this is the best way to do it. Getting the help of a certified public accountant and/or an attorney can save you a lot of grief and many problems in the futre.

YOUR TEAM

You have heard the saying "No man is an island." This is so true, especially when it comes to starting your own business. If you think you can go it alone and do everything that needs to be done to start a successful business, you have a fool for a partner. This doesn't mean that you need to have a co-owner in your business. It simply means that you need the right kind of help. This comes in the form of God, family, partners, employees, and your advisors. You should also consider your vendors and customers part of your success team.

God and family you are blessed with, and advisors you choose. You need to choose your advisors in a completely objective way. I suggest that you use a "Request for Proposal" (RFP) process, which is discussed below. Before we discuss the selection of your advisors, let's discuss the most important partners in your business: God and Family.

GOD

The first "partner" that you need in business is God. Without God, you would be better off giving your total investment to the guy by the highway onramp holding the sign "Will work for food." You need to consult God before starting a business and every day that you are in business. Having God as a partner does not ensure your success in business (remember free will?), but not including God in your life decisions (including your business) can cause you to lose something more important than your business.

If God is truly your partner, then you will operate your business under some basic

Biblical principles. Here are some minimum standards that should guide every Christian businessman that has God as his partner:

- Reflect God in all of your business practices
- Treat your customers fairly
- Render a fair product for a fair price
- Treat your employees fairly
- Treat your creditors fairly
- Remember that all belongs to God

Always involve God in all of your business affairs. Take him with you to all your business meetings. Remember, he is looking over your shoulder when you sign vendors' contracts; he is standing beside you when you deal with your customers, employees, and vendors. He's always there. Remember, you invited him. If you don't feel him there at all times, do what a paint store owner in my neighborhood did. He hung a sign in each room of his establishment that simply says "I AM HERE." If you are like me, a gentle reminder is a good thing. The sign also enables him to witness to people who frequently ask about the signs.

If you are in business with God, let the world know about it. You should take every opportunity: through your business to the world and to your employees. The California-based fast-food chain, In-N-Out Burger, has witnessed to their customers and employees since 1987. They include tiny notations from Bible verses in some of their burger and drink packaging. Look at the bottom of one of their soft drink cups and see "John 3:16." In-N-Out Burger is probably one of the most successful fast-food companies in Southern California. Don Chang, the deeply religious founder of clothing chains "Forever 21" and "XXI," saw the In-N-Out Burger reference to John 3:16 and now includes it on the bottom of his stores' shopping bags. Another example is David Green whose craft chain, Hobby Lobby, plays only Christian contemporary music in its 362 stores. One last example is S. Truett Cathy who advertises that Chick-fil-A sandwich shops, nationwide, are closed on Sundays to free employees to focus on faith and family.

FAMILY

You can't expect your family to be understanding and supportive of your entrepreneurial activities unless they know what is going on. You will always let your investors know what and how your business is doing, and you will report to the government what your business is doing. Does your family deserve any less than your investors or the government? I think not. Even if your family is not involved on a day-to-day basis, they need to be kept abreast of what is going on with your business. Each day, when my wife gets home from her job and I get home from the office, for 15 minutes, I give her highlights of my day and she gives me highlights of her day. I also include her in all my important business decisions. I also keep our children involved so that they have an appreciation of the trials and tribulations of starting and running a small business. By doing this, I not only have their support when I might have to work a few extra hours, but some of our best product ideas have come from my wife and children. I also encourage every member of my family to drop by whenever they want, and if they do, I just might put them to work.

I personally do not advocate giving your children monthly profit and loss statements, but it's good to keep them involved by letting them know what's going on in the business on a summarized basis. I tell them about the new products I am developing, which ones are about to come out, which stores the products are in, new customers that have been acquired by the company, and other aspects of the operations of the company.

When it comes to your spouse, God says in Genesis 2:24 (American Standard Version), "Therefore shall a man leave his father and his mother, and shall cleave unto his wife: and they shall be one flesh." Nowhere in the scriptures does it say to exclude business issues. I have found, through the years, that my wife has been a key factor in many of my good decisions. And she reminds me of this often. I am only kidding, but seriously, consider including your spouse in your business decisions. You have the benefit of wise counsel and the benefit of a greater understanding from your spouse of what you are going through on a daily basis. As stated by Larry Burkett in his great book *Business by the Book*:

> "...sometimes a wife doesn't want to know anything about the business. I would answer, 'That isn't an option according to God's word. When a wife takes on the responsibilities of a helpmate, she must be willing to learn enough to help.' "[18]

It is your responsibility to make sure that your spouse has the tools necessary to have a positive impact on your business. This includes training and constant up-to-date information on your business. Notice that I say "spouse" rather than "wife." There are more and more women going into business, and husbands have the same obligation that wives do to help their spouses with their businesses.

18   Larry Burkett, *Business by the Book*, Nashville: Thomas Nelson Publishers, pg. 12, 1998.

PARTNERS

In a lot of ways, a partnership is like a marriage. There are a number of verses in the Bible that apply both to marriages and to partnerships. Consider the following few verses:

> "Do not be yoked together with unbelievers. For what do righteousness and wickedness have in common? Or what fellowship can light have with darkness? [15] What harmony is there between Christ and Belial? What does a believer have in common with an unbeliever?" 2 Corinthians 6:14 (NIV)

The Bible is very clear on "yoking together with unbelievers." You be the judge, but these verses do not need interpretation or discussion: to yoke yourself with an unbeliever will not be a good thing. Rationalize any way you wish, but the Bible is pretty clear on this issue.

Here are some questions that you should ask potential partners and receive appropriate responses:

1. Do you believe in God?
2. Do you believe the Bible is the infallible word of God?
3. Do you believe that Jesus is the Son of God?
4. Do you believe that our assets are all God's and only loaned to us?
5. Will we sue to collect debts?
6. Will we let all potential employees know that they are applying to work at a company that is Christ-centered?
7. Will we evangelize through the business?
8. Do you believe in paying tithes?

Having a partner who is a Christian will not guarantee that your partnership will survive, but being yoked to a nonbeliever as a partner is starting your business off on the wrong foot.

EMPLOYEES

You may or may not have employees when you first start your business. As your business grows, you will probably need to start hiring employees. As discussed in the chapter on risk management, hiring the right employee is critical to the success of your business. Good employees will help you minimize the risks associated with starting and running a business and will also help you grow your business. Keeping good employees is also important. The turnover of key employees can cost you a lot of resources. Some jobs that you have in your business will always have turnover. You may hire high school or college students for certain positions and expect them to move on to other jobs. But, it is critical that you be able to retain your key people. If you treat your people in accordance with Bible principles, they will stay with you for the long haul. WWJD (what would Jesus do) is a good principle for running all areas of your business and, in particular, for the way you treat your employees.

You will want to hire someone who can do the job better than you can. Hire good people who can help you build a business that can run without your direct day-to-day involvement. If you cannot delegate select tasks as you begin to grow, then you have hired the wrong employees.

Employee retention and motivation has long been the subject of many surveys, studies, books, and articles. Frederick Herzberg and Abraham Maslow have often been quoted in business literature documenting the factors important to retaining and motivating employees. Herzberg, a psychologist, proposed a theory about job factors that motivate employees. Maslow, a behavioral scientist and contemporary of Herzberg's, developed a theory about the ranking of various human needs. These two studies are a little theoretical but have been tremendously useful to employers for almost 50 years.

To better understand employee attitudes and motivation, Herzberg performed studies to determine which factors in an employee's work environment caused satisfaction or dissatisfaction. He published his findings in his 1959 book *The Motivation to Work*. His findings are still highly relevant. His two motivational theories were what he called the "Hygiene Theory" and the "Motivation Theory." The Hygiene Theory includes elements that do not lead to higher levels of motivation, but without them, there is job dissatisfaction. These factors are:

> Company policies—Clear, understandable, and well and evenly executed?
>
> Supervision—Is the supervision evenly applied, and is it respected?
>
> Working conditions—Clean environment with the proper tools to do the job?
>
> Salary—Is the employee compensated comparable to similar jobs and

at the appropriate level within the company? Contrary to popular belief, salary is not a motivator but can be a de-motivator if below standards.

Status—Is respect paid to the person and the position according to what it deserves within your organization?

Security—Does the employee have to worry if he has a job tomorrow? Can he feel secure within his position and within the company?

The second part of Herzberg's motivation theory involves what people actually do on the job. These are motivators. These are tools you can use to get your employees to perform better:

Achievement—Does the employee see the end result of his good work?

Recognition—For work well done

Work itself—Is it significant, important?

Responsibility—Is the employee given a well-defined area of responsibility?

Advancement—Is there advancement for employees who become more valuable to the company?

Growth—Positive change and forward movement in the job, company, environment?

The important point to remember is that there are certain things that must be present for a satisfactory job environment (these are not motivators, but can be de-motivators); but there are other things that motivate an employee to perform. As a Christian building a Bible-based business, all of these principles should come naturally to you.

In 1954, Maslow published a book entitled *Motivation and Personality* that introduced his theory about how people satisfy certain personal needs in the context of their work. He theorized that there is a general hierarchy of needs, recognition, and satisfaction that people follow. His theory reflects increasingly sophisticated levels of satisfaction a person can have once he has met the needs of satisfaction at his current level. As an example, the most primitive and basic needs are for satisfaction of thirst, sex, and hunger. According to Maslow's "Hierarchy Theory," the highest level of satisfaction one can achieve is to fulfill one's potential as a human being.

Level	Type of Need	Example
1	Physiological	Thirst, sex, hunger
2	Safety	Security, stability, protection
3	Love and Belongingness	To escape loneliness, love and be loved, and gain a sense of belonging
4	Esteem	Self-respect, the respect of others
5	Self-Actualization	To fulfill one's potentialities

Although the Herzberg and Maslow theories are about 50 years old, they still ring true today. You need to create a work environment that helps your employees reach the level of self-actualization.

According to a recent poll conducted by Harris Interactive, Inc. for Age Wave, an independent think tank that counsels business and government, there is a lot of dissatisfaction with employers. This is, in large part, a countrywide reaction to corporate scandals, very high executive salaries, accelerating outsourcing, and continuing downsizing. According to the study, only 36% of workers said they believed top managers acted with honestly and integrity. Even fewer (29%) believe management cares about advancing employee skills. A full one third of the surveyed employees felt they were in dead-end jobs. This same report found that job security, health care coverage, and professional development were more important than salaries. Also interesting was the fact that small-company employees felt far more engaged in their work than their large-company counterparts.[19] This author validated completed a ramdom survey and has found that these results are still valid in 2010.

You know intuitively that you want to keep good employees who have been trained at your company. Many studies show that it normally costs a lot more to bring in a new employee, train them, and get them integrated into your company environment than it does to keep a well-fitting current employee satisfied. Turnover is estimated to cost 10–20 times the person's weekly wage to replace them. Turnover costs include ads, employment agencies, interviews, reference checking, medical exams, orientation, training, and the

19   Dr. Ken Dychtwald, *New Employer/Employee Equation Survey* (poll conducted by Harris Interactive, Inc. for Age Wave, an independent think tank and Concours group, a global consultancy advising senior executives). Dr. Ken Dychtwald is the founder of Age Wave. http://sideroad.com/cs/

uncertainty of trying out a new person. Here are some ways to motivate and retain your current employees in addition to the ones mentioned by Herzberg and Maslow:

- Give recognition by thanking an employee for a job well done. Leaving a handwritten note or recognizing their accomplishments in a company newsletter costs you nothing.
- If you can, offer flexible work schedules. This shows that you care about their personal life as well as what they do for you while at work.
- Remember birthdays and important anniversaries.
- Get input from your employees and reward any input that saves you money or generates more revenue.
- Professional development is important for you and for the employee. Some employers fear increasing the attractiveness of their employees to other companies. Treat them right, and they will stay with you.
- Don't make your employees guess at what they are supposed to do. Have really good, comprehensive job descriptions written for all positions.
- Let your employees know exactly how they are evaluated.
- Hire the right person for the right job. This should be obvious, but this principle is violated often.
- Celebrate all major holidays. Decorate the offices, store, and warehouse with your employees' help. They are your extended family.
- Treat all employees fairly in hiring, retention, and termination. Show no favorites.
- Recognize the power of diversity in the workplace. Diversity is one of the most important strengths of America. It should be reflected in your business.
- Be visible on the front lines. Employees need to see you with your sleeves rolled up.
- Use a coaching approach rather than an authoritarian approach. You might find that your employees have some better ideas than you do. Don't let this bruise your ego; remember, you own the company. Also, remember to reward them for their ideas.
- Provide regular, consistent performance feedback.
- Never use the threat of firing. Employees know, without being told, that you have the ability to fire them.

- Find out what the industry standards are for fringe benefits (e.g., vacation, jury duty, family time off, medical, dental, training, flextime, etc.) and exceed the standards. Many studies show that exceeding the industry standards will result in enhanced performance of employees.
- Always be accessible no matter how big the company gets.
- Show you trust your employees. Let them take risks. Always make sure that you have a safety net so that their failed decisions are never fatal to them or the company.
- Offer personalized rewards. Your recognition rewards should reflect their individuality to show that you put some thought and effort into the reward.
- If you have employees who use uniforms, your company might launder their uniforms for them.
- My company actually has a free Starbucks coffee card that the receptionist keeps for any employee to use whenever they want it.
- DreamWorks, the film company, feeds their employees lunch. You cannot get a better lunch in the area, so why would an employee leave the lot to go eat out?
- Emergency child care. When the need arises, have it ready for them.
- Create a fun place to work
- Keep them informed, on a consistent basis, as to business performance.
- Provide opportunities for expanded roles and responsibilities.
- Eliminate all "busy work."

We Christians love the Ten Commandments. Here are ten commandments for making your employees feel special:

1. Show them respect.
2. Be considerate of their personal lives and needs.
3. Care about employees as individuals.
4. Always be fair.
5. Trust your employees.
6. Share the wealth and pay them a fair wage for a fair day's work.
7. Involve employees and keep them informed.
8. Recognize their accomplishments.
9. Make their jobs interesting.
10. Remember WWJD.

When it comes to fringe benefits, employees have come to expect a certain basic level from their employers. A study from the U.S. Department of Labor stated, "Among the most frequently observed benefits provided to full-time employees in small private establishments...were medical care, life insurance, holidays, vacations, and paid jury duty leave. The majority of full-time workers in these small establishments received each of these benefits. In contrast, less prevalent among full-time workers were such benefits as personal leave, dental care, defined benefit pension plans, short-term disability insurance, and long-term disability insurance."[20]

Benefits sited in the Labor report were:

1. 79% of full-time employees had weekly work schedules of 40 hours, based on five 8-hour days.
2. Vacation leave was the most prevalent type of paid time-off benefit in the survey. Paid vacations, provided to 7 out of 8 full-time employees, averaged 8 days after 1 year of service, 14 days after 10 years of service, and 16 days after 25 years of service.
3. Four-fifths of the workers were provided paid holidays, averaging 8 days per year.
4. Just over half of the workers were eligible for paid leave to attend funerals for family members (usually 3 days).
5. Nearly three-fifths of the workers were covered by jury duty leave, the majority on an as-needed basis.
6. One-seventh of the workers were provided paid personal leave averaging 3 days per year.
7. Almost nine-tenths of covered workers were allowed a fixed number of paid sick days per year, with an average of 8 days after 1 year of service, 10.5 years after 5 years, and 10.9 after 25 years.
8. 29% of all workers were covered by short-term disability benefits, with benefits typically available for up to 26 weeks.
9. Medical care was among the most widespread benefit for full-time employees in small private establishments: 64% of workers participated in such plans.
10. Other health-related benefits were less widespread: 31% of full-time

20   U.S. Department of Labor, *Employee Benefits in Small Private Establishments*, Bulletin 2507, April 1999 - 2010.

employees participated in a dental care plan, and 12% had vision care coverage.

11. Just over one-half (52%) of all medical care participants had to contribute to the cost of their individual coverage. Three-fourths paid at least part of the cost for family coverage. When workers contributed to the cost of medical care, their fixed monthly premiums averaged $43 for individual coverage and $182 for family coverage.

12. Almost two-thirds of medical care participants were covered by non-traditional plans, nearly always health maintenance organizations (HMOs) or preferred provider organizations (PPOs).

13. Life insurance protection was available to 62% of full-time employees. Employers paid the full cost of the basic life insurance for 4 out of 5 full-time employees with the benefit.

14. 46% of all full-time workers in small private establishments were covered by at least one retirement plan.

15. About 39% were eligible for job-related education assistance; assistance for non-job-related training was rare.

16. Almost 15% were eligible for employee assistance programs (referral or services for alcohol and drug abuse; marital difficulties; and financial, legal, and emotional problems).

The bottom line is that you have to take care of your employees. It is Biblical and it makes good business sense. There are a number of ways to take care of your employees. Employee turnover is a costly result of not taking good care of your employees. Employee retention and motivation is not all about money.

ADVISORS

The primary advisors to include on your team are your accountant, attorney, and risk-management advisor (e.g., insurance broker). These advisors will often be referred by family and friends. It is great to get referrals from these sources, but make sure that you remain as objective as possible in selecting these advisors. One proven approach is the "Request for Proposal" (RFP). This approach gives you an objective way to gather, analyze, and select outside advisors.

Another approach I have seen new entrepreneurs use is the "spaghetti" approach. When I was in the Army, the cooks would often (more often than anyone ever wanted) serve spaghetti. As a new recruit, I was required to serve on KP ("kitchen police") duty. Basically, it meant that you peeled the potatoes, mopped the floors, and performed other equally important duties. I remember watching a cook throw spaghetti noodles at the wall. Some would stick and some would not. When I asked why he was doing this, he said that if they stick to the wall, they are done. This is the way many people select outside advisors for their business. They "throw their options against the wall and see what sticks." Not a good approach to selecting advisors.

Using the RFP for Selecting Advisors

The typical RFP process follows an organized number of steps. You can use the same process for selecting an accountant, attorney, or insurance broker.

1. Compile a list of potentially qualified advisors.
2. Check the background of professionals with their regulatory state agencies.
3. Develop a Request for Proposal.
4. Develop a system for ranking the proposals.
5. Send out invitation letters.
6. Send out RFPs to those advisor candidates who have responded to invitation letters.
7. Evaluate the proposals.
8. Contract with the selected professional.

Compile a List of Potentially Qualifying Professional Advisors

Where do you find a list of potential advisors? There are a number of places to locate a list of qualified (or at least preliminarily qualified) insurance brokers.

Word of Mouth from Friends and Neighbors

When a family member or friend refers a professional advisor to you, make sure they understand that you will be performing an objective search process and their referral may or may not be selected. This can save some hard feelings later on in the process.

Professional Associations within Your Industry

All industries have local and national associations. These are typically associations that provide independent business people combined buying power, representation to governing bodies, and other useful functions.

Newspaper Classified Ads

A number of professionals advertise in the classified section of the newspapers. Don't forget to look at your local paper, national newspapers, and specialized newspapers such as your local business newspapers. As an example of a really good local business newspaper, Los Angles has the *Los Angeles Business Journal*.

Yellow Pages

"Let your fingers do the walking" is a term you've heard many times. As with newspapers, there are general yellow pages and specialized yellow pages. The Yellow Pages will often break attorneys, accountants, and insurance brokers into specialized areas.

Chambers of Commerce

Chambers of commerce are more than willing to supply new businesses with names of their members who might fit into your list of potential professional advisors. After all, the chambers are there to promote business in their area.

Your Existing Professional Advisors (e.g., accountant, attorney, insurance broker)

The same caveat applies to this referral source as to the friends and family referral source. They need to understand that you will be conducting an objective RFP process and that their referral may or may not be selected. Some major positive aspects of getting referral sources from your current advisors is that they are familiar with your business needs and they may have already worked with their referral professionals on other engagements.

The Internet

We sometimes forget what life was like "B.I." (Before Internet). The Internet is an incredible source of information. All professionals will have their information on the Internet. If they do not have a Web site, you should hesitate to include them on your list of potential advisors. To get a list of potential professional advisors, go to a search engine and enter in the type of advisor you are looking for, your location, and maybe a specialized area you are looking for. As an example, if you were looking for an accountant in Sherman Oaks, California, you would key the following into your search engine search box: "accountant, Sherman Oaks, California." You might find that you need to broaden your search for accountants to include areas outside of Sherman Oaks. You might want to try going to www.Christianbr. com. It is the Web site for Christian Business and Ministry Resources and is a good source of Christian business connections. A good Christian search engine is www.Crossdaily.com.

Christian Business Associations

There are a number of solid Christian business associations in the United States. Type "Christian business associations" into any search engine, and you will come up with a good list of associations that can refer you to professional advisors.

State Regulatory Agencies

All states have agencies that regulate accountants, attorneys, and insurance brokers. These agencies typically perform these functions:

- Administer uniform tests
- Control licensing of these professionals
- Establish minimum standards of performance
- Establish and administer minimum continuing professional education standards
- Review consumer complaints
- Administer disciplinary actions regarding substandard performance by professionals

Professional Associations

Accountants, attorneys, and insurance brokers all have national and local associations. These associations all have directories of their members. The majority of accountants, attorneys, and insurance brokers join their professional associations.

Accountants

American Institute of Certified Public Accountants
1211 Avenue of the Americas
New York, NY 10036-8775
tel. 212.596.6200
fax 212.596.6213
www.aicpa.org

Attorneys

American Bar Association
321 North Clark Street
Chicago, IL 60610
tel. 312.988.5000
www.abanet.org

Insurance Brokers

Independent Insurance Agents and Brokers of America
127 S. Peyton Street
Alexandria, VA 22314
800.221.7917
703.683.7556 – fax
www.aba.org

This list consists of the most widely recognized national associations for accountants, attorneys, and insurance brokers. There are also state and local associations for these professional groups.

Church Referrals

Most churches do not compile and publish listings of their members nor do they publish listings of business services offered by their members. With this being said, you can normally get a good referral from the business pastor at your church and from fellow members. I have personally had really good luck with this referral source. If you are a "pew warmer" at your church and do not like to get involved, then you may have a more difficult time getting referrals from your church staff and fellow members. This is not the only reason you should get involved with your church, but it can be a side benefit to getting involved. Don't be a pew warmer!

Check the Background of Professionals with Their Regulatory Agencies

Even before checking the resumes of the accountants, attorneys, and insurance brokers on your candidate lists, you should check their professional status with their state regulatory agencies. Just call your local State Department of Insurance. Many states require all agents and brokers to include their Department of Insurance issued license number on all business cards, premium quotes, and printed advertisements. If this is not the case in your state, ask the company for this information. They should be willing and happy to provide this information. Your State Department of Insurance should be able to provide you with the brokers' current licensing status, any disciplinary actions taken against them, and a profile of each broker.

You will be checking to see that they are properly licensed and that they have no disciplinary actions against them.

Develop a Request for Proposal (RFP)

There are typically three ways that most business owners select their professional advisors from their list of candidates.

By selecting the lowest bidder. Save money selecting this method, and you will still be playing Russian roulette. When selecting an insurance broker, the lowest is not always the best choice. By focusing too much attention on the price, you may end up selecting an inappropriate insurance broker. They may have the lowest costs, but they may have bad claims handling, may not understand your industry, or may have other negative issues.

By selecting friends and family. At first, this seems like a viable way of selecting a broker. But what happens when it's time to terminate the relationship and possibly go with another broker? It will be harder to end the relationship. Also, friends and family will not normally be qualified to refer a broker to you.

By using a Request for Proposal (RFP). The process of placing your insurance package out to bid via an RFP is the most objective way of dealing with and getting the best deal on insurance coverage. The RFP, if properly conducted, can get you the most-qualified broker and the proper insurance. The RFP process does require a little more work on your part, but it substantially increases your odds of getting the right insurance coverage for your business.

The RFP can be a powerful tool in selecting a broker or any other professional goods or services. It forces you to be more precise in defining what you want from your professional advisor. This, in turn, can assist your advisor in better serving you and will assist you in keeping your costs down.

An RFP will normally include the following sections:

1. Company Overview
2. Candidate Minimum Qualifications
3. Scope of Work
4. List of References
5. Pricing
6. Evaluation Criteria
7. Proposal Delivery Requirements

Company Overview

This section will describe your company, its industry, history, and revenue and include a discussion of major competitors and your market share. This section will also discuss the key assets and liabilities of your company. It should include information on your current insurance program. The executive summary section of your business plan will supply much of the information needed in this section. (See the chapter THE BUSINESS PLAN AND OPERATING YOUR BUSINESS.) Provide summary information only. Too much detail will drive up the price of the potential advisors' services.

Candidate Minimum Qualifications

Prepare this section carefully so that you can eliminate proposals of unqualified advisor candidates. You will want to include such things as:

- Experience in your particular industry
- Current licenses
- No disciplinary actions outstanding
- Years the advisor candidate is in business
- Any specialized skills needed
- Bondable
- Geographical location
- Professional society memberships
- Malpractice insurance
- Continuing professional education requirements
- Accessibility in regard to time of day/week
- Internal quality control standards

Scope of Work

This section describes the work to be performed by the selected advisor. This section is basically a job description for the advisor, listing the particular services you want the advisor to provide during the period of the contract. This will normally include the following minimum requirements in addition to other requirements particular to the area in which you are requesting proposals (e.g., accounting, legal, risk management).

- Start date
- End date
- Detailed description of services requested
  - Accounting (see details below)
  - Legal (see details below)
  - Insurance (see details below)
- Details of potential other nonrecurring services
- Reporting requirements for services performed
- Frequency of face-to-face meetings
- Delivery requirements for the services rendered

The scope of work must be well defined so that you can make sure the proposals that you get from potential advisors are what you need. A well-defined scope will also make the proposals that you receive more comparable to each other. Take some time to carefully construct this area of your RFP.

List of References

When it comes to reviewing proposals, I never give much weight to reference letters or letters of recommendation. No advisor is going to give you any negative letters of reference. A letter of reference will basically tell you that that the person submitting the letter was satisfied with his services. Almost every prospective advisor will have at least one client that will agree to provide them with a "glowing" letter of recommendation. A much better and much more reliable approach is to ask for a list of 10 of their current large clients who are in your line of business along with their contact information. You should then call each client and review the scope of work and evaluations with them.

Pricing

The advisor proposals should have concise pricing for scope of work performed. Normally, you will want to get a detailed breakdown for the individual elements specified in your scope of work. You will also want to get a separate price list for items included in the scope of work and rate for nonrecurring goods or services.

Evaluation Criteria

You should always include the evaluation criteria. I have heard of people who issue RFPs without including evaluation criteria. Their reasoning was that they were afraid that the people responding to the RFPs would mold their response to accommodate the criteria. My response is "Okay, so what is the problem? Isn't this exactly what you want them to do?" To do otherwise is playing games with your prospective advisors and wasting their time and yours. You will get much better proposal submissions if you let your potential advisors know exactly how you will be evaluating them. Make sure that you develop your evaluation criteria independent of any one potential advisor so that you do not unfairly weight the criteria in their favor. The easiest and most objective way to construct your evaluation criteria is to give each key area a weight and points for "exceeds requirement," "meets requirement" and "does not meet requirement." See the following discussion of "Developing a Ranking System" for a discussion on setting up your evaluation criteria.

Proposal Delivery Requirements

You should tell your prospective advisor candidates exactly what you expect to see in the final proposal that they deliver to you. You should include the following information in your RFP:

- Cover formatting – information to include on the cover page
- Page formatting – font, line spacing, margins
- Binding (e.g., spiral binding, Velo® binding)
- Number of copies to be delivered
- Exact date the proposals are due
- Preferred method of delivery
- Use of graphics within the presentation
- Use of appendices and exhibits

Develop a Ranking System

The key to keeping your evaluation of the proposal submissions from your prospective advisors as objective as possible is to distill your evaluation criteria elements down to a numerical ranking system. To illustrate this approach, let's say that you are evaluating the proposals submitted by potential accountants for your new company.

Here is your weighted average criteria list ranking schedule (an abbreviated sample):

	Weighted Relevance	Advisor Ranking					Advisor Weighted Computed Score				
		ABC	DEF	AAA	ZZZ	XYZ	ABC	DEF	AAA	ZZZ	XYZ
Price	15.00%	3	5	2	4	1	0.45	0.75	0.3	0.6	0.15
Experience in your industry	25.00%	2	4	1	5	3	0.5	1	0.25	1.25	0.75
Overall proposal appropriateness	15.00%	1	3	5	4	2	0.15	0.45	0.75	0.6	0.3
Detailed response to detailed scope of work	30.00%	4	2	3	1	5	1.2	0.6	0.9	0.3	1.5
Services outside of primary scope offered	10.00%	5	1	2	3	4	0.5	0.1	0.2	0.3	0.4
Reporting related to services	5.00%	5	4	1	2	3	0.25	0.2	0.05	0.1	0.15
Total	100.00%	20	19	14	19	18	3.05	3.1	2.45	3.15	3.25

Important Points:

5 different advisors submitted proposals
Advisor DEF got the best rating for the lost price (price only)
Advisor ABC got the best raw score
Advisor XYZ got the best weighted average score and will be the most like
   advisor proposal selected.

Fig.7 – Advisor Ranking System

Notice a few things about the example ranking schedule:

- It is prepared using Microsoft Excel® so that the calculations can be automatically calculated for you.
- The criteria (e.g., price, experience in your industry) are given a percentage in the "Weighted Relevance" column based on the relative importance of the individual elements.
- The "Advisor Ranking" given to each advisor is a number (1 through 5) (since there are 5 advisor candidates in the example) with 5 being the best score.
- The "Advisor Weighted Computed Score" is calculated by multiplying the "Weighted Relevance" times the ranking number to arrive at the "Advisor Weighted Computed Score."
- Notice that advisor "ABC" has the highest raw ranking score, but advisor "XYZ" has the highest "Advisor Weighted Computed Score," which is more important. The reason for this is that advisor "XYZ" scored better on the two most important evaluation criteria: "Experience in Your Industry" and "Detailed Response to Detailed Scope of Work." In the example, advisor "DEF" scored best for price but did not have one of the best overall "Advisor Weighted Computed Scores." This Weighted Computed Scoring method can be used for evaluating a multitude of decisions where multiple candidates are being evaluated.

Send Out Invitation Letters

The Invitation Letter will be sent out to prospects on your list without the RFP. The letter will invite the prospect to submit a proposal. The letter will include the following key dates:

- Date information will be sent out or made available
- Date for question-and-answer meetings
- Date for tours or candidate information meetings
- Date written proposals are due
- Date for oral presentations if part of the process
- Date for selection of advisor

The Invitation Letter will instruct the advisor candidate to proceed if he is interested in getting a copy of the RFP.

Send out RFP

Once you get responses back from the candidates, you will send out RFPs to the candidates that have requested them.

Evaluate the Proposals

After you have received the proposals back from those advisor candidates that have requested copies of your RFP, take the following steps to evaluate them:

1. Apply your ranking system that you developed above to the proposals that you received.
2. Call the references given to you in the RFPs.
3. Narrow down the list of candidates to the best two or three based on your ranking system,
4. Arrange for a face-to-face interview or a phone interview for the final candidates. This is important. Some people are much different when you directly communicate with them as opposed to getting written information from them.

Contract with the Selected Advisor

You should probably select your attorney before the other advisors so that you can utilize his services to review any contractual documents you may be contemplating signing with your selected advisors. Below is a checklist of typical provisions for a personal services contract. Use this checklist as a guide to help you help your attorney draft your contracts. I will say it again: have your attorney review all of your contracts—do not try to enter into a contract that you have drafted yourself that has not been reviewed by an attorney.

1. Legal names of the parties.
2. Term of the contract, including a specific beginning and end date.
3. Purpose of the contract.
4. What is expected of each party, including any time requirement for their performance.
5. Remuneration to be paid or consideration to be offered.
6. Both parties have provided something of value (e.g., cash payment for some product/service).
7. Payment schedule and any requirements for payment, including some manner for determining when payment is to be made (e.g., specific dates when payment is to be made, payment to be made within thirty days of receipt of invoice, etc.)
8. Signature lines for execution by appropriate parties.
9. Any other conditions considered essential in order for the contract to occur.
10. Additional rights and/or responsibilities of each party.
11. Requirement of receipts if payment for expenses is being made, statement of any requirements for reimbursement, and a limitation on payment.
12. If one party is collecting money and paying a portion to the other party, the amount or percentage should be clear, and the contract should always include the right to review and audit the records of the party collecting money.
13. Clear identification of the party who will be responsible for any costs associated with the contract.
14. Limitations of damages in case of default, preferably cap damages at the contract price.
15. Your company should be named as an insured if the other party is providing insurance.
16. Clear statement of which party will be held responsible if there is loss or damage under the contract.
17. Statement of what will happen to the contract if another event or contract this contract is contingent on does not occur.
18. Attachment of any underlying contract a party is required to follow the terms or conditions of.

19. Statement of incorporation of any RFP and the other party's response to that RFP that the contract is based on.
20. Clear specification of the rights of the parties to any intellectual property at issue.
21. Specification of ownership of any equipment or asset after the contract is ended when equipment or anything of value is to be developed or purchased as part of the contract.
22. Statement of conditions that would result if the contract is terminated early; inclusion of cancellation clause (30 days' written notice, etc.)
23. Specification of anything that must take place when the contract terminates (i.e., return of equipment, etc.)
24. Force majeure (events out of the control of either party that would result in a delay in the performance of the contract for which neither party would be liable)
25. Entirety clause (the written contract includes all of the agreements between parties)
26. Assignment provisions (parties do not have the right to assign their rights and responsibilities without the other party's approval)
27. Enforceability clause (if party does not enforce its rights under the contract at a particular time, this will not constitute a waiver of its right to enforce the terms and conditions of the contract at any later date)
28. Independent contractor clause (describes the legal relationship between parties)
29. Notice clauses (specifies the manner in which notice should be given under the contract, including person and address where notice should be received)
30. Applicable state law controlling the contract (try to always make your state the controlling state)
31. Venue (your city and/or county)
32. Vague and/or indefinite terminology (e.g., party is supposed to do something "promptly" or no end date)
33. Indemnity and hold-harmless clauses (can leave hold harmless if necessary; if absolutely necessary, can leave indemnity clause by adding "To the extent allowed by the laws of the jurisdiction state")
34. Attorneys' fees (can be left in the contract if necessary by adding "to the extent allowed by the laws of the jurisdiction state")
35. Arbitration clauses
36. Confidentiality agreements
37. Change "warrant" to "agree"

38. Agreement for advisor entity to purchase or provide liability insurance
39. Agreement for advisor entity to enter into a partnership or agree to be the agent for another party, or vice versa.
40. Statement of assumption of personal liability on the part of whoever signs the contract, if applicable.
41. Exclusivity clauses (unless exclusivity is desired, then keep term short)
42. Non-solicitation of employees.

Your Advisors Have a Fiduciary Responsibility to You

Your advisors (e.g., accountant, attorney, insurance broker) have a fiduciary responsibility to you, their client. "Fiduciary" is derived from a Latin word meaning "trust." Your advisors' fiduciary duty should be at the heart of their relationship with you. Your advisors typically have greater knowledge and expertise about their chosen profession than you do; this is why you hire them. They are held to higher standards of conduct and trust than is a stranger. They must avoid self-dealing. Their conduct should be guided by what is best for you, their client.

Your Accounting Advisor

Unless you are a trained accountant starting a business, you need to start your business with a good accountant as a resource. But you are not hiring him to make decisions for you. He is there to validate your decisions. You are the one who succeeds or fails in your business—not your accountant. Once you select an accountant, you might have to occasionally remind him of this fact. There are basically three different types of individuals whom you can employ to perform your accounting/bookkeeping services:

> Bookkeeper
>
> Normally, a bookkeeper is employed once your accounting systems have been set up by an accountant. Sometimes, a bookkeeper can also set up the accounting systems. Bookkeepers typically do not have academic training in accounting. One way to keep your accounting cost down is to employ a bookkeeper to perform your periodic accounting (e.g., weekly, monthly, quarterly, or annually) and have an accountant review the bookkeeper's work periodically. Bookkeepers cannot represent you before the IRS or other governmental bodies. Certified Public Accountants can represent you.

Accountant or Bookkeeping Service
This is a category of accountants that are not certified by their local state governments. They typically will have college degrees (but not always) and have had some experience in setting up accounting systems and recording accounting transactions. They are typically not closely regulated by any governmental agency. They will often specialize in certain industries. On a recent search of the Internet for bookkeeping services, I found a service that specialized in accounting for pet-sitters, and another that specialized in restaurants, one that specialized in Amway® dealers, and still another one that specialized in bookkeeping for flea market vendors. This category of bookkeeper/accountant cannot normally represent you before the IRS or other governmental bodies.

Certified Public Accountant (CPA)
This category of accountants will have four-year college degrees from recognized institutions and often have advanced college degrees. They are licensed by their states and have passed a rigorous set of exams. Less than 45% of exam takers qualified to take the exam actually pass the exam. Another positive aspect of using a CPA is that they are required to meet continuing education requirements in order to continue practicing public accounting. Most CPAs will actually prefer that you or your bookkeeper do your bookkeeping. They most often feel, and justifiably so, that they can better serve you in areas other than bookkeeping.

What Services Should an Accountant Perform?

Accountants and bookkeepers are able to perform more than just bookkeeping services. Here is a list of services normally performed by bookkeepers, accountants, and CPAs.

Record daily transactions for sales, cash receipts, expenses, cash disbursements

Post daily transactions to general ledger

Reconcile general ledger accounts

Prepare financial statements

Process payroll

Reconcile bank accounts

Tax reporting

  City business licenses

  Property taxes

  Sales taxes

  Payroll taxes

  IRS

  State income taxes

  Secretary of State filings

  Quarterly/monthly estimated tax filings

Regulatory reporting

  Labor relations board

  Census forms

Check writing and invoicing services

Maintain client Accounts Receivable and Accounts Payable and coordinate with client to ensure timely payment and collection

Cash flow management

Periodic review of internal controls

Set up accounting systems

Assist you in making management decisions based on sound accounting records

Audit your bookkeeper's work on an annual basis (CPAs only)

Review and analysis of bookkeeping performed by bookkeepers

Provide periodic analysis of your business and recommend areas of improvement

Business plan preparation (typically, this type of work is performed by accountants or CPAs)

Analysis of lease or buy decisions

Analysis of merger and acquisition decisions

Preparation, review, and analysis of business deals

Preparing budgets and forecasts

Representation before the IRS and state taxing agencies (CPAs only)

As noted, CPAs can perform a greater array of services than noncertified accountants or bookkeepers. At a minimum, you'll want monthly profit and loss statements prepared as well as a balance sheet and a cash flow statement. You'll also need some basic analysis of your financial statements. If you have payroll, you will need someone to file your payroll tax returns. The IRS and most state governmental agencies are unforgiving when it comes to late or missing reports. You'll also want someone to reconcile your bank accounts, preferably at the end of each month.

Why Hire an Accountant?

You will probably start your business because you believe you have something special to offer the world. Sitting behind a desk doing your bookkeeping probably won't be the best use of your precious time. In addition to the time it can take you away from other aspects of your business, you probably do not have accounting/bookkeeping skills and probably don't want to learn them. Also, it's good to have an independent set of eyes looking at your business's performance, offering an independent perspective. Accounting is the language of business, and accountants are the best at understanding this language and helping you use it as a competitive advantage. Relevant, accurate, and timely (R.A.T.) accounting can keep your investors and governmental reporting agencies happy with the periodic required reporting that you submit. And finally, how can you manage and grow your business without R.A.T. accounting? You can't.

Selecting a Bookkeeper and/or Accountant

When you are just starting out, every dollar is important, so you don't want to overspend in any area. You won't want to pay for more advisor services than you need. Many people will use a bookkeeper for all of their bookkeeping needs and use a CPA to review their work on a quarterly or annual basis.

Accountants are qualified to perform more than bookkeeping and/or accounting services. They can breathe life into the numbers that they generate and can advise you on complex business, accounting, planning, and tax matters.

Selecting the right accountant is critical. Here is a short checklist of items to consider when looking for an accountant:

1. Do you want to work with a large accounting firm or small accounting firm? The advantage of a large firm is more diversified resources at your disposal. The disadvantage is that you are probably going to be a really small fish in a really large pond. And remember, someone has to pay for all of the fancy overhead.

2. Does the accountant have experience working with entrepreneurial start-up companies?

3. Do you want to work with a bookkeeper for day-to-day bookkeeping and have an accountant review the bookkeeper's work on a periodic basis?

4. What are the exact services that you want the accountant/bookkeeper to perform?

5. Can the accountant guarantee R.A.T. (relevant, accurate, and timely) services?

6. The accountant should prepare financial statements in conformity with GAAP (Generally Accepted Accounting Principles).

7. Check references of companies similar to yours that have used the services of the accountant under consideration.

8. Check on the validity of the credentials being presented to you by the prospective accountant (e.g., education, government certification, etc.).

9. Document all aspects of your relationship with your new accountant in writing.

10. Make sure that you get a definite fee amount from the accountant for recurring services and special services. These services should be documented in detail.

11. Check on the availability of the accountant for answering quick questions.

12. Determine, through questions, that your prospective accountant's workload isn't so large that he couldn't adequately handle your needs.

13. Make sure that your prospective accountant has the ability to grow with you, at least for your first few years.

14. Your prospective accountant must be technologically savvy. Don't even consider any accountant that is not totally comfortable with automated business systems.

15. If your prospective accountant tries to sell you goods or services outside of accounting (e.g., such as tax shelters, etc.), immediately take him off of your prospective list.

16. The accountant/bookkeeper should be willing to sign a document in which he agrees not to disclose any of your confidential information to anyone without your specific written authorization.

17. Some accountants will set up your books for free if they are going to be doing your bookkeeping/accounting over a period of time.

18. Your accountant should be aggressive and proactive. A reactive accountant will be of little use. A good analogy is "You want an accountant who will guide you around potholes in the street, not one who can fix your flat tire caused by the pothole."

19. Is your prospective accountant familiar with your industry and its reporting requirements?

20. Determine if your accountant has relationships with other professionals that might be of use to you in the future (e.g., how well connected is he?)

21. Do you need your accounting services on a weekly, monthly, quarterly, or annual basis? How much of the bookkeeping can you do yourself without cutting into your management and building of your company?

22. Does the accountant keep up with his continuing education requirements?

23. What type of continuing education courses has the accountant taken?

24. Does the accountant have professional liability insurance?

25. Does the accountant have a periodic peer review?

26. Has the accountant received any special awards; what are they?

27. What speaking engagements has the accountant been invited to over the last couple of years?

28. Does the accountant do work for any other company that could prove to be compromising to your business? This is, at first glance, a seemingly odd question, but I had an associate who secured

the services of an accountant in the San Fernando Valley area of Southern California. Shortly after hiring the accountant, my friend found that they specialized in accounting for companies in the adult entertainment industry. He had a very difficult time explaining this to his wife (who was his office manager), his children, and to select members of his church when his new accountant was interviewed in the local newspaper.

The California State Board of Accountancy Web site has a checklist of recommendations to keep in mind when hiring a CPA.

When selecting a CPA, the California State Board of Accountancy (http://www.dca.ca.gov/cba/slectcpa.htm) recommends that you do the following:

- Check the license status from our Web License Lookup, or call the California Board of Accountancy at (916) 263-3680. Specifically, make sure the license is current and active (renewed with continuing education).

- Check whether there have been any enforcement actions against the licensee and how long he or she has been licensed.

- Interview the prospective CPA either by telephone or in person. A common inquiry is "what type of accounting work do you typically perform?" Compare the CPA's experience to your service needs.

- Ask about the office hours of the CPA; determine whether the office is open year-round; inquire if the CPA is available to take telephone inquiries. Ask what type of continuing education the licensee has taken recently.

- If the services you require include either reviewed or audited financial statements, ask the CPA if he or she participates in a peer review or quality review program. If yes, ask the year and month—and the result—of the most recent review.

- Effective January 1, 2002, some CPAs are authorized to perform a full range of accounting services including signing reports on attest engagements. Attest engagements include an audit, a review of financial statements, or an examination of prospective financial information. Others will be authorized to perform a full range of accounting services, including accounting, compilation preparation, and management advisory, financial advisory, and tax and consulting services, but will not be authorized to sign reports on attest engagements.

- Licensees are required to comply with Section 54.1 of the California Board of Accountancy Regulations. This regulation provides that no confidential information obtained by a licensee shall be disclosed without the client's permission. Therefore, you should ask whether the CPA discloses any of your confidential information to persons or entities outside the United States in connection with outsourcing any services provided by the licensee on your behalf. While other persons or entities may provide you with financial services, including tax preparation, it is important to be aware that Section 54.1 of the Accountancy Regulations pertains only to licensees of the California Board of Accountancy.

- Before any work is done by the CPA, it is important to make certain that you receive an engagement letter detailing the work to be performed for you, who will specifically be performing the work, including whether the work is outsourced, confirming that all private and personal information is secure, and specifying the cost of the services.

DEFINITIONS

Attest Engagement: One in which the practitioner is engaged to issue, or does issue, a written communication that expresses a conclusion about the reliability of a written assertion that is the responsibility of another party. Attest services include an audit, a review of financial statements, or an examination of prospective financial information; however, attest services do not include the issuance of compiled financial statements. See California Business and Professions Code Section 5076.

Audit: Examination of a client's accounting records by an independent Certified Public Accountant (CPA) or Public Accountant (PA) to formulate an opinion on financial statements and/or financial information. The auditor must follow generally accepted auditing standards.

Compilation Preparation: Presentation of data in financial statement format without the accountant's assurance.

Continuing Education: Acceptable continuing education (CE) is a formal program of learning that contributes directly to the professional competence of a licensee in public practice. For additional information on acceptable CE, see Continuing Education.

Financial Statement: Contains financial information about an organization. The required financial statements are balance sheet, income statement, and statement of cash flows. They may be combined with supplementary information to depict the financial status or performance of the organization.

Peer Review: The study, appraisal, or review conducted in accordance with professional standards of the professional work of a licensee or registered firm by another licensee unaffiliated with the licensee or registered firm being reviewed.

Review of Financial Statement: To perform an inquiry and analytical procedures that permit a Certified Public Accountant or Public Accountant to determine whether there is a reasonable basis for expressing limited assurance that there are no material modifications that should be made to the financial statements in order for them to be in conformity with generally accepted accounting principles or, if applicable, with another comprehensive basis of accounting.

Keeping Your Accounting Fees as Low as Possible

Accounting fees can grow to painful amounts if you're not careful. On the other hand, don't beat up your accountant to the point where all you are getting is the same basic service year-in and year-out. Most CPAs will do your accounting for really reasonable monthly fees so that they can have the basic accounting records on which to base their more specialized services for you such as income taxes and consulting. Here are some ways to keep your accounting fees down:

1. Do some of the bookkeeping work yourself. Accountants have a special acronym "PBC" (prepared by client) that they use for the work that their clients prepare for them. Depending on the level of skill you have in the area of accounting and/or bookkeeping, there are a number of schedules you can prepare for your accountant:

   A. complete trial balance or completed financial statements. If you have the ability to do this, your accountant will then be able to review them and make adjustments for accuracy and to increase their utility. If these financial statements do not need adjustment, then he may spend his time analyzing them, preparing governmental reports from them, and giving you ideas for improving your profitability.

   B. Some accountants can prepare R.A.T. (relevant, accurate, and timely) financial statements from select schedules that you provide, such as cash disbursement listings, cash receipt listings, invoice registers, and accounts payable registers.

2. Some entrepreneurs will not need monthly financial statements and can run their businesses fine with only quarterly or annual financial statements prepared by their outside accountants. Even if you feel quarterly or annual financial statements are adequate for your company, you will still need to prepare certain inside reports on your own to keep track of your business. You will always want to know your cash balances, your accounts receivable detail and balances, and your accounts payable detail and balances.

3. You may want your accountant to only do select tasks for you so that you can keep track of your business:

   A. Bank reconciliations
   B. Accounts receivable and accounts payable reconciliations
   C. Payroll preparation and reporting
   D. Monthly/quarterly reporting
   E. Calculation of quarterly income deposits
   F. Year-end income preparation

4. Divide up your accounting work between a bookkeeping service and your accountant. Bookkeeping services typically charge less than one fourth of what an accountant will charge for the same service. If you need

monthly financial statements, consider having a bookkeeping service compile your monthly financial statements and having your accountant review their work on a quarterly basis.

5. As with any professional service provider who is rendering services to you on a paid basis, don't call him every time you have a question unless the particular question is critical. Save your questions until you have a number of them, and ask them all at once.

6. Get to know your accounting system thoroughly. This includes your chart of accounts so that you can properly record all of your cash disbursements and receipts to their proper general ledger account. Every time you write a check, review your chart of accounts to see what expense account the expenditure should be charged to and record this on your check stub.

7. Most accountants will work with a monthly fixed fee arrangement based on your volume of transactions. This is good for you in that you can then effectively budget for these expenses.

As discussed below, in the process of selecting an insurance broker, you should consider selecting your accountant via the Request for Proposal (RFP) process. I suggest that you periodically put your insurance needs out to bid as you are buying product (insurance policies) from your insurance broker, but you are basically getting professional services from your accountant. I suggest that you always watch your accounting fees closely; but normally you will keep your accountant on board for a number of years, since he will get to know your business better over time.

Your Insurance Broker (Risk Management Advisor)

Risk management in business is much more than just getting the right insurance policies; but a big part of risk management is all about insurance. Insurance is an area where new entrepreneurs try to cut cost. I have seen way too many people starting businesses without giving any consideration to insurance and risk management. This is like playing Russian roulette; any mistake, act of nature, or otherwise adverse situation can put you out of business if you are not adequately insured. On the other hand, you don't want to be overinsured.

One of the most important decisions you face in starting your business is the selection of an insurance broker. An insurance broker is an independent go-between who searches the marketplace for an appropriate policy in the interest of clients and is not an insurance company employee. The broker represents you, the customer. Insurance brokers today don't just provide you with a way of purchasing insurance coverage. If an insurance broker is good, he will offer you ways to keep your insurance costs down and will also provide other risk management services. Securing the services of a good insurance broker is as important as having a good accountant and a good attorney on your team. Don't just assume that you can give all of your insurance needs to your brother-in-law because he just became an insurance broker.

Objectively selecting your insurance broker is critical to the long-term success of your company.

One part of your risk management plan is to make sure that you are always running your business under the Grace of God. One of the most important parts of your risk management plan is daily morning prayers.

What Services Should the Insurance Agent Perform?

Duties before purchasing insurance would include:
1. Gain a detailed understanding of your insurance needs for all areas of your business.
2. Have a complete understanding of the available insurance products for your given industry and company size.
3. Shop your insurance needs to the appropriate insurance carriers.
4. Negotiate the best possible rates for your insurance needs.
5. Obtain coverage that suits your needs with the scope outlined and within any time frame that is stated in your written guidelines.
6. Find an appropriate insurer and pay attention to the financial standing of that insurer.
7. Communicate with you if they are not able to completely meet your insurance needs as outlined by you.

Duties after purchasing insurance would include that they:
1. Check to make sure that the policies provide the coverage requested by you before the insurance carrier sends them to you.
2. Track your insurance coverage to make sure that it does not lapse so

that you and/or your company are never in an uninsured status.

3. Notify you about mid-term alterations to the policies promptly.

4. Advise you if the financial condition of the insurer deteriorates, thus exposing you to risks.

5. Keep you informed of any development that may affect the efficacy of your insurance policy coverage.

6. Keep up-to-date on all changes in the insurance industry that could directly affect your business.

7. Provide you with those totally useless little wall calendars that insurance companies are notorious for sending out at Christmas time (only joking).

As an important member of your management team, your broker should interact not just with you but with your accountant and attorney. To keep costs down, your insurance broker should interact with your other advisors through you. It is a good idea to get your accountant, attorney, and insurance broker together for a meeting once a year to review the last year's results with them and plan for the upcoming year.

Selecting an Insurance Broker

You should review your insurance needs annually and put your insurance coverage out to bid every couple of years. This is because your business changes continuously, and the insurance industry changes continuously. As part of this periodic review, you should put your insurance needs out to bid. This bidding process accomplishes a number of things:

1. Helps keep rates down

2. Forces you to review your insurance periodically to make sure that you are adequately protected

3. Keeps your broker on his toes

4. Keeps you abreast of the complex insurance market

5. Your company's operations may have changed since the last time you renewed your insurance policies. Changes in operations include downsizing, new products or product lines, strategic change in mission, change in equipment and/or personnel.

6.   Laws may have changed since your last insurance review and may require different amounts and coverage.

There are over six thousand insurance companies licensed to do business in the United States. You need a broker to connect you up with the right insurance company and to get the appropriate coverage.

Keeping insurance costs down

I once asked the question at a seminar, "How can we save money on insurance?" and a gentleman from the back of the room answered, "Don't buy any." I never got an opportunity to speak with this man on a face-to-face basis, but I did worry for him. Insurance is a "must have" expense for your business. You should be insured, but not over-insured or underinsured. The level to which you insure your company requires a fair amount of analysis, but it also requires that you determine subjectively just how much risk you are willing to take. The amount of risk you are willing to take will have a significant impact on the cost of insurance for your business. According to the Insurance Information Institute, about 40% of small business owners have no insurance at all, because they claim they are cash-constrained. The uninsured may be buying into a common misconception that small business insurance is expensive. The truth is that not having insurance can cost a lot more than your annual premiums—you can end up losing everything. Here are some ways to help keep your insurance expenses as low as possible:

1.   Identify sources of potential losses (casualty and theft losses, fraud and embezzlement, injury claims, acts of God, loss of income, etc.).
2.   Evaluate the financial risk posed by ease exposure (how often it occurs, how severe the impact). In the chapter on risk management, you will find a discussion on matrix analysis for evaluating your financial risk of perils that you might face.
3.   Determine how to treat the risk (can you eliminate it, minimize its impact, or can you transfer the risk to someone else e.g., clients, insurance company, etc.?).
4.   Keep track and monitor the above three steps.
5.   Start your search for insurance with a trade association related to your business. These associations will often offer discounted insurance deals to their members.

6. Keep your deductibles sufficiently high, but not high enough that it would cause you to have cash flow problems if you had to pay them. Your deductible is the amount that you have to pay before your insurance kicks in for an insurance claim. Your insurance broker should give you estimates of your premiums where the only variable is the amount of your deductible so that you can determine the effect of higher and lower deductible amounts.

7. Always make sure to keep your asset lists current so that you don't pay insurance for assets that you no longer actively deploy in your business. Make sure that you know their depreciated values and estimated market values.

8. Train all employees in the proper use of machinery and equipment.

9. Have regular inspections of your facilities, looking for potential hazards.

10. Keep all equipment in proper working order.

11. Put your policies out to bid at the end of each policy term.

12. Make safety and risk management every employee's business.

13. Have a regular safety and risk management training program.

14. Self-insure up to the limit that you can afford. This is closely related to your deductible and your tolerance for risk.

15. Make your insurance broker one of your best friends. I am joking about this, but you do need to talk to your insurance broker more than once a year. The insurance industry is constantly changing, and insurance products are constantly changing, so you need to stay current on the changing industry. This is part of what you pay your insurance broker to do.

16. Buy a package policy. Sometimes, it can be less expensive to buy a package policy instead of buying individual policies for your complete insurance coverage. In the insurance section of this book, we discuss Business Owner Policies (BOPs), which combine types of insurance most often carried by businesses.

Your Attorney

According to Dictionary.com, an attorney is "A person legally appointed by another to act as his or her agent in the transaction of business, specifically one qualified and licensed to act for plaintiffs and defendants in legal proceedings." Attorneys are typically licensed to practice law in specific states, after passing a rigorous exam. If you start a business or are in business, somewhere, somehow, sometime you will need an attorney. It is better to hire your attorney before you need him so that he can become familiar with you and your company and then be able to be much more effective on your behalf.

The Constitution of the United States gives you the right to represent yourself in court. It takes an incredibly unique person to defend himself in court. He must have the ability, initiative, guts, time, and fortitude to fight a battle in court. Usually, a person will choose to defend himself out of financial necessity. The person who can successfully be his own attorney is definitely the exception rather than the rule. Here are some reasons a person should not be his own attorney:

- Lack of objectivity
- An attorney can help keep you out of court in the first place.
- Attorneys are trained in the "fine points" of the law.
- An attorney is more than your advocate; he is a member of your "success team."

The good news is that there are over 1,000,000 lawyers in the United States, and the bad news is that there are over 1,000,000 lawyers in the United States. To be exact, according to the American Bar Association, there are 1,116,967967 lawyers in the United States. As we discussed in chapter 1, *OVERVIEW OF SMALL BUSINESS IN AMERICA*, there are 22.9 million businesses in America. So let's stretch our analysis a little bit. If each lawyer filed 20 lawsuits in a year, there would be enough lawsuits to get every single business in American involved in at least one lawsuit annually.

Here are some more interesting statistics and facts from the website *The Freeman*[21]:

The United States has 70% of the world's lawyers but only 5% of the world's population.

The United States has thirty times more lawsuits than Japan, one of America's primary trade competitors.

---

21 Joseph S. Fulda and Patrick J., *Are There Too Many Lawyers?* ,http://www.thefreemanonline.org/columns/are-there-too-many-lawyers/print/, 2010.

The threat of litigation has caused 47 percent of manufacturers to withdraw products from the market.

In Japan, the ratio of engineers to lawyers is 20 to 1, but in this country it is 2.5 to 1

It is a fact of life that although you may conduct your business in a Christian manner, there are people who will not do so. Churches that wish to keep their doors open and continue to do God's work must have attorneys in today's environment. If you are to properly protect the assets that God has loaned you to manage, you must have an attorney as part of your team.

What services should your Attorney perform?

An attorney performs three broad categories of complex and difficult services for you. An attorney acts as your legal advocate, legal advisor, and legal analyst.

Attorney as an Advocate

When most people think of attorneys, they think of them in the capacity of a spokesperson for their clients. Most people visualize an attorney serving their client by advocating their positions before a judge, a jury, or directly to an opposing party. An attorney can serve as advocate in many situations. There are a number of federal, state, and local commissions, agencies, and other organizations where an attorney can represent a client's interest. It's often a good idea to let your attorney negotiate for you in major transactions such as buying a business. There are a couple of reasons why this is a good idea. For one, they know the law. An equally important reason is that in negotiations, they can normally be more objective and assertive. Sometimes during the negotiation process, the parties will get angry with each other. Let them get angry with your attorney instead of you.

Attorney as an Advisor

Often, you will present a set of facts and problems to your attorney, and he will be able to recommend a useful course of action. Your attorney can advise you on how to use the appropriate tools so that you can solve your own problems.

You will often have problems that have multiple possible solutions. In these cases, your attorney's role is to help you understand the advantages and disadvantages of each possible solution. A good attorney can assist you in clarifying what matters most to you, as well as explain the broader implications of each possible solution.

In some instances, you may find yourself facing possible legal situations. A good attorney can advise you of your options should you get involved in a legal action and can also advise you of ways to avoid legal action.

Attorney as an Analyst

Sometimes, the most important function your attorney can perform is to provide a comprehensive review and analysis of your problems. Your attorney's analytical tests include probing the facts by asking you all the proper questions about them. Sometimes, the facts that you think are important to you are possibly irrelevant to the problem you are trying to solve, and you may have missed or discounted some more important facts.

Specific Areas Where an Attorney Can Help You:

Arbitration and Mediation

Business/Corporate Planning

Complex Business Negotiations

Commercial Collections

Contract Drafting

Copyrights/Trademarks/Patents

Corporate Filing, Tax & Representation

Distributor Agreements

Employment/Labor Law

Entity Dissolutions

Franchise Agreement Reviews

Going Public

Incorporation/LLC Formation

Leases & Contracts

Licensing

Litigation

> Personal Injury/Wrongful Death
> Business Issues
> Corporate Defense
> Complex Litigation
> Directors', Officers' & Executives' Liability
> Employment Disputes
> Intellectual Property Litigation
> Trade Secret Litigation

Mergers and Acquisitions

Partnership Disputes

Partnership Formation

Private Placements

Product Liability

Public Company Compliance

Purchase & Sale of Business

Representation before government boards, commissions, and other entities

Securities

Vendor/Supplier Agreement Reviews

Venture Capital Acquisition

Workers' Compensation

Zoning and Development

Why Hire an Attorney?

If you plan to start a business in the United States, you must have a good attorney on your team. There are three good reasons to have a good attorney on your team:

> To protect you and your business while operating in the extremely litigious business environment of the United States.
>
> To make sure that you operate your business in compliance with the laws of American commerce. Your attorney can be your guide through the complicated business maze.
>
> If you find the right attorney, he or she can be very useful as business advisors.

The flip side of hiring a good attorney is the danger of hiring the wrong attorney. Don't hire an attorney who:

- Says, "Agree to it now, and we will change it later."
- Says, "We can get the whole thing done for $399.00."
- Says, "Let's make them beg for mercy."
- Says, "I have the judge in my pocket."
- Says, "You have a 'sure win' case."
- Says, "We can always appeal."
- Says, "Let's go for the jugular."
- Says, "We have their backs against the wall, so let's keep the pressure on."
- Is always late.
- Wants an equity interest in your business to represent you.
- Charges you for every minute of every phone call.
- Refuses to negotiate particular points on your behalf in the way you wish them done.
- Automatically rejects any suggestion or request from the other side of the transaction.
- Prefers to fight rather than settle issues without litigation, if possible.
- Is never available for consultation.
- Never visits your place of business.
- Can't remember your name.
- Is disorganized and always losing your files.
- Has ungodly business practices.

The bottom line is that your attorney, no matter how good he is, cannot guarantee any particular outcome for you. Examining his track record will give an indication of his past performance. This will give you an indication of his abilities but will not guarantee his success in your particular situation. As a Christian, you do not want an attorney representing you who always "goes for the jugular." There are "win, win" ways of doing business, and you want your attorney to reflect this "win, win" philosophy.

Sometimes an attorney will decline becoming your attorney for the following reasons:
- Has a competing company as a client
- Believes you are not being upfront with him
- Believes that you will not follow his advice
- Does not feel comfortable with your industry
- Believes that you perceive everything as an emergency
- Is too busy to take on any new clients
- Believes you are not communicating with him
- Only does litigation and does not handle non-litigation work
- Thinks your style and his style are not compatible
- Believes you cannot afford his legal fees
- Believes your expectations are not reasonable or flexible

Attorney has a conflict of interest. Never take it personally if an attorney does not want to become your legal advisor. Of all your advisors, you will probably have a longer relationship with your attorney than any other advisor. This is why you and your prospective attorney should comprehensively evaluate your prospective relationship. Frequent changes of attorney will weaken the utility of your legal advisor. I know of many businesses that have never changed attorneys.

Selecting an Attorney

Your attorney is probably the most important advisor that you will hire when you start your business, and he will continue to be valuable as long as you have your business. As you business grows, you will face issues related to real estate, employment, intellectual property, taxes, securities law, possibly law suits, and other topics. There is often the temptation to get a few self-help books and pre-printed forms and attempt to be your own lawyer. As we have said elsewhere in this book, "The person who tries to be his own lawyer has a fool for a client." With this being said, there are certain things you can do to keep your legal fees down, as you will see in the following section entitled "Keeping Attorney Cost Down."

Things to consider when selecting an attorney:

1. Will you be charged for your initial consultation?
2. Does the attorney have experience in working with entrepreneurial start-up companies?
3. Does the attorney have experience in your industry?
4. Do you want a large, diversified practice or a small firm to handle your legal needs? Remember, a large firm might be impressive, but the fancy stationary and the big lobby with the smiling receptionist to offer you mints is going to cost you.
5. Have you ever worked with this attorney in another capacity?
6. How many matters like yours has the attorney handled in the past?
7. Does the attorney have any references that he can readily supply?
8. Do you know anyone who has worked with the attorney in the past, such as your accountant, your pastor, your insurance broker?
9. Does the attorney advertise? Why? Some people have concerns with attorneys that advertise. They feel that the attorney may deal in quantity of clients rather than quality of relationships with clients. You decide.
10. Is the attorney current on his continuing education?
11. Has the attorney been a speaker at any colleges, professional organizations, etc.?
12. Does the attorney have any information, positive or negative, on the Internet?
13. Does the attorney represent any of your close competitors?
14. How much does the attorney charge per hour?
15. Will the attorney personally work on your legal matters, or will they be assigned to junior lawyers or a paralegal?
16. If work is assigned to junior lawyers or a paralegal, what will be the billing rates?
17. Will the attorney always give you an up-front estimate of the amount he is going to bill you for select legal tasks he is going to perform for you?
18. Will the attorney be the type that always "goes for the jugular" (translated as "LITIGATION"), or will he be a dealmaker/peacemaker?
19. Does the attorney object to the client's doing some of the work for the attorney (e.g., research, etc.) to help keep his costs down? If so, why?
20. Will the attorney bill you for "out-of-pocket" costs at actual costs?

21. Has the attorney had any official complaint proceedings filed against him?
22. Has the attorney ever lost his license, and if so, for what reason?
23. Does the attorney receive referrals from his peers for his area of expertise?
24. Is the attorney licensed in any other state?
25. Has the attorney ever received any honors? If so, can he give you a list of the honors and what the honors represent?
26. What seminars has the attorney attended in the last couple of years as part of his continuing education?
27. Has the attorney ever had anything published? If so, what?
28. Does the attorney ever refer work to other attorneys for areas in which he lacks expertise? Can the attorney supply a list of such attorneys?
29. Does the attorney have a peer review done of his practice?
30. Does the attorney have malpractice insurance? If not, why not?
31. Is the attorney listed in the Martindale-Hubbell directory?
32. Is the attorney a litigator, or does he have a professional relationship with a litigation attorney?
33. As mentioned above, in the "Selecting an Accountant" section, you want to make sure that your attorney does not represent any unsavory-type clients. If your attorney will not answer this question, say "NEXT."

Keeping Attorney Costs Down

Legal fees are an area that can get out of control very fast. Because legal fees don't relate directly to the cost of your products, it's easy to pick up the phone, call your attorney, and let the "meter start ticking." Lawyers are great listeners, and they often are great advisors about general business matters. This can make it easy for you to get a really unpleasant surprise when you open the monthly bill from your attorney. Here are some ways to keep your legal fees under control:

1. Get an estimate from your attorney in advance for each major project that you ask him to complete.
2. Have a cap that is not to be exceeded without your express written permission.
3. For recurring tasks other than normal business transactions that he might perform for you, have him set up standard forms for you so he doesn't have to re-create the wheel each time he performs the same task. Examples of these types of tasks are employment contracts, notes payable, employee loans, and other recurring legal tasks.

4. Establish, ahead of time, how your attorney will bill you for select transactions. Attorneys typically use four types of fees: hourly, contingent and deferred fees, and retainers. Try to get your attorney to utilize a fixed-fee approach for tasks that can easily be measured.

5. Make sure that you get a detailed, itemized statement from your attorney each month.

6. Make sure that tasks performed by lower-level attorney staff are billed at a lower rate.

7. Make sure that out-of-pocket costs are billed at cost and are reasonable. If they are not, ask to see the supporting invoices.

8. Never visit your attorney unless you are totally organized, prepared, and ready for the topic at hand.

9. Make sure you remember that the attorney is working for you. He should provide you a budget, keep you informed, and complete the work on time.

10. "An ounce of prevention is worth a pound of cure." It is always easier and cheaper to prevent a legal problem than to deal with a problem with litigation. Try to solve problems before they become BIG problems. Make sure you have an attorney with the same philosophy.

11. Group together your legal affairs needs. You will save money if you visit your attorney about several legal matters at one time.

12. Do a lot of the work yourself. As an example, you can use one of the three major patent software packages on the market to draft a rough copy of a patent before meeting with your attorney. He can "redline" it and you can make the revisions, and then let him do the final polish. Keep in mind that, while doing this, you may be saving money, but you are taking time from your daily management duties.

13. Be as informed as possible concerning the legal aspects of your business. This will help you help your attorney be more efficient.

14. Use nonlawyer professionals for select legal matters. There are certain legal tasks that other, less expensive professionals can sometimes do even better than lawyers and at less cost. Some of these professionals are real estate brokers, insurance brokers, appraisers, CPAs, paralegal agencies, etc.

INITIAL GOVERNMENTAL FILING REQUIREMENTS ━━━━━━━━━━━

There are a number of governmental agencies that you will need to notify when you are going to start a business. You will need to file a variety of forms with these agencies before you start your business. If you are doing business in the United States, you will be required to report your business activity to a number of government agencies. This book is not intended to be a comprehensive tax guide but rather a high-level overview of your governmental reporting requirements. You can order publications from the various agencies that will guide you through the various requirements. You also need the services of a good accountant to help guide you through the numerous land mines that are included in the various tax codes and regulations. Listed below are a number of governmental agencies that you need to notify when you start your business.

FEDERAL REGISTRATION AND FILING REQUIREMENTS

For Federal income tax purposes, you need to select a legal form for your business, choose a tax year, and choose your accounting method. It is also useful to get an Employer Identification Number from the IRS for your company.

Select a Business Structure

Go to the "LEGAL FORM OF YOUR BUSINESS" chapter for a discussion of the various legal form options that you have at your disposal. It is best to decide which legal form you want to use to operate your business when you start your business. As you will see in "LEGAL FORM OF YOUR BUSINESS," I cannot see very many situations where you wouldn't want to incorporate your business upon its initial formation.

Choose a Tax Year

You must figure your taxable income and file an income tax return based on an annual accounting period called a *tax year*. A tax year is usually 12 consecutive months. There are two kinds of tax years. There is the calendar year, which ends on December 31 of each year, and a fiscal year end, which is 12 consecutive months ending on the last day of any month except December. There is no way around filing a tax return if you have business income.

If you file your first tax return using the calendar tax year and you later begin business as a sole proprietor, become a partner in a partnership, or become a shareholder in an S corporation, you must continue to use the calendar year unless you get IRS approval to change it or are otherwise allowed to change it without IRS approval. You must use a calendar tax year if:

1. You keep no books.
2. You have no annual accounting period.
3. Your present tax year does not qualify as a fiscal year.
4. You are required to use a calendar year by a provision of the Internal Revenue Code or the Income Tax Regulations.

If you have never filed an income tax return, you adopt either a calendar tax year or a fiscal tax year. You adopt a tax year by filing your first income tax return using that tax year. You would select a tax year different than a calendar year if you had a business that had a business cycle that made it difficult to use the calendar year. As an example, a swimsuit manufacturer might want, and be granted, a tax year-end on September 30, since the bulk of their revenue would be generated in the last quarter of their fiscal year. There are some specific rules that you should consider that are beyond the scope of this discussion that you should review with your accountant before deciding a tax year-end.

Employer Identification Number

Since the federal government uses the Employer Identification Number (EIN) for a lot of its reporting, you probably should apply for one even if you answer "no" to all of the questions below. These questions are direct from the Internal Revenue Service Web site (www.irs.gov). According to the IRS, you do not have to secure an EIN number unless you answer "yes" to one of the questions below.

You will be submitting income tax withholdings, FICA, FUTA, etc., to the Internal Revenue Service periodically.

You will need an EIN if you answer "Yes" to any of the following questions. Additionally, if you provide health insurance for your employees, you may need a National Standard Employer Identifier (NSEI) for your electronic health transactions, which is the same as your EIN.		
Do you have employees?	YES	NO
Do you operate your business as a corporation or a partnership?	YES	NO
Do you file any of these tax returns: Employment; Excise; or Alcohol, Tobacco and Firearms?	YES	NO
Do you withhold taxes on income, other than wages, paid to a non-resident alien?	YES	NO

Do you have a Keogh plan?	YES	NO

Are you involved with any of the following types of organizations?
  Trusts, except certain grantor-owned revocable trusts, IRAs,
    Exempt Organization Business Income Tax Returns
  Estates
  Real estate mortgage investment conduits
  Non-profit organizations
  Farmers' cooperatives
  Plan administrators
	YES	NO

EIN (employer identification number) – How to Apply

Apply by EIN Toll-Free Telephone Service

You can obtain an EIN immediately by calling the Business & Specialty Tax Line (800-829-4933). The hours of operation are 7:00 am to 10:00 pm local time, Monday through Friday. An "assistor" takes the information, assigns the EIN, and provides the number to you over the telephone. Have the SS-4 form below filled out when you call so that you can be sure to have all of the information that you need while you are on the phone.

Apply By Fax

You can fax a completed Form SS-4 application to you state fax number. If it is determined that the entity needs a new EIN, one will be assigned using the appropriate procedures for the entity type. If you include a fax number, a fax will be sent back to you with the EIN within four (4) business days.

Apply by Mail

The processing time frame for an EIN application received by mail is four weeks. Ensure that the Form SS-4 contains all of the required information.

Apply by EIN Online

You may also apply for an EIN via the Internet. Once all the necessary fields are completed on the online form, preliminary validation is performed, and you will be alerted to any necessary information that may not have been included. An EIN will be issued after the successful submission of the completed Form SS-4 online.

Form **SS-4**	**Application for Employer Identification Number**	OMB No. 1545-0003
(Rev. July 2007)	(For use by employers, corporations, partnerships, trusts, estates, churches, government agencies, Indian tribal entities, certain individuals, and others.)	EIN
Department of the Treasury Internal Revenue Service	► See separate instructions for each line. ► Keep a copy for your records.	

Type or print clearly.

1 Legal name of entity (or individual) for whom the EIN is being requested

2 Trade name of business (if different from name on line 1)	3 Executor, administrator, trustee, "care of" name
4a Mailing address (room, apt., suite no. and street, or P.O. box)	5a Street address (if different) (Do not enter a P.O. box.)
4b City, state, and ZIP code (if foreign, see instructions)	5b City, state, and ZIP code (if foreign, see instructions)

6 County and state where principal business is located

7a Name of principal officer, general partner, grantor, owner, or trustor	7b SSN, ITIN, or EIN

8a Is this application for a limited liability company (LLC) (or a foreign equivalent)? . . . . ☐ Yes ☐ No   8b If 8a is "Yes," enter the number of LLC members . . . . ►

8c If 8a is "Yes," was the LLC organized in the United States? . . . . ☐ Yes ☐ No

9a Type of entity (check only one box). **Caution.** If 8a is "Yes," see the instructions for the correct box to check.

☐ Sole proprietor (SSN) _____
☐ Partnership
☐ Corporation (enter form number to be filed) ► _____
☐ Personal service corporation
☐ Church or church-controlled organization
☐ Other nonprofit organization (specify) ► _____
☐ Other (specify) ►

☐ Estate (SSN of decedent) _____
☐ Plan administrator (TIN) _____
☐ Trust (TIN of grantor) _____
☐ National Guard   ☐ State/local government
☐ Farmers' cooperative   ☐ Federal government/military
☐ REMIC   ☐ Indian tribal governments/enterprises
Group Exemption Number (GEN) if any ►

9b If a corporation, name the state or foreign country (if applicable) where incorporated | State | Foreign country

10 Reason for applying (check only one box)

☐ Started new business (specify type) ► _____
☐ Hired employees (Check the box and see line 13.)
☐ Compliance with IRS withholding regulations
☐ Other (specify) ►

☐ Banking purpose (specify purpose) ► _____
☐ Changed type of organization (specify new type) ► _____
☐ Purchased going business
☐ Created a trust (specify type) ► _____
☐ Created a pension plan (specify type) ► _____

11 Date business started or acquired (month, day, year). See instructions.	12 Closing month of accounting year

13 Highest number of employees expected in the next 12 months (enter -0- if none).	14 Do you expect your employment tax liability to be $1,000 or less in a full calendar year? ☐ Yes ☐ No (If you expect to pay $4,000 or less in total wages in a full calendar year, you can mark "Yes.")
Agricultural Household Other	

15 First date wages or annuities were paid (month, day, year). **Note.** If applicant is a withholding agent, enter date income will first be paid to nonresident alien (month, day, year) . . . . ►

16 Check **one** box that best describes the principal activity of your business.
☐ Construction ☐ Rental & leasing ☐ Transportation & warehousing ☐ Health care & social assistance ☐ Wholesale-agent/broker
☐ Real estate ☐ Manufacturing ☐ Finance & insurance ☐ Accommodation & food service ☐ Wholesale-other ☐ Retail
☐ Other (specify)

17 Indicate principal line of merchandise sold, specific construction work done, products produced, or services provided.

18 Has the applicant entity shown on line 1 ever applied for and received an EIN? ☐ Yes ☐ No
If "Yes," write previous EIN here ►

Third Party Designee	Complete this section **only** if you want to authorize the named individual to receive the entity's EIN and answer questions about the completion of this form.	
	Designee's name	Designee's telephone number (include area code) ( )
	Address and ZIP code	Designee's fax number (include area code) ( )

Under penalties of perjury, I declare that I have examined this application, and to the best of my knowledge and belief, it is true, correct, and complete. | Applicant's telephone number (include area code) ( )

Name and title (type or print clearly) ► | Applicant's fax number (include area code) ( )

Signature ► | Date ►

For Privacy Act and Paperwork Reduction Act Notice, see separate instructions.   Cat. No. 16055N   Form **SS-4** (Rev. 7-2007)

Fig.8 – Employer ID Number

Selecting an Accounting Method for Federal Income Taxes

There are 3 permissible accounting methods for Federal income tax reporting purposes:

1. Cash receipts and disbursements
2. Accrual
3. Hybrid

Cash Receipts and Disbursements Method

Income is recognized when it is actually or constructively received, and expenses are deductible when they are paid. There are some exceptions to this rule for prepaid expenses where their benefits exceed one year. In this case, the expenses must be capitalized and amortized over the period that they cover. Also, if you sell inventory and it is a substantial element of your profit calculation, you must use accrual accounting for sales and cost of sales.

Accrual Method

Using this method, you recognize income when it is earned, and expenses are deductible when there has been economic performance for the expenditure made. The recognition of revenues and expenses does not have any relation to the actual cash received and the cash payments made. As an example, let's say you sell a complete house of furniture to a customer on November 1, 2009. The customer establishes a charge account with you and charges his purchase to his account. He does not pay you until January 1, 2010. The sale is considered made in 2009, even though you do not receive the cash until 2010. It is the same for expenditures. If your janitor bills you on December 31, 2009 for janitorial services but you do not pay him until January 30, 2010, it is a 2009 expense because he rendered economic benefit to you in 2009.

Hybrid Accounting Method

The Hybrid Accounting Method of accounting is just what it sounds like; it is a combination of cash and accrual accounting. It is generally used when inventory is a material factor in your business. If this is the circumstance in your business, accrual accounting is used to determine the gross profit from inventory, and cash accounting is used to report other income and expenses.

Other Special Circumstance Accounting Methods

There are a couple of other methods that are acceptable to IRS under certain circumstances. If you realize income over a period of time of more than 12 months from a single transaction, you will want to use installment accounting. If you have long-term contracts with your customers, you may want to consider the percentage of completion method or the completed contract method. Home construction and certain other real estate construction contracts would qualify for the completed contract method of revenue recognition. Most other non-real estate, long-term contracts would qualify for the percentage of completion method of accounting. Under the percentage of completion method, a portion of the gross contract price is included in income each year as the work progresses.

US IMMIGRATION AND NATURALIZATION SERVICE

Proof of Residency Requirement: Employees hired after November 6, 1986 must provide proof of eligibility to work in the United States.

US CUSTOMS AND BORDER PROTECTION (CBP)

If you export or import goods or travel to foreign countries in your business, you will need to know US Customs and Border Protection regulations. The importance of this federal agency has increase substantially since 9/11. There is a list of publications available at http://www.customs.ustreas.gov/xp/cgov/toolbox/publications/ that you will want to review if you are going to engage in exporting or importing. Some of the key publications are:

Modernization Monitor
ACE (Automated Commercial Environment) has hit the road running. With new features like e-Manifest Trucks, ACE participation continues to rise. In this edition, learn more on the latest capabilities and how to participate in ACE.

Informed Compliance Publications
CBP has a number of Informed Compliance publications (ICPs) in

the "What Every Member of the Trade Community Should Know About: ..." series. As of the date of this posting, the subjects listed are available for reading or downloading.

CBP Today
CBP Today, the official employee newsletter of the U.S. Customs and Border Protection, is published monthly by the Office of Public Affairs.

Know Before You Go
Regulations for U.S. Residents. As an international traveler, you should be aware of the rules for bringing items back from your trip.

Visiting the United States
Publication# 0000-0511, Welcome information from the U.S. Customs and Border Protection

International Mail Imports
Publication# 0000-0514 answers international travelers' questions on mailing merchandise into the United States.

U.S. Import Requirements
Publication# 0000-0517 explains import requirements for a person interested in establishing an importing business or a person who may be importing something for personal use only—not for resale

Importing into the United States
Publication# 0000-0504 explains the process of importing goods into the U.S., including informed compliance, invoices, duty assessments, classification and value, marking requirements, etc.

Plant Protection and Quarantine Manuals
ACE: Modernization Information Systems

Improving border security and the flow of trade, the Modernization Program has reached a major milestone with the implementation of the Automated Commercial Environment (ACE). Find out what ACE is, when it will affect you, and how it is being developed.

Most of the publications from the US Customs and Border Protection are available in electronic form for download or available for order as hardcopy.

There are possibly other federal reporting requirements, especially with the new administration in Washington, D.C. restructuring federal infrastructure.

STATE REGISTRATION AND FILING REQUIREMENTS ━━━━━━

In addition to federal registration and filing requirements for your new business, there will be a number of state registrations and filings that you will be required to make upon starting your business. Taking Nevada as an example, although they do not have a state income tax, there are a number of other state registrations and filings that you will be required to perform before doing business there. Below, we are using California as an example, but all states have similar governmental requirements.

EMPLOYMENT DEVELOPMENT DEPARTMENT

Registration Form for Employers: Required to file a registration form within 15 days after paying more than $100.00 in wages to one or more employees. No distinction is made between full-time and part-time or permanent and temporary employees in meeting this requirement. You will be submitting employee taxes, employer-paid training taxes, and disability insurance assessments and unemployment taxes to this department or one similar to it.

Franchise Tax Board

State Income Tax Information: Businesses should obtain the appropriate state income tax forms from the Franchise Tax Board. All businesses are required to submit a Business Income Tax statement annually.

Department of Industrial Relations

Wage/Hour Laws: Businesses with employees must comply with laws establishing minimum standards for wages, hours, and working conditions. Workers' Compensation Information: Businesses with employees must maintain Workers' Compensation Insurance coverage on a self-insured basis or provided through a commercial carrier or the State Workers' Compensation Insurance Fund.

State Board of Equalization

Sales & Use Permit (Seller's Permit): All businesses selling or leasing tangible property must obtain a Seller's Permit.

Cal/OSHA Consultation Services

Occupational Safety and Health Information: Businesses with employees must prepare an Injury and Illness Prevention Plan. The state provides a no-fee consultation service to assist employers with preventing unsafe working conditions and workplace hazards.

Department of Consumer Affairs

The mission of the California Department of Consumer Affairs is to protect and serve consumers while ensuring a fair and competitive marketplace. They protect and serve consumers by making available information that educates consumers about their rights and responsibilities. They help ensure a competent and fair marketplace by establishing minimum standards of competency in over 100 business and 200 professional categories, including doctors, dentists, cosmetologists, contractors, and automotive repair shops.

Department of Fair Employment and Housing

Discrimination Law: Harassment or discrimination in employment is prohibited if it is based on a person's race, ancestry, national origin, color, sex (including pregnancy), sexual orientation, religion, physical disability (including AIDS), mental disability, marital status, medical condition (cured cancer), and refusal of family care leave. Discrimination in housing, public services, and accommodations is also prohibited.

Employers must post the Harassment or Discrimination in Employment notice (DFEH 162) and provide their employees with a copy of the DFEH information sheet on sexual harassment (DEFH 185) or a statement that contains equivalent information. Employers must also provide notice for an employee's right to request pregnancy disability leave or transfer as well as notice to request a family and medical care leave (CFRA). Employers with 5 or more employees must maintain all personnel records for a minimum of 2 years.

Secretary of State

Corporation, Company, or Partnership Filings: If you are considering becoming a corporation (either stock or nonprofit), a limited liability company, or a partnership (limited or limited liability), you must file with the Secretary of State's Office. Also, if you are conducting business as one of the following, you must file a bond with the Secretary of State's Office: immigration consultant, credit services organization, dance studio, discount buying organization, employment agency, employment counseling service, invention developer, job listing service, nurses registry, or auctioneer or auction company.

CITY AND COUNTY REGISTRATION AND FILING REQUIREMENTS ━━━━━

In addition to the Federal and State registration and filing requirements, there will be registration and filing requirements at the County and City Levels.

Building and Construction Permit: Required for all new and remodeling construction, including change of occupancy.

Business License (Business Tax Certificate): Required for all entities doing business within city limits. See "County Unincorporated" for businesses located outside of city limits.

Zoning (Land Use) Approval: May include Conditional Use Permit, Variance, Zone Change, Sign Permit, Parking Regulations, etc., to conform to zoning provisions.

Business Personal Property (normally a county tax): Property used in the operation of a business such as machinery, equipment, trade fixtures, etc., is taxable and subject to assessment. Business operations need to file a Business Property Statement annually with the Assessor declaring property on hand as of January 1 of each year. Generally, those businesses with personal property and fixtures with a cost less than $100,000 are not required to file a property statement.

Fictitious Name Filing (DBA) (normally a county requirement): Required if fictitious name is used.

OTHER POSSIBLE ANNUAL FEES

Universal Product Code

All products now have Universal Product Codes (UPCs) (www.uc-council.org) attached to them. This is a machine-readable code that tells the price, manufacturer, and other information in a twelve-digit sequence. The right to use this code will cost you an initial $750 for up to a block of 100 UPCs. And you will be charged an annual renewal fee of $150.

International Standard Book Number

The International Standard Book Number (ISBN) is the number used by book publishers to identify their books on bookshelves in stores. If you sell books, you will have to acquire an ISBN. They are available from RR Bowker (www.bowker.com). You will get a block of ten numbers for a fee of $225. For more information, go to www.isbn.org.

SETTING UP A BUSINESS BANK ACCOUNT (it ain't as easy as it seems) ━━━

You might think that setting up a business bank account is easy if you have cash to deposit. This is not at all true. You will need the proper documentation to set up a business bank account. Banks want to know that you are starting a real business.

Typically, you will have to supply them your federal employer ID number, fictitious business name filing, articles of incorporation (if you have set up your business as a corporation), and the first board minutes authorizing you to open a bank account (again, if you are doing business as a corporation). If for some reason you started your company before using the same federal employer ID number and left your prior bank account with some difficulties, the bank may decline opening a new account for you. Many banks use a rating service that is tied to your federal employer ID number. Once you get on this rating service as a problem account, it is almost impossible to get off of it. If you can't get off of the "problem account" list, you may be forced to apply for another employer ID number or go to a bank that does not use this rating service.

The bottom line is that once you establish a business bank account, treat it with kindness since it is a valuable asset. It is the starting point of establishing a solid relationship with your bank. Once you have opened your business bank account, your bank will naturally start offering you additional services (of course, for additional fees). Here are some of the services offered by a bank after you have established your account and have had a good track record:

1. Wire transfers – You might think that you'll never need this service, but someday you might. Some out-of-the-country vendors require payment via wire transfer. Also, if you need to get money to a vendor fast, you will probably send it to them via wire transfer. To send a wire transfer, you will need all of their banking information, including name of business, address of business, contact name, bank routing number, bank account number, possibly a correspondent bank's (intermediary bank) name and information, and the amount of the wire. Wire transfers are expensive, ranging from $25 to $50 for each individual transfer. Always build this into your quotes to vendors and customers. If you have large sales of product to companies or people outside of the United States, you may want to have them wire their payments directly into your bank account.

2. Corporate credit card – These credit cards are normally more robust in the information that they provide to you on your monthly statement. They normally provide you with more detail as to classification of expenditures. They will help you keep your personal expenditures separated from your business expenditures.

3. Line of Credit – Cash flow is not always positive in small businesses, especially in start-up businesses. You may have had great sales, but most of them could have been on credit, and thus, you may not have received the cash. So you made the sale and probably had to pay for the merchandise you sold, since you are a new business and your vendor probably would not give you credit. So now you need cash from your bank until the cash comes in from the sales you have made. Be careful when using lines of credit. If the sales are just not coming in and you are using a line of credit, eventually that line of credit will have to be paid back. Even if you start operating your business as a corporation, most banks will probably require that you personally guarantee your corporation's line of credit.

4. Small Business Loans – Almost all small businesses eventually need to get a small business loan. If you have an established relationship with a bank, it should be much easier to get a small business loan with them.

5. Specialized bank accounts. One such account is the zero balance account. Once you have substantial amounts of cash coming into your business checking account, you might want to consider a zero balance bank account. Using a zero balance bank account, the funds coming into your account are automatically "swept" into a savings account leaving your checking account with a zero balance. This allows you to maximize the interest earned on your funds. Similar arrangements can be made with your business disbursements.

6. Ancillary relationships – Your banker will typically know a lot of people in the business community. Your banker can often network you into other businesses that will benefit your business. It is in your banker's best interest that you grow and prosper, because it makes him grow and prosper.

RENTING OFFICE OR OTHER BUSINESS SPACE

Many people feel that they need a big, impressive office or retail presence to feel like they are really in business. Many businesses really do not need offices or any physical presence at all. If you don't need an office or retail space, don't rent it. I know of many businesses that rent post office boxes with impressive addresses and conduct their businesses out of their homes.

If you occasionally see clients or customers and need a conference room or office, there are a number of companies that provide what are called "Efficiency Suites." These are offices that you can rent on an "as needed" basis.

RESEARCHING YOUR NEW LOCATION

First of all, researching your business location may be as simple as walking into your spare bedroom and deciding where to put your desk and bookcase. If you don't need an office or physical location to start your business, don't feel compelled to have an office outside of your home. There are many successful businesses operated out of homes. Here is a quick checklist of items to consider when locating a location for your business.

Area Considerations

1. Is the area zoned for this type of business?
2. Are there a number of churches in the area? If there are a number of churches in the area, it may indicate that it is a good family area and possibly a better place to have your office or retail business.
3. What is the crime like in the area? Is it trending up or down?
4. Is there public transportation available for customers and employees?
5. Is the area in a flood zone?
6. Is your prospective location in the flight path of the airport?
7. Is there a major freeway in close proximity?
8. Are there competitors in the area?
9. Do you have easy access to the closest freeway (convenient on and off ramps)?
10. Is the area growing, established, or declining?
11. What is the cultural and ethnic breakdown for the area, if you are a retailer?
12. Do surrounding businesses properties appear to be well maintained?
13. What is the mix of businesses in your area of consideration? Are there high-end retailers in your area? Are there quality boutique shopping areas near your proposed premises? Are there bookstores in your area?
14. Is there a police station or police substations near your proposed premises?
15. Are there businesses that are open after 5:00 pm, or are most businesses closed during evening hours?
16. Are the traffic patterns in your prospective area compatible to your business?

17. Are the streets well maintained?
18. Are the streets well lit?
19. Are the wages in this area similar to or lower than other areas' you are considering?
20. Is the area a tax-free enterprise zone?
21. Is housing availability in the area under consideration?
22. Is there local taxation burden (e.g., special levies, etc.)?
23. Lifestyle factors?
24. Community and cultural events?
25. Is there a fire station close to your proposed premises?
26. Is there an active chamber of commerce in the area?
27. Are there Starbucks in the local area?
28. Will the local governmental entities give special considerations for you to locate your business in the area (e.g., tax breaks, building assistance)?
29. Is there a local Economic Development Commission?
30. Is there potential for brown-outs or black-outs?
31. Have there been any situations of civil unrest in the past?

Resources

1. Are there qualified employees in the area?
2. Are there colleges and other training institutes in the area for training prospective employees?
3. Is it important to have suppliers in your area?
4. Are there suppliers in your area?
5. Are there convenient shippers located in your area (e.g., Federal Express)?
6. Are the rates for transporting goods similar to or lower than other areas' rates?
7. Is there an airport in close proximity for emergency shipments?
8. Are there quality hotels for people visiting your business?
9. Are there quality meeting facilities available close to your establishment?

Facilities

1. Are the utilities needed for your business available?
2. Does the cost of this facility in this location compare favorably with the cost in

other areas you are considering?

3. Is the area suitable for expansion?
4. Is there adequate parking for employees?
5. Is there adequate parking for customers?
6. Will the landlord pay for necessary leasehold improvements?
7. Do the premises project the image that you need for your particular business?
8. Is there room for expansion on the premises?
9. Is there on-site management for the premises?
10. Are the facilities safe for your clients and customers?
11. Is the security for the premises adequate?
12. Cost per square foot?
13. Common area maintenance charges?
14. Building service/lease provisions?
15. Physical suitability and condition of the building and grounds?
16. Projected quality of site for the next 10 years?
17. Cost of insurance required compared to other areas?
18. Compliance with the American with Disabilities Act (ADA)?
19. High speed Internet connectivity available?
20. Population density?
21. Competition?
22. Signage rules and regulations?
23. Types and quality of other tenants in your building, mall, or shopping center?
24. Are utilities above ground or below ground?
25. Is there adequate storage available?
26. What is the age of the building?

Customers

1. Is the site close to the markets served by your prospective business?
2. Are there businesses in the area that can direct customers to your business?
3. Do you depend on foot traffic for your business?
4. Proximity to customer generators?
5. Demographics of potential customer base?
6. Are there adequate advertising media for reaching your potential customers (e.g., local newspapers, radio, billboards, signage, buses, bus benches, etc.)?

7. Will your customers consider your business a destination, or will they shop at your place of business as part of a multi-stop shopping trip?

Additional Considerations if You Plan to Manufacture Products

1. Does the area allow for disposal of hazardous materials?
2. Will your business be disruptive to the local community?
3. Is there adequate storage for raw materials?
4. Is there access to rail shipping?
5. Are there sources of raw materials in the area of your manufacturing facility?
6. What are the EPA (Environmental Protection Agency) standards for the area?
7. Are there major trucking companies in the vicinity?
8. Is there adequate warehousing in the vicinity?
9. Is the community manufacturing-friendly?

DETERMINING YOUR SPACE AND OTHER NEEDS

At the start of a search for office, retail, or manufacturing space, a real estate broker will invariably want to know right away how much space will be needed by the prospective tenant—you. But, how do you determine how much space you will really need now, next year, and the year after? At first blush, you might compute the number of offices or the square feet of selling space you will need, but you may or may not be accurate.

Here are some things to consider when determining what kind and how much office space or retail space you will need:

1. Local rules and regulations. Sometimes, cities will specify the square footage and design required for your chosen office or retail space you will need.
2. You must make sure that you comply with equal access laws to include the American Disabilities Act (ADA).
3. Plan for growth. If the lease is for 3 years, will the space you are leasing accommodate your business growth over the term of the lease?
4. Plan for non-staff, but necessary space. This would include file cabinets, lunchroom for employees, copy room, bathrooms, entry,

storage, conference room(s), cost room, first-aid room, professional library, stockroom, and other ancillary square footage.

5.   If you are looking for retail space, you have to consider what the competition is doing (e.g., wide isles, eye-level shelves, cash register stations)

6.   If you are looking for office space, you have to give consideration to electrical outlets, Internet connections, lighting, heat/air vent placement, windows, privacy, staff interaction, office traffic patterns, and other aspects of staff productivity.

7.   Will you want an open, bullpen type of setup, or will you want individual offices and cubicles? The current trend seems to be toward an open work environment.

8.   When using systems type furniture, lay out your plan carefully, making sure to include any columns and irregularities in your prospective space.

9.   Plan your cabling/wiring for telecommunications and electronic equipment carefully. Make sure each workspace will be adequately equipped and no cables will be running down or across aisles.

When you buy office furniture or retail furniture and fixtures, the manufacturer or reseller of the furniture will often assist you in determining the amount of space that you will need for your current and future operations.

NASA, in their Headquarters Office and Workstation Space Assignment Policy, states that each executive is allowed the following square feet of office space for their staff:

1.   Associate Administrator   300 SF for private office
2.   Associate Administrator Conference room   200 SF
3.   Deputy Associate Administrator   200 SF for private office
4.   Senior Executive   150 SF for private office
5.   General Merit Employees   75 SF workstation

This is meant to show you that you have to plan for your office usage before you actually secure your premises so that you get the space you need rather than try to stuff your business into some space that you may soon find out is just not the right size for your operations. You can always adjust your space requirements once you find out what is available.

The standard estimate for office space is USF (usable square feet) in the amount of 175 USF per person for densely planned arrangements. For larger, more spacious offices, 325 USF is used.

Generally, offices take up more space on a per-person basis than cubicles. Your philosophy on privacy can have a substantial impact on the total space required for your operation.

According to anan article by Virginia Gibson, a professor at The University of Reading in the UK, here are criteria most often considered (in order of importance) when selecting leased office space:[22]

> Location
> Cost of property (rents, rates)
> Ability to vacate/exit
> Other occupational costs
> Length of commitment
> Expansion/contraction capabilities
> Efficiency of layout
> Speed of occupation
> Opportunity to promote branding and identity
> Inclusive package of real estate, fit out, and services

Most people believe that location is the most important thing to consider when finding office/retail space. This is not surprising in that location can make or break a retail business. Office space must be close to the employment base that it utilizes to be effective.

THINGS TO LOOK FOR IN A LEASE

One of the most important documents you will sign as a new businessperson is your real property lease. You need to be very careful when signing a real property lease. Most landlords will require that you sign a multiyear lease. It's easy to get locked into a location that you can't afford, or you may find that it's not a good location for a number of reasons. I would never recommend signing a lease without doing a lot of homework on the location. And always have your attorney review the lease before signing. Sometimes,

---

22 Virginia Gibson, *Evaluating Office Space Needs and Choices,* Reading, UK: The University of Reading, pg.18, 2001.

your attorney can get a better deal on your lease if you let him negotiate it for you. Sometimes, your professional real estate broker (PREB) can also negotiate a better deal for you once he knows your parameters such as how much you are willing to spend and your physical needs in the way of real property. Listed below are some important things to look for in your real property lease. This is not an exhaustive list, but it covers areas that you should pay particular attention to when reviewing and negotiating a lease.

Some of the clauses that are discussed below are overlapping, but their discussion is meant to alert you to possible problem areas in a lease and not to serve as a guide for drafting real property lease clauses.

Brokerage Commissions

It is necessary, more often than not, to use a professional real estate broker (PREB) to find just the right real property lease for your business. Only use a PREB if they do not charge you anything. Normally, the landlord will pay the PREB commission. Verify that before signing any documents.

Competition

If you are renting retail space, you may want to have a provision in the lease that prevents your landlord from renting to competitive businesses. You will want to have your rights outlined expressly in the lease agreement if your landlord does violate the "competition" clause.

Commencement date

The date the lease actually starts is defined as *lease commencement*. This may or may not be related to the actual delivery of the premises and may not be the same as the possession date. Be sure to have these dates clearly stated in your lease agreement.

Common Area Charges

Most business leases in which you are part of a mall, strip mall, or high-rise building have provisions that specify how you will share in the expenses of maintaining the common areas of the leased premises.

Construction

Does the landlord warrant that the building conforms to all local building codes and laws? Will the landlord take the necessary steps to make sure that the building does comply with local codes and laws before you take possession of the building?

Delivery access—elevators, ramps, etc.

Make sure that you have adequate shipping and receiving access. This will include access for semi truck and trailer rigs for delivering merchandise to your store. Make sure that the hours that you are allowed to accept delivers will accommodate the hours that your vendors will be making deliveries. If you ship product out, make sure that you can do so on an uninterrupted basis.

Destruction/Condemnation

You contract should be specific in this area. Make sure that destruction is well defined. What is the landlord required to do if the premises experience destruction or is condemned? Will your rent be abated? Can the lease be terminated if your premises are partially destructed?

Enforcement

What are the rules if there is a breach on the part of the lessee or lessor? Are there specific damages listed in the contract? Who pays the cost of attorneys for enforcement of the contract? What is the state law controlling the contract if the landlord is out of state? Is there a stated period for remedy of breaches?

Escalation Clause

All multiyear lease agreements will have some type of escalation clause in them. Determine if this clause is keyed to actual increases of expenses of operating the building or if they have keyed it to some index. There are advantages and disadvantages to each. If there are some larges repairs that have to be made, the janitors negotiate a large increase in pay, or a significant increase in the cost of operating the building occurs, you will have your rent raised to compensate for these increased operating expenses. Under most circumstances, having your escalation tied to an independent index will be more predictable.

Estoppel Certificate

Generally speaking, a broad definition of the Estoppel Certificate is "An acknowledgement certificate that generally contains very pertinent information found within the lease along with the status of the tenant's and landlord's rights and obligations under the lease." At the very least, the minimum requirements of any Estoppel are:

Verification of the lease commencement and expiration dates
The rent payment status—current or past due

The status of any defaults by the landlord
Modifications to Lease, i.e., Amendments
Information about possible expansion options

Expense Allocation

Clearly operating expenses, even nonrecurring operating expenses before the tenant moves in, should be the sole obligation of the landlord. After the tenant takes possession of the leased property, the expenses may become the partial responsibility of the tenant. These expenses may be included in this section of a lease and/or a clause covering common area charges; but these expenses typically cover expenses that are directly associated with the tenant's leased premises. There are some costs that are often not clearly covered in a lease, such as periodic testing, minor system (e.g., air conditioning units, and heating units) and other costs. Make sure that it is clearly stated who is responsible for these expenses.

Grace Period

There should be stated grace periods in the lease for such things as default on rent and other stated deadlines. Naturally, try to get these grace periods as long as possible, and try to get the lease to include required notification on the part of the landlord as to the start of any grace period.

Governmental Reports

Various federal, state, and local agencies will require that tenants and landlords report on various aspects of their businesses. This will include the storage of hazardous chemicals and other matters. It would be important for you to know if any of your fellow tenants are storing hazardous materials. It would also be important for you to know if one of your fellow tenants has had fire department violations. You should try to get a provision in your lease that would require your landlord to supply you with copies of these governmental documents.

Hold Over

At the end of your lease, you may have to stay a little past the last day of your lease before your new lease at another location allows you to move in. This is called a "holdover" period. Most landlords understand this need and will accommodate you. But, to be safe, make sure that the amount of rent during this holdover period and the length of time you are allowed to hold over are provided for in the lease.

Indemnity

The basic indemnity clause frees the landlord from any liability resulting from your actions as a tenant. The main problem with this element of a lease is when it becomes a separate clause. When this happens, a landlord tends to expand it to a level that can be troublesome for you as a tenant. A landlord will often use the opportunity of a stand-alone indemnity clause to state that the landlord is not liable for the actions of the tenant or for his OWN actions. If you see this type of clause, you absolutely must have it modified.

Internet, High-Speed Connectivity, and Wiring

It is difficult for almost any business to be effective without high-speed Internet. Make sure that you have it clearly stated in the lease that you have access to high-speed Internet throughout your premises rather than in a selected area. Also, try to get any connectivity for high-speed Internet covered in your leasehold improvements.

Landlord Solvency

When you are negotiating your lease, you never really think about your landlord's becoming insolvent, but it happens more often than you could imagine. You need to have language in your lease that will protect you in this. The main problem with landlord insolvency is that they will often stop providing services that they agreed to provide such as janitorial, electricity, etc. At the very least, you want to be able to cancel your lease if it is in your best interest.

Legal Compliance

Your lease might include a provision whereby you agree to comply with all present and future federal, state, and local laws, including future environmental laws affecting your leased premises. This is one lease provision that you probably will not be able to get around, and if worded fairly, is an appropriate clause to have in your lease. The wording should state compliance with governmental laws and regulations, not with subjective rules and regulations that are difficult to understand and too difficult to maintain compliance with.

Leasehold Improvements

Your space must be functional to your particular needs and have the "look and feel" that will help propel your business forward. Every business will be different, because every tenant will be different. How your space is configured and constructed is important. If you move into an older building, your premises may need extensive leasehold improvements. Leasehold improvements may be as simple as painting walls and laying new carpet or as complex as adding fixtures, moving doors, windows and walls, and more. If the work is extensive, the landlord may request that you enter into a construction contract that will become part of your new lease. Your leasehold improvements clause will typically include the following points:

1. Your plans and specifications
2. Timetable for your plans, approval process, and the actual construction
3. Construction work to be completed by the landlord and the landlord's contractors
4. Construction to be completed by you, the tenant
5. Costs that are to be paid by the landlord
6. Costs that are to be paid by you
7. Payment schedule
8. Final work acceptance—when you can take possession and occupy the premises

Liens on Tenant's Property

Never sign a lease with a clause that gives the landlord the remedy of a lien on your property. This type of clause specifies that the landlord will have a lien on all of your personal property including, but not limited to, all of goods, wares, fixtures, furniture, and equipment of your business. This can create an incredibly onerous burden on you. Your PREB may even try to get you to sign such a clause. If so, change your PREB, as he is not looking out for your best interest.

Insurance

This section of the lease will specify who is responsible for what insurance and in what amounts. It will specify who is responsible for liability insurance, theft insurance, fire insurance, and other casualty insurance. In the area of insurance, be sure to look closely at any clause that looks or smells like a "hold-harmless" provision. You never want to be held liable for any harm caused by the landlord.

Maintenance and Repairs

The information included in this paragraph may be included in another paragraph of your lease, such as expense allocation. There are leases that are referred to as "full service gross" leases where the landlord covers maintenance, janitorial, utilities, trash collection, gardening, and other expenses of upkeep of your premises. I personally prefer a lease where the landlord is responsible for all premises upkeep so that I can concentrate on the business of my business. Whatever type of lease you plan to enter into, make sure that it clearly lays out who is responsible for which expenses.

Major Tenant Clause

Some leases refer to this as the "going dark" clause. If you are located in a building, mall, or shopping center based around a major anchor store or other major company, losing that anchor store could have a substantial impact on your business. In today's economic environment, this is a real problem. Try to negotiate a clause that will allow you to relocate, cancel your lease, or at least get a rent reduction if a major tenant moves out of your building, mall, or shopping center.

Nature of Lease

What is the nature of the lease? Is it a lease for commercial purposes that allows you to have customers buying merchandise on your premises? Is it a triple net lease that demands you pay all maintenance, janitorial, etc., or is it a full-service gross lease that states your landlord will be picking up all of these expenses?

Notices

This is a clause that is often ignored. It is ignored primarily because it is pretty straightforward, and after negotiating the other sections of the contract, this one is often overlooked. This clause specifies what constitutes notice to you and to your landlord. This clause is particularly important when it pertains to the notices for sending and receiving your monthly lease payment, the landlord's notice of default, your intention to renew your lease, sublet your premises, and other matters of communication between you and your landlord.

Parking

This can be an important point, even if you are not in a retail business. You want to make sure that you have enough parking for you, your staff, and visitors. If you will be receiving customers at your place of business, make sure that you have adequate customer parking. Parking will often be assigned stalls and/or tandem parking spaces based on the number of square feet you are going to lease. Find out if the parking is assigned, if you have to pay for it, and if you can rent additional stalls.

Phone Equipment and Wiring

Make sure that you have adequate phone connections in the space you are going to lease. If not, make sure they will be installed as part of leasehold improvements.

Purchase Option

You just might like your leased premises enough to buy the place. If this is feasible, make sure that you have a purchase option clause drafted into your lease agreement. Make sure that your agreement includes the option price and when and how you must exercise the option.

Quiet Enjoyment and Nondisturbance

These are two separate, but somewhat related, lease clauses. The quiet-enjoyment clause is a promise by the landlord that as long as the tenant pays his rent and abides by the provisions of the lease, he will peacefully enjoy the full possession of the premises without molestation or hindrance by the landlord or any other party over which he has control. The nondisturbance clause is a bit more complicated. For total protection, you need to have additional "quiet enjoyment" clauses from any third party, apart from your landlord. Specifically, this refers to a mortgage lender or a future building purchaser. There is some question about the value of this clause, since the landlord typically cannot create a liability for actions on behalf of a third party.

Renewal

If you can get renewal language into your lease, this is a good thing. You can basically obligate the landlord without obligating yourself for a long lease period. You should ask about the terms of the renewal and what must be done to exercise the option to renew.

Rent

Make sure the monthly payment amount is clearly stated, including the amount, the due dates, and when it becomes delinquent. Also, make sure that you have an exact address and payee listed in your lease agreement.

Right of Entry

At first thought, you may be inclined to want to limit your landlord's right to enter your premises as much as possible. I have never seen a landlord abuse this right. It is normally in the best interest of the tenant to allow the landlord entry to the premises on an as-needed basis. This should be allowed even if it is somewhat inconvenient to you. If for any reason the landlord must close your premises, you should, if possible, have a provision in your lease agreement for some abatement of rent during the period your premises are closed.

Security and Rent Deposits

It is sometimes possible to get the security and rent deposit dropped, but this doesn't happen often. In the event of your default, your landlord will have the right, but not the obligation, to use or retain all or any portion of the security deposit for the payment of any base rent or additional rent or any other monetary sum for which you are in default. The landlord can also take all or a portion of your deposit to repair damages to the premises or the building (as specified elsewhere in the lease). Normal wear and tear on the property should not be deducted from your security and rent deposits, and this should be spelled out in your lease agreement. Sometimes, a landlord will ask for first and last months' rent and a security deposit equal to the amount of your monthly rent payment. This mean that you would have to come up with three times your monthly payment before you could move into your new premises. Try to negotiate this away or to make it as low an amount as possible. This money will go into your general ledger as an asset, but you will not have access to it until you move out of the premises and have satisfied your landlord's move-out condition requirements.

Signs and Directory Listings

Sometimes, you will not find signs and directory clauses in lease agreements. You will often agree to abide by the tenant rules and regulations associated with the building. If your lease has a separate signs and directory clause, make sure that it meets with your needs for establishing your presence in the building. You also want to make sure that it controls signs and directory listings to your satisfaction so that your fellow tenants are not allowed to have signage or directory usage running contrary to your best interest.

Space

Usable square footage is different from rentable square footage. What you rent is not necessarily what is useable by you. You will have spaces under stairwells, columns, windows, doors, and corners with odd angles that all affect your usable square footage. Also of importance is your ability to expand your current square footage. Can you be given first right of refusal when adjacent space becomes available in your building? Can you relocate to a larger area in your current building or to another building that your landlord owns?

Subletting and Assignment

These are your rights to sublease a part of your premises or assign your total rights in a lease to another tenant. Typically, it is best to have nothing in the contract in regard to subletting or assignment. If no contrary language exists in the lease agreement, you are free to sublease or assign the lease to whomever, whenever you choose. If there is some restrictive language in the lease, have your attorney review it and get a complete understanding of your obligations under a subleasing and/or assignment clause. Remember that even though you sublease or assign your premises in your lease, you will probably still have some liability.

Subordination and Attornment

Subordination refers to the fact that one document has priority over another document and that one of the documents is less important than the other document(s). In a lease agreement, this clause means that the rights of a tenant will be subordinate to all mortgages and related documents. This clause is more important to the mortgage holder than to you. Attornment is related to subordination. *Attornment* is your automatic acceptance of, and paying rent to, a new landlord or owner. This provision in a lease is important to both small and large tenants. This provision will keep a new landlord from kicking you out of your premises in the event of foreclosure on the original landlord.

Subrogation

This is an important clause that you will find in most leases. The term *subrogation* refers to any situation where a creditor substitutes its rights for the rights of another creditor and has all the rights of the original creditor. For example, a landlord has damage caused by a tenant and turns it into his insurance company. His insurance company pays him for his claim and then turns around and sues the tenant for the amount of the paid claim. This is subrogation.

Surrender of Premises

Most leases are design to end without incident at the end of the lease period, with surrender of premises assumed. But, from the tenant's point of view, this clause can be important when it comes to disposition of furnishing, fixtures, and equipment and leasehold improvements on your lease premises. These assets, in addition to keys and locks, will normally be required to be returned to the landlord in good, clean condition, subject to normal and reasonable wear and tear. Be careful with this clause as you might end up being financially responsible for the removal of fixtures and furniture. This should be the responsibility of the landlord, but I have seen some leases that sneak in the provision that the removal of assets by the landlord can be charged against the tenant's security deposit.

Taxes and Expenses

Your lease should state who is responsible for all taxes and general maintenance. If you are responsible for maintenance, make sure that you are free to contract with whomever you wish. Also, make sure the lease is clear on who is responsible for extraordinary or structural repairs and maintenance.

Term of Lease

This clause should normally be short and sweet, specifying when the landlord's and the tenant's obligations to each other begin and end. Remember that the delivery of premises date may not be the same as the lease commencement date, and may also differ from the occupancy date. You don't want the lease commencement date to be substantially sooner than the occupancy date.

Termination of Lease

Make sure that that you can fulfill all of the requirements of termination of the lease. Make sure that you have a provision in the allowance of normal wear and tear on the premises. You have to button this provision down so that you can get your security and rent deposit back at the end of the lease. Many small businessmen rely on the refund of their terminating lease security and rent deposit to help them get into their new lease. If you are one of these lessees, you must be sure to fully understand and comply with the termination provisions of your lease.

Use Restrictions

There is a positive and a negative side to this provision in lease agreements. It will restrict what you can use the property for, and it can also restrict what your fellow tenants can use their premises for, which is probably a good thing. If you are going to be using hazardous chemicals or dangerous equipment, you need to know this restriction before signing a lease that could possibly preclude you from using these types of assets in your business.

Utilities and Waste Disposal

Utilities and Waste Disposal expense will normally be covered in the taxes and expenses clause of your lease, but make sure it is addressed somewhere in your lease agreement. Normally included with this clause is the cost of janitorial and other building operation expenses recurring monthly.

Warranties and Representations

Be careful with warranties and representations. Your landlord may want you to agree to take your premises on an "as-is" basis. Who knows what can go wrong in this type of situation? There are often conditions that are not visible on a walk-through that could cause you grief in the future, so be ever so careful of "as-is" warranties and representations. If you are desperate and insist on signing a lease with an "as-is" clause, have your landlord specify any problem of which he is already aware.

Wireless connectivity

Make sure that the lease allows you to utilize high speed wireless connectivity without interruption from other tenants. If you don't think you are going to be using wireless communication, think again. Remember that things change rather quickly in the communication/computer arenas, and you may want to use it in the future.

Zoning

Your lease probably will not have any clause related to zoning. But be aware of the zoning laws applicable to your premises. And they can change. Once you find a good physical location with a lease that you can tolerate, be sure to check the zoning laws before getting too deep into the lease negotiation process.

Working with a Broker

You might get lucky on your own and find the perfect place to lease, negotiate the perfect lease, and move in without any problems—OR NOT. It's possible to secure your own leased property, but it's not nearly as effective, efficient, and economical as working with a real estate broker. Real estate brokers will not cost you anything, and their knowledge of the real estate market in your community will be a great asset to you. They know the areas that will best fit your needs and budget. They are familiar with local zoning and tax laws.

Once they find a number of locations that are potentially good for your business, they will then help you objectively narrow down your selection. Once you choose a location, they can negotiate the best terms possible and complete the mountains of paperwork for you. It is in their best interest to make sure that all leasehold improvements are completed, all inspections are completed, and all paperwork is completed, since they will not get paid until this is all done.

Although many states let PREBs (professional real estate brokers) complete leases, it is a good idea to also have your attorney review the lease. Remember, these are legal documents, and they will possibly lock you into a relationship with your prospective landlord for years.

Financing Your Business

Most people starting a new business do not have enough funds to start it, but they do it anyway. There are lots of stories about people who started businesses with a dollar in their pocket and an idea. This does indeed happen, but you can increase your odds with solid planning and with proper resources. You have probably heard the saying "The more prepared I am, the luckier I seem to get." Unfortunately, a lot of great products and business ideas never happen because the entrepreneur did not have incredible luck or did not look at the total picture before trying to get their product to market or before trying to get their business idea off the ground. Being prepared and adequately funded can significantly increase your "luck" and increase your odds for success. Even more important than finances is making sure that God is in your corner. By the time you are starting to raise funds for your venture, you should have already put your business idea before the Lord. You should include the Lord in all of your business decisions, large and small.

The chapters entitled THE BUSINESS PLAN AND OPERATING YOUR BUSINESS and GROWING YOUR BUSINESS deal with the aspects of putting together a solid business plan and budget. The chapter on building a business plan is presented separately from this chapter, because a constantly evolving business plan should be a part of your normal management process and should be completed each year (and constantly updated) even if you are not seeking funding. Completing an annual business plan is a very useful management tool to keep you and your business focused. I will assume that you have read these chapters and know the amount you need to finance your new business venture. It is worth reiterating that after starting a business, it almost always takes longer than you estimated to become profitable. And always remember that you need to include in your funding estimate the amount of money you need to live on while you are taking your business to a profitable level.

LIABILITIES ASSOCIATED WITH OBTAINING FUNDING

Never accept any kind of investment into your company without having your attorney involved. When you accept money from organizations and/or individuals, there are certain liabilities that you assume in addition to paying back the funds. There are certain steps you can take to minimize your liability. One example: make sure any individual investing in your business is a qualified investor according to the definition given by the Securities Exchange Commission (see "EXISTING BUSINESS FINANCING" below). And there is responsibility to a higher authority. Never give a bad name to doing business in a "Christian-like manner."

HOW MOST FUND THEIR NEW BUSINESSES

In a recent survey conducted by the U.S. Chamber of Commerce,[23] new entrepreneurs get their funding from a variety of sources with personal savings being the leading source of new business capital:

Personal savings	81%
Bank loans	18%
Credit cards	15%
Family loans	8%
SBA loans	3%
Revolving credit	3%
Venture capital	2%

From the listing, you can see that there is overlapping of the sources of new business capital that new entrepreneurs use. As an example a new entrepreneur may use bank loans and personal savings to finance a new business or any other combination of sources. Most new business owners use a combination of these sources, getting their

---

23   U.S. Chamber of Commerce Statistics and Research Center, *Access to Capital: What Funding Sources Work for You?*, May 2005.

funding any way they can that is legal and Godly. Be very careful during this stage, because the wrong financial decisions can either haunt you while you are in business or can completely wreck your business. While desperately looking for funding, you might take in an equity partner that is not a good choice or obtain a loan that cripples your chances for survival. I know of an eager Christian inventor of consumer products that took in two partners to help minimize the risk of starting a new venture. As they were starting to achieve a level of success, they were approached with what appeared to be a financially rewarding deal with an adult film company. His two partners wanted to "take the money and run," and the one Christian partner did not. After being in business together for a couple of years, this single transaction caused the partnership to break apart at a critical juncture in their company development. The single Christian partner did stay in business, but this setback almost totally destroyed his dream company.

The best position to be in is to not need funding. But if you have to pursue funding for your new venture, debt funding is normally preferred over equity funding if you want to maintain unencumbered control of your business. This is not to say that equity funding is a bad thing. You only have to look at the major stockholders of Google. Equity funding has made them billionaires. Use outside funding judiciously, as there are no "free rides."

DETERMINING HOW MUCH FINANCING YOU NEED

Determining how much financing you will need depends on a number of factors. You will need to determine if you are going to be starting your business on a full-time or part-time basis. You may not initially know if you are able to start on a full-time basis. Once you have analyzed your cash flow situation and the amount of cash needed to start your business full-time, you may decide to keep your day job while you build your business. You will need to determine what resources you have at your disposal, and you will need to have a good idea of what your personal and business financial needs are going to be. You may find that you need a number of "rounds" of financing at different stages in the growth of your business. The initial financing that you need to start your business is often referred to as "seed capital." Make sure that you read the chapter entitled THE BUSINESS PLAN AND OPERATING YOUR BUSINESS.

Here is an example of a cash flow analysis for XYZ Company, Inc. for one year. This is an incorporated entity, so the entrepreneur's salary is incorporated into the model as salary.

Twelve-month cash flow

XYZ Company, Inc   Fiscal Year Begins: Jan-06

	Pre-Startup EST	Jan-07	Feb-07	Mar-07	Apr-07	May-07	Jun-07	Jul-07	Aug-07	Sep-07	Oct-07	Nov-07	Dec-07	Total Item EST
Cash on Hand (beginning of month)	10,000	81,950	57,956	26,461	4,217	26,472	19,728	19,733	28,989	40,244	48,750	54,505	62,511	62,511
CASH RECEIPTS														
Cash Sales	0	5,000	5,000	20,000	30,000	60,000	75,000	90,000	100,000	105,000	110,000	115,000	120,000	835,000
CASH PAID OUT														
Purchases (merchandise)	2,500	2,500	10,000	15,000	30,000	37,500	45,000	50,000	52,500	55,000	57,500	60,000	7,500	425,000
Gross Margin	-2,500	2,500	-5,000	5,000	0	22,500	30,000	40,000	47,500	50,000	52,500	55,000	112,500	410,000
Gross wages (exact withdrawal)	0	10,000	10,000	10,000	10,000	10,000	10,000	10,000	10,000	10,000	10,000	10,000	10,000	120,000
Payroll expenses (taxes, etc.)	0	2,500	2,500	2,500	2,500	2,500	2,500	2,500	2,500	2,500	2,500	2,500	2,500	30,000
Outside services	0	1,000	1,000	1,000	1,000	1,000	1,000	1,000	1,000	1,000	1,000	1,000	1,000	12,000
Supplies (office & oper.)	0	250	250	1,000	1,500	3,000	3,750	4,500	5,000	5,250	5,500	5,750	6,000	41,750
Repairs & maintenance	0	0	0	0	0	0	0	0	0	0	0	0	0	0
Advertising	0	5,000	5,000	5,000	5,000	5,000	5,000	5,000	10,000	15,000	20,000	20,000	20,000	120,000
Car, delivery & travel	250	250	250	250	250	250	250	250	250	250	250	250	250	3,250
Accounting & legal	0	1,250	1,250	1,250	1,250	1,250	1,250	1,250	1,250	1,250	1,250	1,250	1,250	15,000
Rent	0	2,000	2,000	2,000	2,000	2,000	2,000	2,000	2,000	2,000	2,000	2,000	2,000	24,000
Telephone	300	300	300	300	300	300	300	300	300	300	300	300	300	3,900
Insurance	0	250	250	250	250	250	250	250	250	250	250	250	250	3,000
Interest		2,000	1,989	1,977	1,966	1,954	1,943	1,931	1,919	1,907	1,896	1,884	1,872	23,238
Miscellaneous														
TOTAL EXPENSES	550	24,800	24,789	25,527	26,016	27,504	28,243	28,981	34,469	39,707	44,946	45,184	45,422	396,138
CASH FLOW FROM OPS	-3,050	-22,300	-29,789	-20,527	-26,016	-5,004	1,757	11,019	13,031	10,293	7,554	9,816	67,078	13,862
Loans (Cash In)	275,000	0	0	0	50,000	0	0	0	0	0	0	0	0	325,000
Cash Available	281,950	59,650	28,167	5,934	28,201	21,468	21,485	30,752	42,019	50,537	56,304	64,322	129,589	129,589
Loan principal payment		1,694	1,706	1,717	1,729	1,740	1,752	1,763	1,775	1,787	1,799	1,811	1,823	21,096
Capital purchase (specify)	175,000												50,000	225,000
Other startup costs	25,000													25,000
Reserve and/or Escrow														0
OTHER CASH PAID OUT	200,000	1,694	1,706	1,717	1,729	1,740	1,752	1,763	1,775	1,787	1,799	1,811	51,823	271,096
Cash Position (end of month)	81,950	57,956	26,461	4,217	26,472	19,728	19,733	28,989	40,244	48,750	54,505	62,511	77,766	77,766

Fig.9 – 12 Month Cash Flow

We are assuming that the entrepreneur in this sample cash flow projection can live on the $10,000 a month listed as his monthly salary. This is a simplified cash flow projection with the following assumptions:

1. The gross margin on products sold is 50%.
2. Cost of Goods Sold is paid for in the month before the sale.
3. The $300,000 that is needed for the business is to be used as follows:
    i. $175,000 for equipment
    ii. $25,000 for other start-up costs

      iii. The loan is for 36 months and has a 6.50% interest rate.

      iv. The balance of the loan is to cushion operating expenses.

4. This entrepreneur assumes that he will be cash flow (from operations) positive in the month of September. He is timing his marketing entry so that he can ramp up his activity for his busy season, which starts in August/ September.

5. He is anticipating a tight cash flow during the month of August and September since he has had to prepay for the inventory associated with his increased sales in September and October.

Here are the steps that you would normally follow in constructing your cash flow projections:

1. Estimate your start-up costs. This would include:
   i. Rent deposits
   ii. Building repairs
   iii. New equipment
   iv. Beginning supplies
   v. Permits and licenses
   vi. Beginning inventory
   vii. Miscellaneous expenses

2. Determine the amount of money you will need to keep you in a cash-flow-positive position.

3. Compile your recurring expenses
   i. Rent
   ii. Insurance
   iii. Supplies
   iv. Repairs and maintenance
   v. Advertising
   vi. Other expenses

4. Determine your projected sales. Realistically, you would have more than one product, so you would want to build a worksheet that shows the various products that you will be selling and their associated cost of sales to arrive at a weighted average gross margin. Part of your

projected sales computation is to determine the effect of seasonality for each month of your projection. You need to determine the sales that you need to generate to cover, ongoing expenses.

5.   Compile your recurring expenses
   i.   Rent
   ii. Insurance
   iii. Supplies
   iv. Repairs and maintenance
   v.   Advertising
   vi. Other expenses
6.   Determine your personal cash needs.
7.   Determine what you desire for net income.
8.   Compute your cash shortfall and determine how you are going to cover it, or revise your cash needs by repeating the prior steps.

Determining what you need to start a business is as much art as it is science. It's important to commit your analysis to writing. Using Microsoft Excel® to set up a proper spreadsheet will help you create a much clearer picture. . This approach also enables you to do a "what if" analysis. Once you complete the worksheet, you can change certain amounts to reflect different approaches to solving your projected cash flow issues. As an example, if you find that your cash outflow is too high, you can ratchet down your monthly salary or ratchet down one of the other expense line items. Always keep in mind that it usually takes longer than you originally anticipated to get your monthly business activity to a positive cash flow position. It seems to be a law of nature. The example presented is just one of a number of ways you can estimate your beginning cash needs.

FUND WITH DEBT, EQUITY, OR INTERNALLY (Personally) ━━━━━━━━━

Funding for your new venture will be one of three types: it will either be debt, equity, or internal financing. You may get offered funds that are considered a "gift" or a "grant," but this happens so seldom that we won't discuss these sources of funding. Also, keep in mind that there are very few things in life that are free, and gifts and grants normally come with strings attached. Your funding options change after you have been in business for a while. If you have become cash flowflow positive and have accumulated some assets, you will have some additional options for financing at your disposal.

You might wonder why you should seek external funding when you seem to be doing okay using only internal funding. If you can borrow funds that have a lower interest rate than the rate of return from your business, it makes sense to borrow the funds. You will then earn the difference between your cost of debt money (interest you pay) and the return that you receive from the additional income generated by your business using the extra funds. I had one client that used similar logic to keep expanding his chain of franchised fast food restaurants. He started out with one franchise unit that returned approximately $10,000 net income per month. He calculated the cost of the money that he would need to borrow to open a second unit, which, in turn, also began to generate approximately $10,000 per month. The last time I saw this client, he had 13 units that each averaged $10,000. He was now earning a monthly net income of $130,000 instead of $10,000 a month.

Debt financing is funding that you will have to pay back, with interest, at some future, specific date. You will owe the money regardless of the success of your venture. If you are just starting out, you will probably have to personally guarantee the debt for your corporation if your new venture is incorporated. Equity financing is where you give up part of your business for funding. Your investors assume most or all of your risk. If your company fails, they lose their money, and you don't owe them anything. But if it does well, they typically make a much better return on their investment than if they had lent you the money. Another way to look at it is that equity financing is far more expensive if your company is successful, but far less expensive if it is not successful. Using internal funds is the best way to finance your venture if you don't have to "bet the farm" (jeopardize your family's financial security).

You will often hear people say "OPM" or "other people's money" is the best way to finance anything. Just remember that OPM always come with S-T-R-I-N-G-S, and no one likes to dance on the end of someone else's strings. Using other people's money is not necessarily a bad thing, and lots of solid, profitable businesses have been built using OPM. But, as Christians, we try to minimize our debt to others (and risk) and use "YOM" or "your own money."

If you have been in business for a while, you have some options that you don't have if you've never been in business. There are basically three stages in which you will want funding for your business: Seed Capital, Expansion, and Acquisition. If you are seeking funding for a start-up (seed capital), your situation is unique, since you will typically not have a verifiable track record. It will be a lot harder to attract venture capital and venture capital interest. Once you are past the initial phase, you will more easily attract capital. You will be able to tell your potential investors/lenders that you want to grow your already successful or potentially successful business. Having a track record makes it easier to quantify your projections and the need for additional capital. Based on these facts, you can usually obtain more capital. It seems that the less you need funding, the more you can get, especially from banks. In the exit phase, you will be looking for someone to buy your successful business, or at least a major portion of it, so that you can enjoy the fruits of your labor.

There are a number of factors to consider when deciding between debt and equity or a combination thereof. The first three factors are the amount you need, how badly you need the money, and what type of funding is available to you. As a start-up, you will not have all normal sources of business financing available to you.

	Debt	Equity
Risk	higher	lower
Involvement from funding source	lower	higher
Cost	lower	higher
Complexity	lower	higher
Accessibility to entrepreneurs	lower	higher
Funding periods	shorter	longer
Ease of exiting the transaction	easier	harder
Dilution of owner's equity	none	can be substantial
Effect on cash flow of business	must be repaid	none
Restriction of future fund-raising	higher	lower

If you use debt to finance your new business venture, it can negatively impact your cash flow. When you pay back a loan, the payments you make are not an expense, but they are reductions in cash.

A great idea alone will not get you funding. No one will finance a "great idea" by itself. They need to see how this great idea will translate into profits. This is where your well-written business plan and your resume will come into play. You may have a great business plan that you researched well and/or paid an "expert" to write for you, but if your investors don't believe that you can execute the business plan, then the only thing you will have is a well-written business plan and no funding. So, along with your great business plan, you can increase your odds of obtaining financing by having a resume that supports your business plan. If you are an accountant who wants to start a bakery catering company, your accounting resume probably won't impress potential financiers. Sure, you can keep a mean set of books, but can you bake a mean apple pie?

THE IMPORTANCE OF YOUR PERSONAL AND BUSINESS CREDIT RATING

If you can't get financing for a car or a house, you probably will not get outside financing for your business venture. You need to get a copy of your credit rating and make sure that you take care of any derogatory issues on your credit report. Almost all lenders and most equity funding sources will be very interested in your credit report. A good credit rating can also substantially influence the terms of the business loan that you may be trying to get. Your credit rating or credit score, as it is often called, is a value based on a number of criteria used by lending institutions for decisions on giving credit to individuals. The criteria used include the amount you owe on non-mortgage-related credit accounts such as credit cards, your payment history, and your credit history.

Lenders use a credit score referred to as FICO to gauge the risk that you represent as a borrower. Your credit score is just one component of your credit evaluation, but an important one. Two borrowers with the same above-average FICO score of 750 may end up getting different interest rates on their business loans based on their current debt load and other current factors. The Fair Isaac Corporation, known as FICO, created the first credit scoring system in 1958, for American Investments, and the first credit scoring system for a bank credit card in 1970, for American Bank and Trust.

You will also want to make sure your business is registered with the major reporting companies such as Experian and Dun & Bradstreet. Check to see if businesses that your company does business with report to the major credit reporting agencies. This is very important to your company, as you can have a great track record for paying all of your bills on time, but if it's not being reported, then it will not factor into your credit rating.

PERSONAL FUNDING SOURCES ━━━━━━━━━━━━━━━━━━━━━━━

As stated above, the best place to get financing for your new business venture is from internal resources, but only if you can do it without jeopardizing your family's financial security. This will also be your quickest source of financing. The process of securing funding from outside sources can take several months. If you have incorporated your business, which is normally recommended, you can either give resources (including cash) to your business or you can lend them to your corporation. If you give them to the corporation, it will be considered equity. If you lend them to your corporation, you will record them as a liability on the corporate books. Recording them as a liability on the corporate books can be advantageous to you personally. If they are recorded as a liability, the corporation can pay you back, and the payments you receive will not be a taxable event but merely giving you back an asset that you lent to your corporation.

Although outside cash will cost you resources and possibly some equity, you will need to secure outside funding sometime in the life of your company. Most companies must get outside funding help to achieve rapid growth. Recall the example I used earlier of my client who started with one fast food restaurant that generated an average of $10,000 per month, borrowed the funds to buy a second unit that also generated $10,000 a month, and continued to do so until he had 13 units generating about $130,000 per month net income. It would have taken him 10 years to achieve this growth without outside financing. With outside funding, he did it in 3 years.

As a start-up, you may not have options available to you outside of your own personal, internal funding.

YOUR PERSONAL SAVINGS AND OTHER PERSONAL ASSETS

You will eventually probably seek out a business loan even if you don't secure one to start your business. When you do, most lenders will want to see that you have invested some of your own funds into your business. You won't have much of a chance of securing a business loan if all the lender sees on your balance sheet is debt and no equity. (See the accounting equation that is reviewed in the chapter entitled KEEPING TRACK OF YOUR BUSINESS (ACCOUNTING AND OTHER FUN THINGS) Assets = Liabilities + owner's equity.)

If you are going to invest your personal savings into your new business, first gain agreement from your spouse. Remember, your spouse is your business partner even if he/she does not participate in the day-to-day operations of your business. Make sure that the money you will be using is not earmarked for your children's college or major repairs to your house. Many people will go through life thinking everything is great financially until they realize that they have not set aside savings for unanticipated home repairs or other emergencies. Investing in your new business does not qualify as an emergency.

When people think of taking personal assets to start a business, they think of personal savings.   But, everyone has personal assets other than their savings accounts. Take stock of what you have by taking a complete inventory of your financial and physical assets. The easiest place to start is your financial assets. Things you would include in this category are savings accounts, checking accounts, IRAs, retirement plans, loans to strangers, friends and family, time share interests, vacation homes, whole-life insurance policies, stocks, bonds, deposits, patents, copyrights, interest in other companies, stock option plans, trust accounts, equity in your house, and anything else that can be readily turned into cash.

Next, take an inventory of your physical assets and assign them a realistic value. Include items such as motor homes, travel trailers, camping equipment, boats, jet skis, power tools, sporting equipment, cars, vacation homes, computers, printers, furniture, TVs, books, etc. You will be surprised at the amount of "stuff" you own. A lot of these items can be converted into cash. These days, it is very easy to convert physical things to cash with Web sites like eBay.

Once you have a list of all of your financial and nonfinancial personal assets, you should classify them with the following information:

1. Current value
2. Any encumbrances (any money owed on the assets to outsiders)
3. Your willingness to part with the asset (1 = easy, 2 = you can part with the asset if you have to, 3 = you can't part with the asset)

Total up the assets that you have available to start your business. Even if you don't have enough, you can either scale back your plans or obtain additional funding from one of the other ways listed in this chapter. Using your personal assets is not a long-term funding approach. You will want to develop a long-term plan that encompasses some of the other methods. You will also want to discuss with your attorney and accountant how you should contribute these assets to your new company.

If you use personal funds, you will be blurring the line between your personal wealth and the development of your business. Ideally, it is best to keep a clear distinction between your personal wealth and your business. If you use personal funds to finance your new business venture, you should include, within your plan, a way to repay these assets. Just because you already own them doesn't mean that they are "free." Bringing personal assets into your business complicates your risk picture. You can place your family at greater personal risk if you encumber your life insurance, borrow against a retirement account, or get a second loan against your personal residence. These sources of capital for your new business should be viewed as temporary and not as an ongoing source of capital.

HOME EQUITY LOAN

This personal funding source is often used for starting new businesses. You have to be careful using this source. It's important, when starting your new business, to keep your personal living expenses to a minimum. A lot of new entrepreneurs are able to start their businesses because they have low mortgage payments after being in their existing house a number of years. I remember one new entrepreneur that had a conversation with his wife about the new business he wanted to start. His wife was more interested in moving to a larger house. His business was eventually successful. He got his way, and now they live in a really BIG house. You can get the extra cash out of your house by putting up your house's equity for the loan, or you can refinance your house. There was a period in the United States when interest rates were relatively high. If you refinanced during the 2000 to 2006 time period, the chances are that you might have been able to refinance your house without taking out a second loan on the house and get a smaller payment plus the funds for financing your business.

START YOUR BUSINESS PART-TIME

You have heard the saying "Keep your day job." This might be a worthwhile strategy for you if you are considering starting a business. There are some obvious benefits to this approach:

1. A "try-before-you-buy" approach. Wouldn't it be awful if you quit your job, started your new company, and found that you wished you had your job back again?
2. You still have the security of your "day-job."
3. A well-managed transition from your day-job to your dream company

is most often better than abruptly quitting your job one day and starting your company the next day.

4. You won't feel the mental pressure of putting all of your eggs in one basket.

Structure Your Business to Your Finances – You may want to start selling products on a smaller scale than you originally anticipated.

MOONLIGHTING

This "financing technique" is closely related to the technique above of starting your business on a part-time basis. The difference is that you will not let your new business venture interfere at all with your day job. When you moonlight, you are working your new business venture around all of the other aspects of your life; whereas in starting your business part-time, you have made more of a commitment to turn your part-time venture into a full-time pursuit.

LIVE ON YOUR SPOUSE'S INCOME

Many spouses have supported their mates as they have built businesses. Living off of one income after having two full incomes can be a major adjustment for a couple. I was fortunate to have a wife that allowed me to quit my well-paying job to start a business. There were times that it looked like the business would never become profitable, but God had a different timetable than I had, and I was just not listening. Once I started listening, the process of building the business became more enjoyable. Half of the fun of building a business is enjoying the journey. If you elect to use this approach to building your business, both you and your spouse have to be realistic about your goals and how long it will take to reach them. It is vitally important to keep your spouse totally informed about what is going on in the business so that they feel part of it. Don't just tell them all of the good things that happen, but share the negative things as well. Try to include your spouse in all of your important business decisions. Building a business can actually help build your relationship with your spouse, just as your relationship can help you build your business. You will probably both enjoy the process more if you are sharing the details of the journey.

It's extremely important to share realistic goals and milestones with your spouse so he/she can see your progress and maintain confidence in you and your venture. They, in turn, will be able to boost your confidence and offer valuable insights and fresh perspective to your business decisions.

BOOTSTRAPPING

This can occur when you do not qualify for loans or equity investments. It means finding money and resources by any means possible including begging, borrowing, bartering, sharing, and leasing just about everything you need in your business. It is estimated that 75% to 85% of all new entrepreneurs use bootstrapping to start their new businesses. You are bootstrapping when you pull out all of the stops and use personal assets, lease all of your equipment, and get your financing from whatever source (as long as they are legal and Godly) you can find. If you use bootstrapping to start your business, the initial rate at which you can grow your business will probably be limited.

Bootstrapping implies that you have cobbled together all of your available funding resources. But, the biggest source of funding in bootstrapping is spending less on items where you can, making the decision to forego certain items, squeezing money out of accounts receivable, and paying bills at the last minute. If you are able to do this and show some progress in your business growth, you might be able to have a good story to tell a potential funding source. Funding sources love to hear successful bootstrapping stories. It demonstrates that the company (really the person) that they are about to invest in has tenacity and is resourceful. These are two qualities an entrepreneur must have to be successful. Bootstrapping holds a certain amount of romance for investors and lenders.

SEVERANCE PAY

Severance Pay is a term that's used much more often around the world now than ever before. As recently as the 1970s, people would work at one, maybe two jobs throughout their entire career. A recent report by the Bureau of Labor Statistics reveals the average American worker will hold 8.6 jobs between the ages of 18 and 32. Other study results vary, but the average number of jobs a person will have during their working years is more than 12—and that number is on the rise.

If you were anticipating separating from your employer and you don't need the severance pay while looking for a job while unemployed, then severance pay could be a good funding source for your new venture. Severance pay will often come with strings attached to it. You should consult with an attorney before accepting a severance package from your employer, as employment law can be very complex.

CREDIT CARDS

We've all heard stories of individuals who have used credit cards to finance their businesses. Today, credit cards are easier to obtain than ever. It's actually harder NOT to get a credit card than it is to get a credit card. Most mailboxes are glutted with offers from credit card companies. I knew of one entrepreneur who signed up for a couple of credit cards, then ran up the balances, and then used new credit cards to pay off the old credit cards. This is a risky way to use credit cards and will often catch up with you and cause you to ruin your personal credit. It can takes years to fix bad credit. Credit rating companies will notice how many credit cards you have applied for and how many you have in your wallet.

Using credit cards properly can be a good ancillary source of funding for your new business. Credit cards can be used for fixed asset purchases or for short-term working capital needs. If you need to purchase a new computer or office supplies, use your credit card, but using them to finance your business over the long term does not make good business sense. Using one card to pay off another and so on can lead to out-of-control debt.

START YOUR BUSINESS ONLINE

As discussed in the chapter entitled GROWING YOUR BUSINESS, it costs very little to put your business online. If you have a reasonably fast computer, a DSL or cable modem hookup, you can be in business. You don't need to know anything about computer programming to set up a great Web site. You can go to Yahoo.com, 1and1.com (currently the largest Web site host in the world,) or any other Web site hosting company and be online and transacting business in a day or two. For under $50 a month (not counting your DSL expense, which you probably already have), you can launch your business. Once you have proven that people want what you are selling, you can decide if it makes sense to open a "brick-and-mortar" store. There are very few businesses that cannot start online and transition to a physical presence.

MOVE BACK A STEP OR TWO IN THE SUPPLY CHAIN

You may have developed a great idea for retail products and are hoping to open a retail store. After preparing your business plan, you discover that you just don't have enough money or funding to open a retail store. An alternative to abandoning the entire project is to move somewhere else on the distribution chain.

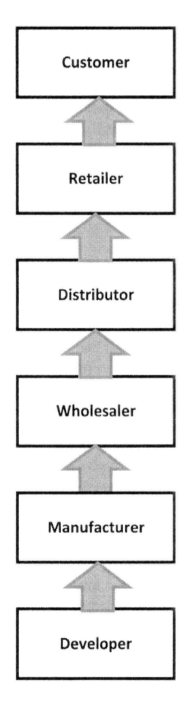

Fig.10 – Distribution Chain

If you don't have the funding for opening a retail store, then consider selling your unique products to the existing retailers. Or you could sell to a distributor or wholesaler. You might even consider licensing your unique product to a manufacturer that has its own sales and distribution divisions. Easy Brain Labs, Inc. was a company that had some unique product ideas and originally sold their products to retailers. They soon realized that this approach was extremely difficult and required a lot of cash. Instead, they started licensing out their ideas of toy and consumer products to large companies. This turned out to be an overall wise business decision.

DEBT FINANCING

There are a number of different types of debt financing, and there are a number of sources of debt financing available to the new small businessperson. Banks, credit unions, savings institutions, and other financial organizations are not all the same, although changes in regulations over the last couple of decades have made them become more alike. There are, still, some subtle differences.

COMMERCIAL BANKS

Commercial Banks are in the money business to make a profit. They accept deposits and lend money. According to the Federal Deposit Insurance Corporation (FDIC), there are more than 8,000 commercial banks in the United States. Some big names that you might recognize in the commercial banking world are Wells Fargo Bank and Citibank.

Most commercial banks do not service the start-up market with loans. As with most things in life, there are exceptions. Banks really do want to lend you money, since that's how they make money. But banks are also conservative, because they are risking their depositors' funds.

Even though banks may not seem very friendly when it comes to lending money to you for your start-up business, it is important to start developing a relationship with a bank as soon as you start your business. In addition to bank loans, your commercial bank has a number of other services that you will need in your business:

Checking Accounts – You would be hard-pressed to do business anywhere on the planet without a checking account. Not all checking accounts are created equal. Take a look at your bank statements. I have seen some that even I have a tough time understanding, and I'm a Certified Public Accountant. Most bank statements, though, will be fairly easy to understand. You should have a beginning balance that agrees with the ending balance on your prior statement. You should then have all of your checks, withdrawals, transfers, and account fees listed in detail and totaled. The statement should list all deposits in detail as well as the total. These figures will facilitate reconciling your monthly bank statement. Never wait more than a couple of weeks after receiving your bank statements before reconciling them to your accounting records. It's critical to verify that you don't have any unauthorized transactions and to make sure that your bank agrees your records when it comes to your cash balances.

There are some special features that you will probably want to consider along with your checking account that are listed below. Zero balance and sweep accounts and overdraft protection are some special features that you might want to consider with your basic vanilla business checking account.

Online Banking – As incredible as it may seem, some banks still do not offer online banking for their commercial customers. Once you have used online banking, you will wonder how you ever managed without it. You have access to your bank account activity on a 24/7 basis. I can remember when I had to pick up the phone and call a bank representative if I wanted a copy of my bank statement, and then they would only send me a copy in the mail. A few years ago, most banks instituted automated phone systems so that you could instantly check on individual debits and credits to your bank account. Now, almost all banks allow you to go on line and keep track of your banking activity. This is incredibly valuable and a "must have" for the new business, since cash management is so important. I would not use a bank that does not offer online banking. You just can't effectively manage your cash flow without online banking as a tool.

Savings Accounts – If you have a need for a savings account when you are starting up your business, you are better off than most other entrepreneurs. Business savings accounts are similar to personal savings accounts with the exception that they are typically more accessible than personal savings accounts. Banks will typically allow you to have a certain number of withdrawals per month before you are penalized.

Overdraft Protection – Banks normally charge for overdraft protection. They do this partly to keep you from using the service. It is also a source of revenue for banks. Make sure you know what the charges will be if you're going to add an overdraft protection feature to your account. Typically, it will be similar to the Non-Sufficient-Funds (NSF) fees with some distinct advantages. With NSF charges, whoever you wrote the check to will be notified that your check "bounced." This is not a way to build a trusting relationship with vendors and others you do business with. With overdraft protection, you will never know that you overdrew your bank account. If you do this very often, it may point to a bigger problem of spending more than you take into your business.

Credit Card Payment Processing – If you are a retail company or you have lots of customers and have lots of transactions, you will want to accept all of the major credit cards. Major banks will help you get your credit card processing set up and operating smoothly. See "Direct Response Marketing" in the chapter entitled GROWING YOUR BUSINESS for a more complete discussion of credit card processing.

Collection of Federal and State Payroll Taxes – This is a convenient way to submit your payroll tax deposits for amounts you withhold from employees and the amounts that you must pay for employment taxes. Many commercial banks are authorized by the Internal Revenue Service and state taxing authorities to accept these types of deposits and report them to the appropriate taxing authority.

Zero Balance Banking – Zero balance bank accounts enable you to link one or more accounts to your main checking account. During the business day, activity in your accounts will result in a positive or negative intra-day balance. At the end of the day, your bank will tabulate all transactions and move funds sufficient to bring all of your subaccounts back to a zero ledger balance. This eliminates any worries on your part about which account to move the funds to that day. You just need to ensure that your main-concentration account has enough funds for all of your daily activity. The most popular use of this service is for Payroll Accounts.

Sweep Accounts – At the end of the business day, excess collected funds are swept into an overnight investment. Funds automatically transfer back to your checking account as needed, based on a predetermined target balance. A sweep account enables you to make sure that you don't have idle cash in your bank accounts that could be earning interest.

Lines of Credit – Using a line of credit is really like setting up a standing loan for those times when you need extra cash in your business. You can probably qualify for a business line of credit for your new business with some caveats. If you are a corporation, you will have to personally guarantee the balances drawn on the line of credit. Once you set up a line of credit, it's easy to "draw down" your credit line. The amount you draw down your line of credit will reduce the amount that you can subsequently draw down, until you repay the amount drawn out. It is a convenient tool to use when cash flow requires it. Consider it a temporary fix that will be repaid after you have sufficient cash flow. Never draw down on a line of credit unless you are certain of future receipts to cover the drawdown.

Safe Deposit Boxes – This is one of the oldest services offered by banks. The basic theory for using a safe deposit box is that it is safer than storing valuable documents and jewelry at home under your mattress. Safe deposit boxes cost next to nothing, and they afford a high level of protection for important documents.

Wire Transfers – If you have to get cash someplace fast, this is the way to do it. You will need the banking information of the person or company you are sending the cash to. You will need the following information to send wire transfers:

1. Amount of the transfer in currency you agreed to transfer funds in
2. Name of person to whom you are sending funds
3. Name of company for which the person is serving as receiving agent
4. The address of the company to receive the wired funds
5. The bank account number
6. The bank routing number
7. The bank address
8. The name of a bank officer at the receiving bank
9. The receiving bank's phone number
10. The corresponding bank's identification information if needed (your bank may be a small bank and not have a direct correspondence relationship with the bank to which you are wiring funds)

Wire transfers will cost you approximately $50 for each wire transfer. You can use wire transfers for domestic or international transfers of cash.

Commercial Letters of Credit – These financial instruments are used to ensure your overseas suppliers of your company's credit standing for the full amount of issued letters of credit. A commercial letter of credit undertaking, usually on the part of your bank, will list a payee (beneficiary - your international customer) to receive a specified amount of money if he presents documents in accordance with the terms and conditions that you specified in your letter of credit.

Standby Letters of Credit – These are used to ensure your customers of payment in the event of nonperformance or default. These are letters of credit that you do not (normally) expect to be collected. They are normally only called with you have not done what you said you were going to do.

Bankers' Acceptances – A bankers' acceptance starts as an order to you to pay a sum of money at a future date, typically within six months. At this stage, it's as if you have postdated a check. When your bank endorses the order for payment as "accepted," it assumes responsibility for ultimate payment to the holder of the acceptance. At this point, the acceptance may be traded in secondary markets, much like any other claim on the bank. Bankers' acceptances are considered very safe assets, as they allow traders to substitute the bank's credit standing for your own. They are used widely in foreign trade where your creditworthiness might be unknown to your trading partner. Acceptances sell at a discount from face value of the payment order, just as US Treasury bills are issued and trade at a discount from par value.

Documentary Collections – Your bank can assist you in processing your foreign receivables, improving control of shipping documents, collection of drafts, and follow-up of delinquent transactions.

Foreign Currency Exchange – Your bank can help you process international transactions when your customers use a different currency than the U.S. dollar.

Foreign Drafts – Offer you a safe, effective way to convey funds by mail or by courier.

CREDIT UNIONS

According to the Credit Union National Association (CUNA), a credit union "is a cooperative financial institution, owned and controlled by the people who use its services. These people are members. Credit unions serve groups that share something in common, such as where they work, live, or go to church. Credit unions are not-for-profit, and exist to provide a safe, convenient place for members to save money and to get loans at reasonable rates." You can usually get better rates on loans and on deposits with credit unions, because the depositors are the owners. Commercial banks are in business to earn money for their owners and not for you, their customer. There are some drawbacks in using a credit union. The big one is that they do not offer as many services as banks offer. This is changing, but credit unions are not as robust as commercial banks. Also, credit unions don't generally provide commercial checking accounts.

FINANCE COMPANIES

Finance companies, which supply credit to businesses and consumers, are often categorized as non-depository institutions, along with mortgage bankers and brokers, because they make loans without taking in deposits. They acquire funds to make these loans largely by issuing commercial paper and bonds, and securitizing their loans. As financial intermediaries, finance companies compete with banks, savings institutions, and credit unions.

There are different types of finance companies. Some are "captive," which are affiliated with companies such as motor vehicle companies (GMAC, General Motor Acceptance Corporation) and appliance manufacturers. Another type of finance company is a consumer finance company. Consumer finance companies normally make small, secured, personal loans. These loans are typically for only a few thousand dollars. Loans from consumer finance companies normally have higher interest rates and processing fees than the typical bank or credit union, because their loans are smaller and riskier. They are comparatively less conservative and may possibly offer a high-interest loan for candidates with poor credit histories. You probably will not consider consumer finance companies as your first choice for loans because of the higher costs. These finance companies make loans directly to consumers for major purchases. There are also finance companies that specialize in making loans directly to businesses. Because commercial finance companies typically offer only loans secured by commercial assets, these institutions are used primarily by established businesses, not start-ups.

SAVINGS INSTITUTIONS

This category of financial institution includes savings and loan associations and savings banks. Savings and loan associations are federally chartered banks. Savings banks are like savings and loan associations but are chartered by various states. They are often mutually held, meaning that the depositors and borrowers are members with voting rights and have the ability to direct the financial and managerial goals of the organization. Modern savings and loan associations tend to look and feel like any other bank participating in retail banking. Recent changes in U.S. regulations allow them to refer to themselves as banks or savings banks. The services offered today to individuals are similar, if not identical, to services offered by commercial banks or credit unions. I World Savings is an example of savings and loan associations.

FRIENDS AND FAMILY

Friends and family is typically the first place that entrepreneurs go for financing. There is one very important piece of advice to follow if you borrow money from these sources and that is to put your financial arrangement in writing. Write a formal business plan, make out a promissory note, draw up a formal repayment schedule, and stick to it. Such documentation cuts the default rate on private loans in half and makes it easier for both parties to claim their tax benefits. This type of documentation will also go a long way in saving your relationships with your family and friends. Loans from friends and family are much more popular than equity investments. Regardless of your relationship with your family and friends, it is a must that you document your financial arrangements with them.

SMALL BUSINESS ADMINISTRATION (SBA)

The SBA offers numerous loan programs to assist small businesses. It is important to note, however, that the SBA is primarily a guarantor of loans made by private and other institutions.

Basic 7(a) Loan Guaranty – Serves as the SBA's primary business loan program to help qualified small businesses obtain financing when they might not be eligible for business loans through normal lending channels. It is also the agency's most flexible business loan program, since financing under this program can be guaranteed for a variety of general business purposes.

Loan proceeds can be used for most sound business purposes, including working capital, machinery and equipment, furniture and fixtures, land and building (including purchase, renovation, and new construction), leasehold improvements, and debt refinancing (under special conditions). Loan maturity is up to 10 years for working capital and generally up to 25 years for fixed assets. The primary customers for these SBA loans are start-ups, existing small businesses, and commercial lending institutions. These loans are obtainable through commercial lending institutions. The SBA offers multiple variations of the basic 7(a) loan program to accommodate targeted needs.

Certified Development Company (CDC), a 504 Loan Program – Provides long-term, fixed-rate financing to small businesses to acquire real estate or machinery or equipment for expansion or modernization. Typically, a 504 project includes a loan secured from a private-sector lender with a senior lien, a loan secured from a CDC (funded by a 100% SBA-guaranteed debenture) with a junior lien covering up to 40% of the total cost, and a contribution of at least 10% equity from the borrower. These types of loans are for small businesses requiring "brick and mortar" financing and can be obtained through certified development companies (private, nonprofit corporations set up to contribute to the economic development of their communities or regions).

Micro-loan, a 7(m) Loan Program – Provides short-term loans of up to $35,000 to small businesses and not-for-profit child-care centers for working capital or the purchase of inventory, supplies, furniture, fixtures, machinery and/or equipment. Proceeds cannot be used to pay existing debts or to purchase real estate. The SBA makes or guarantees a loan to an intermediary, who, in turn, makes the micro-loan to the applicant. These organizations also provide management and technical assistance. The SBA does not guarantee the loans. The micro-loan program is available in selected locations in most states. These loans are for small businesses and not-for-profit child-care centers needing small-scale financing and technical assistance for start-up or expansion. They are delivered through specially designated intermediary lenders (nonprofit organizations with experience in lending and in technical assistance).

Loan Prequalification – Enables business applicants to have their loan applications for $250,000 or less analyzed and potentially sanctioned by the SBA before they are taken to lenders for consideration. The program focuses on the applicant's character, credit, experience, and reliability rather than assets. An SBA-designated intermediary works with the business owner to review and strengthen the loan application. The review is based on key financial ratios, credit and business history, and the loan-request terms. The SBA's Office of Field Operations and SBA district offices administer the program. These loans are designated for small businesses and are delivered through intermediaries operating in specific geographic areas.

COLLATERAL LOANS – USE YOUR OWN ASSETS

As mentioned above, banks will normally require some collateral if you want their money. You will either have to guarantee your company's loan from a bank, or you will have to put up collateral with which the bank can feel comfortable. You may have a valuable painting or sculpture, but it may not qualify as collateral. Banks require collateral that they can easily control and liquidate in the event you default on your loan. Assets that can typically be utilized as collateral are certificates of deposit, land, buildings, stocks, and bonds. If you are seeking a loan for a specific asset, such as a company car, you can normally use the asset as collateral for the loan. There are thousands of companies that offer collateralized loans. These companies range from pawnshops (I would stay away from the pawnshops) to big, prestigious banks like Chase Manhattan.

BORROWING AGAINST CASH-VALUE LIFE INSURANCE

There are four basic types of insurance coverage: term, whole life, universal life, and variable life. Term insurance offers a death benefit only. Whole life, universal life, and variable life are versions of cash-value insurance that combine a death benefit and cash value, which is generally accessible through loans against your policy. Term life insurance is "pure" insurance—it pays a death benefit if the insured person dies during the term of the policy but does not build any cash value.

"Borrowing" money from a cash-value life policy is an absolute last resort. Check your insurance company to see if you have options other than borrowing against your life insurance policy to get money from your life insurance policy. Also, ask them how much you can actually borrow against your policy. The amount available to you depends on how much cash has accumulated in the policy. That, in turn, depends on how long the policy has been around, how much you've paid into it, and other factors. For example, if you have a $500,000 policy with a cash value of $150,000, your borrowing capability will be based on the $150,000 cash value. Understand that when you borrow against your cash value, you must pay interest on the amount you borrow. The interest you pay does not go into your cash value, as many people think. Instead, it goes back into the pockets of the insurance company.

You don't have to pay back your loan against your insurance policy if you don't want to, but you must be willing to have a reduced death benefit for your beneficiaries when you pass away. You will also pay interest on it for the rest of your life. To add insult to injury, any interest you owe on your loan will be deducted from the payout. Check with your accountant before borrowing against your life insurance policy. Depending on the particulars of your individual policy, borrowing could create a taxable event for you.

EQUIPMENT LEASE FINANCING

As a start-up, you may want to consider leasing rather than buying equipment. Leasing gives you access to many types of equipment: computers, copy machines, fax machines, trucks, and more. Leasing won't bring cash in the door, but it will reduce the amount of cash you'll need to raise for your business.

When you lease equipment, a manufacturer, dealer, or lender either buys or already owns the equipment you want. In exchange, you make monthly payments to the owner (lessor). The monthly payment structure typically enables you to treat the payments as tax-deductible business expenses.

Leasing some of your equipment may make it easier for you to keep pace with constantly changing technology. This is especially important if your business relies upon cutting-edge technology to generate revenues and to effectively compete. A series of short-term leases will cost you less than buying new equipment every year or two. Some leases even have yearly computer upgrades built into them, eliminating the problem of whether you can afford to upgrade or not.

If you need equipment right away, leases are approved much more quickly than loans and typically involve less paperwork and have more-relaxed credit requirements. Many equipment vendors provide lease financing, as do a number of banks. For early stage businesses, equipment lease financing is more easily obtained from a vendor than a bank. Ultimately, leasing will likely prove more costly than buying; but if cash flow is your main issue, then leasing is an attractive alternative.

WHEN LEASING, BE SURE TO CONSIDER THE FOLLOWING POINTS: ━━━━━━━

Term of Lease – What is the lease term? The length of the lease will affect the amount of your monthly payment, with a longer lease term usually meaning a lower monthly rent.

Up-front payment – What is the size of any up-front payment? Can you reduce the up-front payment and amortize it over the life of the lease?

Monthly payments – Are the monthly payments reasonable? You can analyze the amount of the payment by determining the interest factor associated with the lease.

Return rights – For vendor-leased equipment, under what circumstances can you return the equipment if there are problems?

Early termination – Do you have the right to terminate the lease early? Most lessors will be reluctant to do this, but you may be able to negotiate an early termination right in exchange for payment of a fee.

Option to purchase – Try to negotiate a right to buy the equipment. Equipment lessors will often give you this right at the end of the lease term, usually for a fixed price (e.g., 10% of the purchase price of the equipment) or at fair market value.

If you decide to lease equipment, keep the term short—two years is ideal. Try to negotiate a "modern equipment substitution clause" that lets you update or exchange your equipment so you don't end up paying for obsolete technology. And insist on a cancellation clause that lets you pay a fee to cancel the lease. Be sure to note the cost of any cancellation penalty.

Maintenance Contract – On equipment such as computers and other electronics, you might want to have a maintenance contract included in your lease agreement. Some maintenance contracts will require that you take the equipment into a repair shop, and some will have provisions for repairing the equipment on your premises.

Credit Cards

Credit cards are discussed above in the section entitled PERSONAL FUNDING

SOURCES, but no matter how you slice it, using your personal credit cards to finance your business is still debt financing. If you use your personal credit cards to finance some of your business needs, you should record these transactions in your business general ledger as liabilities to you from your company. It is better to have a separate credit card for business expenditures. If you qualify for a personal credit card, you can qualify for a business credit card. You will be guaranteeing your business credit card with your personal credit.

Debt Consolidation Loans

This is a personal funding source and debt financing. Debt consolidation programs are usually just a big loan that pays off other smaller loans. They can be very beneficial to borrowers, but these programs also have their pitfalls. Debt consolidation programs are good for a few situations. If you are paying several different loans off, your life may be easier if you consolidate everything into one loan. It's good to simplify when starting a new business. You'll want as few complications in your life as possible. You'll only get one monthly statement and make one payment. Also, you'll find that your monthly debt payments decrease if you use a debt consolidation program that stretches your payments out over a longer period of time. By paying out less each month, you can free up some cash. Using a debt consolidation program to eliminate various high-rate revolving debts can be a good financial strategy.

Debt consolidation programs can also hurt you. The new smaller payments that you will likely have upon consolidation can trick you into going into even more debt. You should be very aware that these programs only shift your debt—a debt consolidation program does not eliminate your debt. You will have to pay it back sooner or later.

Line of Credit

Lines of credit vary in how they are set up. For example, business lines of credit are typically asset based, meaning hard assets are used as collateral. Such credit lines can also be based on receivables and, in some cases, inventory (although this is less common, since the value of inventory can decline very quickly and is therefore seen as a greater risk to the lender). The interest rate can also differ, since commercial rates may be equal to or exceed the prime lending rate (also based on the level of risk as perceived by the lender). Therefore, it is advisable to shop around. While seeking such a line of credit, make sure that the interest is only on the money being borrowed, as opposed to being calculated on your borrowing limit or in any other manner. Also, inquire whether or not deposits are made directly to the outstanding balance, which reduces the amount of interest you will have to pay. For additional discussion concerning line of credit financing, see above.

A revolving line of credit enables you to always have available funding and gives you peace of mind as a business owner.

Borrowing from Your 401(k) Retirement Plan

Many companies offer 401(k) retirement plans to their employees. If you are fortunate enough to work for one of those companies, you can borrow from your own 401(k) plan. A loan is different from a withdrawal. You can normally borrow up to 50% from your plan. There are a number of important things to consider before you borrow from your 401(k) plan:

1. Your contributions to your 401(k) are pretax, but the payments you make to repay your loan are made after taxes.
2. The interest on your 401(k) loan normally is not tax-deductible as is a home equity loan or a mortgage.
3. If your business becomes successful and you leave your employer prior to paying off your loan, you will be required to either pay the entire balance due immediately, or the balance will be subject to taxes and penalties like a withdrawal.
4. The money you borrow will only earn you the interest you pay on your loan. For instance, if your 401(k) is currently earning an annual rate of 7% and you borrow half of your account for a prime rate of 5%, you will be losing interest on the money you borrowed along with any compounding interest.

Consider these points carefully before you borrow from your 401(k) plan.

EQUITY FINANCING

If you have a lot of self-confidence in your ability to make a business and you have ranked well in the entrepreneur questionnaire in the chapter entitled DO YOU REALLY WANT TO BE AN ENTREPRENEUR?, you will be more inclined to seek out debt funding rather than equity funding.

ANGEL INVESTORS

An angel investor is a high-net-worth person who's willing to make a private equity investment in an emerging-growth company. The amount of money that an angel investor is willing to put into a business venture will be based on the potential for financial return and his personal interest. Given the risks that the angel investor is assuming with his investment, he is normally looking for a substantial double-digit return on his investment. Angel investors will want to get their money back and have good return on their investment, but there is an intangible factor that must appeal to the investor. If the investor has no interest in sports, you probably will not get him to invest in your sports venture. This type of investor is not necessarily a professional investor. His money may come from any number of sources. You will find that the process for securing an investment from an angel investor is much less formal than working with institutional investors. One major negative is that angel investors typically will want to be more involved in your business than would an institutional investor.

Once you find an angel investor, make sure that he is treated well. Angel investors are few and far between. I have found that once you have given a fair return to your angel investor, he will be there for subsequent investments, and he is willing to introduce you to other investors when your business grows and your financing needs become more substantial.

SMALL BUSINESS INVESTMENT COMPANIES (SBIC)

See the discussion below concerning SBICs. A number of SBICs will fund, for small amounts, start-up companies.

TAKE ON A PARTNER

Sometimes, it does not make sense to go it alone. I know of a small company that started with three entrepreneurs. The lead entrepreneur was starting a Web site that was going to download filmed content. He had the business knowledge but did not have the technical expertise to build a Web site and did not have the contact in Hollywood to secure filmed content. He took on two partners who covered these areas. He could not afford to employ a Web site builder and he could not find access to filmed content. His business grew much faster than if he had tried to do all three functions by himself. The downside was that they were not spiritual and they were unequally yoked, which led to the business falling apart.

Although taking on a partner to share your risk, bring talents that you don't have, and possibly bring resources that you don't have can be an attractive idea, it can cost you long-term in often unexpected ways.

EXISTING BUSINESS FINANCING

Once you have your business up and running, there are additional funding sources available to you.

INVESTMENT GROUPS

This financing source is exactly what it sounds like. It is a group of investors, either formal or informal. They can be private or loosely connected to a governmental agency. They typically only invest in existing businesses and have multiple financing sources available to them. Many of these groups require that their members meet the Securities and Exchange Commission standards for an accredited investor:

> "Any natural person whose individual net worth, or joint net worth with that person's spouse, at the time of his purchase exceeds $1,000,000"; and "Any natural person who had an individual income in excess of $200,000 in each of the two most recent years or joint income with that person's spouse in excess of $300,000 in each of those years and has a reasonable expectation of reaching the same income in the current year."

If you solicit money from a group and have the investment club certify that all of its investors are accredited investors, you will take some liability off of yourself. At some point, presenting risky investment propositions to people who are not accredited can be a problem. Consult with your attorney before you present investment opportunities to any investment group. Be careful about jumping into a financing deal that subjects you to potentially tremendous heartache. If you oversell your investment opportunity and an unsophisticated investor later loses his money, you could endanger your business. You can find investment groups through your accountant or lawyer, or simply type "investment groups" in your Web browser.

STRATEGIC ALLIANCE

If you have a product or service and it is compatible with a product or service of someone you know, then you might want to consider teaming up with them in a strategic alliance. A strategic alliance is not a partnership but is taking advantage of an associate's resources (in a positive way) and enabling him to take advantage of your resources. As an example, I know of a certified public accountant (CPA) who was starting his accounting practice. He met another CPA at a CPA association meeting who complained that he was dreading the coming tax season because he was overworked and couldn't find good help. They struck a deal in which the new CPA would use the established CPA's office and equity for free, and the established CPA would use the new CPA for his overflow work. This arrangement worked well for them for a number of years.

Another example: a couple of young men wanted to open a Tae Kwon Do studio to teach martial arts, but they couldn't afford the cost of renting and furnishing a studio. They approached a local private grammar/middle school chain and proposed that they start offering Tae Kwon Do at their schools. This became a "marriage made in Heaven." The fact that the school now offered Take Kwan Do was a big pull for parents and students considering going to their schools. Now, the young men have three studios on separate campuses of the school, and they have a built-in customer base with the students on campus.

BARTERING

Bartering is exchanging one commodity for another commodity that someone else owns. Bartering is NOT a way around recording income and paying taxes. Here is what the Internal Revenue Service has to say about bartering:

> Bartering occurs when you exchange goods or services without exchanging money. An example of bartering is a plumber doing repair work for a dentist in exchange for dental services. The fair market value of goods and services exchanged must be included in the income of both parties.
>
> Income from bartering is taxable in the year in which you receive the goods or services. Generally, you report this income on Form 1040, Schedule C *Profit or Loss from Business*. If you failed to report bartering income on returns you have already filed, you should correct this by

filing an amended return, <u>Form 1040X</u> (PDF), for each year involved. For information on amended returns, refer to <u>Topic 308</u>.

A barter exchange is any person or organization with members or clients that contract with each other (or with the barter exchange) to jointly trade or barter property or services. The term does not include arrangements that provide solely for the informal exchange of similar services on a noncommercial basis.

The Internet has provided a medium for new growth in the bartering exchange industry. This growth prompts the following reminder: barter exchanges are required to file Form 1099-B for all transactions unless certain exceptions are met.

If you are in a business or trade, you may deduct any costs you incurred to perform the work that was bartered. If you exchanged property or services through a barter exchange, you should receive a Form 1099-B, Proceeds from Broker and Barter Exchange Transactions. The Form 1099-B or other statement generally will show the value of any cash, property, services, credits, or scrip you received from the exchange during the year. The IRS will also receive the same information.

Even though bartering income is taxable, it is an excellent way to develop assets that you need for your new business. As an example, if you are starting your bookkeeping service and your attorney needs accounting services, you can barter an exchange of services. But, remember this type of transaction is taxable.

INCREASING SALES TO EXISTING CUSTOMERS

You have spent time and other resources to get your customers. You can generate additional revenues from existing customers a lot faster and a lot more economically than you can from trying to develop new customers. Study your customer base to determine what they are buying, when and how often they are buying, and in what quantity they are buying. From this analysis, you might be able to sell them more of what they already buy from you, or you might be able to sell them some new products.

This is why it is good to keep in constant contact with your customers via emails, newsletters, or whatever other means you have at your disposal.

VENDOR FINANCING

It is in your vendors' best interest to help you out when you need financing, because you are buying and selling their products. If you are a small business, you may not be in a position to ask a major supplier for help in traditional financing, but there are some creative ways your vendors can help you. But, don't completely rule out getting financing from your vendors.

Terms – Your vendors can give you better terms. As a new business, you may have to pay for goods in advance or with really tight terms. You might be able to approach some of your vendors to give you better terms. Often, vendors will have rigid terms and may be unwilling to be flexible with you, but you don't know if you don't ask. You can sometimes get better terms if you pay a little more or are willing to report to them on a more comprehensive basis than you normally do.

Consignment – Some of your vendors may consider placing product with you on a consignment basis; they give you product to sell, but you don't pay for it until it sells. This is also a way for you to get into outlets that wouldn't otherwise be willing to take a chance on selling your product.

CUSTOMER FINANCING

This is actually using your customer to help you with financing. This type of financing assumes that you are selling to other businesses and not directly to consumers. If your customers are making money from selling your products, they will have an interest in making sure you are successful. Let's say that you need a particular piece of equipment to manufacturer your products. A customer may be willing to finance the particular piece of equipment and lease it to you to make sure that their supply of products is not disrupted. Maybe a customer's business is growing faster than you can accommodate. He might be willing to fund you to increase your output capacity so that you could keep pace with his needs.

ADDING NEW PRODUCTS OR SERVICES

When you are in need of funding, it is sometimes difficult to add new products or services. Then again, you can use one of the other techniques mentioned here (e.g., get a vendor to supply you goods on a consignment basis). If one of your vendors is already supplying you with a number of products, he might be willing to use the "try before you buy" approach and give you the new products on consignment. You will have certain fixed cost (e.g., rent, utilities, etc.) that you have to pay month in and month out. It is normally a good business practice to spread these expenses across as many sales dollars as possible. As an example, if your rent is $2,000 a month and you currently have 2,000 transactions, one dollar of every sales transaction goes to cover your rent. If you increase your sales transactions to 4,000 a month, only fifty cents of each sales transaction goes to cover rent.

PRIVATE PLACEMENT FUNDING

In a private placement, you sell ownership in your company, normally in the form of common or preferred stock, to a small number of private individuals and organizations. You can't solicit investments from the general public with a private placement. You will definitely need a good lawyer who understands securities law for this type of fund-raising. A private placement will normally be your third or fourth round of financing after you have been in business for a while and have already utilized funding from friends and family and possibly an angel investor.

These private placements are often referred to as "Reg D" fund-raising. Reg D refers to Regulation D and Rule 4(2) of the Securities Act of 1933. Some people refer to Reg D offerings as Private Stock Offerings. Even though a Reg D offering is not a public offering, it has been used for raising anywhere from less than $50,000 to several million dollars. They can be used to raise funds via debt, equity, or a combination of both.

A private placement offering (Reg D) can be substantially faster and much less expensive than raising funds through a venture capitalist or through selling stock in an IPO (Initial Public Offering). If you consider this form of fund-raising, remember there are some strict rules about whom you can offer your opportunity to and how you can offer it to them (no advertising).

REVIEWING PRODUCT PRICING STRUCTURE

You should be reviewing your pricing and comparing it to your competition on a continual basis. You might want to look at new ways to price your products:

1. Offer goods bundled with other goods to increase each sale.
2. Sell bigger packages like the big-box stores
3. Sell multi-packs like the big-box stores.
4. Sell unopened cases.
5. Consider putting together premium packs of your standard products.

6. Review your products to make sure that you are pricing right and not leaving money on the table. The lowest price is not always the best price.

SEEKING OUT COMPETITIVE BIDS FOR SOURCING YOUR PRODUCTS

Competitive bidding is something that you should be doing even without raising funds. It is a good business practice to make sure that your suppliers are being competitive. After you have been with a supplier for a number of years, there is often the tendency for them to give new customers better pricing to lure them in. I have also seen cases where vendors realize price drops from their suppliers and fail to pass these price reductions to their customers. An industry that is well noted for this is the electronics industry. Electronic components almost always come down in price and suppliers tend to be really slow in passing these savings on to their customers.

EXPANDING HOURS OF OPERATION

This seemingly obvious method of increasing your cash flow is often overlooked by new business owners. You will have a number of fixed costs regardless of how long you stay open during the day. You will pay the same amount of rent, insurance, and other fixed costs, so it might make sense to spread these fixed cost over a greater number of operating hours. In your analysis, calculate all of the costs that would increase if you stayed open longer. Although rent is normally a fixed cost, some landlords will charge more if a merchant stays open past the hours originally agreed upon. Measure all of these increased costs against your projected increased revenues from the extra hours. Also, remember to measure the effect of these increased hours on your family life and other commitments that you have made to the Lord.

BUSINESS INCUBATORS

Business incubators may be a way for you to get your business off the ground and in operation relatively quickly. A business incubator provides more than money: it is a place where you have access to many resources necessary for success. Not all incubators will invest in your new entity, but they may provide you with other valuable resources such as the following:

- Seed capital for starting your company
- Office space
- Lobby and reception space and personnel

- Meeting and conference space
- Internet, faxing, and phone connectivity
- Web site hosting
- Furniture
- Equipment (computers, fax machines, printers)
- Delivery services
- Consulting services in the areas of marketing, accounting, manufacturing, distribution, and legal
- Interaction with other entrepreneurs
- Reference libraries
- Networking with investors, service provides, and others

For example, let's consider the Business Technology Center of Los Angeles County, the largest technology incubator in California:

> The Business Technology Center (BTC) is a business innovation center with a mission of assisting start-up and early-stage technology firms grow and prosper. Opened in October 1998, the BTC is a 40,000 square foot facility with a state-of-the-art communication infrastructure. The BTC offers key support services, including access to capital, business consulting, and mentoring from an Advisory Committee that has a wide range of skills, experience, and contacts in Southern California.

> Located just 2 miles from the world famous Jet Propulsion Laboratory in Pasadena, the BTC currently houses 30 high-technology tenants with specialties ranging from software development to commercializing federal lab technology. BTC firms have raised over $75 million from angel and venture capital investors.

Incubators typically work with pre-revenue stage companies and early-stage companies. The very fact that you have been accepted by an incubator can attract investors. Many of the incubators are for high-tech companies. Some are directed to women and minorities. You can find a list of incubators at the National Business Incubation Association Web site (www.nbia.org).

ENTERPRISE ZONES

Enterprise Zones (sometimes called Empowerment Zones or Incentive Zones) are particular geographical areas that are designated by state or federal governments to attract businesses. These governmental entities attract businesses by giving them special incentives for locating their businesses in these zones. If you operate your business in one of these zones, you may be eligible for tax credits, financing assistance, streamlining of the permit process, or a number of other financial and operational benefits. Some of the potential benefits are:

- Possible access to funding (not often the case)
- Hiring tax credits
- Sales/use tax credits
- State income tax credits
- Low interest loans
- Permit fast-tracking
- Governmental contract preferences
- Technical assistance

Enterprise Zones are often more attractive to established companies thinking about relocating all or a portion of their business or expanding their business. Established businesses that already have revenue streams can more effectively utilize the tax credits and allowances afforded by some enterprise zones. Some enterprise zones operated by local, federal, and state entities also offer business incubation benefits (See Business Incubators above).

EXPANDING INTO NEW MARKETS

If you are looking for investment funds, you might wonder how you can expand into new markets. If you are profitable or are pointed to profitability, you may find it easier to get an investor if he sees you are going to use the funds to expand into new markets. There are alternative ways of expanding into new markets other than your current ways. As an example, if you are a retailer and you have one retail store that's doing great sales, but you do not have the funds to expand into other markets, you may have other ways to do so. The very fact that you have a successful retail outlet tells a good story to investors. You might consider letting someone sell your product in other areas. You might want to consider letting other retailers sell your unique products in their stores. You might want to use some of the unused floor space in noncompetitive stores to sell your product. Even if you have to lease some of this unused space, it might be cheaper than renting an entire store.

Franchising is another way of expanding into other markets. See the chapter entitled DO YOU REALLY WANT TO BE AN ENTREPRENEUR for a discussion on franchising. This method of expansion is more than a decision to expand into other markets—it's a major change in the way you do business.

MERGERS

When an existing business merges with another existing business, one of the entities survives the merger, or a completely new company is formed. This is a complex approach to building and financing your business and definitely requires the use of a well-qualified Certified Public Accountant and lawyer.

There are a number of reasons that two companies would merge:

- Expansion into new geographical areas
- Growing vertically (a manufacturer merges with a wholesaler)
- Diversifying
- Synergy between assets each company has on their balance sheets
- Economies of scale
- Acquiring the use of another company's technology
- Increased efficiency
- Battling new and aggressive competition

There are several complex issues that need to be worked when and if you decide to merge your company with another company. One major issue is deciding how each company will value itself for the merger. There are several methods of evaluation:
- Capitalized Earning Approach
- Cash Flow Method
- Cost to Create Approach (Leapfrog Start-Up)
- EBITDA Method
- Excess Earning Method
- Industry Specific Valuation Method
- Rule of Thumb Method
- Tangible Assets (Balance Sheet) Method
- Valuation based on Synergies

We won't go into the details of each of the valuation methods commonly used to value a company. This list of valuation methods will give you an idea of the complexities in just one area involved in bringing two companies together. Areas other than financial that need to be reviewed in contemplating a merger are:

- Communications
- Corporate culture
- Customer relations
- Government authorization to merge
- Integration of all systems
- Joint legal and accounting issues
- New structure of management (who runs the company)
- Overlapping resources
- Public perception of the merger
- Shareholder value after the merger
- The new shared vision
- Trust building, internally and externally
- Vendor relations

Not to discourage you from looking into merging your company with another company, but it is estimated that approximately 70% of all mergers fail. If you are considering merging with another company, do not skimp when it comes to doing your due diligence. Often, things uncovered during the due diligence process will give you an entirely different perspective on your potential merger partner.

REORGANIZING YOUR COMPANY

After a company has been operating for a number of years, many entrepreneurs are reluctant to make any changes. The philosophy of "if it ain't broke, don't fix it" sets in. I have seen smart small businesses decline potential new business because it did not "fit their business requirements." As an example, a small Southern California toy distribution company has a corporate requirement that any product that they distribute has to have a 40% gross margin or they won't distribute it. This means that if they sell a product to retailers at $10, they want to realize a 40% gross margin. They had the opportunity to sell a new product with a wholesale price of $100 a unit that only generated a 30% gross margin. They turned it down. They missed out on millions of dollars of revenues because of their rigid structure. On analysis, they decided to reorganize some of the ways they do business. They had been using sub-distributors to sell all of their products to retailers. Over the years, the toy business had changed so that many smaller companies were going directly to major retailers and bypassing distributors. The distribution company failed to keep up with the way the industry evolved and thus had an outdated way of doing business. They had to reorganize the way their company was doing business.

SELLING COMPANY ASSETS

If you have been in business for a while, you may find that you have some assets that are not being used. If this is so and they are just getting in the way, consider selling them. When selling assets that you don't need, keep in mind that they will sell for a fraction of what you originally bought them for.

SMALL BUSINESS INVESTMENT COMPANIES (SBIC)

These investment firms are connected to the Small Business Administration. These are private investment companies that leverage their financial resources by joining forces with the Small Business Administration. Their relationship gives them access to funds on favorable conditions that they can then lend to small companies. Disadvantaged companies such as minority and woman-owned are particularly interesting to SBICs, as they are of special interest to the SBA. Some SBICs fund start-ups with small loans. There will be a lot of paperwork in dealing with an SBIC, because you are dealing with a private investment company and the SBA; but the paperwork could be worth it if you get the financing you need to build your company.

LICENSING A PRODUCT

If you have been in business for a while, you should have a number of great ideas for great products. If you believe you have a great idea but don't have the money or time to fully develop it, you might consider licensing it for a royalty. See the subsection "Intellectual Property Overview" in the chapter entitled *RISK MANAGEMENT* about protecting your ideas. A basic rule of thumb in the area of licensing ideas is that the closer you can get to the finished product, the easier it is to sell your idea. At the low end of the chances of selling your idea is the "back-of-the-napkin" approach. If you had artist sketches of your product idea, the presentation of your idea would be greatly improved. Still better would be "works-like, looks-like" models. The ultimate would, of course, be working prototypes.

A typical deal for licensing would be anywhere from 3% to 10% of the wholesale price. If you have a new toy that has a retail price of $20 and you can sell it to retailers for $10, your royalty would be a percentage of the $10. If you negotiate a deal for 5% of wholesale selling price, you will get fifty cents for every unit sold. This may not seem like a lot per unit, but it can add up quickly. Most people who would be interested in a toy product in this price range would not complete a deal with you unless they thought they could sell at least 100,000 units during the first year. Continuing with our example, assume you licensed this product idea to a company that can get the product into 10,000 stores (there are approximately 40,000 stores in the United States that sell toy products). Let's further assume that each store can sell at least one product unit per store per week. If you do the math, you will see that this equals 520,000 units from only 25% of the available units that could sell your product. This would result in a royalty to you of $260,000. If they sold 10 units a week, this would be a royalty to you of $2,600,000.

Sometimes, you can also get an advance against future royalties when you sign the deal. The advances can be almost any amount up to the estimated amount of the first year's royalty. You'll want to negotiate an advance, because it helps ensure that the Licensee has invested in your product and will help ensure that he works hard to recoup the advanced royalty that he has paid to you. If you are new to product licensing and have little or no track record, getting an advance may be somewhat difficult.

SELLING A PORTION OF THE BUSINESS

There may be part of your business that was important when you originally started your company but now serves as more of a distraction and is no longer part of your core business. This is the perfect time to sell off part of your business. Even if that part of your business is no longer profitable for you, it could be profitable for someone else. Although the part of the business you are considering selling is not making a net income, make sure that it is not making some other contribution other than direct profits. Some examples are:

- Giving your business the appearance and "feel" of a broader-based business and thus attracting customers.
- Covering a significant portion of your overhead.
- Fulfilling some contractual requirement from landlords, major clients, financing sources

- Some key clients may utilize the part of the business you are considering selling.
- It may bring in customers that buy your other products.
- It may enhance consumers' positive image of your establishment.
- It may be a product or service that is desperately needed by certain customers.

GOVERNMENTAL FUNDING

There are many different kinds of financial assistance available from a wide range of governmental departments. One Web site for finding grants and other funding sources is www.grants.gov. The charter of Grants.gov is to provide a simple, unified electronic storefront for interactions between grant applicants and the federal agencies that manage grant funds. There are 26 federal grant-making agencies and over 900 individual grant programs that award over $400 billion in grants each year.

Appalachian Regional Commission
Christopher Columbus Fellowship Foundation
City of Orlando
Corporation for National and Community Service
Department of Commerce
Department of Defense
Department of Health and Human Services
Department of Homeland Security
Department of Labor
Department of State
Department of Veterans Affairs
Department of the Interior
District of Columbia
Environmental Protection Agency
Grants.gov System Integrator
Institute of Museum and Library Services
James Madison Memorial Fellowship Foundation
Japan-United States Friendship Commission
Marine Mammal Commission
National Aeronautics and Space Administration

National Archives and Records Administration
National Council on Disability
National Credit Union Administration
National Endowment for the Arts
National Endowment for the Humanities
National Science Foundation
Small Business Administration
Social Security Administration
State of Minnesota
State of Texas
U.S. Election Assistance Commission
U.S. Department of Education
U.S. Department of Transportation
U.S. Agency for International Development
U.S. Department of Energy
U.S. Department of Housing and Urban Development
U.S. Department of the Treasury
U.S. Institute of Peace
U.S. Department of Agriculture
U.S. Department of Justice
Woodrow Wilson Center
California State Controller's Office

Although this Web site is for nonprofit entities looking for grant money, it is useful to see a list of governmental entities that give grants and loans for social purposes. One social purpose of many governmental entities is the creation of jobs. New businesses, like yours, create jobs. When you look at the individual Web sites of these and other governmental entities and the grants that they disburse, you should also look at the entities that receive and administer these grants. An example of one of the entities listed above, The Department of Housing and Urban Development (HUD), has a number of programs to assist small and disadvantaged businesses. The Office of Small and Disadvantaged Business Utilization (OSDBU) within HUD has been organized to help small businesses. Here is the stated purpose of the OSDBU on their Web site:

The OSDBU is responsible for ensuring that small businesses are treated fairly and that they have an opportunity to compete and be selected for a fair amount of the Agency's prime and subcontracting opportunities. The Secretary of Housing and Urban Development is committed to providing universal access to both small businesses and large businesses. The Agency recognizes that small businesses are of vital importance to job growth and the economic strength of the country. A successful and strong business community is an integral component of the Department's overall mission of job creation, community empowerment, and economic revitalization.

HUD has an extensive list of opportunities for small business assistance. This assistance takes the form of loans, grants, and small business set-asides for their contracts.

The California State Controller's office has a great free publication entitled *California and Small Business*. It is a resource guide to financial opportunities within the state government. For example, it lists the Small Business Loan Guarantee Program, which will guarantee up to 90% of a loan amount, with the guaranteed portion not exceeding $500,000.

The guide can be found at www.ocsbdc.com/resources/images/Small_Bus_Guide. pdf. It is definitely worth printing out and reviewing.

If you would like to explore opportunities with the federal government, go to www. FedBizOpps.gov. FedBizOpps.gov is the single government point-of-entry (GPE) for Federal government procurement opportunities over $25,000. Government buyers are able to publicize their business opportunities by posting information directly to FedBizOpps via the Internet. Through one portal—FedBizOpps (FBO)— commercial vendors seeking federal markets for their products and services can search, monitor, and retrieve opportunities solicited by the entire federal contracting community.

FACTORING

The process of selling a company's accounts receivable at a discount to a funding source is called *factoring*. In a factoring transaction, one or more invoices are sold to a funding source called a *factor*.

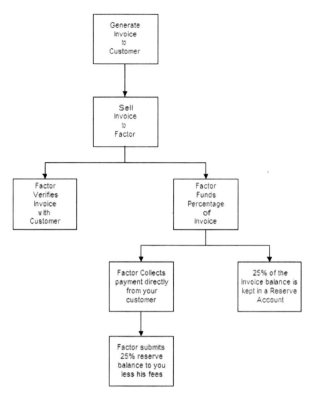

Fig.11 – Factoring

The cost of getting your money immediately instead of waiting for your customers to pay you is a fee charged by your factor company. You will sell individual invoices to your factor. They will immediately submit funds to you, less the amount of a reserve that they hold back and retain. Then, they will submit the reserve to you, less their fees, when they collect from your customers. Here are the accounting entries that you would make in your books if you had a $100 sales transaction:

Submission of invoice to factor company:

	Debit	Credit
Cash	$75.00	
Reserve	$25.00	
Accounts Receivable		$100.00

Factor collects your customer's invoice:

Cash	$15.00	
Factor Expense	$15.00	
Reserve		$25.00

Factoring is not an inexpensive way of financing, but if properly used, it can greatly improve your cash flow. If you find that you are factoring frequently, you need to include it in your product pricing.

PURCHASE ORDER FINANCING

This type of financing is very similar to factoring accounts receivable. Let's say that you are lucky enough to get a huge order for your consumer product that you sell for $20 to retailers and you manufacture in china for $10 a unit. You get an order for 100,000 units. You get excited, because this one order alone is for $2,000,000 dollars. Then, reality sets in. You realize that you must first pay for the product before it ships to your retail customers. The invoice from your factory is $1,000,000, and you have exactly $47.17 in your corporate checking account. This is when purchase order financing comes in to save the day. Here is the basic process:

- Your customer submits a purchase order to you.
- You submit the purchase order to factor for purchase order factoring.
- The purchase order factor makes a payment on the purchase order directly to your supplier. The payments are worked out with your supplier to accommodate timely completion of your products.
- The supplier delivers the finished goods.
- You deliver the products to your customer.
- After you have shipped the products to your customer, you   submit an invoice corresponding to the purchase order to the factor.
- The factor submits your invoice to your customer.
- When the factor receives payment on your invoice from your customer, the amount of the invoice advance and the factoring fee are deducted, and the remainder (the invoice reserve) is paid to you.

GOING PUBLIC

The IPO (initial public offering) is exactly what the name implies. It is a first-time offering of stock to the public. Even non-business people have heard of and know about IPOs. Beyond being a tremendous way to raise money, for the right company, they are a tremendous marketing tool. Because IPOs are closely followed by the press, they raise the public's awareness of your company. Very few companies ever go this route, because IPOs are very complex and closely regulated by the Securities and Exchange Commission. A company can go public without an IPO. Even without the cost of an IPO, there are increased cost and liability associated with being a public company.

BEING A PUBLIC COMPANY CAN GIVE YOU THE FOLLOWING ADVANTAGES:

Access to Capital – Being a public company can give potential investors more confidence in investing in your company. When your stock has a public price, it gives you a listed price for your stock to raise capital. Potential investors can go on the Internet or call a broker and get a quote of your company's stock price.

Increased Valuation – Statistics published by the United States Chamber of Commerce show that sellers of private companies receive an average of 4 to 6 times their net earnings. By comparison, public companies sell at an average of 25 times their net earnings.

Liquidity – In general, stock in a public company is much more liquid than stock in a private enterprise. Investors in the company MAY be able to buy or sell the stock more readily.

Merger and Acquisition – Your stock can be used in acquiring other companies because it will have a "value" associated with its ability to be traded on the open market. I have seen a number of small companies use the "public" stock to acquire controlling interest in other small companies.

Compensation – Many companies use stock and stock option plans as an incentive to attract and retain key employees. Many companies use a combination of stock and salary to attract employees. If your stock is publicly traded, then it can serve as a bigger carrot.

Window Dressing – A public offering of stock can help a company achieve a perception of stability. Being a public company can make it easier to get credit and make vendors and customers more agreeable to doing business with your company.

Here are some real disadvantages in going public:
The Fish Bowl – Once you are a public company, your business transactions are open

to the public. If you like privacy in your business transactions, going public probably wouldn't be a good option.

Administration – You will spend a lot of your time satisfying the reporting requirements of the SEC. The SEC is strict when it comes to the reports that you have to file with them. You will definitely need the continuing services of an attorney and a CPA that specialize in consulting to public companies. In addition to the SEC reporting, you will spend a lot of time "handholding" your stockholders. Since the stock is publicly traded, people you might not want to do business with may end up with your stock and become "part of the family." As an extreme example, say that you have a small public company that produces kids' videos. Let's also say that you are extremely successful. Nothing would prevent an adult film company from investing in your company.

Shareholder Value – You will spend a lot of time making sure that your decisions are improving shareholder value. The problem with this is that improving shareholder value may run contrary to some transactions that you may want to do. As an example, what if you wanted to dedicate part of your facility to your church for a Saturday youth program? Stockholders may not view this as improving their value.

Increased Liability – Your liability increases geometrically when you take your company public. You now have a whole new set of laws that you have to worry about. You also have liability to people whom you might not even know.

Increased Costs – It cost more to maintain a public company with the increased reporting requirements. The cost of an IPO can be several hundred thousand dollars.

You have probably heard of going public via a "reverse merger." This is when you buy a defunct public company that is still in compliance with SEC reporting requirements. You merge your company into the purchased shell and change the name of the shell to your company name. Be very careful with this approach. It does not create a market for your stock, the inherited shareholders are not familiar with your industry or your company, there are potential unseen liabilities in the shell company, and there is a big stigma regarding these in Wall Street.

VENTURE CAPITAL

Venture capital is money invested by professionals who invest in young, rapidly growing companies, like yours, that have the potential to develop into significantly profitable companies. Venture capitalists expect higher than normal return on their investment given the risks they are taking. Venture capitalists (VCs) are professional firms that are typically organized as limited partnerships or as closely held corporations.

They develop pools of investment capital by creating portfolios of funds provided by various investing firms such as banks, institutional pension funds, foundations, insurance companies, and individual investors that are looking to diversify their portfolios. Most VCs will require that individual investors be accredited investors as defined above. VCs will often syndicate their investments in companies to other VCs to offset some of their risks. VCs are different than your regular investors. While a regular investor will not get directly involved in your business, a venture capitalist will get very involved. Most venture capitalists will have experience and knowledge that can be beneficial to the growth of your company. Most venture capitalists will invest in new and fast-growing companies. One problem that many entrepreneurs run into when looking for VCs is thinking too small. A VC will have to put just as much work into a deal asking for $1,000,000 as he will for a deal asking for $10,000,000. Always find out what range of investments your potential VC likes to invest his resources in.

If you really want to get a meeting with a VC, don't send them unsolicited business plans. It will normally be a waste of your time and a waste of paper. It is best to get a referral by someone that has worked with them. With this being said, I have seen entrepreneurs do their research and find a good fit with a VC. Many VCs specialize in industries that they know and feel comfortable with, so make sure that you are a good fit from an industry perspective. Keep in mind that most VCs see hundreds, sometimes thousands, of business plans a year; so know that many of your business plans will end up in their round files. See the chapter entitled THE BUSINESS PLAN AND OPERATING YOUR BUSINESS for a discussion on preparing your business plan and for getting your business plan noticed.

FINANCING YOUR BUSINESS—A FINAL ANALYSIS

In this chapter, we have explored a number of ways of financing your new business enterprise. We have looked at the factors involved in determining how much financing you will need. We have discussed a number of different options of financing your business using equity and debt. If you want to maintain your independence and you have confidence in your abilities, it is almost always better to finance with debt. Once you pay back your debts, you will own the business. With equity, you bring in other "owners." We have discussed being equally yoked with people who have your love of God and share your business philosophy and principles. This is an intangible part of your analysis but probably the most important part. Our business life should never get in the way of your walk with the Lord; so be very careful in choosing which way you finance your new business. At some point during the growth of your business, you may need outside funding. It's not a sin to borrow for growing a business that God has allowed you to start, but be prudent in financing your business. As with all other areas of your life, the first step in the financing process is spending time on your knees asking for wisdom and guidance.

Business with a Purpose
Volume II - Keeping Track of Your Business
and Building It

Keeping Track Of Your Business
(Accounting And Other Fun Things)

WHAT ARE ACCOUNTING AND BOOKKEEPING?

Accounting is the language of business. If it is properly understood and utilized, it can tell you where your business has gone financially, where your business currently is financially, and where your business is going financially. So, whether you like it or not, you have to know the language of accounting. God commands that we take good care of the resources that he has lent to us. A proper knowledge of accounting will help greatly in managing the Time, Talent, and Treasures that God has given to us.

There is a difference between accounting and bookkeeping. This author's grandmother used to refer to me as "my grandson, the 'certified public bookkeeper.' " My designation of CPA (Certified Public Accountant) did not impress her at all. It kept me humble. So, what is the difference between accounting and bookkeeping? Good old *Funk and Wagnall's Standard Dictionary* defines each word as follows:

Accounting – the system of recording, classifying, and summarizing business and financial transactions.

Bookkeeping – the practice of recording business transactions systematically.

There are some critically important differences between these two definitions. Accounting manipulates (this is meant in a strictly positive "non-Enron" sense) and interprets the data that has been recorded by bookkeepers. Accountants properly interpret the financial transactions recorded by the bookkeepers. The transactions must be properly summarized on a relevant, accurate, and timely (R.A.T.) manner. And the transactions must be recorded in a consistent manner to allow for comparison from period to period.

Recording of transactions in a consistent manner also enables you to compare your business with other similar businesses. This comparison can be a vital tool in making sure that you are headed in the right direction in regard to revenues and expenses.

The transactions should be recorded in the accounting system (general ledger) consistent with the way other, similar businesses record their transactions. This is so that the summarized financial transactions can be compared to other, similar businesses by governmental agencies, potential purchasers of your business, your team members, and others. There is a set of universal guidelines that promote the uniform recording of financial transactions. This set of guidelines is referred to as Generally Accepted Accounting Principles, commonly abbreviated as *GAAP*. These guidelines are codified in a uniform body of rules and regulations by the Financial Accounting Standards Board (FASB) and supported by the United States Securities and Exchange Commission (SEC).

Once the accountant makes sure that all of your financial transactions are properly recorded, he interprets them and assists you in making decisions about your business.

HISTORY OF ACCOUNTING AND BOOKKEEPING[24]

Formal accounting was invented by a Franciscan friar named Luca Pacioli in 1494 in his paper "Summa de Arithmetica, Geometria, Proportioni et Proportionalita" ("Everything About Arithmetic, Geometry and Proportion").

The treatise described double-entry bookkeeping -- that for every credit entered into a ledger there must be a debit, a concept created by Florentine merchants and hailed by Goethe as "one of the most beautiful discoveries of the human spirit."

Three traits shared by successful merchants, Mr. Pacioli wrote, were access to cash, a constantly updated accounting system and a good bookkeeper. His contemporary Christopher Columbus apparently knew that: On his voyage to the New World, he took a royal accountant to track his "swindle sheet when he started to figure the cost of gold and spices he would accumulate," according to Alistair Cooke's 1973 book "America."

The craft changed little until the industrial revolution, when accounting advanced from pure recordkeeping to a means of survival. Josiah Wedgwood, Charles Darwin's grandfather, kept his British pottery factory alive during the depression of 1772 through the innovation of cost accounting -- calculating the costs of materials and labor for each step of the manufacturing process, and then setting prices to ensure enough margin to remain viable.

By the mid-19th century, "accompants," as accountants were known, were flourishing in Britain. The Cooper brothers, whose name lives on in Price Waterhouse Coopers, ran

---

24   Taylor, Jeffrey. *Self-Help Books and Tools: History of Accounting,* http://wwww.executivecaliber.ws/historyofaccounting, 2010.

a Dickensian operation of screeching supervisors lording over clerks toiling long hours for scant pay. The industry followed European investments to the New World, and in 1887, 31 accountants formed the predecessor to the American Institute of Certified Public Accountants. A decade later, they created a standardized test, bestowing on a man named Frank Broaker the honor of becoming the first CPA.

In the early 1930s, after the financial scandals of the '20s and the corporate failures of the Great Depression, the industry sought to formalize consistency, transparency and trust in the profession. Already, in 1922, AICPA had banned its members from advertising, saying it wasn't dignified. The group also forbade accountants to poach each other's clients.

The profession got its own governing board and a manual called Generally Accepted Accounting Practices -- GAAP for short. The profession also won the responsibility for auditing public companies, though not without an intense congressional debate.

Accountants had become moral guardians -- an image reinforced in the public's imagination in the 1930s, when Price Waterhouse was enlisted by the Academy of Motion Picture Arts and Sciences to count ballots for the Academy Awards.

In lieu of the hard sell, accountants networked at the country club and sat on the boards of nonprofit organizations and chambers of commerce.

In the 1970s, the federal government, amid questions about some companies' accounting procedures, set up the Financial Accounting Standards Board to oversee accountants. But it soon also removed a lot of the restrictions that had prevented big firms from competing with each other.

In the late 1970s, the Federal Trade Commission, concerned about anticompetitive practices, began pushing AICPA to allow accountants to advertise. By 1990, the group had lifted most restrictions on ads.

ACCOUNTING AND BOOKKEEPING BASICS

Before you can set up your accounting records, you need to determine what types of business transactions you will be generating. From this transactional analysis, you can determine what journals you will need. The most typical types of transactions will be:

Cash
Sales
Cash Receipts
Expense
Cash Disbursements
Contributions to Capital

Accounting is the method in which financial information is gathered, processed, and summarized into financial statements and reports. An accounting system can be represented by the following Accounting Flow of Transactions:

Accounting Flow of Transactions

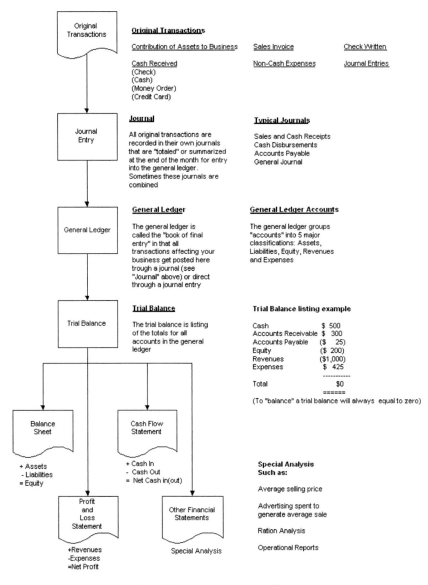

Fig.12 – Accounting Flow

To properly track what your business is doing from a financial perspective, your business transactions will normally follow the sequence outlined in the flowchart above. It should be kept in mind that this transaction flow is for a manual record keeping system. Almost everyone will be using a computerized booking and accounting system, but it is a good idea to understand the language of accounting and how the transactions you record physically flow through the accounting systems.

ORIGINAL TRANSACTIONS

Every accounting entry is based on a business transaction, which is usually evidenced by a business document, such as a check or cash received, a check written or a sales invoice. These original transaction documents must be kept in an orderly filing system for future reference. You may also be required someday to prove the accuracy of the numbers that you record on your tax returns and financial statements. Examples of documentation for original transactions are:

Cash Received Transactions – Documentation Requirements

Contributing cash to your business – your cancelled check (Sales and cash receipts journal).

Check received from a cash sale –cash register tape or copy of invoice (Sales and cash receipts journal).

Credit card sales – copy of credit card receipt and statement from credit card company (Sales and cash receipts journal).

Cash Disbursement Transactions – Documentation Requirements

Check written for business expenses – check stub stapled to copy of invoice and cancelled check (Cash disbursements journal).

Cash paid for business expenses – copy of receipt/invoice. On the rare instance when you cannot get a receipt, a log entry in your calendar with date, time, who was paid, and what was received will suffice (Cash disbursements journal).

Cash paid to owner for personal use – signed receipt from owner showing amount received by the owner. The transaction will be recorded differently depending on whether the business is a sole proprietorship or a corporation. If a sole proprietorship, the transaction will be a "draw" from the cash of the business. If a corporation, it will be a loan from the corporation to the "owner"/stockholder/employee (Cash disbursements journal).

Sales Transactions – Documentation Requirements

Sales made "on account" – copy of sales receipt. When a business makes a sale to a customer/client without receiving cash, the sale is made with the promise of being paid at a later date (Sales and cash receipts journal).

Sales for cash, check, credit card (sales and cash receipts Journal).

Purchasing Goods and Services on Account without Paying for Them in Cash – Documentation Requirements

Purchase of supplies without paying cash – a copy of the invoice (Accounts Payable Journal). There are a number of manual accounting systems, sometimes referred to as one-write systems (such as Safeguard bookkeeping systems), that will write to the Accounts Payable Journal as well as make an entry to the individual vendor's ledger card. If you use a manual or semi-manual accounting system for accounts payable such as Safeguard, you will be making entries to a journal that will be totaled and posted to the general ledger (discussed later) at the end of the month. These types of manual systems normally include a feature where you insert the individual vendor's ledger card into the writing mechanism so that as you write in the Accounts Payable journal, you are also writing on the vendor ledger card. One big disadvantage to manual systems is that you must reconcile the individual vendor ledger cards to the total in the general ledger at the end of each month. With an automated system such as QuickBooks, the reconciliation process is automatically done for you, and the individual ledger accounts for individual vendors always agree with the balance in the general ledger.

Nonrecurring transactions – Documentation Requirements

From time to time, there will be business transactions that are not in the normal course of operating your business. Examples of these types of transactions are:

Contributing Equipment to your business that was originally personal equipment. This type of transaction should be supported by the original invoice. Keep in mind that if you contribute an asset that you have owned for a while, its value to be recorded in your accounting records will probably not be the amount you paid for it. Most assets depreciate and thus will be recorded for a lower amount. You will normally record contributed assets at the lower of original cost or fair market value. As an example, say you contribute your personal computer to the business that you paid $2,000 for two years ago. Also, say you can purchase a similar new computer like your old computer for $1,000 now. You would record the value of the computer at $1,000 in your accounting records. You would want to have your original invoice and evidence to support the current value (e.g., copy of store advertisements) filed in your accounting records (General Journal).

BOOKKEEPING JOURNALS ━━━━━━━━━━━━━

A journal is a place to record daily or recurring transactions of a business. The original transactions listed above are all recorded in one of the journals listed below. ALL business transactions must be entered into one of the journals below. The purpose of the journals is to collect similar transactions, summarize them, and post the summary totals of the journals into the general ledger, which will be discussed below. The general ledger is called the *book of final entry*. It's where all the aforementioned journals are summarized to at the end of each accounting period. The typical journals used to record the chronological, day-to-day transactions are the Sales and Cash Receipts Journal, Cash Disbursements Journal, and Accounts Payable Journal (sometimes called Purchases Journal). There are other journals that businesses may find necessary to use. An example is the Payroll Journal. The main point is that all transactions of the business must eventually be entered into the general ledger. A business normally does not enter detailed transactions directly into the general ledger but, instead, accumulates similar transactions in journals, summarizes these journals at the end of each accounting period, and then enters summarized information from the journals into the general ledger. Let's assume in the following journals that you own a small country grocery store.

Sales and Cash Receipts Journal

Sales and Cash Receipts Journal							
				Accounts receivable			
Date	Description	Invoice Number	Cash Debit (100)	Debit (110)	Credit (110)	Sales Credit (500)	Sales Tax Payable Credit (205)
1/2	Mr. Car - sale on account	IN1001		$1,080.00		$1,000.00	$80.00
1/3	Daily cash sales		$540.00			$500.00	$40.00
1/15	Cash rec'd on acct. - Mr. Bus	CR4005	$250.00		$250.00		
1/29	Mr. Tractor - sale on account	IN1002		$2,160.00		$2,000.00	$160.00
Total			$790.00	$3,240.00	$250.00	$3,500.00	$280.00

Fig.13 – Sales CR Jr

The example Sales and Cash Receipts Journal reflects the following:

1. A sale on account to Mr. Car for a total sale of $1,000 plus sales tax of $80. The transaction shows that we will bill Mr. Car $1,080. This is for his actual purchase of $1,000 and $80 for the sales tax that we collect from him for submission to the State Sales Tax Agency.
2. The transaction on 1/3 shows that we had $500 of cash sales for that day. Again, we collected $540, which included $40 of sales tax that we collected from customers, that we will then have to submit to the State Sales Tax Agency.
3. On 1/15, we received, in the mail, $250 from Mr. Bus for payment on his account. This transaction shows that we deposited $250 in the bank and reduced accounts receivable by the same amount.
4. We had another sale on account on 1/29.

At the end of the month before posting the totals from the Sales and Cash Receipts Journal to the general ledger, we will make sure that it "balances." In other words, we will make sure that the "Debit" columns are equal to the "Credit" columns.

Cash (Debit)	$ 790	(Increase)
Accounts Receivable Increase (Debit)	$ 3,240	(Increase)
Accounts Receivable Decrease (Credit)	($ 250)	(Decrease)
Sales (Credit)	($ 3,500)	(Increase)
Sales Tax Payable (Credit)	($ 280)	(Increase)
Total	$ 0	(Balanced)

This "balancing" of the journal is normally done by running an adding machine tape of the journal. With an automated bookkeeping system, such as QuickBooks, you will not need to balance the journals as the QuickBooks system always makes sure that your transactions are in balance. It is virtually impossible to get your journals out of balance with an automated bookkeeping system like QuickBooks.

Cash Disbursements Journal

						Cash Disbursements Journal				
Date	Payee	Description	Ck. No.	Ck. Amt. Credit	Postage Debit	Office Supplies Debit	Supplies Debit	Other Debit	Other Account Number
1/1	XYZ Industrial Supply Warehouse	Janitorial Supplies	1005	$150.00				$150.00	
1/5	United States Post Office	Stamps and mailing	1006	$36.00	$36.00				
1/9	Sierra Mountains Realty Company	Rent	1007	$500.00				$500.00	710
1/25	ABC Grocery Supply company	Inventory of Groceries - paid cash	1008	$300.00				$300.00	115
Total				$986.00	$36.00	$0.00	$150.00	$800.00	

Fig.14 – CD Jr

This journal is where you record cash disbursements in the form of checks. If you want to make disbursements in the form of cash, you will normally write a check to Cash to set up a petty cash fund. We will explain the petty cash concept a little later in this section.

The example Cash Disbursements Journal reflects the following transactions:

1. On 1/1, a check was written to XYZ Industrial Supply Warehouse for janitorial supplies in the amount of $150.00. When entering the check into the Cash Disbursements Journal, we must enter all of the following information:

   a. Date check was written

   b. The Payee – whom the check was written to

   c. Description – what the check was written for

   d. Check number – the printed number on the check

   e. The check amount

   f. Enter the check amount again in the appropriate column of expense. Check amounts can be entered into multiple columns of expense as long as they total to the amount of the check written in the Check Amount column. As an example, if the check to XYZ Industrial Supply Warehouse was written for $150 for supplies and $150.00 for office supplies, the amount in the

Check Amount column would be $300.00. On the same line in the Cash Disbursements Journal, you would have $150.00 in the Supplies column and $150.00 in the Office Supplies column.

2. Check 1006 was written on 1/5 for $36.00 of postage. The $36.00 was entered into the Postage column.

3. Sierra Mountains Realty was issued check number 1007 on 1/9 for $500.00 as payment for our rent. The amount was entered into the "Other" column. The reason that we used the "Other" column is that we only write one check a month to rent, and it would not make sense to have an entire column dedicated to "Rent." The expense account for rent in our example is 710.

4. The last check in our example Cash Disbursements Journal written on 1/25 to ABC Grocery Supply Company for $300.00 was entered into the "Other" column, and shows that it is to be charged to inventory. Normally, inventory purchases would go through the Accounts Payable Journal as we normally buy our inventory on account and pay for it at the end of the month. Since we are buying inventory for sale to our customers, it is not technically an expense when we buy it, as we have really exchanged on asset (cash) for another asset (inventory). Inventory is an asset account on the balance sheet and not an expense on the profit and loss statement. As products are sold, they are taken out of inventory and entered into Cost of Sales in the profit and loss statement.

At the end of the month, as with all journals, before posting the totals from the Cash Disbursements Journal to the general ledger, we will make sure that it "balances." Again, make sure that the "Debit" columns equal the "Credit" columns.

Check Amount (Cash)	(Credit)	($986)	(Decrease)
Postage Expense	(Debit)	$ 36	(Increase)
Office Supplies	(Debit)	$ -0-	(N/A)
Supplies Expense	(Debit)	$150	(Increase)
Rent Expense	(Debit)	$500	(Increase)
Inventory	(Debit)	$300	(Increase)
Total		$ 0	(Balanced)

As mentioned above, if you are using an automated system like QuickBooks, this balancing and posting to the general ledger is done automatically for you.

Accounts Payable Journal (Purchases Journal)

				Accounts Payable					
Date	Vendor Name	Description	Purch Order/ Return No.	Debit	Credit	Grocery Inventory Debit (Credit)	Non - grocery Inventory Debit (Credit)	Other Debit (Credit)	Other Acct No.
1/2	ABC Paper Supplies	Paper bags and other supplies	1005		$30.00		$30.00		
1/10	XYZ Industrial Supply Warehouse	Grocery Supplies	1006		$100.00	$100.00			
1/15	ABC Grocery Supply company	Return bad peas	1007	$20.00		($20.00)			
1/25	ABC Grocery Supply company	Inventory of Groceries - on account	1008		$800.00		$800.00		
Total				$20.00	$930.00	$80.00	$830.00		

Accounts Payable (Purchases Journal)

Fig.15 – AP Jr

This journal is sometimes combined with the Cash Disbursements Journal. If your business does not make a large number of purchases on account, you might want to combine this with the Cash Disbursements Journal. An important thing to note is that the Journal, as with all journals, has serially numbered control documents. This makes it easier to control all transactions. You generate a Purchase Order/Return document for each order. When the goods ordered come in, you can readily locate the transaction and make sure that you received what you ordered. It is also an excellent control system for credits on returned merchandise.

The example Accounts Payable (Purchases Journal) reflects the following transactions:

1. On 1/2/XX, $30 of non-grocery inventory was purchased from ABC Paper Supplies. The description says that paper bags and other supplies were purchased.
2. XYZ Industrial Supply sells us $100 of groceries on account. You will hopefully then sell the groceries at a markup.

3. On January 15, you had to return some bad peas that were purchased from ABC Grocery Supply Company. The Accounts Payable (Purchase Journal) shows that we have a decrease in Grocery Inventory (Credit) and a decrease in Accounts Payable (Debit).
4. On January 25, you ordered $800 of groceries for resale to customers.

At the end of the month, as with the other journals discussed above, before posting the totals from the Accounts Payable Journal (Purchases Journal) to the general ledger, we will verify that it "balances." To do this, we combine the "Debit" columns with the "Credit" columns. The total should be zero.

Accounts Payable	(Debit)	$ 20	(Decrease)
Accounts Payable	(Credit)	($930)	(Increase)
Grocery Inventory	(Debit)	$ 80	(Increase)
Non-Grocery Inventory	(Debit)	$ 830	(Increase)
Total		$ -0-	

General Journal

The last journal that we will discuss is the General Journal. It is the place where you record transactions that don't happen very often and do not fit the definition of transactions for the standard journals that you are using. If you find that you have recurring transactions that are happening with great regularity and/or are overburdening your existing journals (discussed in this section), you might want to set up a separate journal for these transactions. A good example of a transaction that companies use when the number of transactions in their payroll grows is a Payroll Journal. A general journal is typically a two-column journal.

General Journal					
Date	Acct No.	Account Name	Debit	Credit	Description
1/30	780	Postage Expense	$20		Reclassify Rent Exp
1/30	740	Supplies Expense		$20	Reclassify Rent Exp
1/30	750	Deprec Exp	$5		Record montly deprec
1/30	135	Accum Deprec		$5	Record montly deprec
1/30	100	Cash	$75		Rec sale meat slicer
1/30	130	Equip and Furn		$200	Rec sale meat slicer
1/30	135	Accum Deprec	$160		Rec sale meat slicer
1/30	800	Other Income		$35	Rec sale meat slicer
1/30	600	Cost of Sales	$1,000		Transfer cost from Inventory
1/30	115	Inventory		$1,000	Transfer cost from Inventory
1/30	760	Insurance Exp	$50		Transfer Ins exp from Prepaid
1/30	120	Prepaid Insurance		$50	Transfer Ins exp from Prepaid
1/30	770	Bad Debts Exp	$20		Write of Mr. Car's AR bal.
1/30	110	Accounts Rec		$20	Write of Mr. Car's AR bal.
1/30	720	Utility Expense	$15		Accrue Utility Expense
1/30	230	Accrued Expense		$15	Accrue Utility Expense
		Total	$1,345	$1,345	Balanced

Fig.16 – Gen Jr

Some transactions that would be candidates for inclusion in the General Journal are:

1. To correct previously recorded erroneous transactions

    Occasionally, you may make mistakes in your journals that need to be corrected. The way to do this is through "journal entries" in your General Journal. Let's say that you erroneously recorded a Postage Expense check of $20 as Supplies Expense. To correct this expenditure in the general ledger, you would make the journal entry as recorded below:

2. To record depreciation of Equipment and Furniture

Most businesses use some sort of equipment. For illustration purposes, let's say that you purchased a meat slicer for your grocery store. You bought it last year for $300. At the time of purchase, you were buying a business asset, and it was not recorded as an expense. When you bought it, you didn't use it up all at once, but it will be used over a number of years until it wears out. Let us say that the useful life of the meat slicer is 5 years. This means that you will take 1/5 of the $300 that you spent for the meat slicer into expense each year. Each year, you will record $60 as expense. If you prepare monthly financial statements for your business (highly recommended!), then you will make a journal entry for $5 of depreciation expense each month. In reality, you will have a number of assets that will be depreciated. You will have an Excel spreadsheet or software package that keeps track of your depreciable assets, including the following information:

1. Asset name

2. Any distinctive information such as serial number

3. Who purchased from

4. Date of purchase

5. Estimated useful life of asset

6. Depreciation method: straight-line depreciation, accelerated depreciation. Although depreciation methods are beyond the scope of this book, you should realize that IRS requires businesses to depreciate (take to expense) business assets over regulated periods of time. The IRS also allows certain assets to be depreciated on an accelerated basis.

7. Accumulated depreciation (depreciation taken from the purchase date of the asset to the current date).

3. To record sale of Equipment and Furniture that is used in your business

There are occasions when you will want to sell some of your business's assets. Continuing with our grocery store example, let's say that you have a meat slicer that you would like to retire. Assume that the meat slicer cost $200 four years ago. You recorded the meat slicer in your general ledger at a cost of $200. You were depreciating it at the rate of $40 a year ($200 divided by five years equals $40 per year), and since you had it for four years, you recorded depreciation in the amount of $160 leaving a "book value" of $40. Since the book value is $40 and you sell it for $75, you make a net profit of $35.

4. Record cost of sales taking the cost of sales out of Inventory

There are a number of ways to deal with the issue of recording Cost of Sales. The two most common and simple ways for small businesses to deal with it are:

A. Record all inventory purchases as inventory and not as Cost of Sales. This means that you are considering all inventory purchases as an asset on the balance sheet. At the end of each accounting period, you will take a physical count of your inventory on hand. You will then determine the value (units times unit costs) of the inventory on hand at the close of the accounting period (usually the end of each month). You will then make a journal entry in the general journal to transfer Cost of Sales out of Inventory by adjusting the balance in the general ledger to agree with the balance you determined in your physical count.

B. The other way that many small business owners handle the Inventory/ Cost of Sales issue is to record all inventory purchases as Cost of sales. They then follow the same procedure discussed above for initially recording purchases as Inventory on the general ledger.

5. Write-off of prepaid expenses

Sometimes, you will pay expenses that will cover more than the current accounting period. An example is insurance. You might pay an annual premium that covers 12 months. To record this expenditure as expense for the current period would be inappropriate, and it would distort your financial statements. For our example, if you paid $600 for an annual insurance policy, you would record it initially as $600 of Prepaid Insurance Expense. Each month, you would make a journal entry transferring $50 from Prepaid Insurance to Insurance Expense.

6. Write-off of bad debts

Even if you know most of your customers, you will have bad debts. Sometimes someone just cannot pay their bill. If you let someone buy groceries "on account," this means that you initially recorded a sale in your Sales and Cash Receipts Journal, and at the end of the month, the Journal was summarized and posted to your general ledger. For this example, let's assume that Mr. Car had $20 left on his account that he was unable to pay. You would make a journal entry to reduce Accounts Receivable, an asset (credit Accounts Receivable, because it normally has a debit balance), and increase Bad Debts, an expense.

7. Accrual of certain expenses and reversal of those accruals

Sometimes, you will not get a bill on a timely basis from a vendor. You will want to estimate it and record it so that you can keep your financial statements as accurate as possible. As an example, if you did not get your electric bill this month, you will want to estimate it and make a journal entry to record your Utility Expense for this month. If your normal monthly amount for electricity is $15, you would make a journal entry recorded as Utility Expense for $15 and record $15 to Accrued Expenses. The "Accrued Expenses" account is separate from Accounts Payable. When you record an Accounts Payable amount, it is because you actually got an invoice. Accrued Expenses are estimates of expenses you didn't get invoiced for on a timely basis. You also keep these estimates separate, because you will want to reverse them after the close of the current accounting period and because you will be getting an invoice that will be recorded as an expense, and you don't want to book double expenses.

Normally, at the end of each month, the transactions in each of the journals are totaled, and the monthly totals for the journals are recorded in the general ledger. If you are using a computerized bookkeeping system such as QuickBooks, this is normally a seamless process that is done for you by the computer software.

Here is the General Journal for all of the transactions described above:

General Ledger

While a journal records transactions as they happen, a ledger groups transactions according to their type, based on the accounts they affect. The general ledger is a collection of all balance sheets (asset, liability, and equity), income, and expense accounts used to keep a business's accounting records. At the end of an accounting period, all journals are summarized and transferred to the general ledger accounts. This procedure is called "posting."

Trial Balance

A trial balance is prepared at the end of an accounting period by adding up all the account balances in your general ledger. The sum of the debit balances should equal the sum of the credit balances. If total debits don't equal total credits, you must track down the errors.

Here is the trial balance BEFORE posting our transactions above to it:

Trial balance BEFORE recording this months transactions:

	Debit	Credit
Cash	$10,000	
Account Receivable	$5,000	
Inventory	$1,000	
Prepaid Expenses	$600	
Office Equipment	$6,000	
Accum Deprec.		$300
Accounts Payable		$100
Sales Tax Payable		$0
Notes Payable		$0
Mortgages Payable		$0
Accrued Expenses		$0
Capital Stock		$22,200
Revenues		$0
Cost of Sales	$0	
Rent Expense	$0	
Utilities Expense	$0	
Payroll Expense	$0	
Supplies Expense	$0	
Depreciation Expense	$0	
Postage Expense	$0	
Insurance Expense	$0	
Bad Debts Expense	$0	
Misc Expense	$0	
Other Income	$0	
Balance	$22,600	$22,600

Fig.17 – Trial Balance before transactions

Notice that it balances.

Here is our trial balance AFTER we post our monthly activity from above:

Trial balance AFTER recording this months transactions:

	Debit	Credit
Cash	$9,879	
Account Receivable	$7,970	
Inventory	$1,210	
Prepaid Expenses	$550	
Office Equipment	$5,800	
Accum Deprec		$145
Accounts Payable		$1,010
Sales Tax Payable		$280
Notes Payable		$0
Mortgages Payable		$0
Accrued Expenses		$15
Capital Stock		$22,200
Revenues		$3,500
Cost of Sales	$1,000	
Rent Expense	$500	
Utilities Expense	$15	
Payroll Expense	$0	
Supplies Expense	$130	
Depreciation Expense	$5	
Postage Expense	$56	
Insurance Expense	$50	
Bad Debts Expense	$20	
Misc Expense	$0	
Other Income		$35
Balance	$27,185	$27,185

Fig.18 – Trial Balance After Transactions

Notice we are still in balance.

An often helpful way of looking at a general ledger is to use "T" accounts. T accounts are graphical representations of the activity in a general ledger. The accounts are grouped according to their account type (e.g., Asset, Liability, Capital, Revenue, and Expenses). The T accounts have been color-coded to the journals above and the following financial statements to give you an idea of the flow of transactions.

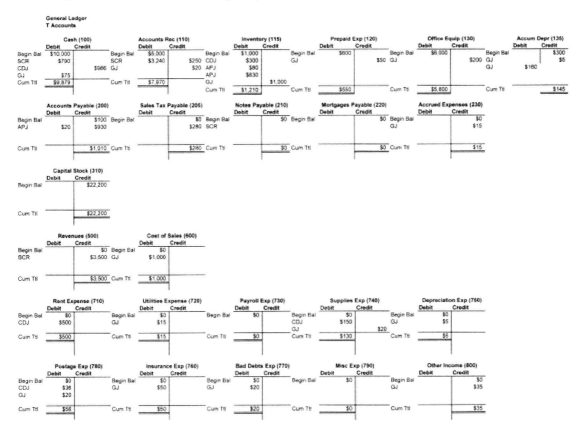

Fig.19 – T Accounts

Financial Statements

Finally, financial statements are prepared from the information in your trial balance.

The above steps are what would occur if you had a manual accounting system. The cost of computer programs such as QuickBooks computerized accounting should be on the "must-have list" of all new business people. It's good to have a basic understanding of the "manual" method of bookkeeping to get a feel for how all accounting processes, records, and their resultant financial statements relate and interact with one another for solid business decision making.

Income Statement for the Month of January	
Income	$3,500
Cost of Sales	$1,000
Gross Income	$2,500
Expenses	
Rent Expense	$500
Utilities Expense	$15
Payroll Expense	$0
Supplies Expense	$130
Depreciation Expense	$5
Postage Expense	$56
Insurance Expense	$50
Bad Debts Expense	$20
Misc Expense	$0
Total Expenses	$776
Net Income from Operations	$1,724
Other Income	$35
Total Net Income (loss)	$1,759

Fig.20 – Income Statement

Your accounting records are important, because the resulting financial statements and reports help you plan and make decisions. They may be used by some third parties (bankers, investors, or creditors) and are needed to provide information to government agencies, such as the Internal Revenue Service.

```
Balance Sheet
As of January 31

ASSETS

Current Assets

Cash                                             $9,879
Accounts Receivable                              $7,970
Inventory                                        $1,210
Prepaid Expenses                                   $550

Total Current Assets                            $19,609

Fixed Assets

Office Equipment                                 $5,800
Accum Depreciation                                 $145

Total Fixed Assets                               $5,655

Total Assets                                    $25,264

LIABILITIES AND EQUITY

Liabilities

Accounts Payable                                 $1,010
Sales Tax Payable                                  $280
Notes Payable                                        $0
Mortgages Payable                                    $0
Accrued Expenses                                    $15

Total Liabilities                                $1,305

Equity

Retained Earnings      (From Inc Statement)      $1,759

Capital Stock                                   $22,200

Total Equity                                    $23,959

Total Liabilities and Equity                    $25,264
```

Fig.21 – Balance Sheet

A FEW WORDS ABOUT CASH FLOW ━━━━━━━━━━━━━━━━━━━━━━━━

Every entrepreneur will use his financial statements differently to manage his business. Most entrepreneurs will be highly concerned about cash flow, especially during the formative years of the business. When you start your business, you will, like most other business owners, be short on cash. We won't go through the mechanics of preparing a cash flow statement, but it's important to track and know what your current cash inflows and outflows are and what you project them to be for the next accounting period. A good way to help you develop these numbers is to look at the change in each of your noncash balance sheet accounts from the beginning of the period to the end of the period and analyze these changes for their impact on the change in your cash balances.

Another way to determine operating cash flow is to start with net income and add back expenses that did not result in inflows or outflows of cash. The most common noncash expense is depreciation. When working with historical figures, adjusting net income with depreciation and other noncash expenses is much simpler than determining all the revenues and expenses that require or provide funds.

Next, you identify all the balance sheet accounts that are associated with operations and determine the *change* in the account from the end of the last period to the end of the current period. What balance sheet accounts are we referring to? Let's take another look at the operating cycle to see which accounts to include.

Operating cash flow will include all the balance sheet accounts that are a part of normal operations. Trade receivables and payables as well as accrued expenses, prepaid expenses, and other current assets that are a part of day-to-day operations are included in operating cash flow as we'll show in the example.

But what about the other balance sheet accounts—how do they fit into this picture? The remaining balance sheet accounts will either be investing activities or financing activities. Once again, you determine the change in each balance sheet account from the beginning of the period to the end of the period, tally them up, and there you have it—a complete picture of the cash flow for your company.

Here is a sample cash flow statement.

Cash Flow Statement For the Month of January	
Net Income after taxes	$1,759
Depreciation	$5
(Increase) decrease in Accounts Receivable	($2,970)
(Increase) decrease in Inventory	($210)
(Increase) decrease in Prepaid Expense	$50
Write off of fixed asset	$200
Write off of accumulated depreciation	($160)
Decrease (Increase) in Accounts Payable	$910
Decrease (Increase) in Accrued Expenses	$15
Decrease (Increase) in Sales Tax Payable	$280
Increase (decrease) in cash	($121)
Beginning Cash Balance	$10,000
Ending Cash Balance	$9,879

Fig.22 – Cash Flow Stmt

ALL ACCOUNTING SYSTEMS ARE THE SAME BUT DIFFERENT ▬▬▬▬

Although the basics of accounting and bookkeeping will be the same for all businesses, debits always equal credits, there will be differences in the specific types of transactions and the way that they are recorded and subsequently analyzed. Another factor that comes into the equation is the individual owner's particular management style.

Say that your business is a grocery store. You will want to have the following elements tracked in your bookkeeping system:

1. Inventory by item so that your bookkeeping system can assist you in determining when you need to reorder specific products.
2. Revenue reporting by product line so that you know how much each type of product is generating in revenues.
3. Cost of sales by product line so that you can determine the product line profitability and possibly how much floor space to dedicate to each product/product line. As we will discuss later under the topic of analysis, numbers must be considered in light of subjective factors. As an example, in grocery stores, milk and dairy do not yield the highest net profits for grocery stores. BUT, you will also notice that most grocery stores put the milk and dairy sections prominently at the back of the stores. This is because customers will often come in for a carton of milk, running to the back of the store, passing higher-profit products and picking them up on their way back to the checkout registers.
4. Normal monthly operating expenses such as rent, utilities, taxes, payroll, payroll taxes.

If your business is an insurance company, you have no real need to track any inventory of any kind. In service businesses, the accounting is normally much less complex than in companies that require tracking of inventory. In an insurance company, you would probably want to track the revenues and profitability of the various lines of insurance that you carry. You might also want to track things such as which zip code your clients come from to effectively deploy your marketing dollars in the right geographical area.

The most complex type of business from an accounting system perspective is a manufacturing business. This type of business must track the constant flow of raw materials going into goods manufactured at various costs to determine the costs of goods sold and costs of finished goods put into inventory. There are many good books on the market today that can show you how to perform the accounting function for a manufacturing entity. This topic is beyond the scope of this book.

Below, an example abbreviated Chart of Accounts for a service business that does not track inventory. Notice the absence of accounts to track inventory and Cost of Sales.

100	Cash
110	Accounts Receivable
120	Prepaid Expenses
130	Office Equipment and Furniture
135	Accumulated Depreciation
200	Accounts Payable
205	Sales Tax Payable
210	Notes Payable
220	Mortgage Payable
230	Accrued Expenses
300	Retained Earnings (If the company is not incorporated, Retained Earnings and Capital Stock will be replaced with Owner's Equity.)
310	Capital Stock
500	Revenues
710	Rent Expense
720	Utilities Expense
730	Payroll Expenses
740	Supplies
750	Depreciation
760	Insurance Expense
770	Bad Debts Expense
780	Postage Expense
790	Misc. Expense
800	Other Income

An abbreviated Chart of Accounts for a company that has the need to track inventory, such as a grocery store. If a business is tracking inventory, they will probably also track cost of goods sold. Some businesses will want to track cost of goods sold by product line to tell which product line is generating the most profit. As we will discuss later, profit by product line could be a very helpful number to generate. If a store owner has been generating cost of sales by product line, he can analyze gross profit by square foot to see if he is effectively utilizing the square footage in his store.

100	Cash
110	Accounts Receivable
115	**Inventory**
120	Prepaid Expenses
130	Office Equipment and Furniture
135	Accumulated Depreciation
200	Accounts Payable
205	Sales Tax Payable
210	Notes Payable
220	Mortgage Payable
230	Accrued Expenses
300	Retained Earnings (If the company is not incorporated, Retained Earnings and Capital Stock will be replaced with Owner's Equity.)
310	Capital Stock
500	Revenues
600	Cost of Sales
710	Rent Expense
720	Utilities Expense
730	Payroll Expenses
740	Supplies
750	Depreciation Expense
760	Insurance Expense

770	Bad Debts Expense
780	Postage Expense
790	Misc. Expense
800	Other Income

Accounting for manufacturing companies is probably the most complex type of accounting. Not only do you need to track inventory and cost of goods manufactured, but you have to track various stages of inventory production. You will normally have finished goods, works in process, and raw materials. Some automated accounting systems such as QuickBooks do a pretty good job of tracking cost accounting elements of your business. If you are contemplating starting a manufacturing company, you should solicit the services of a professional accountant to help you set up your accounting system and to monitor it periodically.

100	Cash
110	Accounts Receivable
115	**Inventory**
	115.5 **Finished Goods Inventory**
	115.10 **Works in Process Inventory**
	115.15 **Raw Materials Inventory**
120	Prepaid Expenses
130	Office Equipment and Furniture
135	Accumulated Depreciation
200	Accounts Payable
205	Sales Tax Payable
210	Notes Payable
220	Mortgage Payable
230	Accrued Expenses
300	Retained Earnings (If the company is not incorporated, Retained Earnings and Capital Stock will be replaced with Owner's Equity.)

310	Capital Stock
500	Revenues
600	**Cost of Goods Manufactured**
710	Rent Expense
720	Utilities Expense
730	Payroll Expenses
740	Supplies
750	Depreciation Expense
760	Insurance Expense
770	Bad Debts Expense
780	Postage Expense
790	Misc. Expense
800	Other Income

COMPUTERIZED ACCOUNTING

Once you understand the basics of accounting, you need to know a little about computer hardware and software. I personally feel that it is almost impossible to run a business nowadays without a computer.

There are a lot of accounting packages on the market. In this author's opinion, the best three are QuickBooks, Peachtree Accounting, and Simply Accounting. I personally use QuickBooks.

As with any major purchase, you have to do your homework. There are a number of things to consider in buying your first computerized accounting system.

BUYING YOUR ACCOUNTING SOFTWARE PACKAGE

How Much Am I Willing To Spend On A Computer And Accounting Software?

This is not an easy one to answer. You computer can perform a lot more tasks than accounting. Here are some things that you will probably use your computer for:

- Accounting
- Spreadsheet tasks (Excel, Lotus, etc.)
- Word processing
- Creating advertising brochures and literature
- Product demonstration
- Product design
- Interface with cash register
- Internet connection
- Many other uses

How Much Will It Cost For Support?

Many accounting software suppliers offer telephone support programs, at least during the initial setup and the initial use of the software. Then again, some companies charge for support. Find out before you buy if the software is supported, if the support costs anything, and how good the support is that is being offered. This can be found out on the Internet, and sometimes you can find a knowledgeable sales clerk at a computer store to give you his opinion as to which one is best.

Will The Software Do Your Payroll?

If you use payroll, what will it take to keep the tax tables current? Some suppliers offer a tax update program, and if there are any changes in federal, state, or local tax laws, the necessary changes are incorporated into an update to load onto your system. If your software of choice does not keep you tax table current do you have the expertise to keep the tables and forms current? Payroll forms such as W-2s usually change frequently and this will require a software update for them to print correctly. Another item to consider , is that various states have specialized reporting requirements. Will the system print these specialized reports or will you have to do them by hand? If you have more than a couple of people on the payroll, you might want to consider an outside payroll service such as ADP. They complete all of your payroll reporting forms, which can be very complicated.

Network

If you need a network, is the software network ready right out of the box? And who will maintain your network? Of course, this will only be an issue if you have other things that you want to attach to your computer, such as another computer, and you want to make the accounting software available to that computer. Most accounting software packages offer multiple computer versions.

Passwords and Security

Also, you might want to consider the levels of password protection that are available. This is helpful in blocking employees from restricted data such as payroll or financial information. You want to be able to not only block others completely out of your accounting software package, but you also want to be able to grant limited access to select employees. As an example, you might want to give an employee access to the accounts payable module of your accounting software so that they can process vendor invoices for you, but not let them have access to the entire accounting system. You will want to be able to give or deny access in the following areas:

A. By accounting module
    a. Accounts payable
    b. Accounts receivable
    c. Payroll
    d. General ledger
    e. Cash disbursements
    f. Cash receipts
    g. Sales
    h. Reporting
B. By administrative access
    a. Company information
    b. Password administration
    c. Customer detail information
    d. Vendor detail information
C. By input/output access
    a. Viewing select modules
    b. Printing out reports from various modules
    c. Printing reports
    d. Viewing reports on screen

Inventory/Sales Issues

Make sure it will handle your inventory costing method such as last-in first-out, first-in – first-out, average costs or ther methods. You might also consider what kind of inventory tracking it performs. The latest version of Peachtree will even track by serial numbers. Will it tell you how many units of select products you sold to a specific customer last year or what that customer's previous purchase was? Even if you do not need to track inventory now, you may need to do so in the future.

Job Costing/Estimating

Do you need Job Costing and/or estimating applications?

Job Costing is used mainly in the Construction and Manufacturing Industry. It consists of assigning income and costs to specific jobs. This is helpful in determining profitability for a specific job. Will the software give you the reports you need? Estimating will enable you to give clients/customers estimates and retain these estimates to measure them against actual costs.

Depreciation

Depreciation is an income tax deduction that enables you to recover the cost or other basis of certain property. It is an allowance for the wear and tear, deterioration, or obsolescence of a property.

Be sure the system will calculate depreciation for income tax purposes and for financial reporting purposes and will be able to reconcile the two different calculations. The system should give you a depreciation schedule that will track each individual piece of equipment being depreciated.

Audit Trail

Do you need an audit trail? This function tracks all the changes made by user. This is helpful when you need to determine who made what entry and establish a paper trail. This is an important function. You will inevitably enter a transaction in your system and forget how or why you did it. A good audit trail will enable you to easily track down why you entered the transaction into your accounting system.

Specialized Software

Many industries have the need for specialized software. As an example to be competitive you would want to purchase specialized loan orgination software.

BUYING YOUR ACCOUNTING COMPUTER

Minimum Requirements

Most software packages have minimum requirements for the software to run properly. As an example, Microsoft Vista (they have recently stopped supporting Window XP and Windows 7) has the following minimum system requirements for its home edition:

- 2 GHz 32-bit processor
- 2 GB of system memory
- 200 GB hard drive (one terabyte of memory is now very inexpensive)
- Support for Direct X graphics and 32 MB of graphics memory
- DVD-ROM drive
- Audio output
- Internet access (high speed)

You can now buy computers that have memory in the 200 gigabyte range for under $1,500. I suggest that you don't buy a system that meets the minimum requirements of your software but instead buy the most robust computer you can afford. You will want to do this so that your computer system can last and service your needs for at least 3 years. You will probably want to buy a computer that has a terabyte of memory.

Operating System

An operating system makes your hardware components communicate with each other. There are several different operating systems out there. The most common are Microsoft Windows and Apple. Be careful when selecting an operating system, as all the programs you buy must be compatible with your operating system. By far, Microsoft Windows has the greatest number of applications available, and about 90% of all small computer users use Microsoft operating systems. I am writing this book with Windows Vista.

Hard Drive

A hard drive is a physical component of your computer (hardware). Hard drives have come a long way in the last few years. I can remember when a 200 MB (megabyte) drive was considered huge. Currently, it is the norm. By the way, a gigabyte is a 1,000 megabytes. This is an adequate amount of storage, but memory has become a commodity and thus relatively cheap; hence, buy more than you need now and you will find that you end up using it later. As mentioned above you will probably want to buy a terabyte of memory.

RAM

RAM stands for Random Access Memory. This is temporary memory that is lost when you turn your computer off. This feature helps speed the computer up by enabling it to temporarily put things in memory. If you buy a system today, it will most likely come with a minimum of 2 GB or 4 GB. Pay a few bucks extra and get the 4 GB with an upgrade path to more RAM.

Processor

Processors come in a variety of speeds, and it seems like there is a faster one out every other month. Talk to a computer professional to determine your needs. I personally prefer Intel's Core i7 processor, Extreme edition. Always for the latest processor..

Monitor

The monitor is the piece of hardware that looks like a TV screen. All are now flat screen. Monitors come in sizes from 15" on up. The actual viewing space is slightly smaller. . Look at the monitor before you buy it because you will be spending a lot of time in front of it. These screens typically have a life of 60,000 hours, which is almost seven years of 24/7 usage.

Cd-Rom, Cd-Rw, Or Dvd-Rom

CD ROMs are available in different speeds. They all work alike; some are just a little faster. A CD-RW will also "write" to writeable CDs. These are just starting to become affordable, and they are great for backing up your company's data. A DVD-ROM is mainly for watching movies, but can be used as an additional CD-ROM. Many computers are now coming with DVD players and burners on them. These are useful because they can hold up to 4.7 GB of information where CDs can only hold up to 700 MB of information.

Modem

Modems are the little devices that connect your computer to the Internet (or another modem). If you have a slow connection, have your DSL or cable line checked to see what the fastest transmission speed is. You will not want to have anything less than a DSL-speed connection for your business, even if you run your business from your home. DSL or cable hookup is a basic requirement to running your business.

Software Included?

Be sure to ask what software is included with the system. It essential to have at least a word processing software package, such as MS-Word, and a spreadsheet software package, such as Excel, included with the package.

Computer Support

Computer building is a highly competitive industry. People go out of business every day. Buy your computer from a business that will still be there if you need warranty work. After all, a warranty is only as good as the company behind it. Check around before buying. This author has found that the support offered by Dell Computer is the most reliable. The support that you get from your computer manufacturer is as important as the computer itself. I personally would never buy an off-brand computer, because the support would also be off-brand.

Networking

Networking is hooking two or more computers together. If you plan on doing this go wireless. It is fast and easy and almost anyone can set up a wireless network system. You may also need a multiuser version of the software. For a small network, you can use the Microsoft home network software built into their Microsoft office package. Most people will be able to set this up with a little phone support from Microsoft.

Anti-Virus software

There are people out there that have nothing better to do with their time than devise ways to harm other people's computers.

This makes anti-virus software a must. I personally use Norton Internet Security, which, in addition to anti-virus software, includes a firewall to help prevent people from "hacking" into your system. If you don't buy any other software, buy anti-virus software. There are some really good free anti-virus softwares available also. Try AVG free anti-virus software.

Spyware and Pop-up Ads

Spyware is loaded onto your computer without your knowledge. It is sometimes used to monitor your surfing on the Web. Spybot and Ad-aware are two common programs used to reduce this threat.

Battery Backup

A battery backup will protect your computer during electrical outages and spikes in electricity. Most will give you several minutes to save your work and shut down your computer without incoming electricity. They will also protect your modem from lightning strikes. This is a cheap piece of insurance; get one.

Software Backup

No matter which program you decide on, you will need to back up your company's books on a frequent basis. You can use floppies, CDs, a tape backup system, an external hard drive or an offsite backup service. I use Carbonite that always backs up in the background to their offsite servers. The service is less than $100 and your system is always backed up. The other options are too time consuming. An external terabyte hard drive can be purchased for about $100. You should also make sure that this hard drive will be located in a physically different location in the event of fire or other natural disaster.

OPERATIONS REPORTING AND FINANCIAL ANALYSIS ━━━━━━━━━━

Once you have an understanding and appreciation of bookkeeping and accounting, you can increase the utility of your accounting system and records by performing operational reporting that is based on your accounting information. You should perform analysis of your business at the end of each month, after generating your monthly financial statements. When performing the analysis below, you should always compare your analysis internally to prior periods of analysis, which will give you a trend. Also, there are various sources for comparing your analysis to businesses similar to yours.

LIQUIDITY

Financial ratios in this category measure the company's capacity to pay its debts as they come due.

Current Ratio

Definition: The ratio between all current assets and all current liabilities—another way of expressing liquidity.
Formula: Current Assets/Current Liabilities
Analysis: 1:1 current ratio means the company has $1.00 in current assets to cover

each $1.00 in current liabilities. Look for a current ratio above 1:1 and as close to 2:1 as possible.

One problem with the current ratio is that it ignores timing of cash received and paid out. For example, if all the bills are due this week, and inventory is the only current asset but won't be sold until the end of the month, the current ratio tells very little about the company's ability to survive.

Quick Ratio

Definition: The ratio between all assets quickly convertible into cash and all current liabilities. Specifically excludes inventory.

Formula: (Cash + Accounts Receivable)/ Current Liabilities

Analysis: Indicates the extent to which you could pay current liabilities without relying on the sale of inventory—how quickly you can pay your bills. Generally, a ratio of 1:1 is good and indicates you don't have to rely on the sale of inventory to pay the bills. Although, a little better than the Current ratio, the Quick ratio still ignores timing of receipts and payments.

SAFETY

Indicator of the business's vulnerability to risk. These ratios are often used by creditors to determine the ability of the business to repay loans.

Debt to Equity

Definition: Shows the ratio between capital invested by the owners and the funds provided by lenders.

Formula: Debt/ Equity

Analysis: Comparison of how much of the business was financed through debt and how much was financed through equity. For this calculation, it is common practice to include loans from owners in equity rather than in debt.

The higher the ratio, the greater the risk to a present or future creditor.

Look for a debt to equity ratio in the range of 1:1 to 4:1.

Most lenders have credit guidelines and limits for the debt to equity ratio (2:1 is a commonly used limit for small business loans).

Too much debt can put your business at risk...but too little debt may mean you are not realizing the full potential of your business—and may actually hurt your overall profitability. This is particularly true for larger companies where shareholders want a higher reward (dividend rate) than lenders (interest rate). If you think that you might be in this situation, talk to your accountant or financial advisor.

Debt coverage ratio

Definition: Indicates how well your cash flow covers debt and the capacity of the business to take on additional debt.

Formula: (Net Profit + Noncash expenses)/Debt

Analysis: Shows how much of your cash profits are available to repay debt.

Lenders look at this ratio to determine if there is adequate cash to make loan payments.

Most lenders also have limits for the debt coverage ratio.

Break-even Analysis

The point at which the revenues for your business equal the expenses.
Formula:

$$\text{Break-even point in units} = \frac{\text{Fixed Expenses}}{\text{Contribution margin per unit} \atop \text{(unit sale price - variable expenses per unit)}}$$

$$\text{Break-even point in sales} = \frac{\text{Fixed Expenses}}{1 - \dfrac{\text{Contribution margin per unit}}{\text{Selling price per unit}}}$$

This break-even formula determines how many units the firm must produce and sell to pay for fixed expenses. It subtracts the variable expense per unit from the sales income for each unit. The difference per unit is then applied to fixed expenses. The break-even quantity is the number of units that must be sold to cover expenses.

Example:

The Successful Company sells decal-decorated tee-shirts to its customers for $10.00 each. The shirts cost $4.00 each, and the decal costs $.40. The store pays a $.60 commission to the salesperson. The total variable cost is $5.00. The total of the fixed costs is $1,500 a month.

Using the Formula for Computing Production Needs, we find that dividing the monthly fixed cost of $1,500 by $5 gives a break-even point of 300 shirts per month. If we sell 300 shirts at $10 each, we generate $3,000. Our variable costs total $5 per shirt or $1,500. Adding the fixed cost of $1,500 to variable costs of $1,500 equals $3,000.

$$\text{Break-even point} = \frac{\$1,500}{\$10 - \$5} = 300 \text{ shirt}$$

Analysis:

Break-even analysis pinpoints where revenue equals total costs. To calculate your break-even point, take your most current income statement and identify each cost as either fixed or variable. Fixed costs are independent of sales level, while variable costs rise and fall with sales. Mixed costs involve elements of both. Most costs will fall readily into fixed or variable. For those that don't, allocate 50% to fixed costs and 50% to variable.

Fixed Expenses:	Variable Expenses:
Salaries	Sales commissions
Office expenses	Taxes
Payroll tax	Sales tax
Benefits	Boxes, paper, etc.
Utilities	Travel and entertainment
Rent	Freight
Licenses and fees	Overtime
Operating supplies	Bad debts
Insurance	Cost of goods sold
Advertising	Car/delivery
Legal and accounting	Postage
Depreciation	
Interest	
Maintenance and cleaning	
Dues and publications	

PROFITABILITY ━━━━━━━━━━━━━━━━━━━━━━━━━━━━━━

The ratios in this section measure the ability of the business to make a profit.

Sales Growth

Definition: Percentage increase (or decrease) in sales between two time periods.

Formula: (Current Year's sales - Last Year's sales)/Last Year's sales

Note: Substitute sales for a month or quarter for a shorter-term trend.

Analysis: Look for a steady increase in sales.

If overall costs and inflation are on the rise, you should watch for a related increase in your sales...if not, this is an indicator that your Prices are not keeping up with your Costs.

COGS to Sales

Definition: Percentage of sales used to pay for expenses that vary directly with sales.

Formula: Cost of Goods Sold/ Sales

Analysis: Look for a stable ratio as an indicator that the company is controlling its gross margins.

Gross Profit Margin

Definition: Indicator of how much profit is earned on your products without consideration of selling and administration costs.

Formula: Gross Profit/Total Sales

Gross Profit = Sales less Cost of Goods Sold

Analysis: Compare to other businesses in the same industry to see if your business is operating as profitably as it should be.

Look at the trend from month to month. Is it staying the same? Improving? Deteriorating?

Is there enough gross profit in the business to cover your operating costs?

Is there a positive gross margin on all your products?

SG&A to Sales

Definition: Percentage of selling, general, and administrative costs to sales.

Formula: (Selling, General & Administrative Expenses)/ Sales

Analysis: Look for a steady or decreasing percentage indicating that the company is controlling its overhead expenses.

Net Profit Margin

Definition: Shows how much profit comes from every dollar of sales.

Formula: Net Profit/Total Sales

Analysis: Compare to other businesses in the same industry to see if your business is operating as profitably as it should be.

Look at the trend from month to month. Is it staying the same? Improving? Deteriorating?

Are you generating enough sales to leave an acceptable profit?

Trend from month to month can show how well you are managing your operating or overhead costs.

Return on Equity

Definition: Determines the rate of return on your investment in the business. As an owner or shareholder, this is one of the most important ratios, as it shows the hard fact about the business—are you making enough of a profit to compensate you for the risk of being in business?

Formula: Net Profit/ Equity

Analysis: Compare the return on equity to other investment alternatives, such as a savings account, stock, or bond.

Compare your ratio to other businesses in the same or a similar industry.

Return on Assets

Definition: Considered a measure of how effectively assets are used to generate a return. (This ratio is not very useful for most businesses.)

Formula: Net Profit/ Total Assets

Analysis: ROA shows the amount of income for every dollar tied up in assets.

Year–to-year trends may be an indicator...but watch out for changes in the total asset figure as you depreciate your assets (a decrease or increase in the denominator can affect the ratio and doesn't necessarily mean the business is improving or declining).

EFFICIENCY

Also called *Asset Management ratios*. Indicator of how efficiently the company manages its assets.

Days in Receivables

Definition: This calculation shows the average number of days it takes to collect your accounts receivable (number of days of sales in receivables).

Formula: (Average Accounts Receivable)/ (Sales × 360 days)

Analysis: Look for trends that indicate a change in your customers' payment habits.

Compare the calculated days in receivables to your stated terms.

Compare to industry standards.

Review an Aging of Receivables and be familiar with your customers' payment habits; and watch for any changes that might indicate a problem.

Accounts Receivable Turnover

Definition: Number of times that trade receivables turnover during the year.

Formula: Net Sales/ Average Accounts Receivable

Analysis: The higher the turnover, the shorter the time between sales and collecting cash.

Compare to industry standards.

Days in Inventory

Definition: This calculation shows the average number of days it will take to sell your inventory.

Formula: (Average Inventory/Cost of Goods Sold) × 360 days

Analysis: Look for trends that indicate a change in your inventory levels.

Compare the calculated days in inventory to your inventory cycle. (Learn how to calculate your inventory cycle in our lesson on Using Financial Statements.)

Compare to industry standards.

Inventory Turnover

Definition: Number of times that you turn over (or sell) inventory during the year.

Formula: Cost of Goods Sold/ Average Inventory

Analysis: Generally, a high inventory turnover is an indicator of good inventory management.

But a high ratio can also mean there is a shortage of inventory.

A low turnover may indicate overstocking or obsolete inventory.

Compare to industry standards.

Sales to Total Assets

Definition: Indicates how efficiently your business generates sales on each dollar of assets.

Formula: Sales/ Total Assets

Analysis: A volume indicator that can be used to measure efficiency of your business from year to year.

Days in Accounts Payable

Definition: This calculation shows the average length of time your trade payables are outstanding before they are paid.

Formula: (Average Accounts Payable/ COGS) × 360 days

Analysis: Look for trends that indicate a change in your payment habits.

Compare the calculated days in payables to the terms offered by your suppliers.

Compare to industry standards.

Review an Aging of Payables and be familiar with the terms offered by your suppliers.

Accounts Payable Turnover

Definition: The number of times trade payables turn over during the year.

Formula: COGS/ Average Accounts Payable

Analysis: The higher the turnover, the shorter the time between purchase and payment.

A low turnover may indicate that there is a shortage of cash to pay your bills or some other reason for a delay in payment.

Creative Thinking In Business

WHAT IS CREATIVE THINKING?

Some people like to refer to it as "thinking outside the box." The "box" represents the barriers that have been put up to creative thinking by our modern education systems. Modern education does not promote creative thinking. It promotes learning by memorization. Most modern businesses do not promote creative thinking. A creative thinker in a large company is often thought of as a renegade, a troublemaker. One of my favorite sayings is "Do what you have always done, and you will always get what you always got." While keeping your goal in mind, as well as framing all of your thoughts and decisions using Godly principles, always be willing to try new ideas. Let's see how creative thinking can benefit your goal of starting and running a business:

Deciding what type of business you want to start
Deciding what to name your business
Deciding what products or services to include in your business
Finding finances for your new business venture
Examining various growth opportunities
Where to locate your business
When and how to expand your products and services
Dealing with competitive situations
Creative solutions when needed resources are in short supply
Growing your business

One of the goals of this section is to help you become an idea machine. Not all of your ideas will be good or even executable. I think we can agree that the more ideas you can generate, the better your odds are that one or more of them will be on target to meet your needs. The bottom line here is to learn to go for a quantity of ideas at first and then filter through them, looking for the nuggets.

One of the greatest authors on the subject of creative thinking is Edward de Bono. One of his most famous books is entitled *Lateral Thinking, Creativity Step by Step*. In his book, he explores what he calls "lateral thinking."

> Lateral thinking is closely related to insight, creativity and humor. All four processes have the same basis. But whereas insight, creativity and humor can only be prayed for, lateral thinking is a more deliberate process. It is as definite a way of using the mind as logical thinking— but a very different way… Lateral thinking is quite distinct from vertical thinking, which is the traditional type of thinking. In vertical thinking, one moves forward by sequential steps, each of which must be justified. … In lateral thinking, one may deliberately seek out irrelevant information; in vertical thinking one selects out only what is relevant.[25]

It is this author's belief that lateral thinking is casting a wider net and considering ideas that are not directly related to the objective at hand on the path to generating viable ideas. As de Bono goes on to say, "Lateral thinking is generative. Vertical thinking is selective." We need both types of thinking to develop our pool of ideas.

THE SECRET WEAPON(S) OF SMALL BUSINESSES

Big businesses have a number of major advantages over small businesses in the competitive market place. They can throw more money, people, and equipment at problems and opportunities. One area in which small businesses have the distinct upper hand is in the area of creative idea generation. Most progressive big businesses realize this fact. Mattel Toys, Inc. has over 600 design engineers, yet they get over 60% of their new ideas from small inventor companies, most often with less than 5 employees. Your other secret weapon is starting your day off with prayer and time with the Lord. If you start each and every day in prayer, you can put yourself in a "winner's" zone or state of mind, enabling you to conduct your daily business to the best of your ability.

25   Edward de Bono, *Lateral Thinking, Creativity Step by Step*, New York: Harper and Row, pgs. 9 & 12, 1990.

Creativeness often gets stifled in large businesses for the following reasons:

1. A "not made here" attitude in the executive management ranks.
2. A new product idea rather than a mere improvement to an existing product threatens small internal empires built around existing products, product lines, and services.
3. For ideas to "float" at a large company, they require deployment of resources (e.g., Time, Talent, and Treasures), or they are not considered important. And sometimes it's nearly impossible to get resources redeployed from existing products/ product lines and redeployed into a new idea.
4. The approval process. Really good ideas in large companies often die in the approval chain. The more steps involved in the approval process, the greater the chance that somewhere along the line, someone will say no.
5. If someone in a large company comes up with a new idea that is "outside the box," he is viewed as someone who doesn't play within corporate guidelines, isn't a team player, or doesn't understand the "company way" of doing things.
6. The old "but it has always been done this way" syndrome.
7. Paperwork, paperwork, and more paperwork.
8. Some really successful companies rely heavily on creative thinking by smaller companies and individuals.
9. It's often risky to introduce a new idea to a company. If it works, an executive, higher up, will take credit for it. If it doesn't work, the person who actually brings it up will definitely get all the credit for it. With this being said, it is often safer in a big company to hold back your creativity.

Creative thinking is a useful skill in deciding what business to start, deciding what product to sell, developing new products, enhancing existing products, finding new channels of distribution, and just plain staying ahead of the competition.

HOW TO THINK CREATIVELY

Many people don't believe that they have the ability to think creatively. I believe that if a person can do two things at the same time, like walk and chew bubble gum, they can think creatively. Christians have a major advantage over nonbelievers when it comes to creative thinking. Remember the verse in Hebrews:

"Faith is being sure of what we hope for and certain of what we do not see." Hebrews 11:1

Having faith in God and Jesus puts Christians way out in the lead when it comes to creative thinking as we KNOW there is a GOD and we KNOW that Jesus died for our sins. This is helpful in the creative thinking process, because we know how to exercise our faith and we can utilize it daily in our lives.

If you are reading this book, you can think creatively.

A consultant named Robert Alan Black, PhD, has written a book about creative thinking in which he presents an interesting list of attributes of the typical creatively thinking person. Look at the list. Don't be concerned if you do not have all or even most of the attributes. The list will hopefully inspire you to explore what being a creative thinker is all about.

His book is called "BROKEN CRAYONS and the act of BREAKING CRAYONS." In his book, Alan Black asks, "Are you a crayon breaker?"

1. Sensitive

Being sensitive helps creativeness in many ways:
- It helps with awareness of problems, known & unknown.
- It helps people sense things easier.
- It helps to cause people to care and commit themselves to challenges or causes.

2. Not Motivated by Money

As important as money is in most societies or economies, it is not a driving force for a creative person. Generally, they have an intuitive sense of the amount of money they basically need, and once that need is fulfilled, money stops affecting or driving them.

3. Sense of Destiny

Intuitively, creative people know that they have a purpose, a destiny, or they realize that they can choose or create one to drive them to reach greater heights of skill, ability, or talent.

4. Adaptable

Without the ability to adapt, people could not be creative. But rather than adapt to something, they choose to adapt things to suit themselves, their needs, or the goals they are striving towards.

5. Tolerant of Ambiguity

Two or more things or ideas being right at the same time challenges the thinking of a creative person. They love to be ambiguous to challenge other people and ideas. Ambiguity helps them see things from many different perspectives all at the same time.

6. Observant

Creative people constantly are using their senses: consciously, subconsciously, and unconsciously, even non-consciously.

7. Perceive World Differently

Thoreau talked about some people hearing a different drummer. Creative people thrive on multiple ways of perceiving: seeing, hearing, touching, smelling, tasting, and sensing things. These different perspectives open up their minds to unlimited possibilities.

8. See Possibilities

Average people, people who don't believe they are creative, people who are fearful or resistant to creativeness or creative thinking, prefer to work within limits with limited possibilities. Creative people love to see many, even infinite possibilities, in most situations or challenges.

9. Question Asker

Creative people, especially highly creative types, probably came out of their mother's womb asking questions. It's in their nature to question. Question, yes, not actually criticize. Their questioning nature often mistakenly appears as criticism when it is simply questioning, exploring, examining, or playing with things as they are or might be.

10. Can Synthesize Correctly, Often Intuitively

This is the ability to see the whole picture, see patterns, and grasp solutions with only a few pieces, even with major pieces missing. Creative people trust their intuition, even if it isn't right 100% of the time.

11. Able to Fanaticize

Stop looking out the window, Billy. Susie, pay attention. Teachers, parents, and even friends often tell creative people this. Highly creative people love to wander through their own imaginary worlds. This is one of the major themes of the very popular cartoon strip Calvin and Hobbes. Both Calvin and Hobbes (Calvin's alter ego?) are perpetual CRAYON BREAKERS.

12. Flexible

Creative people are very flexible when they are playing with ideas. They love to look at things from multiple points of view and to produce piles of answers, "maybes" and "almosts" when other people are content with one answer or solution.

13. Fluent

It could be a doorstop, a boat anchor, a weapon, a prop, a weight for holding down papers, etc., etc., etc. This is what a creative person would say about the possible uses of a brick.

14. Imaginative

Creative people love to use their imagination to play, to make seem real, to experiment.

15. Intuitive

The more creative a person is, the more they tap their intuition skills; the abilities to see answers with minimum facts, to sense problems even when they aren't happening.

16. Original

Being original is a driving force for creative people. They thrive on it.

17. Ingenious

Doing the unusual, solving unsolvable problems. Thinking what has never been thought of before. These are all the "ingenious" traits of a creative person.

18. Energetic

Challenges, problems, new ideas, once committed to by a creative person truly excite them and provide them with seemingly unlimited amounts of energy;

imagine Sherlock Holmes in action once he's grasped a sense of the mystery.

19. Sense of Humor

Laughter and creativity truly go together. Many experts believe that creativity can't occur without a touch of humor. They believe that seriousness tends to squelch creativeness or creative thinking.

20. Self-actualizing

The psychologist Abraham Maslow created this term in the 1960s, representing the ultimate motivator of people: the need or desire to become all you can be, to become what you were meant to be.

21. Self-disciplined

This is one trait that appears to be ambiguous in highly creative people. They can appear disorganized, chaotic at times, while at the same time, they are highly self-disciplined. At the same time, they greatly resist the discipline of other people who are not of like creative mind.

22. Self-knowledgeable

During my life, I have read biographies and biographic sketches of over 4,000 people, mostly considered to be the highest of the highly creative in their respective fields. One of the few things they had in common is that they all kept some form of journal and were constantly striving to better understand themselves.

23. Specific interests

This is still another ambiguous trait of creative people. They appear on the surface to be interested in everything, while at the same time they have very specific interests that they commit their true energies and efforts to. By being willing to be exposed to seemingly unlimited interests, they discover more about their particular specific interests.

24. Divergent Thinker

Creative people love to diverge from the norm, to look at things from multiple positions, to challenge anything that exists. Because of this, they are seen at times to be off-key, deviant, atypical, irregular, or uncharacteristic.

25. Curious

Like the Cheshire Cat of Alice in Wonderland, creative people are continuously curious, often childlike.

26. Open-ended

In order to explore many possibilities, creative people tend to stay open-ended about answers or solutions until many answers or solutions have been produced.

27. Independent

Creative people crave and require a high degree of independence, resist dependence, but often can thrive on beneficial interdependence.

28. Severely Critical

Yes, creative people challenge almost everything, every idea, every rule. They challenge, challenge, and challenge some more, to the point that their challenging appears to most people as severe criticism

29. Nonconforming

Conforming is the antithesis, the opposite of creativeness, and in order to be creative, creative people must be nonconforming and go against the norm, swim upstream.

30. Confident

This is another ambiguous trait in creative people. When they are at their most creative, they are extremely confident. When they are in a stage of frustration, when nothing seems to be working, they often lack confidence. After much positive experience, they begin to trust themselves and know that they will become depressed, frustrated, nearly devastated, but their internal subconscious confidence keeps them moving, or at least floating, until they experience or discover an Aha! (a breakthrough idea or piece of information).

31. Risk Taker

This trait is generally misunderstood by many non-creative people or people who fear true creativity. Highly creative people are not really risk takers because they do not see what they are doing as a risk. They simply see it as a possible solution or path towards a solution. They have other possible solutions, often many others, in their head or in their notes if a particular idea or solution does not work. As Thomas Edison once said when asked how it felt to have failed nearly 7,000 times trying to discover the best filament for an incandescent light bulb, "those are not failures, they are solutions to problems I haven't started working on yet."

32. Persistent

Charles Goodyear (discoverer and inventor of vulcanized rubber) and Chester Carlson (inventor of electrostatic copying, the Xerox process: xerography) are two of the best examples of this trait in creative people. Both of them worked over 30 years before finding the solution they were looking for. Creative people do not give up on things that mean a lot to them.

This list of creative-person attributes is included in this book with complete permission of Robert Alan Black, PhD, CSP, reprinted from his internationally noted book, *BROKEN CRAYONS: Break Your Crayons and Draw Outside the Lines*, available on his Web site: http://www.cre8ng.com or in print directly from his publishing company Cre8ng Places Press. It also can be acquired from Amazon.com.

CREATIVE THINKING SYSTEM

I believe, and many authors who have written on the subject of creative thinking will agree with me, that creative thinking can be systematized. At first glance, the term "creative thinking system" may seem like an oxymoron, but it is not.

The goal of a creative thinking system is to serve as a foundation for starting the creative thinking process and organizing your thought process and ideas into usable tools. There are no real rules to the creative thinking system. So, if you can think of a better way to do something we discuss, by all means do it your way. Anything that will get your creative juices flowing and then capture the results of the process is a good thing (again, as long as it is legal and Godly).

I like the way idea expert James Webb Young described idea generation way back in 1960:

> The production of ideas is just as definite a process as the production of Fords; that the production of ideas, too, runs on a assembly line; that throughout this production, the mind follows an operative technique

which can be learned and controlled; and that its effective use is just as much a matter of practice in the technique as is the effective use of any tool. [26]

As stated earlier, we are suggesting a system that can be molded and modified to your own use. The process should evolve as you use it and become as useful as possible. Do not let the process, the definitions, and the techniques become a box to bury your ideas in. Remain flexible and open to new and useful ideas.

The systematic approach to creative thinking includes methods for generating ideas and then massaging them into new, meaningful ideas. A quick example might help here. There is a toy company that sells spy toys for kids. They approached our company and asked us if we had any ideas for spy toys. We looked at their product line and listed all the attributes of their toys. Some of these attributes were:

Toys for listening to faraway conversations

Toys for writing secret notes that can only be read by the recipient

Toys that can detect someone entering the room.

We then starting listing all of the things spies do in all of the spy movies we had seen. This was a long list, as we had seen a lot of spy movies over the years. Then we listed the toys we played with over the years. Keep in mind that since we are talking about toys, the prices of the product ideas have to be low. During our brainstorming session, someone said all junior spies need cameras. They, of course, already had a spy camera in their product line. Then, one of the brainstorm participants reminded us of the periscopes that we used to play with 40 years ago. It was a long box with two mirrors inside at 45 degree angles that enabled kids to peek over fences and around corners. What if we put a camera on a stick that enabled a junior spy to look around corners and take pictures of what they saw? Bingo—they liked the idea.

According to Donna Greiner in her great little book entitled *The Basics of Idea Generation*,[27] we are most often called on to apply our creativity in the following situations:

- Enhancements to existing products and services.
- Breakthrough thinking that leads to new and better products and services.

26   James Webb Young, *A Technique for Producing Ideas,* Chicago: Advertising Publications, Inc., pg. 14, 1940 (A more current edition is available from The McGraw – Hill Companies, Inc.).
27   Donna Greiner, *The Basics of Idea Generation,* New York: Quality Resources, 1997, pg. X.

- Solutions to problems, conflicts, and other difficulties as they arise.
- Strategies for overall betterment of our companies, products, and services.

We want to systematize as much of the creative process as possible without putting ourselves into a box for the following reasons:

- Allows as much time as possible for the truly creative process—the efficient use of our most limited resource—time.
- Generates many more creative ideas.
- Captures the results of the creative process in an efficient manner.
- Filters these creative ideas to get to the ones with true potential.
- Massages the results of the creative process into meaningful solutions, products, and services.

Creative thinking can apply to all areas of your life, from raising kids to planting spring tomatoes.

Here are the simple steps to the creative thinking system I like to refer to as WRITE:

1. (W) Write down your objective, opportunity, or problem
2. (R) Resources—gather relevant resources
3. (I) Idea generation
4. (T) Tailor your list of ideas to meet your needs
5. (E) Energize your short list of ideas

Some of the tools that we will discuss will be usable in one or more of the five listed steps.

WRITE DOWN YOUR OBJECTIVE

If you are already in business and things are going well, you might say that you do not have a problem. This may be true, but you will always have some business objective to be met or some opportunity to make your business better. The first step of the creative thinking system is committing your problem to writing. By "problem," I mean opportunity, goal, objective, desire, need, or whatever end result you are trying to achieve. For the rest of this discussion, I will call the end result we are looking for our "objective."

There is a saying "If you don't know where you are going, how do you expect to get there?" Likewise, if you can't articulate your end goal (objective) for creative thinking, there is little chance that you will obtain your goal. Writing it down in a concise format enables you to have it set in your mind's eye. I personally keep a Palm organizer for my daily tasks, appointments, and contacts. I have a special Task category called "Creative Thinking." Whenever I get a creative thought, I immediately write it down in my Palm Task list. Your objective should be as concise as possible, not more than two to three sentences. With more than two or three sentences, and you will start limiting your potential solutions and put yourself in a box. Don't limit your potential solutions at this stage of the process. You will filter or tailor your list of possible solutions later on in the creative thinking process.

In generating your objective statement, think about the following:

1. Why?
2. What?
3. Where?
4. When?

An important part of this step is the belief that your question has an answer.

It seems that one of the most important components of creative thinking is the conviction that there is an answer to your problem. If you know what you are trying to achieve, whether it is understanding the structure of subatomic particles or finding a way to restore your failing sales figures, you need to believe that it is possible. This seems to fire the creative process. Henry Ford said, "Whether you believe you can, or whether you believe you can't, you're absolutely right."[28] This also applies to you, the budding entrepreneur, considering starting a business.

Sometimes creative thinking about a particular subject or issue will generate unrelated ideas that can lead to unanticipated benefits. I collect these random thoughts for later development. It's important to keep an idea journal. Some people collect their random ideas in their Day-Timer along with their appointments, and some people have a separate journal to collect their random ideas. Whatever technique works for you, use it.

The important point is to collect your random ideas when they happen. They will not always occur at the most opportune time, so be ready to write them down whenever they occur. The famous philosopher Archimedes, according to legend, was bathing when he

---

28   Rose Jay, *The Ultimate book of Business Creativity*, Oxford, United Kingdom:Capstone, pg. 5, 2000.

thought of a way to compute the proportion of gold in King Heron's crown by observing how much water flowed over the bathing stool. He leapt up as one possessed, crying "Eureka!" After repeating this several times, he went running down the street naked yelling, "Eureka!" If he had kept a notebook by his bathtub, he might have saved himself considerable embarrassment.

I keep a small, bound journal by my bed, in my car, in my gym locker, at the office in my top desk drawer, in my garage workshop, and in the kitchen. Someone once asked me why I didn't just keep one journal with me at all times. Well, for one thing, I could not find a pocket protector big enough to fit my journal, and I could not find one that was waterproof. Periodically, I transfer the recorded thoughts to my Palm and cross off the listings in my various journals. I do this because I sync my Palm to my Microsoft Outlook on my desktop every day. This means that I have a copy of my random thoughts on my desktop, in my Palm Organizer, and in my various journals. This might give you an idea of how valuable I feel these random ideas are. Here is what I record every time I am lucky enough to have one of these random ideas flow into my mind:

1. The idea in a couple of sentences
2. A drawing of the idea if appropriate
3. What I was doing when the thought flowed into my mind
4. The date of the idea
5. Possible applications for the idea.

Microsoft is worth a lot of money at today's stock prices. The idea on which Microsoft is founded is priceless.

Let's use creative thinking to help decide what business you want to start, assuming that you only know that you want to be in business for yourself and that you don't yet know what type of business it might be. Remember that all of the techniques we discuss here can also be used if you already have a business. Most of you probably know what type of business you would like to start and can skip this next section. Answering the why, what, where, and when questions below could possibly result in the following objective answers:

1. Why?
    a. To control my own destiny

    b. To be able to participate more in the raising of my young children

    c. To utilize all of my learned skills

    d. Work hours that accommodate my chosen lifestyle

2. What?
   a. Interested in inventing
   b. Interested in science
   c. Want to have a business that is oriented to kids

3. Where?
   a. I want to work from my home
   b. I want to be able to take advantage of a worldwide market

4. When?
   a. I want to start my business as soon as possible
   b. I want to be able to make money while I am asleep

Be careful not to put yourself in a box. Take your objective statement and subject it to a reality check called a situation analysis. This type of analysis will save you some heart-ache later on by helping keep the objective statement real. A situation analysis will consist of two parts:

1. Review of the external environment (often called the P.E.S.T. Analysis).
2. Review of the internal strengths, weaknesses, opportunities, and threats (often called a S.W.O.T. review).

Big companies use this type of situation analysis to formulate their strategic plan and to do a periodic checkup on the direction of their business. As with many of the tools in our discussion of creative thinking, situation analysis can be used during some of the other stages of the creative thinking process.

P.E.S.T. ANALYSIS (REVIEW OF THE EXTERNAL ENVIRONMENT)

A P.E.S.T. is an analysis of the external environment that affects all companies.

P.E.S.T. is an acronym for the Political, Economic, Social, and Technological factors of the external environment. Such external factors normally are beyond the company's control and are often perceived as threats. For those of you who look at most situations as a glass half full as opposed to a glass half empty, you might want to change the acronym to S.T.E.P.

Political/ Law Analysis

- Risk of military invasion
- Risk of terrorism
- Laws regarding contracts
- Labor laws—minimum wage and overtime
- Corporate laws
- Local, State, and Federal income tax laws and tax incentives
- Product labeling requirements
- Domestic and Foreign Trade regulations and tariffs
- Free trade zones
- Local government economic incentives
- Work week
- Political stability
- Intellectual property protection laws
- Antitrust laws
- Pricing regulations
- Industrial safety regulations
- Mandatory employee benefits
- Monopolistic protections (some industries such as garbage collection allow monopolistic practices)
- Hazardous materials laws
- Zoning laws
- Sales tax laws
- Laws regarding selling select items across state lines
- Gaming laws
- Environmental laws
- Discrimination laws
- City laws and ordinances
- Traffic laws
- Political party prominence in your chosen location
- Business-friendliness of your local and national media outlets

Economic Analysis

- Exchange rates
- Stability of your country's currency

- Stability of other countries' currency
- Major companies filing bankruptcy that could affect your business
- Government intervention in the free market
- Skill level of workforce
- Labor costs
- Prime rate
- Major trade agreements with foreign countries that could affect your business
- Comparative advantages of your country compared to other countries'
- Type of economic system (e.g., capitalistic, socialist, etc.)
- Local economic issues that could affect your business
- Stock market in your country and abroad
- Business cycle stage (e.g., prosperity, recession, recovery)
- Economic growth rate
- Discretionary income of your target consumers
- Unemployment rate locally and nationally
- Inflation rate
- Interest rates
- Insurance requirements

Physical Environment

- Threat of earthquakes
- Severity of the seasons
- Cost of water
- Cost of gas and electricity
- Location of business
- Traffic patterns
- Fire hazards
- Flood hazards
- DSL or high-speed connection accessibility
- Extraordinary season weather conditions such as record rainfalls and other acts of Mother Nature
- Major natural disasters
- Ability to expand your operations at your current location
- Cost of getting product from your location to other locations around the world

Social Analysis

- Demographics
- Class structure
- Education
- Culture (gender roles, etc.)
- Entrepreneurial spirit
- Attitudes (health, environmental consciousness, etc.)
- Leisure interests
- Trends in consumer interest (e.g., fashions, fads, toys, etc.)
- Psychographics
- Impact of religion in your chosen industry and at your location

Technological Analysis

- Recent technological developments
- Technology's impact on your product or service offering
- Impact of technology on cost structure of your products and/or services
- Impact of technology on value chain structure
- Rate of technological diffusion
- Acceptance of technological change in your chosen industry
- Acceptance of technology by your actual and potential customers

S.W.O.T. – REVIEW OF INTERNAL STRENGTHS, WEAKNESSES, OPPORTUNITIES, THREATS

Once you have analyzed your objective statement using the P.E.S.T. analysis, you should analyze it with a S.W.O.T. review. S.W.O.T. stands for (S) strengths, (W) weaknesses, and those external to your company that can be classified as (O) opportunities and (T) threats. The S.W.O.T. analysis is great for taking what you have, (S), (W) (internal strengths and weaknesses) and seeing how you can use them to take advantage of opportunities (O) and avoiding threats (T) in the environment in which your business exists (P.E.S.T.). See how it all fits together?

Let's look at some potential internal strengths and weaknesses:

1. A business plan backed by God (known through a prayerful relationship with God)
2. Strong support structure (e.g., wife, children, family, church, community)

3. Strong brand names
4. Cost advantages from internal knowledge
5. Favorable distribution arrangements
6. Patents, copyrights, trademarks
7. Exclusive access to raw materials
8. Exclusive access to particular artists or craftsmen
9. Great location
10. Cool company name
11. Relationships in your industry
12. Relationships in your church or synagogue
13. Relationships in your geographical area
14. First-mover advantage
15. Relationships with major retailers
16. Large cash reserves
17. Favorable credit terms with vendors
18. Exclusive license rights for a hot product or service
19. Proprietary computer systems
20. Efficient accounting and operational reporting systems
21. Low overhead
22. High margins in products that can be passed on to customers or retailers
23. An incredible product
24. An incredible service
25. Relationships with strong outside advisors (e.g., accountant, attorney) with proven track records in building businesses
26. Low employee turnover
27. A workforce that loves you

These attributes can be weaknesses if you don't have them, and strengths if you do have them. Lacking some of these attributes is not fatal to your proposed or existing business, but not being aware of your weaknesses can be fatal. It is important to know what you have and don't have.

Now that you have reviewed your objective using the P.E.S.T. analysis and looked at your internal strengths and weaknesses, let's look at your potential Opportunities and Threats.

Here are some example Opportunities and Threats that would logically come to light while doing your P.E.S.T. analysis and our Opportunities and Threats review.

- An unfulfilled customer need (e.g., no-flat inner tubes for mountain bikes)
- Major event (e.g., longest winter in history, man landing on Mars)
- New technology (new Game Boy on the market, and the public is begging for accessories)
- New governmental regulations (e.g., all bicyclist now must wear helmets)
- Removal of governmental regulations (e.g., removal of restrictions on competing with phone companies, which encouraged small Internet operators to start Voice Over IP phone services on the Internet).
- Removal of international trade barriers
- A new movie comes out creating consumer want for a product (e.g., "Big Fat Liar" caused an increase in consumer awareness for PDAs).

These opportunities can be threats if you are already in business and were caught off guard by one of these opportunities, and another company beat you to the punch. Here are some examples of threats; but remember threats can be turned into opportunities just as opportunities can become threats. Remember mom's saying, "When life hands you a lemon, make lemonade"?

- Rise in the price of gasoline (this could be really damaging for a business that relies on home delivery)
- Emergence of substitute products (e.g., email replacing a large part of snail mail [postal service deliveries])
- Super-cheap desktop computers (e.g., this one hurt desktop publishing businesses)
- "Big-box" stores going into communities and pushing out smaller retailers
- Foreign manufacturers replacing domestic manufacturers
- Shift in consumer taste away from your product or proposed product
- Major negative news about your industry or company

There is no set order to doing the P.E.S.T. analysis and the S.W.O.T. review. As you are doing the PEST analysis, you will be looking for Opportunities and Threats to your new or existing business. I will emphasize often, throughout this book, not to get caught up in formalities. All information that you gather or develop in your analysis must be R.A.T., which stands for relevant, accurate, and timely. Some people develop what I like to call "paralysis through analysis." This means that they spend so much time and so many resources gathering and generating data, that they never actually make a decision, or make it so late that they have missed the opportunity altogether. You will never have complete data in your decision-making process. What separates the real players from the "wannabes" is the ability to make decisions with the <u>best data available</u> and on a timely basis.

RESOURCE GATHERING

Once you have established and tested your objective, you need to gather as much information as possible about your objective. Keep in mind not to get "paralysis through analysis." Also, keep in mind that all of the steps in our creative thinking system are interactive. In other words, you probably had to gather some resource information before you were able to write down your objective or problem statement. Refer back to the chapter entitled STARTING YOUR OWN BUSINESS for some other resource-gathering tools. You will want to gather information to help address the questions raised during your PEST analysis and your SWOT review. The information will address the following questions:

1. The business I am in or contemplating getting into
   a. Products and/or services to offer?
   b. How are products/ services offered?
   c. Products/services pricing?
   d. Potential for growth?
   e. Resources required to get into this particular business?
   f. Resources required to stay in this particular business for a specific period of time before it becomes self-sustaining?
   g. Suppliers and distributors?
2. The competition
   a. Who are they?
   b. What are their advantages and disadvantages?
   c. How can I effectively complete against them?
      i. Price/ terms

     ii. Variety

     iii. Convenience

     iv. Quality

3. The environment
    a. Government?
    b. Geography?
    c. Demographics?
    d. Natural resources?

4. Technology
    a. Technology required for business now?
    b. Future directions of technology?
    c. How will technology affect my products/services?
    d. How will technology affect my way of doing business?

The Internet, local libraries, local junior colleges/ universities, bookstores, and even your competition are great places to gather information. When using these sources, consider finding information under the following topics:

1. Trade associations
2. Better Business Bureau
3. Governmental organizations
4. Demographics
5. Your particular business
6. Small Business Administration
7. Your competition
8. Your potential suppliers and distributors

Continuing with my example objective of "to be an inventor of children's toys working out of my home," here are some samples of the primary resources that I used for researching my objective.

Internet

I keyed in "toy associations" in my Google search engine and found the following resources:

U.S.A.	American Association of Exporters and Importers	11 W. 42nd St., New York, NY 10036 Tel: (212) 944-2230
U.S.A.	American Specialty Toy Retailers Association	206 6th Ave., Suite 900, Des Moines, IA 50309 Tel: (515) 282-8192
U.S.A.	Association of Crafts & Creative Industries	P.O. Box 3388, Zanesville, OH 43702-3388 Tel: (740) 452-4541
U.S.A.	Bicycle Manufacturers Association	3050 K St. N.W., Washington, D.C. 20007 Tel: (202) 945-6697
U.S.A.	Electronic Industries Association / (CEMA)	2500 Wilson Blvd., Arlington, VA 22201 Tel: (703),907-7600 Fax:,(703) 907-7601
U.S.A.	Hobby Industry Association	319 East 54th St., Elmwood Park, NJ 07407 Tel: (201) 794-1133
U.S.A.	Hong Kong Trade Development Council	219 East 46th St.., New York, NY 10017 Tel: (212) 838-8688
U.S.A.	International Licensing Industry Merchandisers Association	350 5th Ave., #6210, New York, NY 10118 Tel: (212) 244-1944
U.S.A.	International Mass Retail Association	1700 No. Moore St., Ste. 2250, Arlington, VA 22249 Tel: (703) 841-2300
U.S.A.	Juvenile Products Manufacturers Association	236 Route 38 West, Suite 100, Morristown, NJ 08057 Tel: (609) 231-8500

U.S.A.	Midwest Association of Toy, Hobby and Trim-A-Tree	176 Crest Rd., Glen Ellyn, IL 60137 Tel: (630) 858-9626 Fax: (630) 858-9635 E-Mail: Blink308@aol.com Attn: Jim Blankshain
U.S.A.	Miniatures Industry Association of America	P.O. Box 2188, Zanesville, OH 43702. Tel: (614) 452-4541
U.S.A.	Model Railroad Industry Association	P.O. Box 28129, Denver, CO 80228 Tel: (303) 989-6468 Fax: (303) 989-2192
U.S.A.	National Association of Miniature Enthusiasts	130 North Rangeline Road, Carmel, IN 46032 Tel: (317) 571-8094
U.S.A.	National Retail Federation	325 Seventh St. NW, Ste. 1000, Washington, D.C. 20004 Tel: (202) 783-7971
U.S.A.	National Ornaments and Electric Lights Association	236 Route 38 West, Ste. 100, Morristown, NJ 08057 Tel: (609) 231-8500
U.S.A.	Pacific Northwest Toy Association	P.O. Box 66900, Seattle, WA Tel: (206) 242-4462
U.S.A.	Radio Control Hobby Trade Association	560 Bonner Road, Wauconda, IL 60084 Tel: (708) 526-1222 Fax: (708) 526-9987
U.S.A.	Society of the Plastic Industries	1275 K Street NW, Ste. 400, Washington, D.C. 20005 Tel: (202) 371-5200
U.S.A.	Southeast Craft & Hobby Association	6175 Barfield Rd., Ste. 220, Atlanta, GA 30328 Tel: (404) 252-2454

U.S.A.	Southwestern Toy & Hobby Association	World Trade Center, POB 580310, Dallas TX 75258 Tel: (214) 748-4032
U.S.A.	Sports Cards Manufacturers Association	236 Route 38 West, Ste. 100, Morristown, NJ 08057 Tel: (609) 231-8500
U.S.A.	Toy and Game Inventors of America	5813 McCart Avenue, Fort Worth, TX 76133 Tel: (817) 292-9021
U.S.A.	The Toy Center Directory	177 Sound Beach Avenue, Old Greenwich, CT Tel: (203) 637-5466
U.S.A.	Toy Knights of America	200 Fifth Ave, New York, NY Tel: (212) 255-6926 Fax: (212) 366-5421
U.S.A.	Toy Manufacturers of America Inc. http://www.toy-tma.org	1115 Broadway, Suite 400, New York, NY Tel: (212) 675-1141 Fax: (212) 633-1429
U.S.A.	Western Toy and Hobby Representatives Association	11100 Valley Blvd., Ste. 340-20 El Monte, CA 91731 Tel: (818) 442-1635 Fax: (818) 442-2146

This was only the first resource listed under "toy associations." There was a long list of resources given in the Google search.

After keying in "toy association," I keyed in various governmental organizational entities such as:

1. California Franchise Tax Board
2. Internal Revenue Service
3. Department of Labor

You get the general idea. Gather information to help you in your search.

IDEA GENERATION ━━━━━━━━━━━━━━━━━━━━━━━━━

What is an Idea?

Here is the definition of "idea" according to my *Merriam-Webster* dictionary:
1 a : a transcendent entity that is a real pattern of which existing things are imperfect representations b : a standard of perfection : IDEAL c : a plan for action : DESIGN

2 archaic : a visible representation of a conception : a replica of a pattern

3 a obsolete : an image recalled by memory b : an indefinite or unformed conception c : an entity (as a thought, concept, sensation, or image) actually or potentially present to consciousness

4 : a formulated thought or opinion

5 : whatever is known or supposed about something *a child's idea of time*

6 : the central meaning or chief end of a particular action or situation

Idea generation is both a quantity and quality effort. The basic approach is to generate as many ideas as you can and then filter through them for ones that will work. I use *Merriam-Webster* almost on a daily basis, and I believe everyone should keep a copy with their personal library resources; but I think we need a more concise definition for "idea." Bill Backer, in his great book entitled *The Care and Feeding of Ideas*, defines ideas as follows:

> A **Basic Idea** is an abstract answer to a perceived desire or need. An **Executable Idea** is a rendering in words, symbols, sounds, colors, shapes, forms, or any combination thereof, of an abstract answer to a perceived desire or need.[29]

Now our definition of "idea" begs the definition of abstract. Going back to our friendly Merriam-Webster dictionary, we find that "abstract" is defined as:

> 1 a : disassociated from any specific instance b : difficult to understand : ABSTRUSE c : insufficiently factual : FORMAL <possessed only an abstract right>
>
> 2 : expressing a quality apart from an object <the word poem is concrete, poetry is abstract>

────────────

29   Bill Backer, *The Care and Feeding of Ideas*. Random House, New York, pg. 11, 1993.

3 a : dealing with a subject in its abstract aspects : THEORETICAL   b : IMPERSONAL, DETACHED <the abstract compassion of a surgeon — *Time*>

4 : having only intrinsic form with little or no attempt at pictorial representation or narrative content

Many of the ideas that you develop will be abstract and not executable. Abstract ideas are often "mind expanders" that get you to think about your objective in a number of different ways. This is okay, because they often lead to a number of executable ideas. Let's take the example of a toy company we have been using for illustration purposes. My objective is to start a toy development company from my home. As part of my information gathering, I called a number of potential toy distribution companies. I found out a number of valuable pieces of information during this process:

1. Almost all large and small toy companies use independent toy inventors.
2. A number of toy companies that manufacture and distribute toys actually gave me shopping lists of toys that they are looking to market next Christmas.
3. A good idea can be presented on the back of a napkin. But, most toy companies would obviously like to see working prototypes.
4. Make sure you protect your ideas with patents, copyrights, and trademarks. Ideas are the genesis of all great products and thus are prone to being misappropriated.

Linus Pauling (Nobel Prize winner) once said, "The best way to get a good idea is to get lots of ideas."

Albert Einstein once said, "The only sure way to avoid making mistakes is to have no new ideas." So don't worry about your ideas being "perfect" or even totally wrong. If you have enough new ideas, there will be a diamond to be mined somewhere among them.

And remember, ideas are a valuable asset for your business. Napoleon Hill once said, "Truly, 'thoughts are things,' and powerful things at that, when they are mixed with a definiteness of purpose, persistence, and a burning desire for their translation into riches, or other material objects."

Idea Generation Tools

Now let's look at some tools for generating ideas. It is important for you to remember not to do any filtering of ideas during the idea generation phase. Write down all ideas no matter how silly they may seem. It is the silly ones that will serve as catalysts for really innovative and executable ideas. To filter will only serve to limit your number of ideas and the quality of your ideas. Before you start your idea generation process, here are some guidelines that work well when working alone or in groups:

1. Set up a definite daily or weekly time for idea generation. Don't let this definitely scheduled time for idea generation stop you from generating ideas while you do other things. I have been told by a lot of people that they keep a pad and a pencil by their bed. It seems that a lot of people get really creative thoughts once their minds and bodies have began to relax in preparation for sleep. Still other people have told me that they get ideas while riding their bicycles. Always have something to record these random ideas in, since they can float away as quickly as they have slipped into your mind.
2. Unplug the phone, turn off your cell phone—eliminate the interrupters.
3. Be as relaxed as possible and suspend your worry list for the duration of the idea generation session. Try not to let your mind constantly drift back to it. I assure you that the list will still be there after you have finished your idea generation session. I find that praying for wisdom and calmness from the Lord before each creative session works wonders. Sit in your easy chair, turn on some nice background music. Do whatever makes you relax.
4. There are no ideas too weird to write down. Sometimes the really weird ideas (abstract ideas) are the ones that can generate truly innovative executable ideas.
5. If you are developing ideas in a group, make sure that no criticizing is allowed. Write down every single idea that pops into your head no matter how ridiculous. Also, groups tend to try to filter ideas during the idea generation phase. Avoid this early filtering or you will end up with a few boring and dull ideas.
6. Be sure to make it fun. Keep humor in your idea generation process. If you get too serious, you'll begin to box yourself into boring, dull ideas.

Brainstorming

One of the most effective ways of generating new ideas is called brainstorming.

In 1941 Alex Osborn, an advertising executive, found that conventional business meetings were inhibiting the creation of new ideas and proposed some rules designed to help stimulate them. He was looking for rules that would give people the freedom of mind and action to spark off and reveal new ideas. To "think up" was originally the term he used to describe the process he developed, and that, in turn, came to be known as "brainstorming." The rules he came up with are the following:

- No criticism of ideas
- Go for large quantities of ideas
- Build on each other's ideas
- Encourage wild and exaggerated ideas (abstract ideas)

He found that when these rules were followed, many more ideas were created and that a greater quantity of original ideas gave rise to a greater quantity of useful ideas. Quantity produced quality.

Using these new rules, people's natural inhibitions were reduced, inhibitions that prevented them from putting forward ideas that they felt might be considered "wrong" or "stupid." Osborn also found that generating "silly" ideas could spark off very useful ideas, because they changed the way people thought.

You can read Alex Osborn's original approach in his book, *Applied Imagination*.

What is brainstorming used for?

Although brainstorming will be your power tool for coming up with ideas for a new business or product, this technique can be used in a multitude of beneficial ways:

- Business strategy
- Advertising campaigns
- Research and development procedures
- Product enhancements
- Patents, copyrights, and trademarks
- New products
- New services
- Marketing strategy and methods
- Service enhancements
- Written documents and articles
- Investment decisions
- Engineering components
- Research techniques

- Government policies
- Operating processes
- Financial reporting and accounting processes
- Consumer research
- Factory locations
- Factory expansion
- Management methods
- Company structure and policy
- Distribution routes
- New industries
- Better insurance policies

Brainstorming has great utility in everyday life:

- Establishing a Bible reading plan
- Inviting a non-believer to church
- Increasing overall attendance at church
- Expanding your sanctuary
- Adding new programs to your yearly church plan
- Increasing community involvement of your church members
- Menu planning for the family
- Getting the family more physically fit
- The list is endless

Most problems are not solved automatically by the first idea that comes to mind. To get to the best solution, it's important to consider many possible solutions. One of the best ways to do this is by brainstorming.

Idea Sparks

It may be hard to get the idea generation session started or it may, on occasion, fizzle out. Here is a list of techniques to jump-start the idea generation process or get it back on track. I personally like to use one or more of these techniques for every brainstorming session. We will go back to our example toy invention company. We have been given the challenge of coming up with toy concepts for a company that needs toys for the junior spy (this is a real example from a real company).

Random Input

    This is one of the more fun and easy-to-use idea sparks. If you come up to a creative mental block, take your Bible in hand and open it randomly to any page. Randomly put your finger on a passage or a single word. I randomly put my finger on Psalm 77:18: "Your thunder was heard in the whirlwind, your lightning lit up the world; the earth trembled and quaked" (NIV). The word that my finger actually landed on was "lightning." We will now try to relate this word to our task of designing a junior spy toy. Most of the time, the more unrelated a random word, the better it is for generation of ideas. So, what thoughts come to mind when relating the word "lightning" to our objective?

- Lightning – electricity – **wireless**, batteries, home, portable, on/off, dam
- Lightning – trees – branches, **fence**, tall, shade, grow, climb
- Lightning – rain – weather station, water, scuba, waterproof, raincoat
- Lightning – sky – fly, bird, cloud, plane, balloon, sound waves, **hear**
- Lightning – storm – protection, rain, run, cover, random, ocean
- Lightning – visual – glasses, sight, eye, spy, **periscope**
- Lightning – thunder – noise, horn, loud, companion, clap, rumble, roll, bump
- Lightning – scary – story, game, dark, unknown, detective, **assignment**
- Lightning – bottle – can, soda, canteen, belt, rocket, message, secret
- Lightning – super heroes – Superman, super powers, **gadgets**, strong, tights
- Lightning – weather man – news, science, computer graphics, wind, TV
- Lightning – weather station – outpost, instruments, gauges, knowledge
- Lightning – outdoors – cold, cover-up, stars, ocean, rugged, climb
- Lightning – bright, **random**, flashlight, night, design, free, white
- Lightning – clouds – shapes, fluffy, moving, smoke, smog, drift, water, rain
- Lightning – static – experiment, comb, brush, hiss, black and white TV
- Lightning – random – bullet points, math, play, unknown, unorganized, organize
- Lightning – kite – fly, tug, wind, string, colorful, box, loose, tethered, tail
- Lightning – key – open, secret, brass, skeleton, **journal,** secret, answer, spy
- Lightning – Ben Franklin – smart, scientist, stove, invention, old, funny, **shoes**
- Lightning – funny shoes – old, walk, run, buckles, black, socks, wet, heel
- Lightning – wire rim glasses – x-ray, **see,** fragile, peer, fold, case, hinge, ear
- Lightning – science – mad, experiment, books, formulas, explore, touch, play
- Lightning – telephone – communicate, secret, wireless, show, Morse code
- Lightning – magic – disappear, hat, rabbit, cards, coins, **fake, box,** tools

Although there is no one correct way to use the random-word approach to start the creative juices flowing, it helps to have some systematic method to help the creative process grow and to record its results. Here is what I did:

1. I used free-flow association with the word "lightning." The free flow encompassed synonyms, antonyms, and related and unrelated words.
2. Then I used the first round of new words to generate a second layer of free-flow words. This process could go on for a number of levels, but I stopped at two levels.
3. I then went through the list of words and related them to possible products and came up with the following candidates:

   a. Wireless – a wireless camera that can be set out in the yard to secretly observe your counter-junior spies
   b. Fence – idea booklet for good ways to hide
   c. Hear – a hearing device that lets you hear conversations at a distance
   d. Periscope – an electronic device for enabling the junior spy to take pictures around a corner or over a fence
   e. Assignment –capsules that have fun random games in them for one spy or a group of junior spies
   f. Gadgets – a series of gadgets that can be used assembled together or separately. A booklet to show the junior spy how to make spy devices that will work in conjunction with the spy gadgets sold by the toy company
   g. Random – a software program in which you select various elements for a "spy assignment," and it puts them together to form a complete assignment
   h. Journal – a spy journal to keep track of all of a junior spy's assignments, and to record clues. Works in conjunction with "e" above.
   i. Shoes – false footprints that the junior spy can put on the bottom of his shoes to make tracks to throw off other counter-junior spies
   j. See – a telescope that looks like a pen and can take pictures
   k. Fake, box – a history book with a built-in recorder and camera

Not all of these ideas will make it to market, but at least three of them are under consideration by a major toy company.

Mind Mapping

Another useful tool to either spark the idea generation process or to put it back on track once it has started is "Mind Mapping." Like the Random Input device above, it is also a good tool to use during any brainstorming process to track progress, encourage tangent ideas, and keep the process going.

How to do a Mind Map

Mind mapping starts out by writing down your central idea in a circle (or square) in the center of a piece of paper. You then add additional circles that contain related ideas. These circles radiate out from the central idea circle. Focus on key ideas and look for branches off of the main idea or one of the "sub-ideas."

Record relationships

In writing down your sub-ideas, you are developing relationships between the central idea and sub-ideas that radiate from it. Sometimes, there will sub-ideas that relate to other sub-ideas. There will also be sub-ideas of sub-ideas, and so on.

Construct your visual mind map quickly without pausing, qualifying, or editing

The purpose of the mind map is to generate ideas and relationships quickly and creatively. You should not be worried about making your mind map a work of art. It can be cleaned up after you have had your idea generation session. There are a number of really good mind mapping software packages on the market. I would encourage you to buy one of these packages, as they make the mind-mapping process go a lot smoother. Remember to only map summary ideas. Do not get caught up in explanations or descriptions.

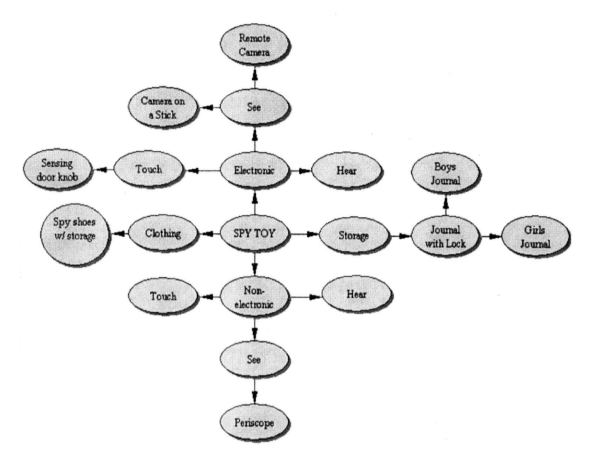

Fig.23 – Spy Toy

This mind map was done with a software package called Inspiration. This is one of many (but probably the easiest to use) mind-mapping software packages on the market today. It will assist you in brainstorming, webbing, diagramming your thoughts, critical thinking, concept mapping, organizing your thoughts, outlining, and organizing your thoughts.

But if a computer is not available or you want to do a group mind-mapping session, you can construct your mind map on a white board or other surface. Be sure to always save a copy of your mind maps for future reference and amendment or additions. The main point is to grow your mind-map tree as wide and deep as you can.

Random Picture

Take any newspaper or magazine and randomly take a picture and relate it to your objective. Use the same approach as used in the Random Input approach or the mind mapping technique.

Analogies, Metaphorical Thinking, Parables, and Similes

An analogy is a statement in which two things are compared because they have something in common. Sometimes, the two things are the same in some way, sometimes they are opposites. A simple analogy would be "Man is to woman as boy is to girl." Another example is "plate is to dish as arms is to weapons."

Metaphors are used extensively in learning. Dictionary.com defines a metaphor as:

1. A figure of speech in which a word or phrase that ordinarily designates one thing is used to designate another, thus making an implicit comparison, as in *"a sea of troubles"* or *"All the world's a stage"* (Shakespeare).

2. One thing conceived as representing another; a symbol: *"Hollywood has always been an irresistible, prefabricated metaphor for the crass, the materialistic, the shallow, and the craven"* (Neal Gabler).

Often, you can draw an analogy between your problem and something else, or express it in metaphorical terms. A metaphor is a simple type of analogy that uses a known thing to represent another thing. As an example, "the construction site was as busy as a beehive." It's a figure of speech that links two apparently unconnected ideas.

A simile is closely related to analogies and metaphors. It is a direct comparison of two essentially unlike things, marking the comparison with the word "like" or "as." Similes state that A is "like" B. An example is, "Jordan's taking the product promised to Sandy and giving it to Pamela is *like* robbing Peter to pay Paul."

A parable is an extended simile. A simile compares the point of similarity (thus, simile) between two unlike things in order to demonstrate and teach that point.

A parable is a brief story that is true to life, comparing the point of commonality between two unlike things, given for the purpose of teaching spiritual truth. Jesus, with his great wisdom and knowledge, often used the parable to simplify a complex thought for man's understanding. Jesus used farming analogies to teach spiritual Truths. The fig tree used by Jesus as a symbol of the nation of Israel . See Luke 13:6-9 as an example.

[6]Then he told this parable: "A man had a fig tree, planted in his vineyard, and he went to look for fruit on it, but did not find any. [7]So he said to the man who took care of the vineyard, 'For three years now I've been coming to look for fruit on this fig tree and haven't found any. Cut it down! Why should it use up the soil?' [8]'Sir,' the man replied, 'leave it alone for one more year, and I'll dig around it and fertilize it. [9]If it bears fruit next year, fine! If not, then cut it down.' "

We can take a lesson from Jesus and use the analogy/metaphor approach to creative thinking. Continuing with our example, we will use this approach to generate ideas for our spy toy company:

Spy toy related	Metaphor Subject
1. Seeing without being seen	Chameleon
2. Camouflage pants and shirt	Changes colors with environment
3. Hearing without being heard	American Indians
4. Electronic ear	Ear to the ground
5. Leaving no tracks	American Indians
6. Rubber shoe prints that strap on to make look like different footprint	Using bear claws to make look like bear print instead of man

You get the general concept. This can be a very useful tool in generating ideas.

Association

We have all played the game of free association where we say a word and others in the group immediately, without thinking, say what comes into their minds. Free Association is the foundation of the association method of idea generation. The mind is a beautiful instrument that will normally associate words based on one of the following three principles:

Next Word – Say the next word that is associated with that would come next. As an example, when someone says, "Bible," you might immediately say, "Jesus." If you say, "communion," someone might immediately say, "body" (as in the body of Christ).

Similarity – Something that is very close or like the word mentioned. If you say, "broccoli," someone will say, "cauliflower."

Opposite -   Refers to a word that is opposite or near opposite the word you said. As an example, if you say Heaven, someone might say Hell.

Association is a very useful tool for a group or an individual. In either case, make sure that you immediately record each word that is said. Also, have more than one word ready to start your Association session. Continuing with our example of starting a business that invents toys for kids, I would start with the following words to come up with a toy invention idea:

Toy   spy   see   hear   hide   secret   games

Opposite Assumption

You will always have basic assumptions that will guide the way you do business. Some of your basic assumptions might be:

Customers want good service.

Customers want cheap prices.

Customers want an enjoyable shopping experience.

These are, in most cases, correct assumptions. But, try looking from the opposite view of your correct business assumption.. Let's take "Customers want cheap prices" and reverse it to say, "Customers do not want cheap prices." Not all customers want the cheapest price that they can get for a product. In Southern California, there is a grocery store chain called Gelson's that does not have the lowest prices, but they are highly successful. In exchange for cheap prices, they offer wider aislesaisles, broader selection, individually wrapped produce and meats, background music, and exceptional service.

Scenery Change

Once, while sitting in church at Shepherd of the Hills and listening to our lead pastor, Dudley Rutherford, talk about getting out of a potential sinful train of thought, he said "Don't try to fight it; go somewhere else mentally." We all have temptations and challenges that are seemingly insurmountable, so maybe we shouldn't try to surmount them but, instead, change the scenery. As an example, if you are tempted to have that second piece of apple pie, instead of sitting at the table and staring at the pie, it might be easier to win over temptation if you got up and took a walk. This also works well with creative thinking and idea generation.

In my prior life, I was a certified public accountant. In the days before computerized accounting, I had to do what was called "running a trial balance." This consisted of totaling all of the accounts in the general ledger. More often than not (this is probably why I am no longer an accountant), the debits would not equal the credits. Often I would just get up out of my chair and do something totally unrelated such as read a little in a philosophy book to get my mind temporarily off of the problem. When I went back to the numbers, I was usually able to zero right into the solution. There is a saying: "You are too close to the trees to see the forest." This is why the Scenery ChangeChange approach works. Divorcing yourself from the problem enables you to look at it from a different angle and thus possibly arrive at a solution from a different view. It's a really good tool if you find yourself faced with a mental block.

Picasso Method

Doodling is good. This is a technique that will often work to unleash ideas when other techniques will not work. There are a number of approaches to using this technique:

Pencil and Paper

This approach is simply to try drawing a solution or perceived solution to your stated problem or objective. As you attempt to draw your solution, you will spark a number of ideas along the way.

Fig.24 – Spy Camera Sketch

These simple drawings helped decide that a periscope or camera on a stick would be a good product. When I thought of spies, I immediately thought of the old Kilroy image of the man peeking over the fence. This led to the idea of a periscope to look around corners and over fences, which then led to the camera on a stick. You don't have to be Picasso. As a matter of fact, being a bad artist may be a benefit, since you will probably draw a more abstract representation of your objective.

Doodles

When you can't come up with any ideas, just start doodling and scribbling whatever comes to mind. This is similar to the random input or random picture approaches mentioned above. Whatever you draw, try to relate it somehow back to your objective. You will be surprised at the number of ideas that random doodling or scribbling will bring up. Be sure to save all of your drawings for future inspiration.

Fig.25 – Scribbling

From my random scribbling (and I promise you that this doodling was random), I get the following ideas for our example of spy toys:

- Spy toys for outside

- Spy toys for in the house

- Disguise spy toys

Mind sketching

This approach is for more than one person. You doodle or scribble your idea representations on a piece of paper during a 5-minute period. You then pass your drawing to someone else who then tries to improve upon your doodling for another 5 minutes. Now, pass your drawing again so that a third person gets your drawing, and you get one of their drawings to improve upon.

Mini-vacation Technique

This approach is similar to the Scenery used here, but it combines visualization and analogy techniques. If you are having difficulty in developing ideas, either in a group or alone, give this approach a try.

Here are the basic four steps to the Mini-vacation Technique:

1. Define your problem or opportunity to the group.
2. Go on an real or imaginary trip – If in a group suggest an idea for a trip. It could be by car, plane, etc. This can be a real or imaginary trip. Make sure everyone pays attention to detail on the trip. As an example you might notice the zig-zag pattern on the flight attendants uniform. Details are important.
3. Have everyone write down their detailed observations from their trip.
4. Now every should try to find analogies between each of their detailed observations and the problem or opportunity at hand.
5. Have everyone evaluate their analogies and zero on on the ones that may have some relevance to the problem.
6. Have each person share their analogies with the group and allow the group to enhance the individuals' analogies without criticism.

If there were some really good ideas then discuss if they are feasible.

Shotgun Wedding Technique

This technique has helped me create some of my best ideas. Start by listing at least ten attributes for the objective for which you are generating ideas. Use your Bible's index and randomly select two topics. Now make a list of ten attributes related to each of the selected topics. Now make the listed attributes of your problem or opportunity relate to the topics listed from your subjects selected from your Bible. Now list a corresponding number of attributes related to these subjects. Now "make" a relationship between the two lists of attributes. This process will squeeze out some interesting ideas.

Someone Not Involved with the Problem or Opportunity

Sometimes the best place to get good ideas is from someone unrelated to the situation. Here are some different groups of people from which you could request ideas:

The Average Individual Not Related to the Problem or Opportunity

Anybody you know who you feel comfortable with and is totally unrelated to your need for ideas could be a gold mine. When preparing them for your idea generation session, give them a generalized description so as not to "put them into a creative box." If I were looking for ideas for a spy toy for kids, I would give the following simple description:

"I am looking for ideas for a spy toy for kids."

I would start with this one line and listen closely as they may come up with categories of ideas that you have not even thought of yet. Another approach, if you feel that you have all the categories that you need, is to give a description of categories within your objective. Following through with our example, we would possibly give the following idea generations description:

I am looking for ideas for spy toys for kids. In particular, I am looking for spy toys in the following categories:

- Seeing
- Hearing
- Game play

I am always amazed at the depth and breadth of ideas that people unrelated to the project can come up with in these simple little idea generation sessions.

A person who is an expert in a particular area that has some effect on your objective

Sometimes people with particular areas of expertise not necessarily in your objective area can have really great ideas that you may not have considered because you don't know all the possible areas that could be useful in developing ideas for your objective. While coming up with ideas for spy toys, I talked to the following "experts":

- Electronic Engineers
- Nano Technology Scientist
- Mechanical Engineers
- Hydraulic Engineers
- Clerks at toy stores
- Police Officers
- Special effects supervisor from a film production company
- A writer of science fiction books

Children

"Out of the mouths of babes" is so true when it comes to developing fresh, new and exciting ideas. When I work with children in the area of idea generation, I always try to keep the description of what I am looking for as abstract as possible. I do this because they are much better at filling in the blanks than adults.

Lotus Blossom Technique

This is a popular method of generating multitudes of ideas. It originated in Japan, developed by Yasuo Matsumura, president of Clover Management Research. Its name is based on the fact that the lotus flower, like all flowers, has petals that radiate from its center. The Lotus Blossom chart is constructed in a similar manner. Using the format, take the following steps:

Idea A related idea 1	Idea A related idea 2	Idea A related idea 3	Idea B related idea 1	Idea B related idea 2	Idea B related idea 3	Idea C related idea 1	Idea C related idea 2	Idea C related idea 3
Idea A related idea 8	Core Related idea A	Idea A related idea 4	Idea D related idea 8	Core Related idea B	Idea B related idea 4	Idea C related idea 8	Core Related idea C	Idea C related idea 4
Idea A related idea 7	Idea A related idea 6	Idea A related idea 5	Idea B related idea 7	Idea B related idea 6	Idea B related idea 5	Idea C related idea 7	Idea C related idea 6	Idea C related idea 5
Idea H related idea 1	Idea H related idea 2	Idea H related idea 3	Core Related idea A	Core Related idea B	Core Related idea C	Idea D related idea 1	Idea D related idea 2	Idea D related idea 3
Idea HD related idea 8	Core Related idea H	Idea H related idea 4	Core Related idea H	Core Idea	Core Related idea D	Idea D related idea 8	Core Related idea D	Idea D related idea 4
Idea H related idea 7	Idea H related idea 6	Idea H related idea 5	Core Related idea G	Core Related idea F	Core Related idea E	Idea D related idea 7	Idea D related idea 6	Idea D related idea 5
Idea G related idea 1	Idea G related idea 2	Idea G related idea 3	Idea F related idea 1	Idea F related idea 2	Idea F related idea 3	Idea E related idea 1	Idea C related idea 2	Idea E related idea 3
Idea G related idea 8	Core Related idea G	Idea G related idea 4	Idea F related idea 8	Core Related idea F	Idea F related idea 4	Idea E related idea 8	Core Related idea E	Idea E related idea 4
Idea G related idea 7	Idea G related idea 6	Idea G related idea 5	Idea F related idea 7	Idea F related idea 6	Idea F related idea 5	Idea E related idea 7	Idea E related idea 6	Idea E related idea 5

Fig.26 – Lotus Blossom Idea Chart

1. Start by writing your primary objective or problem in the center Core Idea square.

2. Now, write eight related ideas in the squares immediately surrounding the Core Idea square. As I have mentioned before, you will want to mix and match the techniques that we discuss in this book. For example, you may want to brainstorm the eight related ideas that go in the boxes around the Core Idea square.

3. Now each of the Core related ideas becomes its own Core Idea. Now, develop related ideas to the "new Core Ideas." The squares can go out even past this point; each related idea for the Core related idea then becomes a Core Idea. As an example, Idea G related idea 7 in the bottom left-hand corner can become a core idea on its own.

Let's complete a sample session using the Lotus Blossom technique of idea generation. We want to create a small handheld device for watching movies.

Good viewing experience	Long battery life	Sale to an existing install base
Designed to appeal to kids	**Kids Handhleld for watching DVD's**	Priced under $49
Must Be portable	Easy for Kids to operate	Rugged For play by kids

Fig.27 – Small Handheld Lotus Blossom Idea 1

Now that we have developed the primary ideas around our core idea, we can take each related idea and develop its related ideas as if they were core ideas. We will take the related idea of "priced under $49" and develop its related ideas:

Sell power supply separately	Sell ear phone separately	Use Game Boy Screen
Minimize pieces in case design	**Priced under $49**	Make device single purpose
Minimize options and switches	Create a line of accessories	Use standard DVD mechanism

Fig.28 – Small Handheld Lotus Blossom Idea 2

This is an actual device that will be on the market by the time this book is published. The idea of keeping the product under $49 was meant to appeal to the parents who would buy the device. The market for handheld media players is hot right now with all the major electronic manufacturing companies entering the market. This particular device has the following MAJOR advantages over the other handheld media players now crowding the market:

1. Priced under $49. This was accomplished by making an adapter that attached to Game Boy® (by Nintendo), and the player uses the Game Boy® screen.
2. The price of $49 puts the adapter in the price range of Game Boy® game cartridges.
3. Kids can play their existing DVDs and won't have to buy another format version of their favorite films.
4. The single focus device means fewer things can go wrong.
5. Although the device is inexpensive compared to other portable DVD players, it has a superior viewing experience, since it uses the host-device screen.
6. The line of accessories is "a line of accessories for an accessory." This helps the adapter appear to have a more stable existence and adds to the bottom line profits.

The Lotus Blossom technique has helped us organize our approach as well as stimulate new aspects of our "blossoming" ideas.

There are a large number of books on the market with hundreds of ideas for idea generation. In my opinion, two of the best books on the market are *The Ultimate Book of Business Creativity* by Ros Jay and *101 Creative Problem Solving Techniques* by James M. Higgins.

TAILOR YOUR SELECTED IDEAS

After an idea generation session, you will have a lot of abstract ideas and maybe even some that are executable. Even the executable ideas will need tailoring to meet your needs. Never discard your ideas. As Heraclitus said, "No man ever steps in the same river twice, for it's not the same river and he's not the same man." (See the chapter in this book "SOME RELEVANT THOUGHTS FROM GREAT MINDS.") An idea generated in one of your idea generation sessions may not work now, but maybe later, under different circumstances, it will be useful.

For an idea to be executable, it must be R.A.T., which stands for *relevant, accurate, and timely*. To be relevant, it has to squarely address your objective or problem. To be accurate, it has to be able to deliver the results that make it worthwhile to pursue. To be timely, it must address your issue and deliver the desired results in the time frame that is desired. As an example, let's say that you have a product that has been a good money maker for you. But now a competitor has come out with a competing product. For purposes of illustration, we will say that your product is the first DVD player on the market for under $100. You have been doing a nice business over the last year and wake up one morning to see two competing DVD players for under $100! After you regain your composure, you sit down and start generating ideas. Based on the current cost of screens (the most expensive part of a portable DVD player), you can't currently get a portable DVD player with a retail price much less than $100. Also, the portable DVD player market is getting crowded with competitors. You have invested a lot of resources in developing your DVD player and do not want to walk away from this investment.

During your idea generation session, one of the ideas generated is to quickly develop and take to market a portable adapter that will allow Game Boys® to play DVDs. Let's see if it meets our R.A.T. test:

Relevant - This potential solution can solve our problem, since there are no adapters currently in the marketplace. Also, there are over 20 million Game Boy® owners in the world—a built-in market. We are also able to take advantage of all the technology we already invested in to create our DVD player.

Accurate - The result is that we are still in the DVD player business but with no present competition. Also, we beat the competition in price, because we utilize the screen on the Game Boy® and are able to lower our price to $39.00 per unit.

Timely - Because we already have manufacturing established with our current DVD player, we only need to design the new interface between the Game Boy® and our DVD player.

If you have generated a lot of ideas (a good thing), divide them into three categories: probable, possible, and not applicable. Remember not to discard the "not applicable" ideas, as they might possibly be useful later. Even if they are not useful later, in the raw state, they can serve as catalysts for other ideas or be modified for future use. In categorizing your ideas, use the R.A.T. analysis along with P.E.S.T. and S.W.O.T. analyses. Some people do this formally and some do it mentally.

Here are a few additional ways of tailoring your list of ideas:

The "Yellow Sticky" Technique

This is actually a method to arrange your ideas, written individually on Post-It®, into rows and columns so that you can see all of them at the same time. Post-it ® notes, got their start in 1968 when a 3M researcher tried to improve adhesive tape. What he created was an adhesive that didn't stick very well. Even so, he knew he had something cool—he just didn't know what to do with it. A few years later, a colleague who was a member of his church choir was getting frustrated because he couldn't keep his bookmarks in his hymnal. He needed something that would stick without being too sticky—something just like that weak glue his colleague had accidentally created. In 1980, the Post-it Note became an official product and a huge hit. This little digression illustrates a couple of points: it took 12 years for the Post-it Notes to become a product (it was a good thing the researcher didn't throw out his idea just because it had no immediate use), and situations change and could give the seemingly useless idea utility at a later date.

Capture All Post-It® Ideas

When you start your "Post-It® note" creative session, write one idea on each sticky and put it on the wall. You can either do this randomly by just putting them on the wall as the idea comes to you or your participants, or by blending this approach with the mind mapping approach, sticking them on the wall in some type of mind mapping pattern. Another alternative is to start forming groups of ideas as they flow from you or your brainstorming group and position similar idea Post-It ® notes into groups. However you decide to do it, the important thing is to get the Post-It® notes on the wall. If more than one person is involved, make sure that you put each person's initials on his or her Post-It® note.

Organize a Ranking Grid on the Wall

This simple process will enable you to group and rank your ideas. In the example below, we have identified 8 categories of potential toys (across the top) that we have generated for our toy development company. Within each category, we have a numbered list from 1 to 10 to rank the toy ideas within each category.

**Product Ideas
Evaluation
Idea Grouping**

Ranking	Major Group	Electronic Toys	Games Non-electron	Dolls	RC Cars	Outdoor Toys	Learning Toys	Plush Toys
1								
2								
3								
4								
5								
6								
7								
8								
9								
10								

Fig.29 – Product Ideas Evaluation Grouping

We will use a "gut" approach to rank all of our ideas within each category column. If you have more than 10 ideas in any one product category column, just add more rows. Your "gut" reaction is, of course, ranking the ideas based on their being R.A.T. (relevant, accurate, and timely).

Using the Post-It® note Method with TK8 Sticky Notes®

If you have grown up using the Post-It® notes, an online company, TK8 Software, (http://www.tk8.com/stickynotes/download.asp) has a really efficient Sticky Note program that you can download for free. The free version has have limitations so spend the extra $25 and the "Pro" version.

Weighted Attribute Ranking

The Post-It® note approach discussed above is useful in most cases, but many of you will probably prefer a little more sophisticated and objective method. Thus, we have the "Weighted Attribute Ranking" method that we discussed above. This method is best done using an Excel spreadsheet, because some calculations will need to be made. Look at the spreadsheet below. Across the top of the schedule, we list the attributes that are important to our toy company ideas. You would list the attributes that are important to you and your analysis. A few explanations are in order to fully understand the spreadsheet.

Play -	This is a measure of the play factor that is so important for toys. We have assigned it a weight of 20% (out of 100%).
Dev. Time -	This is the estimated time to get the product to market from concept stage relative to the other projects being ranked.
BOM -	This is the bill of materials (the per-unit cost of the product idea being evaluated).
NRE -	This is the nonrecurring engineering estimate. This is the cost for getting your product idea from idea/concept stage to finished product, ready for production. As with all of the ideas, this is an estimated number compared to the other products being evaluated.
Expandable -	This is a measure of the revenues that can be generated from accessories that can be sold for the product being considered. Also included in our category here is the potential for consumables. An example of this is a cap gun that needs caps.
Partners -	In our example, we are a small independent toy development company. We must partner with a major toy company to get the product to market. We do not have the resources to manufacture the product or distribute the product.
USP -	The Unique Selling Proposition is the element of the idea that sets it apart from all competitors' or potential competitors' ideas. An idea that is very similar to an existing idea is not

really considered a new idea. This is a critical, subjective measure of differentiation.

Patentable -   Most toy companies prefer that you have an idea that can be protected by a patent, copyright, or trademark.

Gut Reaction -   With all of the analysis that you can do, the final decision is usually based on how you feel in your gut about the idea.

In the example idea, "A" is ranked 1 (out of a possible 5) in Play. This attribute is 20% of our overall attributes that we are looking for to evaluate our product ideas. This gives us a weighted score of 0.20. From the sample spreadsheet below, we can see that idea "A" ranks as 5 out of 5 for NRE and Expandability/ Consumables. The top-ranking product is product "E" with a weighted average score of 3.50.

Product Ideas
Evaluation
Weighted Attribute Ranking

	Play	Devel Time	Bill Of Materials	Non Reoccurring Engineering	Expandable/ Consumables	Partners Available	Unique Selling Proposition	Patentable	Gut Reaction	Total Weight
Weight	20.00%	10.00%	5.00%	15.00%	5.00%	25.00%	10.00%	5.00%	5.00%	100.00%
Raw ranking										
Product A	1	1	2	5	5	3	1	4	1	23
Product B	5	3	4	4	4	1	2	3	3	29
Product C	2	5	1	3	3	2	3	1	5	25
Product D	4	2	5	2	1	4	4	2	4	28
Product E	3	4	3	1	2	5	5	5	2	30
Weighted Avg Ranking										
Product A	0.20	0.10	0.10	0.75	0.25	0.75	0.10	0.20	0.05	2.50
Product B	1.00	0.30	0.20	0.60	0.20	0.25	0.20	0.15	0.15	3.05
Product C	0.40	0.50	0.05	0.45	0.15	0.50	0.30	0.05	0.25	2.65
Product D	0.80	0.20	0.25	0.30	0.05	1.00	0.40	0.10	0.20	3.30
Product E	0.60	0.40	0.15	0.15	0.10	1.25	0.50	0.25	0.10	3.50

Fig.30 – Product Idea Evaluation Completed

Attribute Listing

This technique is used more for product enhancement and innovation rather than for idea generation. Once you have developed a list of ideas and filtered through them, Attribute Listing will help you tailor them to your needs. Let's go back to our spy toy ideas. Let's say that we came up with the idea of creating a "camera on a stick" spy toy. The junior spy uses a camera on an articulated stick that will enable him to take pictures over fences and around corners. He can view the item being photographed on one end of the stick and the camera shutter is on the other end of the stick. To get the product idea closer to reality, we can use Attribute Listing. We will list the attributes that we would like for the camera on a stick to have.

Let's list the attributes of our camera on a stick:

1. Must be inexpensive to manufacture. We must be able to sell the toy for under $29.99 at retail with a $4\times$ markup from the complete bill of materials.
2. A camera lens on one end of the stick
3. A viewer on the opposite end of the stick
4. The stick must be articulated and bendable around corners.
5. The camera must have a way to record a number of low-resolution pictures.
6. The camera on a stick must have a way to transfer pictures to a computer for printing.
7. The camera must be small enough to stick in the junior spy's pocket.
8. The camera should come with a small carrying pouch.
9. It must be a point–and-shoot camera with no focusing or other settings necessary.
10. It must resemble a spy toy with a James Bond look and feel.
11. It needs a handle that can be used to steady the camera while shooting pictures, and the handle needs to fold away.
12. The design of the product should make it obvious what the product is so that it can sell itself off the store shelves.
13. It must come with a one year guarantee.
14. Its design must fit in with the other products in the life of spy toys.

Attribute Listing has enabled us to get a good visual image of the product in our mind's eye. We have put "meat on the bones" of our product idea. Here are some example generic attributes that you will want to consider when using this idea generation/ evaluation tool:

- color
- speed
- smell

- taboos
- self-image of buyer
- motivation to buy the product
- size
- shape
- fad relationship
- competing products
- related products
- cost
- function
- price
- demographics of purchaser
- what needs the product or service will fulfill
- weight
- related social issues (e.g., control)

Sensory Attributes

This is a fun idea generation technique that kids really love. We have five senses that often are dormant when it comes to idea generation. This is one of those techniques that get you to look at your objective from a different perspective. This technique makes you use all of your senses to gain a new viewpoint of your objective. For example, if you are developing a spy toy concept, you could ask yourself the following questions:

What would it taste like?

We aren't going to eat our spy toy, but how does tasting food that you take into your body affect the toy? This leads to the question, What do people put into their mouth? The answer might be junk food, vegetables, vitamins, etc. This led to the development of a bag of large capsules that contained play "top secret" missions to be played by the junior spies.

What does it feel like? Can you touch it?

Take the point of view of a spy. What does it feel like to be a spy? If you close your eyes, can you imagine being a spy for a minute? Maybe as a junior spy, you need some disguises so that people can't tell you are on a secret mission. Using another definition of "feel":

What are some things a spy would feel during his "normal" day, such as his special spy case, his spy gadget belt? Maybe become his fingers and imagine what he would touch on a mission and what gadgets he would need for the things he touched. Maybe you need to become a gadget and "feel" what it is like to be the gadget. If you have developed a gadget, what does it feel like in your hands? Is it smooth? Should it be rough?

What does it look like?

What does a spy look like? What does he see? What does he need to have better than normal vision? If I were a spy gadget, what would I see and what would I look like?

What does it sound like?

What are sounds that a spy would notice? What are sounds that you expect spy gadgets to make: the clicks, the swish of air, the Velcro, etc. If you have a seeing gadget in mind, what does sound have to do with it?

What does it smell like?

What are some smells associated with being a spy? New-leather smell of the seats in your spy mobile? Smell of a seaport as you wait for your contact to arrive on a submarine? These smell sensations can lead to some really interesting ideas.

ENERGIZE YOUR SHORT LIST OF IDEAS

Once you have come up with a "short list" of ideas for your objective, you can grow or energize many of them. As noted earlier, most of the idea generation techniques that we have discussed here can be used in any of the idea generation stages.

Alex Osborn, a pioneer in the area of creative thinking, was the first to identify and record the 9 principle ways of manipulating a subject. They were later arranged by Bob Eberle into the mnemonic SCAMMPERR system[30].

(S)ubstitute something.

(C)ombine it with something else.

---

30   Michalko, Michael, *Thinkpak*, Berkeley, CA:Ten Speed Press, pg. 2, 1994.

(A)dapt something to it.

(M)agnify or add to it.

(M)odify it.

(P)ut it to some other use.

(E)liminate something.

(R)earrange it.

(R)everse it.

To illustrate this technique, let's say our product is a metal paper clip, and we want to enhance it. In this example, we are the original inventors of the paper clip. We find that another company is making paper clips, and we need to expand our product line to give our customers more choices.

(S)ubstitute something.

We can substitute plastic for metal.

(C)ombine it with something else.

Put it on a clipboard and chain.

(A)dapt something to it.

Make paper with a special area that will allow the paper clip to easily slide onto the paper.

(M)agnify or add to it.

Make it a huge paper clip.

(M)odify it.

Make them in various colors.

(P)ut it to some other use.

Use it as a hair accessory or clothing accessory.

(E)liminate something.

Shorten the wire coil at each end to be able to make more clips out of a length of wire.

(R)earrange it.

Make it diamond shaped.

(R)everse it.

Configure it so that it slides on sideways.

This is probably the most powerful technique when it comes to energizing your ideas. As illustrated with the paper clip, a single product idea can be turned into an entire product line using SCAMMPERR. Or maybe you have a product that has been a reliable moneymaker, but it is getting tired and competitors are beginning to take part of your market share. Use SCAMMPERR to see if there are ways to inject some more life into it. SCAMMPERR can also be used for energizing services and for other management decisions.

Take It Apart Analysis

This technique is similar to the Attribute Listing approach discussed above. The difference is that Attribute Listing is what the product is or does, while the "Take It Apart" approach is concerned with the actual physical attributes of the product or product idea. You normally won't have the time or resources to do a "Take It Apart" analysis for all of your product ideas, as it is very detailed in nature and often requires substantial input from outsiders such as engineers and component suppliers. This approach will also help in the actual product design, prototyping, and the building stage. Say that we came up with the idea of a miniature toy race car that's controlled by a light beam rather than radio controlled (RC) (the current rage in toys is RC cars). We would probably want to do both the Attribute Listing approach and a "Take It Apart" (TIA) analysis. The Attribute Listing technique will enable us to develop a listing of attributes that make the Light Beam car a better product than the current RC cars. The TIA analysis will enable us to make the product the best we can. The TIA approach typically includes the following elements:

Document the typical user

It is important to always know your target market. This would typically include the following information:

1. Sex
2. Age
3. Geography
4. Income level

5. Education level
6. Motivation for buying
7. Where they would typically buy your product

Document the user experience

Here, we want to imagine that we are the user. We want to write down how the purchaser of our product will interact with the product we are developing:

1. Seeing the product on the store shelf
2. Taking the product down from the store shelf
3. Unpacking the product once the user gets it home
4. Assembling the product if needed
5. Reading directions for using the product
6. Learning how to use the product through trial and error
7. Playing with the product alone and with others
8. Storing the product

Document the Components

For our RC car example product, we would include the following components:

Plastic

1. Upper body
2. Car chassis/ battery door
3. Wheels
4. Tires
5. Gear sets
6. Transmitter housing
7. Controller button
8. Clutch gear
9. Receiver box

Purchased parts

1. Screws
2. Nut for battery door
3. Battery contacts
4. Metal shaft

5. Video cable
6. RCA jack
7. Clutch spring
8. 49 MHz antenna
9. 1.2 GHz antenna
10. Spring for controller
11. Contact plate for controller
12. Motor

Special material

1. Open box
2. Insert
3. Blister pack

Electronic parts

1. Transmitter/ transceiver
2. PCB (printed circuit board)
3. Transistors
4. Coil
5. Resistors
6. Crystal
7. CMOS (Camera) Imager and Lens
8. CPU
9. LED
10. LCD

The more detailed the information we can compile about our product ideas, the more opportunities we have to make improvements to them.

Document the Component Interaction

When we know the way the components interact, we can more readily explore alternatives for improvement. At this stage of idea energizing, we will see less dramatic enhancements to our ideas. The improvements we see will normally be incremental.

Complete a bill of materials (BOM)

Once we have determined the component descriptions and the component interactions, we can then complete a detailed bill of materials. This will tell us if we have a product that can be sold at a suitable retail price. If we can't get the cost of our idea to an acceptable level, then it won't matter how unique the idea is.

Complete an NRE estimate (Nonrecurring estimate)

As small business owners, we know that we have limited resources. When we develop an idea, we have to determine the cost of getting from the idea/concept stage to a product that is ready for manufacturing. Continuing with our toy RC example from above, we would have to determine the cost of engineering for getting from concept to completed product.

Creative thinking and idea generation are powerful weapons of the small businessperson. These, coupled with a solid relationship with God, are some of the most powerful tools in your arsenal. Anyone can be a creative thinker. Most people are already good creative thinkers, but they just don't manage the creative thinking process adequately. The basic process of creative thinking is to have a system to generate lots of ideas, capture them in writing, modify them to work for you, and then implement them in your business.

Although we have covered a lot of information in the area of creative thinking, we have only scratched the surface. A number of years ago, a comprehensive method of creative problem solving was developed in Russia. The Theory of Solving Inventive Problems (TRIZ, its Russian acronym) was developed in 1946 by Russian engineer and scientist Genrich Altshuller. He analyzed over 400,000 patents from different fields of engineering. Altshuller studied those patents with the *most effective solutions*. His empirical studies revealed objective laws, or trends, in the evolution of technical systems. From these, he formulated his main postulate: the evolution of engineering systems is not a random process but obeys certain laws. From these laws, Altshuller formulated his 8 *Patterns of Evolution* of technical systems. These patterns can be utilized for conscious system development—including problem solving. The TRIZ method is beyond the scope of this discussion, but keep in mind that there has been substantial research in the area of creative thinking, and there is a resultant large body of published work on the subject. TRIZ is an algorithmic approach for solving technical and technological problems.

Christians have the ability to be the most creative people on earth. We believe in a God we cannot see and we have faith that He will be with us in everything we do. God gave us a mind that can visualize what is not, what can be. Sometimes, we just need a little help to climb out of the box. We need to get out of the boat so we can walk on water.

Growing Your Business

You can grow your business in more ways than you may realize. Everything from your daily management of day-to-day operations to your strategic planning for the future, and everything in between, can help your company meet your growth objectives. Growing your business, in the context of this discussion, includes marketing your goods or services and expanding your business internally rather than externally, i.e., through mergers and acquisitions.

As we discuss the growing of your business, keep in mind the title of this book: *Business with a Purpose.* As your business grows, you will be given opportunity to spread the good news about the Lord. As you develop your marketing plans, always think of ways to integrate God's message into your marketing. The way you conduct your business and live your life will be a testimony to the Lord, and if you are creative, you can find many other ways to use your business to spread God's message.

One of my favorite fast food companies, In-N-Out Burger, headquartered in Southern California, sends millions of little reminders of God's grace every year:

> REVELATION 3:20 (burger and cheeseburger wrappers): Behold, I stand at the door and knock: if any man hear my voice, and open the door, I will come in to him, and will sup with him, and he with me.

> JOHN 3:16 (soda cups): For God so loved the world that he gave his only Son, that whoever believes in him should not perish but have eternal life.

PROVERBS 3:5 (milkshake cups): Trust in the Lord with all thine heart; and lean not unto thine own understanding.

NAHUM 1:7 (Double-Double wrapper): The LORD is good, a stronghold in the day of trouble; he knows those who take refuge in him.

Fig.31 – In N Out Burger John 3:16

This is a subtle but effective way of spreading the word of God. When I did a Google search on the Internet by typing in "In-N-Out Bible verses," Google came up with 588 websites that talked about the verses. Notice how something this subtle can generate so much exposure for the Lord.

Fly Alaska Airlines. Here is a little card that is given to passengers of Alaska Airlines with the following explanation:

"The meal prayer card has been a simple tradition on our flights for over 20 years. The quotes have application across many Judeo-Christian beliefs and are shared as a gesture of thanks which reflect the beliefs of this country's founding as in the Declaration of Independence, the Gettysburg Address, Pledge of Allegiance and every U.S. coin and dollar you handle. Alaska Airlines is an international carrier with very diverse customers, and we have no intentions of offending anyone or their beliefs. An overwhelming majority of our customers have indicated they appreciate the gesture, and those who don't are not forced to read it. We do appreciate hearing from you, and look forward to welcoming you on board another flight in the future."

Fig.32 – Alaska Airlines religous ad

The corporate executives at Alaska Airlines have made some real points with the Lord on this one.

If your vendors, customers, employees, and competitors do not know that you are a child of God, then you might want to examine the way in which you are presenting yourself to the world. This may be a perfect time—the moment before you step into a larger world (more customers, more vendors, more employees, more exposure)—to reevaluate your relationship with the Lord and redefine your inner purpose. Dealing with people, there is a larger responsibility in representing your company and yourself. You are always putting out a message. You get to choose if it's conscious or unconscious. That's where the responsibility comes in.

Marketing your business as a Christian requires that you meet ethical and moral standards that are sometimes higher than legal standards. Let's say that you are contemplating buying a new stereo system. You quiz a commissioned salesperson at a local electronics shop at length, knowing that you intend to buy your stereo online. This behavior may be completely legal, but is it ethical? And is it Christian? When growing your business, you will encounter situations that beg these questions of you at every step of the way. Be prepared to answer them.

WHAT IS MARKETING?

Marketing is the function of an organization that does the following:

- identifies its current and potential customers
- creates products or services that meet the needs and wants of the customers
- informs and persuades the customers to purchase the products or services
- delivers the products to the customers
- reinforces the customers' confidence in the purchase they made

It seems as if every college profession that has ever written a college textbook on marketing has a different definition for marketing. Plain and simple, "marketing" is making money by satisfying someone's want or need. I started my professional career out as an accountant. I thought that I had the most important job in business until a salesman told me, "You can't account for it until I sell it. If I don't sell it, you don't have a job." He was right.

Before we go any further, let's look at a few more definitions of what we mean by marketing:

American Heritage Dictionary's Definition of Marketing:

The commercial functions involved in transferring goods from producer to consumer.[31]

American Marketing Association Definition of Marketing:

The process of planning and executing the conception, pricing, promotion, and distribution of ideas, goods, and services to create exchanges that satisfy individual and organizational objectives.[32]

Marketing Definition from *MSN Encarta Dictionary*:

The business activity of presenting products or services to potential customers in such a way as to make them eager to buy. Marketing includes such matters as the pricing and packaging of the product and the creation of demand by advertising and sales campaigns.[33]

Merriam Webster's Marketing Definition:

1 b: The process or technique of promoting, selling, and distributing a product or service

2: An aggregate of functions involved in moving goods from producer to consumer [34]

These definitions tell us that marketing is letting people know that we have something to sell, selling it to them, and getting it in their hands once we have sold it to them.

THE MARKETING MIX

You have a product or service, and you want to sell it to people at a profitable price. This is where the marketing mix comes into the picture. The components of the Marketing Mix are Positioning, Price, Product, Place, and Promotion. Most classic marketing textbooks do not include positioning in the definition of marketing mix. It has been my experience that it is, indeed, an integral part of the marketing mix. All these elements must be just right in order to sell your products or services and maximize your

31   *The American Heritage® Dictionary of the English Language*, Fourth Edition. Copyright © 2000 by Houghton Mifflin Company. Published by the Houghton Mifflin Company.
32   *Ibid*.
33   http://encarta.msn.com/encnet/features/dictionary/dictionaryhome.aspx.
34   Merriam-Webster Online, http://www.m-w.com/cgi-bin/dictionary.

profits. Each element of the marketing mix influences all of the other elements of the marketing mix. No element stands alone. If one of these elements is incorrect, you will not maximize profits and possibly not sell your product. Let's say, for example, that you have an incredible, consumer-friendly price for your product. The problem is that you are actually selling it below your cost. You will possibly sell a great number of units of your product, but you will be losing more money with every unit sold.

Below is a graphical representation of the interrelationship of the components of the marketing mix. All of the individual components are dependent upon one another to maximize the profitability of your target market.

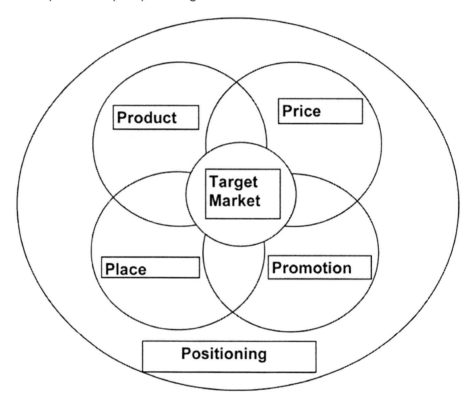

Fig.33 – Marketing Mix

TARGET MARKET

It's important to remember that the focus of marketing is PEOPLE. If you're concentrating your efforts on your products, you are not going to be a successful marketer.

So do not forget that your target market is people with common characteristics that set them apart as an identifiable group. By selecting and concentrating on particular market segments, to the exclusion of other segments, your marketing mix can be tailored for those customers that who are the most likely to buy your products or services.

Type of Market Segment	Shared Group Characteristics
Demographic Segment	**Measurable statistics** such as age, income, occupation, etc.
Psychographic Segment	**Lifestyle perferences** such as music lovers, city or urban dwellers, those that consider themselves spiritual, etc.
Use-based Segment	**Frequency of usage** such as recreational lake usage, church attendance, traveling, etc.
Benefit Segment	**Desire to obtain the same product benefits** such as luxury, thriftiness, comfort from food, etc.
Geographic Segment	**Location** such as home address, business address, school address, church address, etc.

Fig.34 – Marketing Segment Examples

Your target market buys a product at a place, for a price, after promotion brings it to their attention. Your marketing mix will support effective engagement of your target market.

To be truly successful, you need a good picture of who your customer really is. As an example, let's assume that you wish to open an iPod accessory kiosk at a local mall and, if successful, expand to other malls. Here is a brief sketch of your potential customer:

1. iPod owner
2. Early technology adopter
3. Annual income $40,000 to $150,000
4. Shops in upscale malls
5. Why will they be your customer? Because they own an iPod, and you are conveniently located, and you offer contemporary iPod accessories.
6. What do they require from you to remain your customer? They require quality, cutting-edge accessories, and knowledgeable sales personnel.

Since you will be tailoring your marketing mix to your target market, you need to make sure that you investigate and define your target market well. Here are some aspects that you should consider when evaluating a potential target market:

1.   Growth rate?
2.   Can you readily identify and define your target market?
3.   Can you effectively deploy your company assets to meet the needs and wants of this market?
4.   Size of the market?
5.   What will it take to reach the market?
6.   Competition in the segment?
7.   Brand loyalty of existing customers in the market?
8.   Required market share or sales to breakeven?
9.   Profit margin and net profit that you expect to earn from the market?
10. How does the future look for your target market when looking at the effects of politics, economy, society, and technology (the P.E.S.T. analysis as discussed in chapter entitled "CREATIVE THINKING IN BUSINESS")?

See if the target market that you identify and select for your potential market segment can pass the following tests:

1.   Actionable – Can you create a marketing plan that can actually turn your market segment into profits?
2.   Measurable – Can you truly measure this target market and measure the results of deploying your company assets to promote your goods and services to this market?
3.   Accessible – Can you effectively get your message to the selected target market and deliver your goods and services to them?
4.   Worthwhile – Can this target market sustain a demand for your products and services? Does the target market want your product, and do they have the purchasing power to complete the purchase transaction?

Once you select your target markets, you need to be laser-focused on them. There may be people outside of your target market that become customers. This is good, but unless they have great potential, you shouldn't expend much effort to attract them. If you see that these new customers are increasing in strength, then you may need to redefine your target market and redeploy your marketing mix resources accordingly.

POSITIONING

How you want to be perceived in the market will greatly influence the price, product, place, and promotion elements of your marketing mix. To determine this, you need to ask yourself some basic questions:

- How do you want to be known in the market? Describe the way in which you want your target market to perceive you.
- Who are your competitors?
- What differentiates your product from that of your competition? Use elements other than price as your differentiating factor here. Is your product different enough so that customers will actually notice the difference?
- What are your competitors' prices? How are your competitors' products positioned in the market?
- What is your company's market? Will you sell B2B (business to business), or will you sell to distributors or directly to consumers?

Both your individual personality and the market in which you feel most comfortable will determine the position you choose for your company within the marketplace. The position might be based on your prior experiences, or it might be based on a product that you have developed and want to introduce into the marketplace. It might be based on a need you see in the marketplace. Positioning will be based on the type of client or customer you will be serving, the goods and services you will be selling, and how you'll want your company perceived in the marketplace.

PRICE

Pricing your products is an art, not a science. You can perform all of your analysis with great care, perform your planning flawlessly, and implement your strategy with precision, yet still get it wrong. In addition to your analysis, you will probably have a number of trials and errors before you get it right. After you have completed all of your analysis, it will still come down to your "gut" feel. But you can get a much more useful "gut" feel after you have completely analyzed your prices based on the material included in this chapter.

Once you determine what your overall objectives are for your pricing, you can then develop your pricing strategies. The most common price strategies are Premium Pricing, Value Pricing, Cost-Plus Pricing, Competitive Pricing, Penetration Pricing, and Skimming. We will also discuss some pricing sub-strategies. These are tools that you can use along with your pricing strategies to enhance your sales and your bottom line. Your pricing strategies should not be handcuffs; they are your overall approach and guide to maximization of profits for your company.

Price – Objectives

Pricing objectives should only be formulated after you know your company objectives and your marketing objectives. Even if you don't formally commit to all of these objectives in writing, you should at least go through the mental process of reviewing each one and seeing how they all fit together; then you should commit your pricing policies and procedures to writing.

Company Objectives

You go into business to build a profitable company. I have yet to see an entrepreneur who went into business in order to lose money. You want the business to be stable and have a long life. The chapter entitled "DO YOU REALLY WANT TO BE AN ENTREPRENEUR?" discusses a number of reasons a person goes into business. Money is not the only reason that most people go into business. There are many reasons even more important than money for going into business. These reasons will serve as the foundation for your company objectives. Your company objectives will support your mission statement. Wal-Mart's mission statement is "To give ordinary folk the chance to buy the same thing as rich people." Given this mission statement, Wal-Mart's company objective is to give the average person a wide choice of high-quality products and to do this profitably, generating a fair return for their shareholders. Wal-Mart is known for having a big selection of quality merchandise at the best price possible.

Marketing Objectives

Your marketing objectives will support your company objectives. If your company objectives are to be a big-box store like Costco, then your marketing objectives will support your company objectives by selling at the lowest possible cost and in large quantities. Remember that marketing involves advertising, promotions, public relations, and any other efforts that support the growth of your business and your company objectives.

Pricing Objectives

You will have overall pricing objectives that support your marketing objectives and pricing objectives for individual products that support your overall pricing objectives. Continuing with the big-box example above, you may have some products priced at cost (no profits built into their prices) that will get people into your store to buy them and pick up some of your higher-margin products at the same time. You might want to sell a special razor at cost so that your customers will pick up a specific brand of razor blade. You might want to have your razors bundled so that they are attractively priced but sold in quantities. In this case, your overall pricing policy is to sell select products at very low margins that will lead customers to buy your higher-margin products, thus maximizing your overall profits.

Your goals in the market place will impact your pricing decisions. Are you trying to gain market share? Are you trying to introduce a whole new product concept to the market? Are you trying to combat a new company that has moved into the neighborhood? Your pricing decisions must always be sensitive to the external environment (e.g., competition, economy) rather than be a knee-jerk reaction to them. If your pricing decisions are based on a well laid-out and documented pricing policy, you will avoid knee-jerk reactions to changes in your marketplace environment.

Pricing Policies and Procedures

Since pricing product is an integral part of your business model, you will want to have written pricing policies and procedures. Having written pricing policies will help you ensure that the policies are designed in support of your overall company objectives and that they are being consistently applied. Part of your policies and procedures should include pricing models that calculate your prices based on changing parameters. If you have built a pricing model in which you have identified all of your pricing variables, you can easily isolate one variable to see its impact on your profitability. It is best to have standard pricing worksheets built in Excel® so that you don't have to re-create the wheel each time you have to make a pricing decision and so that your policies are applied on a consistent basis. I have seen people develop a pricing model where they had left out a critical cost element that made the price they were charging for their product unprofitable for every unit sold. A well-thought-out and well–laid-out model can reduce the likelihood of this happening. Having written policies and procedures for pricing can help minimize serious errors like this one. Here are some questions to ask yourself when you are drafting your pricing policies and procedures:

- Do you price all of your products at levels that provide for adequate profit margins? If not, why?
- Are your products priced so that there is room for markdowns during sales?
- Do you constantly monitor costs of your products and make price changes to provide for continued profitability?
- Have you analyzed your price-volume combination so that you are maximizing profits?
- Are your prices consistent with your product images?
- When you increase or reduce prices, do you consider your competitors' reactions?
- When you increase or decrease prices, do you consider your customers' reactions?
- Do you price to cover your variable costs, fixed costs, and your desired profit margins?
- Customers often equate the quality of unknown products with their prices. Do you adjust prices accordingly?
- When setting prices, do you consider these factors:
    - Channels of distribution?
    - Competitive and legal forces?
    - Annual volume and life-cycle volume?
    - Opportunities for special market promotions?
    - Effect of markdowns on margins?
- Do your accounting systems give you enough information by product to price effectively?
- Do you practice odd pricing (e.g., $1.94, $2.83)?
- To avoid competitor retaliation, have you tried adding extra services, providing warranties, or paying transportation costs rather than lowering prices?
- Do you give volume discounts?
- Do you develop continuity pricing if someone purchases one of a set and

continues to purchase additional elements of the set at later dates?
- Do you provide different pricing structures for different channels of distribution?
- Do you allow price changes outside of your standard pricing model? If so, under what circumstances?
- Do major price adjustments require your or top-level executive written approval?
- Have you defined "major price adjustment"?
- Do you advertise prices?
- Do you give discounts to special groups: military, clergy, firemen, students, etc.?
- Do you give employees and their relatives special discounts?

Price – Your Ceiling and Your Floor

When you set the prices for your products or services, your prices must be competitive and yet cover your fixed and variable costs and return a profit to you. There will always be a floor and a ceiling for your price. You can go through all of your pricing calculations, but in the end, your price must be between this floor and ceiling.

The cost of your product is "the floor." This includes all of the costs to get your product from its source to your shelves for sale. These costs will normally include the following components if you are buying finished goods for sale:

- Cost of the product from the supplier
- Taxes, customs, and duties
- Any assembly required for the product
- Storage/warehouse costs while your product is waiting to be moved to your store shelves
- Packaging if charged separately from the cost of the product
- Shipping materials and cartons
- Transportation from supplier to your store
- Overhead allocation

There are some reasons for pricing products below or near the floor, and maybe even at a loss. Sometimes you might need a "loss leader" to get people into your store or to get people to visit your Web site. "Loss leaders" are products that are sold either with no profit built in or below cost to bring people into your store or your Web site with the hope that they will then buy other products. There are certain situations in which you will sell products at small margins or at a loss to get people to buy related products. As an example, Nintendo sells Game Boy® at very small margins so that they can sell their Nintendo games, which have good margins. This is often called the "razor/razor blade" approach. Give the razor away so that you can sell more razor blades. Gillette mastered this effective sales approach years ago. Everyone benefits from this sales approach: consumers get the razor they want at a really good price, you benefit because they have to buy your higher-priced razor blades.

If you were manufacturing your product instead of buying finished goods, you would add labor and other manufacturing costs involved to its cost.

The ceiling price is the price customers are willing to pay for your product. If you price your product above this ceiling, your product will gather dust on the shelves. The ceiling price will be greatly influenced by your customers' perceived value of the product, the price being charged by your competition for the same product, and the availability of your product.

If your product is hard to get and the demand is high, your selling price can command a premium. There is a great movie with Arnold Schwarzenegger called *Jingle All the Way*. In the film, Howard Langston, Arnold's character, forgets to get his son "Turbo Man" for Christmas. He tries to find the toy, but Turbo Man is in short supply, and people are paying outrageous amounts for the doll. The film is actually based on the "Cabbage Patch" doll phenomenon. Moms and dads were willing to pay almost any price for the almost impossible to find Cabbage Patch dolls at Christmastime. If you have a popular product and you are the exclusive seller of the product, you will have incredible latitude in setting your price. BUT, with this being said, remember the golden rule of "a fair price and a fair profit." This does not mean that you can't charge a premium for a product, because you won't be able to charge a premium permanently, and you will not be able to charge a premium on all of your products. There are situations where it would be unethical and un-Christian to charge whatever premiums consumers would be willing to pay. In 2005, New Orleans' levies broke, ruining thousands of homes and businesses. Some gas stations increased their prices well beyond what was warranted based on their costs. The United States federal government warned all gasoline suppliers against price gouging. It's much easier to justify premium pricing on luxury products than on "necessity" types of products.

Price – The Starting Point of your Price Analysis – Calculating Breakeven

A good place to start your price analysis is to compute your break-even price for your product. If you are not at least breaking even, you will not have to worry about long-range planning, because you will be out of business soon. In your break-even calculation, you will have fixed costs that are not related directly to the number of units of products that you sell. You will also have costs directly related to the product. These are called *variable costs*. They will vary with the number of units sold.

Keep in mind that each industry and type of business (e.g., service, retail, manufacturing) will have its own rule of thumb for pricing products. As an example, if you are manufacturing a product, you need to see if your final retail price will be in line with consumer expectations and competitor prices. As a rule of thumb, you will want to take all of your variable cost, fixed cost, overhead allocation, and your "built in" profit and multiply this sum by 4. This will give the wholesaler his margin, and it will give the retailer room for his normal margin. If you are just starting out in your manufacturing business, you will probably have to sell to a distributor that will sell to the wholesaler, since many wholesalers will not deal directly with small new companies. So when you are calculating the final retail price, you need to find a product price acceptable to a distributor that will sell to a wholesaler that will sell to a retailer.

Breakeven is a good tool that will show you how many dollars in sales or sales in units you need to break even.

$$\text{Breakeven in sales} = \frac{\text{Fixed expenses}}{1 - \dfrac{\text{Gross margin per unit}}{\text{Selling price per unit}}}$$

Another way to view the break-even formula is to see how many units the firm must produce and sell to pay for fixed expenses. You subtract the variable expense per unit from the sales income for each unit. The difference per unit (contribution margin) is then applied to fixed expenses. The break-even quantity is the number of units that must be sold to cover expenses.

$$\text{Breakeven in units} = \frac{\text{Fixed expenses}}{\text{Sales price per unit} - \text{variable cost per unit}}$$

Example:

The Successful Tee Shirt Company sells decal-decorated tee-shirts to its customers for $10.00 each. The shirts cost $4.00 each and the decal costs $.40. The store pays a $.60 commission to the salesperson. The total variable cost is $5.00. The total of the fixed costs for the Successful Tee Shirt Company is $1,500 a month.

Using the formula for computing breakeven in units, we find that dividing the monthly fixed cost of $1,500 by $5 gives a break-even point of 300 shirts per month. If we sell 300 shirts at $10 each, we generate $3,000. Our variable costs total $5 per shirt, or $1,500. Adding the fixed cost of $1,500 to variable costs of $1,500 equals $3,000.

$$\text{Break-even point} = \frac{\$1,500}{\$10 - \$5} = 300 \text{ shirts}$$

Break-even analysis pinpoints where total gross margin (sales less cost of sales) equals total fixed expenses. To calculate your break-even point, take your most current income statement and identify each cost as either fixed or variable. Fixed costs are independent of sales level, while variable costs rise and fall with sales. Mixed costs involve elements of both. Most costs will fall readily into the fixed or variable category; for those that don't, allocate 50% to fixed costs and 50% to variable.

The simple analysis above assumes that you only have one product. Realistically, you will have a number of products. Not all of your products will have the same contribution (gross margin) to cover fixed costs and profits. Following is an example of a company that has three products. One of the products is a high-ticket item with a good gross margin, but the unit sales are projected to be only twenty units per month.

The first step is to estimate the units of each product or product group that will sell per month. After you determine this information, construct a spreadsheet (this is much easier if you use Microsoft Excel® software.) See Step 1, below. The spreadsheet has the unit selling price and variable costs, and calculates Unit Gross Margin for each product. You should complete a projection for all twelve months of the year and then calculate the average Unit Gross Margin per month. This is necessary, because all businesses have factors that will affect monthly sales, such as holidays. Then you calculate projected dollar sales and dollar gross margin for each product. The Gross Margin (Sales less variable costs) is used to cover fixed costs and profits. Then you divide total gross margin ($61,000) by total unit sales (320) to arrive at the computed unit gross margin (GM). You then calculate the percentage of sales for products A, B, and C as a percentage of your total projected unit sales.

Step 1 - determine weighted average gross margin

	Product A	Product B	Product C	Total	
Unit selling price	$100	$200	$3,000		
Variable costs	$20	$50	$1,500		
Unit Gross Margin	$80	$150	$1,500	Average	$577
Projected unit sales	200	100	20	320	
Projected sales	$20,000	$20,000	$60,000	Total	$100,000
Projected gross margin	$16,000	$15,000	$30,000	$61,000	

Calculation of Weighted Average Unit Gross Margin:

	Gross Margin	Unit Sales	
Product A	$16,000	200	63%
Product B	$15,000	100	31%
Product C	$30,000	20	6%
Total	$61,000	320	100%
Ttl Unit Sales	320	320	
Computed Unit Avg GM	$191 ($61,000/ 320 units)		

Fig.35 – Weighted Average Gross Margin Step 1

In step 2, estimate all of your monthly fixed expenses, or use your profit and loss statements to develop your fixed expense amount. In our example, your monthly fixed expenses are $14,550. You are now ready for Step 3.

Step 2 - determine fixed expenses

Fixed Expenses:

Owner Salary	$10,000
Rent	$1,000
Utilities	$200
Assistant Wages	$3,000
Telephone	$200
Supplies	$150
Total Fixed Expense	$14,550

Fig.36 – Weighted Average Gross Margin Step 2

In step 3, you calculate the weighted average breakeven in units by dividing your calculated average margin (determined in step 1) into your estimated total fixed expense. This results in total units (all three products combined have a total of 76). Then you take the percentage calculated in Step 1 for each product and multiply it by the total calculated units necessary to break even. Combining all of the product unit sales together will give you the number of unit sales per product necessary to reach a total per-unit break-even point. You can double-check the calculation to make sure that your total units for breakeven equal your individually calculated units to break even.

Step 3 - Calculate break even in units

Total Fixed Expense		$14,550
Weighted average Gross Margin		$191
Total Units to sell to breakeven		76
Product A unit sales to breakeven	63%	48
Product B unit sales to breakeven	31%	24
Product C unit sales to breakeven	6%	5
Total units to breakeven		76

Fig.37 – Weighted Average Gross Margin Step 3

Now for step 4, which is really just a proof of your calculations. You can see in Step 4 that your total gross margin equals your total fixed expense. You are in good shape if your projected sales are reasonably accurate. Your analysis shows that you need to sell a total of 76 units of product to break even, and you are projecting that you will actually sell 320 units of product.

Step 4 - Proof

	Units	GM	Total GM
Product A unit sales to breakeven	48	$80	$3,816
Product B unit sales to breakeven	24	$150	$3,578
Product C unit sales to breakeven	5	$1,500	$7,156
Total projected GM			$14,550
Total Fixed Expenses			$14,550
Difference			$0

Fig.38 – Weighted Average Gross Margin Step 4

You can extend this price model out by including your desired profit along with your fixed costs. You can then determine the sales required to cover your fixed costs and generate your desired profit.

Price – Services and Manufactured Products

Developing prices for services and manufacturing products is slightly different than the process used for retail products. The points discussed in this section on Pricing will almost all apply to these three areas of sales, but with a little twist for both the services industry and the manufacturing sector.

Price – Services

In service businesses, your primary "raw material" is labor. You only have so much of it, and you want to utilize it as much as possible at the highest possible rate. In law firms and CPA firms, you will often hear new young professionals walking the hallways talking about "billable hours." In all industries, there will invariably be time that is not billable to clients. Staff must have down non-billable time for continuing education, administrative work, and other non-billable activities.

Let's say the business you want to start is a bookkeeping service. Since you are just starting out, let's assume that you are only going to bill out your time and the time of a part-time bookkeeper who will be working 20 hours a week. You estimate that you will be able to bill out about 80% of her time. Your bookkeeper is costing you $10 an hour, including fringe benefits. You don't have to pay her fringe benefits, but as a Christian, you want to make sure you go above and beyond what is required when it comes to your staff.

Determine how much you want to earn, and temper it with a dose of reality. In this example, further assume that you feel that you would like to open an office rather than work out of your house. Based on this, you calculate that your operating cost for rent, telephone, supplies, etc., is approximately $5,000 per month. Your target income is $120,000 a year or $10,000 a month. You estimate that you can bill your time out at about $40 an hour and your part-time bookkeeper at $25 an hour.

Calculate your monthly cash requirements:

Rent, telephone, supplies, etc.	$ 5,000
Bookkeeper salary, including fringe (80 h × $10)	$ 800
Your target salary	$10,000
Total monthly cash requirements	$15,800
Billing for bookkeeper (80 h × 80% × $25/h)	($ 1,600)
Cash requirement that you have to cover from your billings	$14,200

You estimate that you can bill out at 75% of your total hours worked, because you have to do all of the administrative and marketing work. Hence, you can bill out at about 120 hours per month (160 × 75%). If you bill out at 120 hours at $75 per hour, you will bill a total of $9,000 dollars for the month. You will be able to bill your bookkeeper out for approximately $1,600 per month, but you must pay her $800, leaving $800 of gross profit. This means that you will not break even, since the cash outlays that you need to cover are $14,200 and you can only generate $10,600 in billings. Now, we have to do a gap analysis, which is a measurement of the difference between the cash you must generate in order to cover projected cash outlays and the cash that you can realistically generate.

In our bookkeeping scenario, you cannot cover $3,600 of cash outlays for an average month. You need to either reduce your monthly outlays of cash or increase your billing rate or the number of billable hours. If you are able to acquire the clients, you could increase your billing rate or increase your bookkeeper's billable hours. At the moment, you don't think you can increase your billing rate (based on the competitions' rates), and you don't think that you can increase your billable hours at all. To cover the $3,600 by increasing your bookkeeper's billable hours, you will need to have 360 more billable hours

Calculation:		Proof:	
billing rate	$25	Hours worked	360
billable %	80%	billable %	80%
billable	$20	hours billed	288
Bookkeeper wages	$10	billing rate	$25
Average Gross Margin	$10	Amount billed	$7,200
Deficit	$3,600	Bookkeeper wages paid	$3,600
hours needed	360	Gross Margin	$3,600
		Difference	$0

Fig.39 – Bookkeeper Salary Coverage

These calculations illustrate that you can't just take the hourly billing rate for your bookkeeper and divide them into the deficit of $3,600, because not all of your bookkeeper's hours are billable.

Based on this analysis, you will be short on your cash inflows. This shortage cannot be covered by increasing your billings or by hiring new bookkeepers, since you don't yet have the business necessary to do so. You will need to cover the shortage with your financing until you can acquire new customers. Another option is to work out of your home until you acquire a few more customers.

Price – Manufactured Goods

A detailed discussion concerning manufacturing cost accounting is beyond the scope of this book. Should you decide to start a manufacturing company, there are a number of very good books on the market that discuss this subject in depth. There are two major types of manufacturing costing that will impact your pricing decisions if you are a manufacturing business. One is called *process costing,* and the other is called *job-order costing.* These accounting processes do not determine the price that you need to charge for your product. They help you determine what your products are costing you. Once you can determine your actual costs of your products, you can apply the rest of the concepts discussed in this chapter to determine your proper selling prices.

Process Costing

A process costing system is used when a single, homogeneous product is produced. In a process costing system, total manufacturing costs are divided by the total number of units produced during a given production period, usually a month. Total units produced will include finished goods and equivalent units that are partially completed.

In a process costing system, there are typically 5 steps that you go through to get the costs of your products:

1. Summarize the physical flow of your product units in production.
2. Compute output in terms of equivalent units.
3. Compute equivalent costs.
4. Summarize total costs to account for.
5. Assign total costs to units completed and to units in ending works-in-process.

Examples of industries that use process costing are manufacturers of flour and bricks, major food processors, and oil refining.

Job-order Costing

Job-order costing is used when different types of products, jobs, or batches are produced within a period. In a job-order costing system, direct materials costs and direct labor costs are usually identifiable directly to particular jobs. Overhead is normally applied to jobs using a predetermined rate. Actual overhead is not normally traceable directly to any give job. Examples of industries that use job-order costing are shipbuilding, hospitals, professional service firms such as law firms, movie studios, and other special order types of businesses.

Price – Issues Affecting Price

Although the prices for your products must always be measured against your price ceiling and price floor, there are other factors that have significant impact on your pricing decisions.

Price – Impact of Supply and Demand

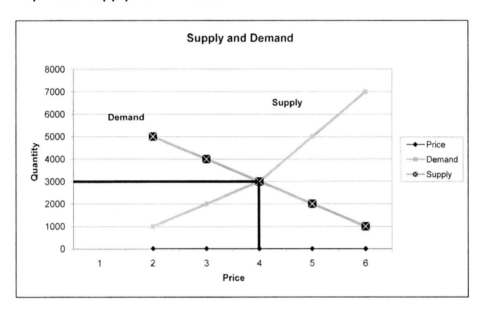

Fig.40 – Suppy/ demand Graph

The market price of your product will be determined by both supply and demand. The graph above shows the following data presented in a "Supply and Demand" chart.

Price	Demand	Supply
$16	1,000	5,000
$13	2,000	4,000
$10	3,000	3,000
$7	5,000	2,000
$4	7,000	1,000

Fig.41 – Supply/ demand Data

The table shows that at a price of $16 for this product, the demand for it would be 1,000 units; but suppliers would be willing to supply 5,000 units at this price. This is not a good situation, and the law of supply and demand will drive the price back down to a lever where customers will begin purchasing it at a greater rate. Supply and demand equilibrium is achieved when suppliers are willing to supply what buyers are willing to buy. In the example, the equilibrium price is $10. At this point, customers will buy 3,000, units and suppliers are willing to supply 3,000 units.

The Supply and Demand model shows that when prices are high, suppliers are willing to supply more and customers are willing to buy less. The converse is also true. When prices are low, consumers will buy more, but suppliers will supply less. This has some rather important implications for you and your product pricing.

Let's take the PDA (personal digital assistant) market as an example. Most people think of the Palm Pilot when they think of the PDA market. Approximately half of the PDAs sold are not Palm PDAs but PDAs based on the Microsoft operating system. In 1996, Palm Computing introduced the Palm Pilot, and that same year, Microsoft introduced its CE operating system for handheld computers. A number of manufacturers, such as HP, Compaq, and Casio, adopted it for their handheld PDAs. The very first PDAs were $300+ in price. Within 24 months, there were over 20 companies producing PDAs. This competition put pressure on the retail price point so that PDAs started appearing on the market for less than two hundred dollars at retail. Although the price point had dropped significantly, the consumer fascination with the PDA had begun to wane, and demand began to fall. With demand falling and weak price points, some manufacturers such as Sony and Toshiba stopped manufacturing PDAs.

With the shift of consumers to more multipurpose devices, PDAs are becoming more business-oriented, and some manufacturers are leaving the marketplace, driving the average price of a PDA back up. According to Gartner (www.gartner.com,), one of the world's leading providers of research and analysis about the global information technology industry, in a news release dated May 4, 2005, the average selling price of PDAs rose 15% to $406, the highest since Gartner began tracking PDA prices in 2000.

This is a classic example of the law of supply and demand at work. Although you may not be a big manufacturer of PDAs, their market position will substantially impact your business if you produce and/or sell PDA accessories such as carrying cases and software. As a small business, there will always be supply and demand trends of big companies that will directly impact your pricing decisions and your business overall.

Price – Impact of Availability

Availability, or the lack thereof, can affect your business at a number of levels. Let's say that you are a small company that has developed a great little electronic product: a picture frame that attaches to your computer and rotates through selected pictures from your computer's picture file. Your picture frame then displays these pictures in an "electronic picture frame" that sits beside your computer. You form a partnership with a manufacturer. The manufacturer uses silicon wafers to produce your integrated circuits (ICs) for your USB picture frame. You read that there is a worldwide silicon wafer shortage because Apple Computing has just announced that it's releasing a new version of its iPod. The prices of your components will go up. Your challenge will be to see if the increased costs of your IC, caused by the silicon wafer shortage, will impact your retail price. And if it does impact your retail price point, will it do so to the point of pricing you out of your primary market?

The point here is that major events involving availability of raw materials and components worldwide can and will affect your pricing decisions, even if you are just a "mom and pop" operation. The previous example was a real-life issue that affected a small consumer electronics development company called Easy Brain Labs, Inc.

Price – Impact of USP (Unique Selling Proposition)

If your product is truly unique and fills a consumer need, a lot of the normal rules of pricing will not apply. If you are the only one who has the product and you can get your message out to consumers, it's a situation of "what the traffic will bear," at least for the short term. If the product is a necessity for consumers, then, as a Christian, you will have moral and ethical constraints not to gouge your customers. If it is a nonnecessity product (e.g., for entertainment), then you will have more latitude in setting your price. Also, keep in mind that what may seem to be gouging at the start of a new product's life cycle will balance out over the life of the product as its price settles into a consumer-acceptable price over its life cycle. Also, you have to consider the pricing of all of your products together when deciding if you are following the Christian principle of a "fair price for a fair product or service." Some of your products may not enjoy good margins, while others may have high margins to offset those that don't. You may also have to charge premium prices to offset front-end development costs.

What traffic will bear. What is the perceived value of your product? This is a very subjective point to keep in mind. When a new and innovative product is first introduced, it will have more perceived value than at any other time in its product life cycle. Early adopters will pay to have the coolest new, exciting, innovative product. Fads fall into this category. Years ago, Ken Hakuta, a.k.a. Dr. Fad, introduced the children's toy called Wacky Wall Walker. It was a totally silly product. Even Mr. Hakuta realized this and stated so in his book, *How to Create Your Own Fad and Make a Million Dollars*. He wrote, "The Wacky Wall Walkers have absolutely no social significance. That's why people buy them—and Mood Rings, and Pet Rocks. They're so dumb, people find them irresistible."[35]

Mr. Hakuta actually went on to make over $20 million off of this silly little toy. It was a little piece of rubber with eight little sprouts sticking out. Mr. Hakutaq said, "When you threw it against the wall, it would stick there for a few seconds, and then it appeared to come alive as it shuddered, let go, flipped over, grabbed the wall again, lurched downward, shimmied, and expired." Mr. Hakuta goes on to say that what starts out selling at Bloomingdales for $3.00 will go on to sell eventually in Kmart for $1.79. It's almost always best to aim for the highest price you can sell your products at, since you may be forced to lower the price during the product's life cycle. You can always go down in price, but it's very difficult to go up once a price is set.

Price – Impact of Customers

Your target customers will naturally have a major impact on your pricing decisions. When you are just starting your business, you may have a good feel for who your customer is. Or do you? You might have a product that caters to the "tweener market" (typically considered to be kids from 12 to 17 years old). You have possibly picked the right demographic, but have you really looked at the psychographic aspects of your target customers? The American Marketing Association defines psychographic analysis as:

> "A technique that investigates how people live, what interests them, and what they like...."

Although the tweener market is generally defined as 12 to 17 years old, they typically have a psychographic description of wanting what makes them feel like a teenager. When studying your target market, study their psychographic characteristics as well as their demographic characteristics. Continuing on with the discussion of the tweener market, they tend to be less sensitive to price than other demographic/psychographic groups. It's normally mom and dad pulling out the credit card to pay for your product.

35   Ken Hakuta, *How to Create Your Own Fad and Make a Million Dollars*, New York: Avon Books, pg. ii, 1990.

Keeping this in mind, you have to capture the imagination of the tweener and his/her parents.

Your customers will influence your pricing decisions, because they can quickly lose interest in your product based on a long list of reasons. They may find it cheaper somewhere else, there may be new technology that pulls them from your product, maybe it didn't measure up to their expectations. You must constantly "read" your customers and be on the lookout for changes in their preference. Your customer will be the major factor in deciding the ceiling price for your products.

Price – Impact of Competition

Your competition will be one of the major forces setting your pricing ceiling. One of the key elements to your pricing decisions is knowing your competitors' prices. It is always a good policy to "shop" your competition at all times. In today's environment, it is relatively easy to keep track of your competition's prices.

Internet	Almost all of your competitors will have Internet sites. Review their sites and check out their prices. Look at their product mix and any special feature to their pricing structure. You can learn a lot about your competition by visiting their Web sites.
Shop the Competition	If you are a retailer, go window shopping at your competitor's place of business. You can learn a lot about how he is merchandising his products. If a big-box store has just moved into your neighborhood, you can see what its disadvantages are by taking a walk down its aisles. The first thing that comes to mind is lack of service, long lines, and bulk pricing (sometimes an advantage and sometimes a disadvantage).
Read Ads	Be sure to keep an eye on his newspaper ads and other printed media and electronic media. Get on your competitors' mailing lists and regularly look through their catalogs.

Don't let your competitor set your prices for you—just keep abreast of his pricing. There are a number of ways to beat your competition other than pricing. You can give better service, better quality products, easier access, etc.

Price – Strategies

Once you have determined what your pricing objectives are, there are a number of strategies that can help you in achieving your pricing objectives. You don't have to choose one strategy exclusively over other strategies. They are merely broad classifications. The most-often-used strategies are Premium Pricing, Value Pricing, Cost-Plus Pricing, Competitive Pricing, Penetration Pricing, Skimming, and Price-Lining.

Price – Strategies – Premium Pricing

Premium pricing is used when your product has one or more unique characteristics. This uniqueness differentiates your product greatly from your competition and creates a significant competitive advantage over your competition, enabling you to charge a premium price for your product. This strategy requires that your product be of high-perceived quality and/or limited availability. As your competitors begin to see that you are able to sustain your premium pricing, they will assume that you have a high margin in your product. They will start to develop products to compete with yours. The length of time that you are able to sustain your premium pricing strategy will depend on barriers to entry for your competitors. If you have developed a unique patent for a product, then you may have created a substantial barrier to entry.

If you think a competitor is going to knock off your product, then you might want to consider creating your own product knockoff. If a competitor is tracking your product and sees another one on the market in addition to yours, he may be more hesitant to enter the market. When I was a controller for a major food company, we owned two companies that produced similar products. This was useful when food store chains wanted to give their customers choices in their meat section: both of our companies' products would be sold in the meat section to give their customers choices.

As part of a premium pricing strategy, you may want to consider producing a less expensive, less-feature-rich product to be sold at different outlets than your premium version. This will help combat a competitor trying to capture some of your market share based on price and will still allow you to keep your premium pricing structure in place.

The more competition you get, the less useful premium pricing becomes as a strategy.

Price – Strategies – Value Pricing

Value pricing is the little brother to premium pricing. If you are experiencing moderate competition, you may want to consider value pricing as a strategy. You would consider using this strategy when there are only a few competitors, barriers to entry are still relatively high, and your customers value the benefits provided by your product. This might be an appropriate strategy when you have products that have competitive advantages that are not sustainable for a long period of time.

Price – Strategies – Cost-Plus Pricing

Cost-Plus Pricing is a pricing method commonly used by many companies, especially those in retail. It is used primarily because it is easy to calculate and requires little information. There are several varieties, but the common thread in all of them is that you first calculate the cost of the product, and then include an additional amount to represent profit.

Calculating Price Using the Cost-Plus Method

Cost-plus pricing is probably the most widely used method of pricing product. This is based primarily on the fact that it's easy to use. There are several ways of determining cost, and the profit can be added as either a percentage markup or an absolute amount. One example is:

$$P = (AVC + FC\%) * (1 + MK\%)$$

where:
P = price
AVC = average variable cost
$FC\%$ = percentage allocation of fixed costs
$MK\%$ = percentage markup

For example: If variable cost (AVC) is $30, the allocation to cover fixed costs is $10 and you calculate that you need a 50% markup, then you would charge a price of $60 computed as follows:

$$P = (\$30 + \$10) * (1 + 50\%)$$
$$P = \$40 * 1.5$$
$$P = \$60$$

To make things simpler, some firms, particularly retailers, ignore fixed costs and just use the purchase price paid to their suppliers as their cost. They indirectly incorporate the fixed cost allocation into the markup percentage. To simplify things even further, sometimes a fixed amount is applied rather than a percentage. I would try to avoid this approach, as it does not give proper weight to the value of the product.

Disadvantages of Cost-Plus Pricing

- tends to ignore the role of consumers
- implicit limits to growth and profit potential
- arbitrary measurement of variable and fixed costs
- variable and fixed costs not analyzed frequently
- tends to ignore the role of competitors
- uses historical accounting costs

Advantages of Cost-Plus Pricing

- easy to use
- leads to profitability if fixed costs and variable costs are analyzed frequently
- an easy policy to establish, set, and use

As long as you pay attention to your price floor and ceiling, and other elements of your pricing decision, Cost-Plus Pricing can be a simple tool to use. BUT, keep in mind that you should constantly be reviewing your pricing elements and your pricing policy so that you do not become complacent (or lazy) when it comes to your product pricing.

Price – Strategies – Competitive Pricing

Tracking your pricing with that of your competitors can be tricky. You must constantly monitor your competition. You will be monitoring your competition anyway, but if you are tying your pricing to your competitors' pricing, you will monitor their pricing even more closely. This pricing strategy can also be imprecise, because you probably will not be aware of their price structure, their volume of product sold, and the spectrum of services that they are giving to their customers.

Pricing Above the Competition

This strategy is possible when price is not your customers' greatest concern. Some considerations important enough for customers to justify paying higher prices include:

- Non-product considerations
  - Shorter lines
  - Home delivery
  - Product assembly
  - Speed of service
  - Satisfactory handling of customer complaints
  - "No questions asked" return policy
  - Employees' knowledge of product and/or service
  - Friendly employees
  - Convenient or exclusive location
  - Ease of ordering (e.g., "one button" ordering Web site)
  - Free wrapping and mailing
  - Free coffee and donuts
  - Product training
  - Easy payment plans

- Product or Service
  - Exclusive merchandise
  - Extensive selection of merchandise
  - Extensive selection of variations of merchandise
  - Focused merchandise line
  - Partnering with compatible products offered by others
  - Higher quality of merchandise
  - Customizable merchandise
  - Small quantities available
  - Large quantities available
  - Special order

Pricing Below the Competition

This is a very difficult strategy to maintain, especially if you are a new small business. A strategy based solely on low price simply will not work for very long if you are just starting your business. Competitors will meet your price and, before long, you may have a price war that you may not be able to win. You have to be aware of your competitors' prices at all times, but always pricing below the competition is not normally a good idea. There is bound to be a competitor who will be able to out-price you based on his buying volume or special relationship with his suppliers. If you are going to price your products below the competition, you must give consideration to the following:

- Obtain the best possible prices for your merchandise.
- Locate your business in an inexpensive location.
- Closely monitor inventory.
- Pay close attention to Economic Order Quantity calculations.
- Limit your products to fast-moving items. At low prices, you cannot afford to have them sitting on your shelves for an extended period of time.
- Your advertising should concentrate on prices.
- Limit your other services.
- Consider customer "self-serve" where possible.
- Give discounts for large-quantity purchases.
- Consider cash only and don't carry accounts receivable.

Pricing With the Competition

You will always give some consideration to your competition's pricing. They will be a factor for your price ceiling. You will not be at parity with your competition all of the time. You will not always be able to price at parity with your competition, as there are too many variables to your competition's pricing structure, and you cannot possibly know them all. He may have gotten a special price on a major purchase of a product that you both sell. While he still has this low-cost item on hand, you could lose a lot of money trying to meet his prices.

Price – Strategies – Penetration Pricing

Penetration pricing is a version of pricing below the competition for the purpose of gaining immediate market share or immediate recognition of your new product. The purpose of penetration pricing is to rapidly attract customers and discourage competition. Eventually, you will have to raise your prices to start making some profit on your products, and when you do, you will find out a lot about your customers' loyalty. Don't approach penetration pricing haphazardly. Do your homework. The margin that you give up in penetration pricing is like spending marketing dollars to attract customers with one big difference—with advertising dollars being spent, you don't have to worry about losing customers when you eventually raise prices. Always consider the option of getting your normal margin and spending more on marketing when you are considering penetration pricing. You might be able to achieve the penetration you are seeking with increased ad dollars rather than penetration pricing. Another option is to offer rebates on your product. This will enable you to get your product out at a lower price while maintaining your pricing structure and maintaining a consistent price perception for your customer.

Unless you have a truly unique product, your competition will soon meet your price, and there will be a general depression of prices for your product. As part of the penetration pricing strategy, you will want to differentiate your product with special services and other elements that have some barriers so that your competition cannot readily copy your approach. As an example, let's look at the discount airline industry. We have all seen a discount airline lower their fees and watched their competition follow suit. One way a particular airline effectively competed was by increasing routes to locations where their competition did not go. Think outside the box when it comes to price strategy.

One justification that is often used for penetration pricing is the fact (hopefully) that increased volumes will lead to lower cost per unit for the seller. Companies that need to use excess capacity will often use penetration pricing.

Price – Strategies – Skimming

Before milk was sold in a homogenized state, it would sit in your refrigerator and the sweet cream would rise to the top of the bottle. You could "skim" the cream from the bottle and have a really good tasting addition to your coffee. Skimming in the sense of pricing strategy involves charging a relatively high price for a short time when a new, innovative, or much improved product is launched onto the market. For some products, especially electronics and toys, "early adopters" are willing to pay extra to be the first of their friends to have the product. Skimming works as long as a demand for the product is inelastic. This means price, within a relevant range, will have no or little effect on the demand for the product. The inelasticity of demand for a product usually lasts for a very short time during the initial introduction of the product. Once your competitors see you enjoying increasing sales and good margins, they will introduce their own competing product, and the prices that consumers are willing to pay will decrease. Skimming, a temporary strategy, will be followed by one of the other strategies listed here.

There are several reasons to consider using Skimming as a normal part of your pricing strategy. If you spent a lot of money for research and development of your product, skimming is a way to recapture some of those funds. Skimming can also offset some of the cost of marketing your new product to consumers. Skimming can also be used to establish a high-quality image for your product.

Segmenting your market can help you maximize the benefits of skimming. As discussed in this chapter, there are a number of ways to segment your market, including geographically and demographically. With segmentation, you can have different pricing strategies for each target market segment or product line.

Skimming pricing also works if you have a superior product, your product is legally protected, you have had a technological breakthrough, or if the product is in limited production.

Pricing – Price Lining

This strategy targets a specific segment of consumers by carrying products only in a specific price range. Both "higher end" sellers and "lower end" sellers use this strategy effectively. At the low end, the "99 Cent" stores in Southern California have successfully used price lining. They sell everything from dog food to auto accessories using price lining. You can go to Rodeo Drive in Beverly Hills and see high-end price lining at work in a number of clothing shops.

Price – Sub-strategies

As well as the price strategies discussed above, there are a number of what I call "sub-strategies" that work with each of the primary strategies. I call them sub-strategies as they typically will not stand on their own but can be a part of an overall pricing strategy. The most important ones are Loss Leader, Razor/Razorblade, Reductions, Shipping and Handling, Segmenting, and Multiple Unit Pricing/ Bundle Pricing. These sub-strategies can enhance your overall pricing strategies. The discussion of Price Reductions is more of a defensive discussion if you are supplying your product to major retailers. They have the clout and the desire to extract reductions of your price. Your efforts will be to minimize these reductions while keeping your products in front of your buying public.

Price – Sub-strategies – Loss Leader

Loss leader pricing is a common practice for retailers. It is really a tool used with the other pricing strategies discussed here. As an example, you will normally find milk and other high demand, lower margin products at the back of grocery stores. To get to the milk, you have to travel down aisles stocked with hundreds of other food products. Many people end up with a shopping cart full of other products when all they really wanted was a gallon of milk.

Price – Sub-strategies – Razor/ Razorblade

This strategy, in conjunction with the other strategies listed in this discussion, is used to get customers to buy products that work in tandem with one of your other products, one that you've sold to them at a low margin, maybe even at a loss. Gillette uses this strategy extremely effectively with their name brand razor. They will sometimes even give away razors, knowing that their customers must then buy their name brand razor blades. Another example is Nintendo's Game Boy. The Game Boy is a sophisticated electronic device that has a relatively high bill of materials cost and thus has a very thin profit margin. But Nintendo sells games and licenses the right to sell games to electronic game companies at good margins. Color printers are sold at really low prices, but the ink cartridges made specifically for the machines by the manufacturer are often pricey, and the costumer has no other option but to buy them. The list goes on and on, which speaks to the success of this type of strategy. A product that has a consumable associated with it can be a gold mine.

Price – Sub-strategies – Price Reductions

There are several different types of selling price reductions. Some of them will be expected by retailers. If you are a retailer, they are another source of income and expense offset that your competition will be using, especially the big chains. If you are going to be selling to a retailer or you are opening a retail establishment that will be selling other companies' products, you need to be aware of these price reductions and their uses, since they will have a substantial impact on your selling price.

- Cash discounts

  This type of discount is given for timely payment of bills if you extend credit to your customers. You have probably heard the term "2% discount, net 30 days." This simply means that if your customer pays by day 30, he can take 2% off of the invoices being paid.

- Trade discounts

  Trade discounts are discounts to channel members (people or companies other than retail consumers) for performing marketing functions that you would normally perform. If you own a local hardware store (remember those?) and you have a neighborhood business that buffs out chrome bumpers, you would most likely give the chrome buffer a "trade discount" on his purchase of steel wool from your store.

- Quantity discounts

  Just as the name implies, the price reductions for this type of discount is granted for large-volume purchases. These discounts are justified on the assumption that large orders reduce selling expenses. This type of discount will either be a "cumulative quantity discount" or a "non-cumulative quantity discount." Cumulative quantity discounts reduce prices in amounts determined by purchases over stated time periods. Many businesses and consumers (i.e., the big-box stores) have come to expect quantity discounts from suppliers.

- Allowances

Allowances resemble discounts by specifying deductions from list prices. Typical categories of allowances are for trade-ins and promotional allowances. Here are some other allowances that retailers often expect:

- Marketing Development Funds

Often referred to as MDF, Marketing Development Funds are usually a budgeted amount dispensed at the retailer's discretion to develop new marketing channels or products. Companies may use MDF to launch new products or to introduce established products to new markets. A retailer and a manufacturer will work hand in hand on planned promotions. MDF programs frequently allow media not covered in co-op programs or will sponsor projects not usually considered advertising, such as business presentations or training classes. MDF will come from your product's price. It can be stated as an amount or a percentage of invoice or a flat amount. Whether you are a retailer or selling other people's products, or you are supplying products to retailers, you will eventually be confronted with MDF.

- Co-op Funds

Here, you will be paying the retailers a percentage of their marketing dollars spent for your product. For instance, you may agree to pay a percentage of the cost of any newspaper ads that feature your product. In a co-op advertising program, you will either pay the retailer directly, or he will deduct the co-op advertising dollars from your invoice. The retailer will normally set an upper limit. Retailers have come to view co-op money as an entitlement and usually use the money for commonplace ads. Manufacturers, given the choice, will normally opt for co-op plans, which are typically more structured and controlled, over MDF plans.

- Special Fund Allowances

If you are selling to retailers, this is where you buy some retailer real estate. Many big retailers give their product buyers special incentive to "sell their marketing real estate." The retailer will often offer you a "special deal" to buy end caps (the high-traffic display units at the end of the aisles) in their stores. These end caps will often generate higher sales, but they will cost you. A small chain/ high volume consumer electronics store charged $500 for each end cap in their twenty stores in 2004. With twenty stores, this amounted to $10,000 for the month.

Slotting Fees

Slotting fees have become a fact of life in the retail world. The mergers of major retailers over the years, and thus fewer shelf space options, have created an environment in which retailers can demand slotting fees for the introduction of a new product. City, state, and federal governmental entities have paid considerable attention to the issue of slotting fees. There is widespread and well-founded concern that slotting fees are reducing innovation, reducing competition, and increasing consumer prices. Slotting fees also contribute to the reduction of the variety of products introduced each year, and thus reduce consumer choices. If retailers demand large slotting fees for the introduction of new products, they squeeze the small manufacturer out of the race.

Slotting fees can be enormous. In 2001, American Greetings paid Kmart a slotting fee of $42 million dollars to be placed in their stores. This was for a five-year period but still an enormous fee. Manufacturers usually pay slotting allowances in cash. Each variation of a product represents a separate SKU (Stock Keeping Unit), and thus normally requires a separate slotting fee.

Slotting fees basically transfer a major portion of potential product failure risk back to the manufacturer.

There was a small company that produced CD-ROMs with video content for Pocket PCs. The major retailer in question demanded an impossible slotting fee. The small company was able to convince the large retailer to take a month's supply of free product instead of cash. The small company was able to do this because the CD-ROM duplicating company that supplied their CDs was actually funding their inventory. This illustrates some of the ways to get around slotting fees. When you are projecting your sales and cost of sales, you must know if and how much your retailers will charge in slotting fees. It is not enough to project your sales and direct costs.

Pay-to-Stay Fees

A second form of access payment sometimes demanded by large retailers is the pay-to-stay fee. It is just what it sounds like. If the retailer charges this fee, you will normally be required to pay in a lump sum at the beginning of the year. Many suppliers believe that pay-to-stay fees will exclude many small suppliers. They are right.

Pricing – Sub-strategies – Shipping and Handling

For some businesses, shipping and handling are major pricing considerations. There are a number of direct response products that are sold on the Internet and on television that make their total profit from shipping and handling. Recently, there was an advertisement on TV for a DVD with 10 classic movies for $9.99 plus shipping and handling of $4.95. The company made little, if any, profit on the actual DVD, but they made an average of one dollar from shipping and handling on each of the 500,000 DVDs that they sold. They charged $4.95, and their average shipping cost was $3.95. Another thing that they got that was incredibly valuable was the contact information of 500,000 people who were interested in their product line. As a Christian, you do not use any deceptive practices in business. You should state somewhere in your advertising that you are charging a flat rate for shipping and handling.

Whenever you can, let your customer pay for shipping and handling; in today's market, people are used to paying a separate fee for those services.

Price – Sub-strategies – Segmenting

For some products, you will possibly have a range of different types of customers. Price sensitivity and elasticity of demand may vary for different consumer segments for the same product. Airlines face this problem. Business travelers have to travel at specific times regardless of cost. Nonbusiness travelers can put off traveling to another time when prices are lower. Business travelers have a more-inelastic demand for travel than do nonbusiness travelers. Airlines charge different prices depending on when you buy your tickets. You can also get better deals if you stay over the weekend, which nonbusiness travelers are inclined to do. You may also provide the same or similar products to consumers and to other businesses.

Price – Sub-strategies – Multiple Unit Pricing/ Bundle Pricing

This involves selling a number of units together for one price. This is frequently used by the big-box stores. This strategy is often used for low-cost, consumable products.

Bundle pricing is closely related to multiple unit pricing. Complementary products are bundled together for one price. A couple of examples are shampoo and conditioner, ice cream and chocolate syrup.

Price – Law

The scope of federal antitrust law is very pervasive and covers virtually every business. You need to beware of its implications for your business. You don't want to use pricing strategies that could be considered illegal, and you want to be able to identify them if they are being used against you.

The various statutes that you should have a working familiarity with are the Sherman Act of 1890 and the Clayton Act of 1914 (significantly amended in 1936 by the Robinson-Patman Act and in 1950 by the Celler-Kefauver Antimerger Act, and the Federal Trade Commission Act of 1914).

The Sherman Act prohibits contracts, combinations, monopolies, and conspiracies in restraint of trade. This act is enforced by the Antitrust Division of the Justice Department.

The Clayton Act deals with specific types of restraints of trade, including exclusive dealing arrangements, tie-in sales, price discrimination, mergers and acquisitions, and interlocking boards of directors. This act is enforced jointly by the Antitrust Division of the Justice Department and the Federal Trade Commission.

Price fixing is a major issue covered by antitrust law. The provisions against price fixing are all-encompassing. Not only sellers but buyers as well are within the law's scope. Large and small companies alike in all industries are covered. Price fixing is basically agreeing with a competitor on a price for his and your products that will be in restraint of trade. Price fixing comes in two flavors, horizontal price fixing and vertical price fixing. Horizontal price fixing occurs between competitors. Vertical price fixing occurs between a company and its suppliers and/or its customers.

Another area covered by antitrust statues is the practice, among competitors, of dividing of markets by territory or by customer. These acts are illegal per se and are considered even more of a restraint on trade than price fixing.

If you enter a market and feel that some company is pricing their product below their cost to keep you out of their market, they may be practicing predatory pricing. Pricing cutting or underselling competitors is not necessarily predatory pricing, but when such techniques are used by a company with substantial market share for the purpose of getting rid of competitors, it is considered to be a misuse of that market share.

Predatory pricing is prohibited by the Sherman Act and by various state laws. An example of a state law prohibiting predatory pricing is found in the California Unfair Practices Act, Business and Professional Code, Section 17043. A company must typically have at least 40% of the market to worry about predatory pricing laws. Then it must be proven that the company was selling its product below cost.

PRODUCT (OR SERVICE)

It is pretty obvious if you are going to start a business that you will need to have a product or service to market. We will use "products" to mean both products and services unless noted otherwise. *Evolution* is a word that most Christians do not use often in their day-to-day conversation, but it is very applicable to your products and services. Your products and product lines will evolve to meet constantly changing consumer needs and wants. This chapter is about keeping your products fresh and in demand by your current and potential customers.

Product – Developing New Products

There are logical steps that you will normally follow in developing new products for your business. Refer to the chapter "CREATIVE THINKING IN BUSINESS."

1. Idea Generation – Conceptualization of a list of new potential products.

2. Idea Assessment – Evaluation of your ideas based on written criteria.
3. Concept Testing – The ideas that have passed your idea assessment are discussed with your clients, users, and your internal testers. At this stage, you do not develop physical products.
4. Idea choice – You select ideas that passed the concept testing stage. These are carefully chosen, as you will be deploying assets in the next stage to further evaluate your chosen ideas.
5. Idea Prototype Development – You develop working models of the products for testing and evaluation.
6. Final Version Development – At this stage, you have fully tested your prototypes and are ready to put select products into production.
7. Commercialization – Here, you start lining up your marketing and distribution resources.

Another important aspect of product development is developing the right product mix. How many, what kind, what size, what packaging, at what times of the year are all important questions that need to be answered to maximize profits.

Product – Developing New Products – Idea Generation

New product ideas can come from almost anywhere. There are some basic principles to follow when generating new ideas. The first and foremost principle of generating a good idea is to generate a LOT of new ideas. Your secret weapon as a small business, when competing against big businesses, is your ability to come up with and execute many good new product ideas. The very fact that you do not have the confines of corporate bureaucracy when it comes to new product development is a major competitive advantage.

In addition to applying the principles and concepts discussed in the "CREATIVE THINKING IN BUSINESS" chapter, you will want to apply the principles and concepts in the Product Life Cycle section below.

Though you will generate a lot of great ideas internally, you will also get a lot of ideas from outside sources. Look for ideas from sources such as:

Internal	External
Salespeople	Customers

Employees	Complaints
Family Members	Requests
Board Members	Market Surveys
Advisors	Focus Groups
Store Survey Forms	Warranty Cards
Accounting Records	Marketing Consultants
Brainstorming Meetings	Vendors/ Suppliers
Existing Product defects	Retailers
Accidents	Competitors
Slow-moving products	Local colleges
	Vendors

Product – Developing New Products – Idea Assessment

When reviewing your product ideas, you will want to ask the following questions:

- How big is the current market for the product you are considering?
- Is the market growing?
- Does the product fit within your overall corporate objectives?
- Does the product complement your existing products?
- What is the unique selling proposition (USP) for this product idea?
- What is the competitive environment for this product?

Part of the evaluation process for your product assessment will be to apply a S.W.O.T. (strengths, weaknesses, opportunities, threats) analysis and a P.E.S.T. (political, environmental, social, and technology) analysis to your product ideas. Both these concepts are more fully discussed in the "CREATIVE THINKING IN BUSINESS" chapter. During the idea assessment phase, you will be prioritizing your ideas, but don't throw out any ideas unless they obviously can't be done or do not fit in with your business objectives. Once you have gotten rid of the ideas that are just not feasible, you need a way of ranking your ideas so you take only the best ideas into the Concept testing phase.

Keep in mind that a product that isn't feasible now could be the "hot" product of tomorrow. When you have an effective idea generation environment, you may get ideas that are ahead of their time and could possibly work at a later date.

Your new ideas will be competing against one another for your valuable and limited resources. You will want a systematic and fair way to measure and compare their viability and potential for your company. One way to evaluate a number of product or service ideas is to set up a ranking matrix as previously mentioned. Let's use a toy development and design company as an example. This matrix analysis was actually used by Easy Brain Labs, Inc.

Product Ideas
Evaluation
Weighted Attribute Ranking

	Play	Devel Time	Bill Of Materials	Non Reoccurring Engineering	Expandable/ Consumables	Partners Available	Unique Selling Proposition	Patentable	Gut Reaction	Total Weight
Weight	20.00%	10.00%	5.00%	15.00%	5.00%	25.00%	10.00%	5.00%	5.00%	100.00%
Raw ranking										
Product A	1	1	2	5	5	3	1	4	1	23
Product B	5	3	4	4	4	1	2	3	3	29
Product C	2	5	1	3	3	2	3	1	5	25
Product D	4	2	5	2	1	4	4	2	4	28
Product E	3	4	3	1	2	5	5	5	2	30
Weighted Avg Ranking										
Product A	0.20	0.10	0.10	0.75	0.25	0.75	0.10	0.20	0.05	2.50
Product B	1.00	0.30	0.20	0.60	0.20	0.25	0.20	0.15	0.15	3.05
Product C	0.40	0.50	0.05	0.45	0.15	0.50	0.30	0.05	0.25	2.65
Product D	0.80	0.20	0.25	0.30	0.05	1.00	0.40	0.10	0.20	3.30
Product E	0.60	0.40	0.15	0.15	0.10	1.25	0.50	0.25	0.10	3.50

Fig.42 – Product Ideas Evaluation Completed

This Product Evaluation Matrix was prepared using Excel so that all of the calculations were automatically computed. Your analysis will be different than the example, based on your industry and other elements relevant to your company, products, and industry.

In the example, the following criteria are considered important in the evaluation process:

Play   Is the toy fun to play with, or will the child play with it a few minutes and go onto something else?

Dev.   TimeHow long will the product take to get from the concept stage to production? This is a guess or an estimate as no real analysis has been completed at this stage. You will want to use what I call a "SWIG" number. This stands for "silly wild informed guess." This means that with a lot of work, you should have a reasonably well thought out answer for this criterion.

BOM

Will this product have an attractive "bill of materials"? This does not necessarily mean the cheapest product to produce, but will you be able to manufacture the product so it will fit well in its expected price range and give healthy margins? Your BOM analysis should include cost of raw materials, labor, overhead, shipping, and packaging. As with the development time criterion above, your BOM (bill of materials) will not be "polished." It will be your best guess. Your BOM will be polished and refined at a later stage.

NRE

Nonrecurring engineering expense. This is the expense associated with getting the product from the concept stage through prototyping, up through the proof of concept stage, and into a product ready to manufacture. Sometimes, the cost of building prototypes and doing preliminary engineering can be out of reach for a small company. If you can't build it at costs you can afford to demonstrate it to prospective funding sources or buyers, then you will give a product a lower rating. In the case of a toy design company, the toy company buyers will always tell you that it is sufficient to bring them your ideas on the back of a napkin. I have found through trial and error that you need to have a prototype that is pretty close to the final product. Leave the napkin at home.

Expandable/
Consumable

A product that requires the consumer to come back to you for additional purchases will get a higher rating on this attribute. A good example of a product that would get a high rating here because it is expandable would be a doll like Barbie®. Once you buy Barbie, you naturally have to buy clothes, accessories, Barbie cars, a Barbie house, and of course, more Barbies. A good example of a product with a high rating because of consumables is the toy Easy Bake® Oven that has its own special line of Easy Bake cake mixes. Another good example is buying an HP printer that requires HP printer cartridges.

Partners
Available

This is a ranking attribute that gauges the product's ability to attract "partners" who can help fund the completion of the product and help get it to market. Going back to Easy Brain Labs, Inc., they needed a partner who would help finance the final development and distribution of the product. They had developed an idea for a really good iPod accessory. They needed a partner who would provide the final $100,000 of product development money as well as the initial inventory cost of $8 million dollars until the product became cash-flow positive. If funding is not a real issue for you, you will either give this attribute a low weight or not include it in your analysis.

USP

Unique Selling Proposition (USP) is a critical feature for any new product. You need to be able to clearly state what makes your new product idea special. How will it stand out from the clutter of other products? This is what sets you apart from your competitors, what makes your customers want to do business with you rather than your competitors.

There are a couple of major benefits in thinking about, developing, and documenting your USP. First, it clearly differentiates your business in the eyes of your current and potential customers or clients. Second, it focuses your company on delivering the promise of the USP.

A good USP can often be put into a slogan with some thought. Here are some good examples:

Fly the friendly skies – United Airlines

Don't leave home without it – American Express

Just do it – Nike

Get a piece of the rock – Prudential

Have you driven a Ford…lately? – Ford Motor Company

99.44/100 pure – Ivory Soap

A diamond is forever – DeBeers Consolidated Mines

Good to the last drop – Maxwell House

It's the real thing – Coca Cola

Is it live? Or is it Memorex? – Memorex Corporation

We bring good things to life – General Electric

Here are some humorous examples from small businesses collected over time:

Plumbers:

"We repair what your husband fixed."

A maternity room door:

"Push, push, push."

A tire shop:

"Invite us to your next blowout."

An optometrist's office:

"If you don't see what you're looking for, you've come to the right place."

A podiatrist's office:

"Time wounds all heels."

Pizza shop slogans:

"7 days without pizza makes one weak."

"Buy our pizza. We knead the dough."

Outside a muffler shop:

"No appointment necessary. We hear you coming."

A veterinarian's waiting room:

"Be back in 5 minutes. Sit! Stay!"

The electric company:

"We would be de-lighted if you pay your bill. However, if you don't, you will be."

A plastic surgeon's office:

"Hello. Can we pick your nose?"

Beware of the "cutesy phrase." Funny is OK, cutesy is not. BUT, don't walk with your nose in the air, or you will trip. In other words, "keep it simple, stupid." Don't use quarter words when nickel words will do. Your USP does not need to be expressed in 25 words or fewer just because our examples above are molded into slogans. It can be a detailed set of performance standards. But a memorable slogan that conveys your USP is, well, memorable. Just remember, the USP stands for *Unique Selling Proposition*.

The dream situation is one in which you create a truly unique product that is not available anywhere else and everyone loves it. But don't be discouraged if you develop a product and are initially rejected by the big companies. We've all heard stories of the entrepreneurs who, after being rejected by the large companies, persisted because they "knew" their products were unique and eventually either found a company who believed in their product or successfully marketed it themselves. Sometimes, you can come up with a product so innovative and cutting edge that you can't sell it. Proper timing of innovative product introductions is critical. The more innovative your product, the more you have to explain it when you introduce it. The history books are full of such products.

Thomas Edison turned down the radio, saying it had "No commercial value."

Western Union turned down the telephone, saying, "It will never be more than a toy."

Kodak turned down the Xerox copier.

Thomas J. Watson, Sr., founder and head of IBM turned down the computer, but Watson, Jr. persisted, and the rest is history.

One of the founders of Mattel, Ruth Handler, proposed Barbie to the ad executives at Mattel and they rejected it, saying it was too expensive and that it had little potential for wide market appeal. She persisted, and it became the most popular doll in history and accounts for a major portion of Mattel revenues.

Mattel rejected another doll line that later was to be called "Bratz." The Bratz, developed by a toy maker called MGA Entertainment, Inc. in Van Nuys, California, were introduced in 2001. Bratz became the biggest selling doll with tweens, an age group of girls that the toy industry had almost written off. Before the introduction of Bratz, Barbie held a market share of 90%. After the introduction of Bratz by MGA, her share dropped to 70%. A designer had introduced the "Bratz" concept at Mattel in 1998, but Mattel did not put it into production. A former member of the Barbie design team, then took his idea to MGA. Mattel has successfully sued MGA over the Bratz doll concept.

Patentable
Can you protect the idea for the new product? It will need some unique features to be patentable. A patented product looks good to outside investors and can serve as a barrier to competitor entry.

Gut Reaction
I am a big believer in analysis, but the final decision is going to be based on your gut reaction to the product idea. I have seen what is called "paralysis through analysis." You can sometimes overanalyze a product idea. Anyone can make a decision if they have all the perfect data that they need. The real magic happens when you can get just enough data to make a good and profitable gut decision.

To use the Product Ideas Evaluation for your company, take the following steps:

1. Develop what you consider to be your important attributes.

2. Weight the attributes. Not all attributes are of equal importance. In the example, we rated the most important attribute to be "Partner

Available." This was done, because no matter how good the product was, we could not go forward with it unless we could get a financing partner. Since these are toy ideas, we then gave the next highest weight to the "Play" attribute.

3. Since there were five toy ideas to rank, each toy idea got a ranking of 1 to 5, with 5 being the best. You can see that product idea "E" got the best weighted average ranking. We actually decided to take Product E and Product D to the next step.

Product – Developing New Products – Concept Testing

At this stage, you have not yet spent the money to build a prototype. Here you will probably complete an artist's drawings of the product, develop product overview sheets, and develop preliminary product component listings. You will give a good overview to your "testers" about the functionality of the product. You'll want to know whether your testers would buy the product, why they would buy the product, and what they would pay for the product. You'll find out what is lacking or missing in the product and why the testers might not want to buy it. You'll probably want to choose testers from select groups such as local university professors, family, friends, vendors, and other people you trust. Part of your evaluation documentation is to commit your tester comments to writing.

Product – Developing New Products – Idea Choice

At this stage, you have generated lots of ideas, assessed them, tested them with select employees and/or outsiders, and now you have to make some choices. Your product choices will be made based on the steps you have already taken. Your choices will be tempered by the resources that you have to allocate to the new products, how the new products will complement your existing products, and your gut reaction. You may also be replacing a product that has become unprofitable.

Product – Developing New Products – Prototype Development

You can skip this stage and go directly to the Commercialization stage if you are selling products that have already been developed. If you have arrived at this point, you must feel relatively certain that you have a potentially commercial product. If not, you need to go back to your prior steps and reevaluate this particular product. If you are evaluating services as opposed to physical goods, you can be a little more liberal at this step. Services typically do not cost as much as physical products in this step of the process.

There are several reasons why you will want to build a prototype of your prospective product:

1. To find possible flaws in its design.
2. To find potential patentable features.
3. To keep the product concept alive and moving forward.
4. To aid in developing an estimated viable bill of materials (the estimated cost to produce and deliver one unit of product).
5. To aid in developing an estimated nonrecurring engineering cost estimate (the cost to get your product developed from concept stage to production model).
6. Licensing your product to a larger company will become a vital part of your selling package. At a large company, you will be selling your concept to a product development person. Most big companies take product idea submissions from outside inventors. But they will not take submissions from just anybody. The best way to convince them that you are a "real" inventor is to show them a complete product/concept package and a prototype. Some additional elements to include in the package are:
   a. Product Overview (a one-sheet selling document with pictures and narrative showing features and benefits).
   b. Bill of Materials estimate (unit product cost).
   c. Nonrecurring engineering cost estimate (what it will take in resources to get from your concept to a product that can be put into manufacturing).
   d. User experience documentation to show how the user will interact and enjoy the product.
   e. Component description – a detailed description of the components of the product.
   f. Component interaction – a detailed description of how the components work together to form the product.
   g. Block diagram – this is particular to electronic products. It reflects how the major electronic components are configured.
   h. A one-minute demo video. These are really easy to produce nowadays with Microsoft Movie Maker®, which comes free with most computers, or similar computer editing applications.
7. You can use the prototype to test its appeal to your potential consumers.

Overview of Prototyping

There are various types of prototypes ranging from relatively cheap to very expensive. Many prototypes can be built from materials that you can find at hardware stores, hobby stores, computer stores, or crafts stores. Being a new businessperson, you will want to start with your lowest common denominator and try to build your own prototypes. Prototypes go from sketches to "works-like, looks-like" models to fully functional prototypes. The goal is to get as close to the final product as possible. As I have mentioned earlier in this book, many new product executives will tell you that you can bring your idea to them on the back of a napkin. This is just not true in most circumstances. From personal experience, I know that many of these new product people just don't have the imagination to translate a bad sketch on the back of a napkin into a final product concept. Imagine sitting in the waiting room of a product development executive with your napkin firmly clutched in the palm of your hand and the guy coming out of the office is pulling his fully working prototype in a wagon. The guy with the wagon will win the deal most of the time.

I have sold product concepts from prototypes I have made myself, and I have had prototypes made by professional prototyping companies. Easy Brain Labs, Inc. sold a board game to a game distribution company based on a prototype that we made in our offices. The board was designed using Microsoft Excel and printed on a large commercial printer at Kinko's. The playing pieces were made from materials bought at a local craft store. This prototype cost about $200 to make.

Easy Brain Labs, Inc. also developed a device that could adapt a Game Boy into a portable DVD player. To sell the concept, we had to develop a "works-like, looks-like" model so that we could demonstrate it to the prospective buyer. The product did not really play the DVD or project a film to the Game Boy screen. We used a ROM cartridge that we inserted into the Game Boy and attached the Game Boy to an SLA prototype of the adapter. When the Game Boy was turned on, this ROM cartridge played a sample movie. The SLA prototype had a CD mechanism (that simulated the DVD mechanism) that had a spinning disk in it. SLA stands for Stereo lithography and is the heart of rapid prototyping, turning your 3D CAD drawing into a solid object. A SLA prototype is a computer-generated nondurable, soft plastic representation of your product. Most stereo lithography prototyping can be completed in as little as 1 to 2 days, with larger projects typically being completed in less than 5 days. Stereo lithography prototypes can be used as master patterns for injection molding core and cavity inserts, thermoforming, blow molding, and various metal casting processes.

The Game Boy adapter SLA prototype cost $3,000 for the first unit and $800 for 4 subsequent units.

Fig.43 – Gameboy Adapter SLA (stereolithography) prototype

An SLA prototype enabled Easy Brain Labs, Inc. to produce a great product overview and enabled us to shoot a one-minute video that we put on a CD and sent to prospective toy companies. Once we sold them on the concept, we presented them with an NRE (nonrecurring engineering) estimate of the cost of getting the product from our prototype stage to a manufacturing model stage. The toy company paid us a mid-six-figure amount to do this.

Before you show your idea to anyone, you should have them complete a nondisclosure agreement, putting them on notice that you are presenting them with confidential information. I recommend that you have your patent filed before you disclose your product idea to anyone in the outside world.

If you find that your product is too expensive to prototype, such as a new motor design or a new motorcycle design, you may want to employ the use of Virtual Prototyping. It is a relatively new and affordable computer-generated animation that shows working models in 3-D. A virtual prototype developer will use various design programs and can create a CD-ROM that you can send to new product executives. You can typically have a 3-D virtual prototype completed for around $1,000, depending on its complexity.

Product – Developing New Products – Final Version Development

During the prototype stage, you have no doubt developed a meaningful BOM (bill of materials) and a meaningful NRE (nonrecurring engineering) estimate for your product idea. In building a final version of your product prior to manufacturing, you will be able to see if your BOM and NRE are accurate. Most products will take anywhere from 3 to 6 months to get from prototype stage to their final version as long as Murphy's Law doesn't come into play. As you probably know, Murphy's Law states, "If anything can go wrong, it will." If you are creating a product that requires plastic parts, the mold design and mold-making process alone can take 6 to 8 weeks to complete. If your product requires electronic components, their final design will be completed concurrent with your final plastic design work.

If you are relatively certain that this product will be commercialized, you will probably start your package design using your prototype as the model. To test the manufacturing of the product, you will have a short run of product produced. You will want to use the short production run to make sure that defects and rejects are below your acceptable tolerance levels. This is a good time to test-market your product. In your test market, you will be testing product appeal, price, advertising media, demographic assumptions, packaging design, and other variables appropriate to your product.

Product – Developing New Products – Commercialization

At this stage, you should have made sure that there are no manufacturing or distribution problem areas. By now, you will have estimated the number of units you can sell and have worked out these projections with your manufacturing and distribution partners. This is important, because there can be substantial differences in cost from 100,000 units to 10,000,000 units. Keep in mind that there will be a ramp-up period for getting your project into full distribution. It will take time for you to get results from your marketing and to build consumer awareness. There will also be ordering lead times for getting your products from your manufacturer or distributor. Whether you are developing your own product or selling someone else's product, you should have test-marketed the product as discussed in the prior section before committing major resources to its commercialization.

Product – Product Mix

Determining the correct product mix is no easy task. If you have more than one product or product line, you need to know what your resources are and how to best utilize them to maximize your profits. This is typically done using rather complex algebraic formulas referred to as *linear programming*. We won't get into the calculation of product mix using linear programming in this book. To give you an idea of its complexity, let's look at a hypothetical situation: you own Big Toy Company, Inc., and you have three products, one machine with constraints, and you have labor constraints.

A = the amount of Magic Bike to produce each month
B = the amount of SuperHero to produce each month
C = the amount of Big Doll to produce each month

We are trying to determine the optimal amount of Magic Bike, SuperHero and Big Doll units to produce in order to maximize profits.

If we assume that product A has a gross margin of $54.95 (selling price less variable cost associated directly with the product), product B has a gross margin of $14.95, and product C has a gross margin of $10.00, we can state our profit maximization equation as:

$$Z = 54.95A + 14.95B + 10.00C$$

We know that our machine and labor take a specific amount of time for each product, so we list our machine constraints as follows:

Machine Time: $50A + 20B + 5C \leq 80{,}000$
Labor Time: $40A + 15B + 5C \leq 60{,}000$

You will also have marketing constraints, as we know that your retailers will only be able to sell so much of product A, product B, and product C; so we must factor in the market constraints as follows:

$$0 \leq A \leq 750; \ 0 \leq B \leq 2{,}000; \ 0 \leq C \leq 2{,}000$$

As you can see, the algebraic formula gets a little complex. In reality, the formula would probably be even more complex, with a greater number of variables.

There is an easier way to solve this problem. Microsoft Excel® has an add-in program called the Solver. We can solve the product mix/profit maximization question in minutes rather than the hours it might take if we used the above algebraic formulas.

In our example, Big Toy Company, Inc. (BTC) is currently budgeted to generate $15,425 profit for the month. After utilizing Excel Solver to determine the proper product mix to maximize profits, BTC shows profits of $39,146. We have more than doubled the profits of BTC with only a change in product mix.

	Product Mix Before Solver	Product Mix After Solver
Magic Bike	500 units	750 units
SuperHero	1,000 units	1,333 units
Big Doll	1,500 units	2,000 units

Big Toy Company, Inc. Product Mix Analysis Before Utilizing Solver

Big Toy Company, Inc.
Product Mix Analysis

	Magic Bike		SuperHero		Big Doll		Unused Capacity	Total
Sales volume (cases)		500		1,000		1,500		3,000
Sales $$	$49,975	$99.95	$29,950	$29.95	$29,925	$19.95		$109,850
Variable costs	$22,500	$45	$15,000	$15	$14,925	$10		$52,425
Contribution margin	$27,475	$54.95	$14,950	$14.95	$15,000	$10.00		$57,425
Fixed costs:								
Production equip time		$2,000		$1,500		$1,250	$2,250	$7,000
Assembly time -direct		$3,000		$1,500		$600	$4,900	$10,000
Allocated expenses								$25,000
Gross margin								$15,425
Standard operating data								
Machine-time utilization per case (minutes)		50		20		5		
Labor-time utilization per case (minutes)		40		15		5		
Resource utilization								
Total machine-time utilization		25,000		20,000		7,500	27,500	52,500
Total labor-time utilization		20,000		15,000		7,500	17,500	42,500
Constraints								
Machine time available								80,000
Labor time available								60,000
Max that can be sold in stores		750		2,000		2,000		

Fig.44 – Big Toy Company Product Mix Analysis

After setting up the above work sheet in Excel, click on Solver in your Excel menu. It's located under the Tools option on the main Excel menu. Since it is an add-in, you may have to install it from your Excel disk. The Set Target cell is the Gross margin cell. The cells to change are the Sales volume cells for each of the three products.

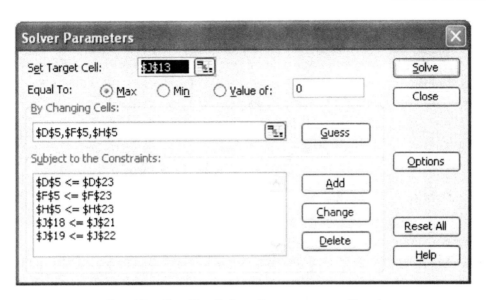

Fig.45 – Big Toy Solver Paremeters in Excel

Once you press the Solve button, you will get the spreadsheet results below.

Big Toy Company, Inc.
Product Mix Analysis

	Magic Bike		SuperHero		Big Doll		Unused Capacity	Total
Sales volume (cases)	750		1,333		2,000			4,083
Sales $$	$74,963	$99.95	$39,933	$29.95	$39,900	$19.95		$154,796
Variable costs	$33,750	$45	$20,000	$15	$19,900	$10		$73,650
Contribution margin	$41,213	$54.95	$19,933	$14.95	$20,000	$10.00		$81,146
Fixed costs:								
Production equip time		$2,000		$1,500		$1,250	$2,250	$7,000
Assembly time -direct		$3,000		$1,500		$600	$4,900	$10,000
Allocated expenses								$25,000
Gross margin								$39,146
Standard operating data								
Machine-time utilization per case (minutes)		50		20		5		
Labor-time utilization per case (minutes)		40		15		5		
Resource utilization								
Total machine-time utilization		37,500		26,667		10,000	5,833	74,167
Total labor-time utilization		30,000		20,000		10,000	-	60,000
Constraints								
Machine time available								80,000
Labor time available								60,000
Max that can be sold in stores		750		2,000		2,000		

Fig.46 – Big Toy company Product Mix Analysis - 2

It is a good idea to periodically do a Product Mix Analysis or have your accountant complete one for you. This is one of those areas that separate the accountants from the bookkeepers. As with all analysis, there are, at times, circumstances that will warrant deviation from your obtained results. For example, a product may not be generating much in the way of profits, but it may be generating sales of other products.

Even if you do not complete a formal analysis like the one above, you should be aware of the fact that the proper product mix can improve your profitability without adding any new resources. This analysis shows how you can allocate limited resources to maximize profits. The algebra may seem a little complex, so the Excel Solver spreadsheet can make your calculations much easier. A still easier way is to have your accountant do it for you.

Product – Pareto's 80/20 Rule

In business, the mathematical principle known as Pareto's 80-20 Rule is a basic rule of thumb. Vilfredo Pareto (1848-1923) was an Italian economist who, in 1906, observed that 20% of the Italian people owned 80% of their country's accumulated wealth. His analytic formula is also known as the "Vital Few and Trivial Many Rule." Called by whatever name, this mix of 80%-20% reminds us that the relationship between input and output is not balanced. In a management context, this rule of thumb is useful when there is a question of effectiveness versus diminishing returns on effort, expense, or time. Although the mix will not always be 80-20, the principle is still the same—the vital few and the trivial many. If you look at the list of products you sell, you will probably find that 20% of your products generate 80% of your profits.

Product – Economical Order Quantity

Other important questions to ask about product mix are how often and at what quantity should you order select product. This is where a little formula called EOQ (economic order quantity) is an effective way of establishing the proper order quantity. This formula will help you decide what quantity and how often you should order product to minimize inventory holding costs and inventory order costs. I have to pause here and say that formulas like this one serve as a reminder of our creator and the creator of everything in the universe. At the beginning of creation, our Lord established many principles of how the infinite elements of the universe work together. The very fact that this formula and thousands of others always work is a testament to the wisdom of our Lord. The EOQ formula was developed in 1915 by F. W. Harris. Man is constantly discovering the laws and principles of math and nature put into place by our Lord. In high school math, we learned that the value of pi is 3.14, information that is valuable in a number of mathematical formulas. All of the mathematical formulas and models that man has "discovered" are further evidence that our world did not happen by accident, but was well laid out by our divine creator.

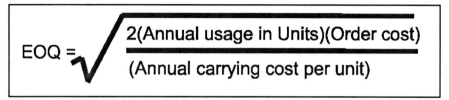

$$EOQ = \sqrt{\frac{2(\text{Annual usage in Units})(\text{Order cost})}{(\text{Annual carrying cost per unit})}}$$

Fig.47 – EOQ Formula

Economic Order Quantity

Annual Demand	24,000
Ordering cost per order	$100.00
Annual carrying cost per unit	$1.50

Economic Order Quantity	1,789
Number of orders per year	13
Length of order cycle in days	27
Average Inventory	895
Annual carrying cost	$1,342
Annual ordering cost	$1,342
Total Annual Cost	$2,683

Fig.48 – Economic Order Quantity Data

This calculation tells you that if you have an annual demand of 24,000 units and it costs you $100 to order the products, and your annual cost to carry the products is $1.50, your EOQ is 1,789. The formula works based on the assumption that the ideal economic order point is when annual carrying cost equals annual ordering cost. The cost of ordering is basically the cost of shipping and any other costs that can be specifically tied to your ordering process. These costs are not associated with the quantity ordered but primarily with physical activities required to process the order.

For purchased items, these costs would include the cost to enter the purchase order and requisition, any approval steps, the cost to process the receipt, invoice processing, and the inbound freight. For a manufacturing company, the order cost would include the time to initiate the work order, time associated with picking and issuing components, all production scheduling time, machine set up time, and any tooling discarded after the production run.

The annual carrying costs are the costs associated with having inventory on hand. It is primarily made up of the costs associated with the inventory investment and storage cost. For the purpose of the EOQ calculation, if the cost does not change based upon the quantity of inventory on hand, it should not be included in carrying cost. The primary components of carrying cost are interest, insurance, taxes, and storage costs.

Product – Life Cycle

All products and businesses go through a life cycle. Some industries and products have relatively short-lived product life cycles, while others have long lives. Take the toy industry for instance. Many toys enjoy major consumer interest for only one season, while others are on kids' "must have" list for decades. Barbie, Matchbox, Hot Wheels, and Tonka are brands that have been household names for many years, while similar toys have come and gone. The length of each cycle will depend on your product, your company, the industry, elements found in your P.E.S.T. (politics, economics, social, and technology) analysis, and your S.W.O.T. (strengths, weaknesses, opportunities, and threats) analysis. The PEST analysis and the S.W.O.T. analysis are both discussed in the chapter of this book entitled "CREATIVE THINKING IN BUSINESS."

Products will begin to decrease in profitability over time, and you need to have fresh, new products ready for introduction throughout the course of your business and/ or adjustments in your marketing mix. It is important to have a basic understanding of your products' life cycles. This will help you manage internal resources used to market the products.

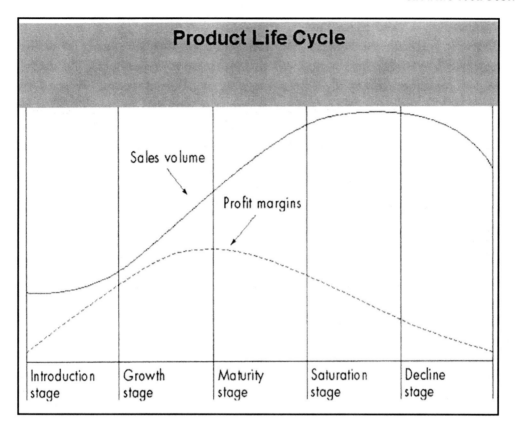

Fig.49 – Product Life Cycle Graph

Total sales of your products and your competitors' products will be different in each stage of the product life cycle but will tend to follow the same pattern. You can't change the individual components of your product life cycles, but you can embrace them as a fact of life and take advantage of them. Even the Barbie doll, which has enjoyed a decades-long run, has gone through a product life cycle. The Barbie currently on store shelves is not the same Barbie originally introduced over fifty years ago. Mattel has adjusted the design and marketing of the doll to appeal to each new generation of girls. Sales and profit will rise and fall at different rates in each phase of your products' life cycles. You will notice that overall industry profits will begin to fall before total industry sales begin to fall because there will be more money spent in the saturation phase, when your industry is trying to wring out sales by spending more in marketing and promotion.

Your marketing mix will change during the product life cycle. For the purposes of this discussion, I have separated "Distribution" out of the "Place" element of your marketing mix, because the product life cycle has a substantial impact on distribution. Your customer's attitudes and needs will change over your product's life cycle. Your product may be aimed at entirely different targets at different stages. A good example is the automobile industry. At one time (when gas was still below $2.00 a gallon), consumers wanted sports utility vehicles. As gas topped $3.00 a gallon, small cars, especially the hybrid vehicles, became the "in" cars. Movie stars were suddenly spotted at the Hollywood "hot spots" driving Toyota's Prius hybrid.

Product Life cycle Matrix	Market Introduction	Market Growth	Market Maturity	Market Saturation	Market Decline
Attributes of the Cycles					
Number of Competitors	Few	Few but growing fast	Stable	Stable	Decreasing
Market Growth	Rapid	High	Low	None	Negative
Market Size	zero to small	Small to modest	Largest	Stable	Declining
Investment	High	High	Stable	Declining	Stopped
Profits	zero	Low but growing	High	Lowering	Low
Prod differentiation	Very high	High	Decreasing	Little	Little to none
Strategic Options	Grow	Grow and maintain	Maintain	Maintain and harvest	Exit
Your Marketing Mix Options					
Positioning	The cutting edge Product	The product the consumer has to have	The market leader	The established market leader	Morphing into new products
Product	One or a few products	Improve product Build brand awareness	Little product differentiation Battle brands	Look for various ways to differentiate	Competitors start dropping out - do you?
Place	Build value chains Build distribution	Build value chains Build distribution	Consolidate channels	Cut costs seek lower cost channels	Cut costs seek lower cost channels
Promotion	Build awareness Build brand Inform public	Build awareness Build brand Inform public	More targeted marketing Differentiate brand	More targeted marketing Differentiate brand Remind public Persuade	Persuade Remind
Price	Skimming Penetration	Value pricing Penetration	Added value Meet competition	Added value Meet competition	Price cutting
Distribution	Direct (factory to customer) Limited distribution to specific customers	Highly skilled Focused channels	Many distributors Alternative channels Foreign sales	Many distributors Alternative channels Foreign sales	Use of existing channels Shrinking channels

Fig.50 – Product Life Cycle Matrix

Always be acutely aware of the life cycle for each of your products and product groups. If you are a consumer electronics retailer, you will have products and product lines in each stage of the product life cycle analysis. If you are a developer of toy products that you license to toy companies, you should stay abreast of the product life cycle for the types of products you are developing. Toy companies actually complete development of their toys in October to bring to store shelves the following October, in time for Christmas. If you were developing toys, this would be the retail cycle that you would consider along with the product and product line life cycles.

Here are some examples of products that might fit into the various phases of the matrix in 2009:

Introduction	Growth	Mature
3G cell phones	Hybrid cars	Personal computers
Conductive ink for consumer products	Legal film downloading	Fast foods
Virtual perception input devices	Wideband wireless devices	Faxes
All "green" products	Video iPods®	Skateboards

Saturation	Decline
Cordless phones	Typewriters
DVDs	Checkbooks
CDs	SUVs
PDAs	Pinball machines

Notice that the products listed above have different product-life lengths. Typewriters, which are in the decline phase of their product life cycle, have had a long history. SUVs, on the other hand, have had a relatively short life span. There will be some companies in each category that continue to make a good profit even if their product group is in the decline stage. In the decline stage, many manufacturers, distributors, and retailers will drop out of the market, leaving room for the few left to make a return on their products.

The typewriter was a revolutionary product that changed more than the way letters were written. It brought the mindset of automation to the office. Let's look at the various stages of the typewriter presented below:

1874 Remington produces the first reliable commercial typewriter.

THE FIRST COMMERCIAL TYPEWRITER
MODEL 1 REMINGTON, SHOP No. 1.

Fig.51 – Remington Typewriter

1950 Electrical typewriters (invented by Thomas Edison in 1872) become widely used.

Fig.52 – 1950 typewriter

1978 Electronic typewriters with "memory" begin to appear.

Fig.53 – Electronic Typewriter

1981 The IBM PC hits the market, and who needs a typewriter anymore?

Fig.54 – IBM PC 1981

The 1874 picture was obtained from http://inventors.com, and the 1950 and 1978 pictures were obtained from http://www.etypewriters.com/history.htm.

The typewriter is an excellent example of the long-lived asset. The original typewriter (of the type we know today) came to market in 1874 when it was considered cutting-edge technology. It fit the "Market Introduction" phase of the product life cycle perfectly. It was one of a kind, it had to be explained to the consuming public, the investment was high to get it developed and to market, and there were no competitors. In 1981, with the introduction of the IBM PC, the typewriter was permanently pushed into the "Market Decline" phase. But an interesting point to keep in mind is that several innovations kept the typewriter a fresh product for over one hundred years.

To maximize your company profitability, you need to manage each product and its related marketing mix. You also must manage your entire portfolio of products as a whole. You need to determine which products or product lines should receive more or less investment. You must develop growth strategies for adding new products to your portfolio, while at the same time, deciding when products should be removed from your portfolio. One useful tool, developed by the Boston Consulting Group, is the BCG Business SBU (strategic business unit) Portfolio Strategy Matrix. An SBU is an identifiable segment of the company, a product line, or a group of products.

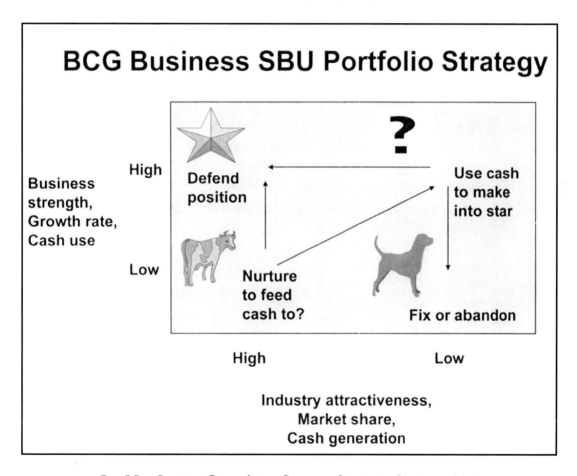

Fig.55 – Boston Consulting Group - Strategic Business Unit

On the vertical axis is business strength, growth rate and/or cash usage. On the horizontal axis is Industry attractiveness, market share and/or cash generation. Start your product portfolio management analysis by dividing all of your products or product lines into four groups:

Stars

Stars are high-growth products or product lines competing in markets where they are strong compared to competing products. In their high-growth mode, they typically need major capital investment to sustain their growth. You will have decided that this group of products warrants your heavy investment based on their potential to become a cash cow for your business. Eventually, their growth will subside or slow down, and assuming they maintain their relative market share, they will mature into cash cows.

You will normally want to aggressively promote products fitting into this category to expand their market share.

Cash Cows

Cash cows are low-growth products with a relatively high market share, most likely built during their "Star" days. These are mature, successful, and well-known products with relatively little need for investment. The profits from these products can be used to support your developing "Stars." These are typically low growth, high market share products.

Question Marks

Products fitting into the "Question Mark" category have low market share but operate in high growth markets. Their position suggests that they have some potential for becoming stars or may slip into the "Dog" category. These products may require substantial utilization of your resources in order to develop into "Stars." You need comprehensive analysis to determine which of your Question Marks deserve allocation of your limited resources to help them develop. Question Marks are high growth, low market share products. You need to decide if you are going to invest more resources or divest yourself of the products.

Dogs

Dogs refer to products that have low market share in less than desirable low-growth markets. These products may break even but have little chance to become Stars, Cash Cows, or even Question Marks. Unfortunately, most companies will at some time have products that fit into the Dog category. This is not a bad thing unless the "Dogs" outnumber the Stars, Cash Cows, and Question Marks most of the time. It can also be dangerous for your business if you have not properly recognized the dogs and you have continued to pump valuable resources into them. If you never have any Dogs, you are probably playing it way too safe in managing your product portfolio. These products are often cash money pits. You will want to identify these types of products quickly and deal with them on a timely basis so that you don't take valuable resources from your other products.

Just as no man is an island, none of your products stand alone. Each one will impact another. You may have a product that is considered a Dog, but it may pull people into your store to purchase some of your Star products. But watch those Dogs closely!

Product – Packaging

Packaging is an integral part of your product. It also impacts your price, promotion, and place as discussed below. If you are manufacturing a product and selling it to a distributor or retailer, it will be a major part of your BOM (bill of materials). When it comes to promotion, a well-designed package can be a strong marketing tool that helps the product "jump off the shelf" and convince customers to take it home. I have also seen great products that have suffered in sales because of poor package design. There are an unlimited number of ways to package your product.

Besides being appealing to your customers, it must be appealing to your distributor and/or retailers (if you are not the retailer.) The retailer will need it to work with his current fixtures. You need to consult with your distributors and retailers when designing packaging. You may have to have more than one packaging design for different retailers. As an example, if you sell to a big-box store, you will probably package your product differently than you will for smaller retailers.

Some of the elements that you will consider when you design your product packaging:

Product – Packaging – Graphics and Color

Your packaging must be pleasant to look at as it sits on your shelves or your retailers' shelves. If you are selling to retailers, your packaging will represent your total company and product image. If your packaging is put together correctly, consumers will recognize your product just from your package design. Part of this ease of recognition will be your logo, color selection, and packaging size. These elements of package design will all support your marketing efforts.

Your packaging color choice is very important. In the United States, an elegant black package with embossed metallic writing and design elements indicates class, but in certain African cultures, it indicates death. Vibrant, bright red packaging may indicate danger in the United States but symbolize abundance and good luck in China. According to Karen Saunders[36], a respected color, design, and marketing expert, color is a magical element that gives feeling and emotion to art, design, and advertising. By understanding color meaning, (or the psychology of color) you can choose the right color to support and emphasize your design.

A dominant color or overall color scheme can determine the tone of your document. Certain colors will help your product, corporate document, or advertisement attract specific audiences and evoke desired responses.

The information below provides generally accepted guidelines on the symbolic meanings of color and how you can use color more effectively in your marketing pieces.

The meaning of the color yellow (including coral, orange, amber, gold)

Symbolizes: Energy, caution, warmth, cheer, joy

Yellows are often associated with the following characteristics: homey, friendly, soft, welcoming, moving, excitement, or adventure. Good for press kits, stationery, and shopping bags.

Use yellow for signage in work situations warning of danger. Yellow is also good for any project that needs to evoke feelings of lightheartedness, humor, or friendliness.

The meaning of the color red (including mauve, magenta, crimson, scarlet, poster red)

Symbolizes: Power, romance, vitality, earthly, energy

Reds evoke highly charged emotions such as aggression, danger, or love. Red makes us pay attention and catches our eye immediately so use reds on items that need to grab attention.

In the financial arena, red symbolizes a negative direction.

The meaning of the color green (including lime, leaf green, sea green, emerald, teal, sage)

---

36   Karen Saunders, *Color Meaning—Unlock the Symbolism and Color Psychology of Common Colors*
      http://www.macgraphics.net/color-psychology-meaning-symbolism.php, 2010.

Symbolizes: life, foliage, grass, trees, water

Greens are sensuous and alive. Green is associated with the following characteristics: friendliness, dependability, freshness, non-threatening, safe, secure, healthy, strong, expensive, and primitive.

In the business world, green symbolizes growth and prosperity.

The meaning of the color blue and purple (including sky blue, ultramarine, violet, purple, azure)

Symbolizes: Peace, law and order, logic, analytical, intelligent, honest, calm, clean, good will, tranquility, compassionate, serious, thoughtful, quiet, reflective, regal, classic, dependable, trustworthiness, tradition, magical

Blues are often used for older, more mature audiences and situations. Blue is common in financial institutions, hospitals, and legal and medical professions. Purples have long been associated with royalty, magic and power Purples are often used with feminine, rather than masculine designs.

Discover what top color combinations really make your designs pop. What if YOU could know the secrets of a 1st class graphic designer that would help you create amazing marketing materials in a few hours, would you want to know how? Find out now at www.BuyAppealMarketing.com

You are welcome to "reprint" this article on the meaning of color as long as it remains complete and unaltered (including my "about the author" section at the end).

Karen Saunders is the author of "Turn Eye Appeal into Buy Appeal: How to easily transform your marketing pieces into dazzling, persuasive sales tools!" Hundreds of business owners have used her simple do-it-yourself design system to create stunning marketing materials.

Product – Packaging – Appropriate for Your Product

You don't package spark plugs in velvet bags, and you don't put Coach purses in clear clamshells for hanging on racks. It is good to be innovative in your packaging, but consumers have come to associate certain types of packaging with certain types of products. Swimming upstream does not equal innovation. Also, retailers have fixtures in their stores that have been built for specific types of products. If your product does not accommodate the design of retail shelves, then it might not be put on display with similar products.

Product – Packaging – Functionality/Versatility

Sometimes packaging is an integral part of the product. When you buy laundry detergent, you use the cap for measuring out the detergent for each load of wash. When you buy mouthwash, you again use the cap for measuring out the proper amount to use. Some types of packaging have uses after the product has been completely used and/or discarded. As an example, you can find coffee cans in many garages filled with nails, screws and other small parts.

You also want to make sure that your packaging is as versatile as possible. A good example of packaging with versatility is the clear clamshell that is designed to be hung on a pegboard and has a flat bottom so that it can be stood on a shelf.

Product – Packaging – Costs

Cost is always an important element of your packaging decisions. Packaging can sometimes cost more than your product. When you develop the bill of materials for your product to determine your total product cost, you will always include the cost of packaging, as it is a variable cost. Your cost of packaging will go up if there is a substantial amount of human involvement needed in the packaging process. Your package design should be developed to require as little human involvement as possible.

Product – Packaging – Purchaser Ease of Use

Have you ever bought a consumer electronics product and had to wrestle for several minutes to extract the product from the clear, bonded clamshell? You will need to balance the need for product security with the ease of opening it by your customers. There will always be some returns of your product. It can be somewhat of a negative if your customer wants to return your product and has to demolish the packaging to extract it; the product can get damaged during the extraction process. I know of one infomercial guru that sells his products in packaging that has been specifically designed so that the packaging CANNOT be reused for returning the product. He believes that this reduces returns. In my opinion, from a Christian perspective, this is not a good way to design packaging, and it is definitely not a way to turn a customer into a repeat customer.

Product – Packaging – Labeling/Legal Requirements

The United States has strict product labeling laws to protect consumers. Make sure that you are in full compliance with the laws that govern your particular product BEFORE you produce your packaging. It could be a major financial hit to you if you found out that you did not comply with labeling laws AFTER production and had to repackage your products. Don't just rely on your packaging consultant. Get your attorney's opinion on your packaging, because federal and state packaging laws, rules, and regulations can be very complex.

Product – Packaging – Shipping/Transportation

Your product packaging must meet the needs of your distributors and conform to their ordering, handling, and shipping needs. You will need to make sure that your product packaging fits into shipping cartons that comply with the storage, human, and machine handling requirements of your shippers. Once your distributors receive your product, it must also comply with their storage, picking, packing, and shipping requirements. Once your product is shipped from your distributors to your retailers, it must comply with their storage requirements and their in-store shelf requirements. If store personnel have a difficult time taking product from their warehouses to their in-store shelves, your product might spend more time in the warehouse than on your retailers' shelves. As you can see, you cannot design your product packaging in a vacuum. You must solicit input from each member of your distribution chain.

Product – Packaging – UPC and ISBN

Most modern accounting and inventory management systems use UPC barcodes for tracking their products. A barcode on the surface of a product is detected and read by a thin laser light that sweeps back and forth over the barcode, identifying the white and black spaces. The laser light reflects back onto a sensor and converts the on/off signals from the information that has been sent to the sensors from the laser light into a flow of digital signals. The UPC consists of twelve characters representing the product manufacturer, product, and a check digit. The Uniform Code Council, Inc. is a nonprofit organization that manages the UPC. In 2005, they changed their name to "GS1 US," but their mission is still the same.

To obtain a UPC barcode for your product, you must become a member of the Uniform Code Council (www.uc-council.org). To become a member, you will have to provide GS1 US with a lot of information including product type, annual revenues expected, and other information. Currently, the initial fee is $750 and up for a block of 100 UPCs, with a $150 per year renewal fee. After you have become a member, you are assigned an identification number licensed for your company's use. You will then use this number to create your own UPC bar codes.

If your product happens to be a book, you'll need to acquire an International Standard Book Number (ISBN) from R.R. Bowker (www.bowker.com). You will not need to get a UPC for your book. ISBNs are issued at a minimum of ten numbers in a block. The fee is currently $225.

Product – Packaging – Production and Materials

Your product must be easy to produce with minimal human interaction to keep your product costs down. The same is true about your product packaging. Awkward shapes and sizes should be avoided when possible. Your packaging must be designed with packaging production machinery in mind. The packaging materials that you choose will depend on a multitude of factors, but it must be appropriate to the product, the product packaging machine requirements, product protection requirements, availability, cost, and supply chain requirements.

Product – Packaging – Getting Your Product in Your Packaging

In addition to your product, you will often have instructions, decals, warranty information, parts, bounce-back cards, coupons, literature about other products, and possibly order forms for reordering consumable elements of your product. All of these additional elements require printing, labor and/or machine time to put them into the packaging with your product. You will also need permission from your supply chain members to include these elements in your packaging. Product assembly and packaging must be included in your product BOM (bill of materials) analysis to determine the contribution to profits and coverage of fixed cost by your products.

Product – Packaging – Environmental Aspects

God gave us this planet to live on and take care of to the best of our abilities. We must be cognizant of the environmental impact of our package design. Many consumer product and toy companies use packaging materials with high amounts of recycled materials in them. Being environmentally aware is taking care of the resources that God has given to us, and it makes good business sense. Consumers like to see companies respect our planet, and if you are using packaging that is kind to the environment, you should tell your customers directly on your packaging. "This Packaging is biodegradable" is not only a definite plus to the environment but a positive marketing attribute.

Product – Packaging – Product Protection

Have you ever excitedly opened a Christmas package only to find the present inside broken? What about the gift that has some missing pieces? Product protection is important for a number of reasons. The primary reason is customer satisfaction. You want to deliver quality products to your customers that are ready to use and definitely not broken. Also, returns are expensive to your company. By the time you have taken the returned product back, researched why it was returned, and sent a replacement to the purchaser, you probably have doubled your product costs. You will find that testing your product packaging for product protection will pay off in the long run. Test your packaging by sending your product to various friends and relatives using various shipping carriers (including the U.S. Post Office). Ask the recipients how the packaging looked when it arrived. Was the packaging still fresh and crisp looking in the shipping carton? Was your product damaged in any way? Was the packaging easy to open? Was the packaging visually appealing? You can learn a lot about your packaging by performing this simple, inexpensive test.

Product – Packaging – Promotional Aspects

If you are a product designer or manufacturer, your product packaging may be the only "face" that the consumer gets to see of your company. Your packaging is more than a container for your product: it is the face of your company. Your product packaging is one of your most powerful marketing tools. It is always selling your product. It is building your brand.

Product – Packaging v. Security

Some products are more prone to theft. As an example, SD cards (the small memory cards that are a little smaller than a postage stamp and are used in PDAs and cameras). The product is so small that it would be easy for someone to slip into their pocket. Most manufacturers of SD cards package their products in 5 × 7 inch or larger clamshells. RadioShack® racks their SD cards in clamshells on racks behind the counter, requiring a sales assistant to get them for the customer. Of course, the large package is also meant to convey value since these little memory cards retail for $29 to $199 depending on their memory capacity.

PLACE

Another important element of the marketing mix is Place. Place can be thought of as the distribution of your products or services in the most advantageous way possible. The key elements in Place are channels of distribution/ channel members, logistics, location, service levels, and market coverage.

Place – Channels of Distribution/Channel Partners

You will be selling your products directly to consumers, retailers, wholesalers, distributors, or manufacturers, or a combination thereof. These are the typical channels of distribution that you have at your disposal.

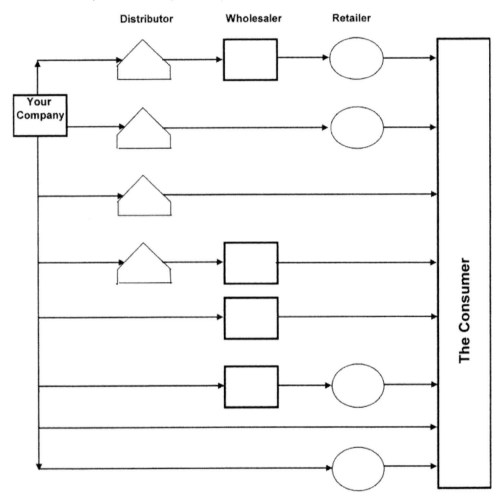

Fig.56 – Channels of Distribution

It is important to establish your channel partners (those entities in your marketing channels that you have joined forces with to sell your products) early on in your new business, as it will impact all other areas of your business. There are many ways to get your product or services directly in front of your customer regardless of which channel you are using:

Permanent Physical Presence – retail stores, merchant show rooms, and kiosks at malls.

Temporary Physical Presence – trade shows, flea markets, bazaars, and crafts fairs.

Internet – your own online store and online stores of others.

Direct Response (DR) – direct mail, infomercials, DRTV spots (30-second and 60-second direct response spots), DR radio, fax marketing, e-mail marketing, and co-op card decks. Direct response advertising typically has what is called a "call to action" ("order now!").

Personal Selling – direct to the end user at their location.

Alternative Selling – bundling your product with other products, consignment selling.

If you are selling directly to the end users of your product, there are no intermediaries between you and the final user of your product. If this is the case, you will most likely be a retailer or service business. Or you may be selling raw materials directly to a manufacturer. The main point is that you are selling to the ultimate user of your product. This channel of distribution is less complex than the other channel arrangements. When you sell directly to the end user of your products, you do not have to extrapolate your product's price to include the profit margins earned by channel intermediaries. If you are not selling to the end user of your product, you always have to include the profits normally earned by your channel members to arrive at the end user's costs. This is a necessary calculation you will make to be sure your product stays competitively priced. Nowadays, even if you have a retail store, you will probably also sell over the Internet.

If you have a product that would work well in retail, you may find that you cannot get retail buying executives to even return your phone calls. Most retail buyers get lots of calls from established manufacturers and distributors that know how to properly present their products to the buyers. I am not trying to discourage you from presenting your products directly to retailers—just letting you know that it can be difficult. Most industries have distribution companies that aggregate products and present them to wholesalers or retailers. The plus side is that you may be able to get your product to consumers by using a distributor. On the negative side, you will not be establishing your company and product with retailers, and you have to add the distributor's profits into your product's price.

Even though you may be forced to use a distributor, you still need to keep your company name and products in front of the retailers to which your distributors are selling your product. Sometimes distributors will take your product into their warehouses, consolidate it with other products, and then ship directly to the retail stores or retailer warehouses. If this is the case, you still should know the retailer buyers' names and keep in contact with them. You can do this by sending out periodic newsletters, product announcements, and other correspondence; remembering their birthdays; and telling them of newsworthy items that are happening in your industry. If your distributor has you drop-shipping directly to retailer warehouses or retail stores, it will be easier to maintain contact with retailers. Once your company and your product are established with your retailers, you may decide to one day go directly to retailers.

Place – Logistics

Logistics involves the actual physical transportation of your product from your manufacturing, distribution, or retail location to you or your channel partner or end user. Although at first your logistical needs may be simple, it is important to have a working knowledge of your logistical options as you continue to grow, as you will always have products or materials coming to you and going from you to your customers. You might be the primary supplier/ manufacturer, or you might be a retailer that markets directly to the end user. Logistics typically includes inventory control and planning, purchasing, physical transportation of product, and warehousing. Logistics is basically getting product from its point of origin to its final destination in the most economical, effective, and efficient manner as possible. The discussion below will apply to your inbound and outbound physical transportation needs. It will be likely that you will have product coming in from your suppliers and then going out to your customers. There are some situations where you will never touch the products that you are selling. Some suppliers will drop-ship your product directly to your customers. I have worked with an online gift company that would send purchase orders along with mailing labels directly to their product suppliers. The suppliers would then bill the gift company and use the mailing labels to send the products directly to the gift company customers.

According to the Federal Highway Administration as summarized on visitdetroit. com[37] transportation is big business in the United States.

- The transportation sector accounts for more than 11.7 million jobs and contributes more than $1 trillion annually to the U.S. economy, generating more than 10 percent of the Gross Domestic Product.

---

37   *Fast Facts | National Transportation Week | Visit Detroit* http://www.visitdetroit.com/index.php/events/ natl-transportation-week/fast-facts, 2009.

- Americans travel almost five trillion miles a year – That's more than 15,000 miles per person, AND enough miles to the sun and back more than 26 thousand times.
- Our nation's transportation network carries more than 12 billion tons of freight every year, or the equivalent of 40 tons for every man, woman, and child in America.
- Every $1 billion in investment in transportation supports 47,500 jobs. Many new business owners do not pay close attention to the logistics of getting their product from their suppliers or to their customers. They often fail to investigate options that can save them substantial amounts of money.

Place – Logistics – Inventory Control and Planning

Your inventory control and planning is an integral part of your logistics. You will rely heavily on your accounting systems when it comes to inventory control and planning. If you only have a couple of products, you can probably adequately control and plan your inventory manually. But if you have a number of products that you sell to customers, you will need a good accounting system that is fully and completely integrated with your inventory control and planning system. If you are a manufacturer, you will positively need a relevant, accurate, and timely (R.A.T.) integrated accounting system. You will want to be able to accurately account for all products coming in (purchasing), being stored (inventory that will appear on your balance sheet), and going out (sales, samples, shrinkage). These physical movements of inventory must be tied directly to your accounting records. There will be times where inventory leaving your store or warehouse may not have been accounted for by a proper sales transaction. Sometimes, this will be the result of theft or just plain and simple sloppy accounting procedures and/or internal controls. A physical inventory (counting your inventory) should be taken periodically and compared with your accounting records. This will help you determine if there is any "shrinkage" (unaccounted for reductions in inventory). If you are experiencing excessive shrinkage, you should call in your accountant to help you "plug the holes" in your accounting system by reviewing your inventory accounting procedures and related internal controls.

Place – Logistics – Purchasing

As a new business owner, you probably will not have a formalized purchasing department in your new business, but you will still have purchasing functions to deal with if you will be making purchases. You need to order the right product, at the right time, and at the right price. EOQ (economic order quantity), as discussed above, is an important concept when it comes to effective, efficient, and economical ordering of inventory. There is a cost every time you order product, and there is a cost of storing inventory. There is also normally significant cost in ordering product on an emergency basis rather on a planned basis; so planning your product needs is crucial.

When you purchase product from your suppliers, you should send them a purchase order. You will retain a copy of the purchase order in an open purchase order file, file a copy in your accounting records, or give it to your accountant. Your purchase order system can be either manual or computerized.

EASY BRAIN LABS, INC.

PURCHASE ORDER

Date	Terms/Conditions
Purchase Order # 0054	Ship Via
Requested By	Ship To
Date Needed By	Account Debited

Stock Number	Description	Quantity	Price/Unit	Total
			$	$
			$	$
			$	$
			$	$
			$	$
			$	$
			$	$
			$	$
			$	$
			$	$
Copy 1 - supplier, Copy 2 – purchase order file, Copy 3 - accounting			TOTAL	$

_____
Authorized Signature

Fig.57 – Purchase Order

There are some important points in regard to your purchase order forms:

1. They should be preprinted (only allow use of your authorized, preprinted purchase order forms).
2. Forms should be preprinted with sequential serial numbers. This way, you can account for all forms. This is an excellent element of internal control, and it will help you track your purchase orders if you know that you can account for all of them. Most forms that you use in your business should be sequentially numbered.
3. All purchase order forms must be signed by you or someone that you designate.
4. Other information that should be on all purchase order forms:
   a. Date issued
   b. Date product required
   c. Terms
   d. Ship to (you might want the product "drop-shipped" directly to one of your customers)
   e. Ship via (you can normally designate the shipping method)
   f. Description of product
   g. Quantity of product
   h. Price per unit
   i. Extended price for each item ordered
   j. Total amount of the order

When you receive the product that you have ordered, you will compare your purchase order to the shipping documents that accompany your received product. Any discrepancies in the product or amount received will be noted on the receiving/shipping documents that you receive with the product.

You will receive an invoice for the product that you received, and you should compare your adjusted receiving/shipping documents to the invoice to make sure that you are being billed only for the product that you actually received. You will also compare the price per unit on your purchase order to your invoice to make sure that you are being billed the correct price.

When it comes to the physical shipment of your product from your supplier to you or from you to your customers, there are a number of choices for your consideration. If you have planned your product needs properly, you can save a substantial amount of money by keeping ordering costs and inventory holding cost as low as possible. You can have your product shipped using a slower method, and thus have your product shipped at a lower rate. Many suppliers will have their own captive shipping companies, and they will include the cost of shipping in the cost of their product. Foster Farms (poultry), which is the largest poultry company on the West Coast, owns its own small railroad company and trucking company. They primarily use their railroad for bringing in the large amounts of feed that they use for their chickens and their trucks for delivering product to their customers.

When ordering product from your suppliers, there are some important variables you should have addressed before agreeing to the purchase of product from selected suppliers. If you are just starting your business, you may be asked to prepay for product before it is shipped. I would recommend that you never do this unless the supplier is a reputable supplier. Always check out the references of your suppliers if they are not nationally recognized.

An important term used in shipping is FOB, which stands for Free On Board. It is a term that indicates that the price for your ordered goods includes delivery at seller's expense to a specified point and no farther. The FOB term is used with an identified physical location to determine 1) the responsibility and basis for payment of freight charges and 2) the point at which title of the shipment passes from seller to buyer. Two terms often following FOB are *Origin* and *Destination*.

FOB Origin

The buyer assumes title and control of the goods the moment the carrier signs the bill of loading. The buyer assumes risk of transportation and is entitled to route the shipment. The buyer is responsible for filing claims for loss or damage during shipment.

FOB Destination

The seller retains title and control of goods until they are delivered and the contract of carriage has been completed. The seller selects the carrier and is responsible for the risk of transportation. The seller is responsible for filing claims for loss or damage.

When you are starting your business, you will probably be buying from suppliers that ship FOB destination, where they either pay for shipping or they have their own trucks that will deliver product to you. If this is the case, you will have little control over the actual shipping of product from your suppliers. On the other hand, if you are shipping your products to your customers, you have a wide selection of shipping methods available to you.

Place – Logistics – Regulation

Transportation systems in the United States are regulated by the U.S. Government in much the same way that the phone and electric industries are regulated. Even the courts have referred to the various transportation modes in the U.S. as public utilities. Railroads were first regulated in 1887 under the Interstate Commerce Act. This act established the first regulatory body in the United States as the Interstate Commerce Commission (ICC). The ICC regulates the railroads, pipelines, motor carriers, and inland water carriers. The Civil Aeronautics Board regulates American air carriers, and the Federal Maritime Commission regulates ocean carriers.

The regulation of all the transportation modes in the U.S. includes a provision that the rates charged must be "just and reasonable." "Just" means that the rate must be fair to the shipper in relationship to what other shippers pay for moving similar commodities under the same approximate conditions. "Reasonable" implies that the carrier shall be allowed to earn a fair return on his investment. The services offered by all carriers are also regulated.

Selecting the right shipper can be very confusing. The complexity is related to "tariffs" which are the books that are used to determine shipping charges. Tariffs are referred to as official publications and there are literally thousands of them. The area of shipping tariffs has become so complex that many companies employ freight bill auditors on a periodic basis to make sure that they have been charged the right amount by freight companies. Freight bills are wrong so often that these freight bill auditors are often paid a salary of 50% of whatever they find in the way of errors. It's safe to assume that the errors are most often in favor of the freight company.

Keep in mind that the lowest cost carrier does not necessarily result in your lowest total cost of shipping. Because of this, you need to constantly and comprehensively evaluate your inbound and outbound shipping. As an example, you might be shipping large volumes of product out and decide the rail transportation is a much cheaper way to get your product to your customer. But you will have to consider how to get your product from your rail shipments to the customers who do not have access to railroads. Also, your customer may not be willing to wait for his order to arrive by rail.

It is also important to be familiar with your shipping options, as they will affect your product pricing, customer service, and overall profitability. As to pricing, your product cost elements do not end when your product rolls off the manufacturer's production line. The product must still make its way to your warehouse or store and then to your customer's warehouse or store. There are substantial costs involved with the movement of your product from its source to its end user. There is also a time factor involved with this movement.

Easy Brain Labs, Inc. licensed a consumer electronics device to a marketing distribution company. The distribution deal was signed in March, and the product had to be available for shipment to retail stores the following Christmas. On the surface, it appeared that this was a slam-dunk transaction. But, let's look at the time line:

Final development from prototype to a product ready for manufacture	60 days	May 30
Mold making and manufacture of first units	60 days	July 30
Shipping by sea from Asia to U.S.	30 days	August 30
Product in customs	15 days	September 15

The retailers wanted the product no later than August 30 for shipment to their stores and regional warehouse in time for the Christmas buying season. Given this requirement, Easy Brain Labs, Inc. needed to find a way to shorten the process by at least 15 days. Also, there was absolutely no cushion of time left for any potential problems. Everything had to go perfectly, which we know seldom happens. As you can see, the movement of your product is critical to servicing your customers' needs. The bottom line is that you need to be familiar with shipping options and their implications for the cost of your products and their timely delivery.

You will want to constantly test your delivery results to make sure your carrier is meeting your agreed-upon standards of delivery. This can be done by using a customer response card on the outside of your packages, asking customers to evaluate your delivery service. You will be surprised by the high participation of customers willing to return your response cards.

You have a number of transportation modes that you can use to ship product or receive product:

Railroads

Railroads still move the bulk of products (measured in tons per mile) in the United States. Railroads are the most efficient mode for moving bulk commodities and durable goods (cars, washing machines, etc.) over longlong distances. There are a very small number of carriers to choose from. Railroads are best used for long haul, large volume shipments. Accessibility can be a problem, as not every company has direct access to the railroad. Transit times are often spotty and are generally long. The service standards for the U.S. rail system are not as high as for other delivery modes.

Motor Carrier

The motor carrier's prime advantage over the other modes is the relatively fast, consistent service, both for large and small shipments. For this reason, the trucking industry concentrates its resources on manufactured goods as opposed to railroads that concentrate on bulk and raw materials shipments. There are a large number of small and large motor carriers Almost all logistics systems use motor carriers somewhere in their system. 82% of U.S. freight is carried by motor carriers. Motor carriers are typically more accessible than other modes of transportation. Motor carriers do not own the rights-of-way to the roads they use. Motor carriers are typically higher in cost compared to rail and water. The trade-off is faster and more reliable service. Transit times are normally quicker than by rail or water. Reliability can be adversely affected by inclement weather. The relatively smaller load capacity of motor delivery vehicles coincides with lower and quick replenishment requirements of their customers.

There are a number of classifications for the motor carriers.

Truckload (TL)

As the name implies, a truckload carrier is one that moves single shipments that fill out the capacity of a truck trailer. They pick up the freight at one particular shipper and deliver it to one particular location. There are a number of advantages to moving freight in truckload quantities. The two primary benefits are cost and time. A truckload volume will almost always result in a lower cost per pound than a less-than-truckload volume. You also gain the advantage of not having intermediary stops, instead going directly from pickup point to final delivery point. A United States coast-to-coast truckload can move from coast to coast in two to three days.

Less-Than-Truckload (LTL)

This is the most widely recognized carrier classification. This is also the one that you will most often encounter in your business. The LTL motor carrier picks up an assortment of small shipments from a number of different shippers over the course of a day. They will then take their total day's pickups back to their terminal for sorting onto trucks going to each intended geographical area. As mentioned above, LTL product shipments can take longer because they will make numerous stops. Also, keep in mind your freight will be handled more often as the truck driver rearranges his load during the numerous product drop-offs. LTL motor carriers will normally take five to six days to move product from one coast of the United States to the other coast.

LTL motor carriers are broken down into two different classifications: long-haul and short-haul. Long-haul carriers will typically service deliveries of over 300 miles or 5 hours of drive time.

Being a small business owner, you will probably at one time or another use a freight broker. They typically will solicit shipments from various carriers and match them up with truck owner-operators looking to fill their trucks. Freight brokers normally do not own any of their own trucks. The broker will bill you as the shipper for your freight shipment and then pay the owner-operator a percentage of the revenue generated from the freight delivery service provided. There are some "fly-by-night" people in the freight broker business, so make sure that you know who you are dealing with before using the services of a freight broker. Ask for a verifiable list of references from owner-operators and from shippers who have used their services. Also, ask that they have their insurance company send a current certificate of insurance directly to you verifying that they have cargo insurance in the event that something happens to your freight while in transit.

Small Package Carriers

Since you are just starting out in business, you will probably be using the services of a small package carrier to get your products sent to you and to send your products to your customers. The choice between Small Package Carriers was much easier a quarter century ago. If you had a small package to ship, your choices were either the post office or United Parcel Service (UPS). Then came Federal Express and DHL Worldwide Express and others. Although there are now scores of small package carriers in the United States, the choice of many shippers is still the United States Postal Service (USPS). It is still one of the best bargains for shippers.

Small package motor carriers are those that move packages ranging in size from a letter to a package of 150 lbs. Depending on the carrier and the type of service requested, they can move your products either by ground or by air. Their ground services are normally economical, while their air services (e.g., next day) can be somewhat expensive. The major players are UPS (United Parcel Service), FedEx (Federal Express), , DHL, Airborne Express, BAX Global, Menlo Worldwide, and Emery Worldwide.

The top three things to look for when evaluating a small package shipper are cost, time in transit, and account management capabilities. As mentioned in the chapter entitled "FORMING YOUR BUSINESS – YOUR TEAM," it is wise to occasionally put your partners/vendors, including small package motor services, out to bid. In order to do this, you have to provide all bidders with accurate information about your shipping requirements. When you are soliciting proposals, you will need the following information:

- Number of shipments, weights, and average retail cost by service level and/or zone.

- Primary shipping locations.

- Dollars spent, by retail location, for each segment of your business.

- Current rate charts and/or contracts.

- A to-and-from Zip/ Postal Code analysis, including number of shipments and weights.

- Your requirements for tracking packages.

- Your reporting needs

- Any special handling needs that you might have.

- Ability to handle your inbound and outbound freight issues.

- International capabilities

Small Package Carriers compete in a market in which there are a lot of choices for shippers like you. You can develop a competitive advantage in your negotiations with them if you have enough freight to be interesting to them. I could ship an average 5-pound package through my wife's international company for $7 dollars, when it would cost me $20 through my own small company. The message here is that volume matters. Some large companies will let their employees ship their packages out at their "super shipper" rates to increase their volume. So while you are starting your new company, you should see if your friends or family has a special rate with a small package carrier that you can use to receive or ship out product. Another option is to form a special company or buying cooperative (preferably a corporation) exclusively for shipping out product for the group members. There can be a substantial savings for volume.

Water

There are basically two types of water carriers: the inland or barge (sometimes called Domestic Water Carriers) lines and the ocean deepwater ships. Water Carriers are very efficient transporters of bulk commodities. Domestic Water Carriers operate along the Atlantic, Gulf, and Pacific coasts, along the Mississippi, Missouri, Tennessee and the Ohio River systems and the Great Lakes. Oceangoing ships operate on the Great Lakes and in international commerce. Water Carriers are a relatively low-cost mode of transportation. They are typically a long-distance mover of low value, bulk-type mineral, agricultural, and forest products. Much of America's consumer products are manufactured in Hong Kong and China, and thus shipped via international water carriers.

When planning the purchase of goods manufactured in these overseas countries, you will have to input an additional 30 days for overseas boat delivery. You will want to add in an additional 5 to 7 days for clearing customs once your products have reached an American port. This is due in large part to increased security measures after 9/11.

Air

Airfreight is still a relatively insignificant percentage of the total ton-miles shipped, amounting to much less than 1% of all freight shipped. Cost structure is highly variable, and carriers do not own rights-of-way. Because of airfreight's relatively high cost, it is used primarily for very valuable or highly perishable products. Typical products include watches, computers, fresh flowers, high-fashion clothing, and live seafood. Airfreight is also used for emergency shipments. I know of one electronics company that had 144,000 units (12 master cartons) shipped from Hong Kong to the U.S. to make sure that they were the first to launch a particular electronics product. Also, keep in mind that airfreight may be able to help you better manage your JIT (just in time) method of inventory management and production. The high cost of transportation can be somewhat offset by reduced inventory holding costs and faster customer service. You will typically use airfreight for products with a high-value-to-weight ratio. Reliability of air transportation is affected by weather more than other transportation modes.

Pipeline

Even though the pipeline industry is second in total ton-miles transported, many people are not even aware of their existence. It is highly unlikely that you will ever transport any of your products using the pipeline industry. Obviously, this mode of transportation has a very narrow type of product that flows through their systems.

Intermodal Transportation

When companies need to move large amounts of durable goods, they will often use "intermodal" logistic transportation models. These intermodal transportation models can be somewhat complex, often involving moving product from a ship to a railroad to a warehouse and then to a motor carrier to get the product to its final destination.

Fig.58 – Intermodel Shipping

An intermodal transportation model will often require the services of a freight forwarder or freight consolidator. If you were required to use an intermodal transportation model, you would want to make sure that you had solid estimates of time and cost for each leg of the trip. As already discussed, when you are selling your product, your customers expect to know when it is going to arrive. You also need to know the total cost of transportation to properly incorporate it into your selling price.

Freight Forwarders

If you plan on selling your products overseas, you will absolutely want to find a good freight forwarder. In addition to the obvious economies of scale, consolidators provide a host of value-added services. These services include package tracking, delivery confirmation, billing, customized rates, pickup, document preparation, and retail fulfillment. Freight forwarders are in the business of getting your products to your overseas customers. They will work with the various modes of transportation to get you lower transportation rates and will prepare your documentation for you. They will also arrange for overseas warehousing and make sure that your customers get your products. The documentation requirements for doing business overseas are very complex; it's important that you have a good freight forwarder as your "partner" in your international logistics process.

In your transportation selection decision, you will give consideration to the following elements of the transportation equation when choosing the mode as well as the individual shipper:

1. Cost
2. Transit time to get your product to you from your supplier or from you to your customer
3. Reliability of the shipping company
4. Track record of shrinkage from loss and damage
5. Shipment expediting ability
6. Shipment tracking
7. Willingness of carrier to negotiate service changes
8. Scheduling flexibility
9. Claims processing
10. Specialized equipment
11. Capability of the carrier
12. Accessibility of the carrier
13. Market coverage of the carrier
14. Reputation of the carrier
15. Security of your inventory while in the shipper's control
16. Financial stability of the carrier
17. Are you shipping bulk or packaged goods?
18. Is your project fragile, requiring special handling and/or packaging?
19. Do you need next day delivery?
20. Comprehensive reporting abilities
21. Size of your shipments (weight, size, number of pieces)
22. Do your goods need to be refrigerated?
23. Can the carrier accommodate intermodal freight transportation needs?

An integral part of the entire logistical process is storage of your product once you receive it. We have already discussed EOQ (economic order quantity) in this chapter. There are costs of ordering products and there are costs of holding products. There is a tremendous cost associated with out-of-stock conditions. If you sell product that is taken from your inventory, you will have the usual functions associated with inventory management and warehouse operations:

Receiving
    Scheduling carrier
    Unloading carrier vehicles
    Inspecting for correctness of order and shortages and damaged product
    Receiving documentation maintenance

Putting Product Away
    Identify products
    Identify storage area
    Move products
    Update your inventory records

Storage of Products
    Have proper equipment on hand
    Maintain equipment
    Stock location decisions
        Frequency of access
        Unit size
        Unit value
    Protection against product damage
    Protection against product shrinkage

Order picking
    Processing order
    Selection of optimum picking method
        Batch picking
        Zone picking
        Pick and assemble
    Proper order picking process
    Proper order picking equipment

Shipping preparation
    Packing orders
    Labeling orders
    Staging orders

Shipping
 Scheduling carrier
 Load carrier vehicle
 Accounting system update
 Shipping documentation maintenance

All of these functions will affect your warehousing needs and the layout of your warehouse. Your warehousing needs will be closely related to your customers' needs, your projected sales, your EOQ calculations, and many other factors.

Place – Location

This is where your customers meet your products. You need to make sure that your products or services are offered in their appropriate location where their target market can have access to them. As an example, you would not want to put a snow ski shop in Jamaica. You would not want your new toy product marketed in the housewares department of a department store. Your customers may meet your products online. Almost all businesses should have a shopping-basket-enabled Web site given the minimal costs of setting up a Web site and its easy operation. If you are a manufacturer or distributor, your customers will be both retailers and the end consumer (via the retailer). The retailers will probably meet your product at their buying offices as introduced by you or your distributors. Your end user consumer will meet your product on the retail shelves. If you sell through retailers, your packaging will be the only face your end user will see.

Here is a list of locations where your customers can meet your product:
Airlines
Airports
Back of the room selling at seminars
Bazaar (popular in Mexican-American communities)
Beach vendors
Big-box stores (e.g., Costco, Sam's Club)
Catalog
Cell phone marketing
Christmas shops
Churches and church bookstores – family friendly products
Consolidators

County fairs

Corporate "giveaways"

Credit card statement premiums

Cruise ship stores

Direct mail

Direct Response (one-minute direct response commercials)

Door-to-door

Door hangers

eBay (this is really hot right now)

e-mail marketing

Fax marketing

Fast food kids' meals toys

Flea markets

Freestanding displays at grocery stores (if you are not a grocery item)

Gift parties

Governmental

Group coupon mailings

Home shopping Networks

Infomercials

International

Internet

License to large and/or international firms

Magazine/newspaper

Mall kiosk

Military base stores

Multilevel similar to Amway

New-car premium giveaway for test-driving cars

Piggyback on other products

Premiums for more expensive products

Premiums in cereal boxes

RadioShack (they often require an exclusive relationship with their 7,000 stores)

Retail store – mass market

Retail store – specialty (e.g., Bed Bath & Beyond)

School and library market

School fund-raising programs (e.g., selling chocolate candy bars door-to-door)

Specialty retail (e.g., gift shops, truck stops, university bookstores)
Street-corner vendors (popular in New York and Los Angeles)
Trade Fairs
Wholesale and let other people sell it

These are just a few ideas. You get the general idea. Don't get locked in to selling your product through one marketing channel. You've spent a lot of resources developing your products and services, so sell them in as many channels of distribution as you can.

Place – Service Levels

Remember the days (you probably will not remember unless you are over 50 years old) when you pulled up to a gas station and someone came out to wash your windows and check your oil and the air in your tires? Before you left, you would also get a handful of S&H Green Stamps or Blue Chip Stamps for purchasing products from gift catalogs. This level of service is only a distant memory at gas stations. The level of service that you give to your clients must be balanced with the costs of the service. This is why today there is no service at gas stations. According statistics from the website for SCORE[38]

- The lowest-ranking employee in a business can lose more customers than can be gained by the highest-ranking employee.
- In the average business, for every customer who bothers to complain, there are 26 other who remain silent.
- The average wronged customer will tell 8 to 16 people (about 10 percent will tell more then 20 people).
- 91 percent of unhappy customers will <u>never</u> purchase good or services from you again.
- If you make an effort to remedy customer's complaints, 82 to 95 percent of them will stay with you.
- It costs about 5 time as much to attract a new customer as it does to keep an existing one.

It is helpful to break services into primary services and ancillary services. Primary services are those services that are necessary to get your product into your customer's shopping bag. Ancillary services are those that are not necessary to the process of

---

38   SCORE *High Cost of Losing A Customer,* http://scoremichigansgreatsouthwest.org/high_cost_of_ losing_a_customer.html, 2010.

getting your product into their shopping bag, but are additional arrows in your quiver of customer acquisition and retention. You may have the greatest product in the world, but with poor services, your great product will not continue to generate sales.

Many of the services discussed here will be oriented toward retail customers. Many of them are also appropriate if you are marketing primarily to wholesalers and retail chains.

Primary services will normally include:

1. Adequate exposure to your product so that customers can make a purchase decision based on "touching" your product. This presents more of a problem for companies that have only an Internet presence. As an example, if you sell books online through a company such as Amazon.com, you would want to make the online purchaser feel as if he has "touched" the book. Book lovers have a need to "touch" their potential product purchase. Amazon does a great job of this by allowing people to view a number of pages inside their books.

2. Product information presented either by personnel, the Internet and/or packaging that gives the purchaser enough information about the product to make an intelligent and informed purchase decision. Continuing with the Amazon.com example, they give the page count and information about the author, similar books, and reviews by people who have purchased the book.

3. A system that will accept your customer's payment, approve his payment, process his order, deliver his order, and follow up with a "thank you" note if appropriate. This all implies a sufficiently robust system that can capture a customer's information.

4. Packaging that will adequately protect your product up to its delivery at your customer's door.

Ancillary services can include:

1. Online ability to track the delivery of customer purchases.
2. Selection
3. Free and convenient parking
4. Convenient-sized packaging
5. Online video telling your customer how to assemble and maximize the benefit from using your product.
6. Coupons for reduced prices for products related to the purchase of your product.

7. Enclosed literature that explains alternative uses for your product other than the uses fro which your product was purchased.
8. Availability of extended warranty.
9. Free samples of similar products.
10. "No questions asked" return policy.
11. Free videotape explaining the use of your product.
12. Coupons for free or reduced-priced consumables related to your product.
13. Coupons for reduced-price or free related products.
14. A company consultant to visit customers' homes or businesses to install or set up the item the customer purchased from seller.
15. Unlimited free phone technical support.
16. Free servicing for the life of the product purchased (e.g., Saturn cars).
17. Free replacement if broken.
18. Discount on product if purchased in prestated time limit.
19. "But wait there is more" "free" products.
20. Free product for a friend.
21. Classes that show your customers how to benefit from their purchase of your product.
22. 24/7 customer support hotline and Web site.
23. Ability to charge their purchase and pay later.
24. "One button" ordering online.

Big-box stores have made major inroads into the retail margin by offering limited service and low price, and making it easy to purchase their products. Two major weapons you have, as a small business, are superior service and unique products. There will always be a demand for both high volume/limited service stores such as Costco, and for the service-oriented, independent small stores.

Many of the services listed above will also apply to your customers if you are selling your products to retailers and others in your marketing channels that are not the final users of your products. Here are some additional services that can be applicable to your "non-retail" customers:

Order tracking

Comprehensive invoicing

Liberal terms

JIT (just in time delivery)

Small order size purchasing

Support for their customers for your products

Training their personnel in the proper use of your products

Training of their personnel in maximizing the sale of your products

Low defect rate in your products

Display units provided

Pass-through purchase incentives

Place – Market Coverage

An important decision you will have to make is market coverage. You may want to distribute all of your products to all available markets. There are a number of reasons that you will not chose to distribute all of your products to all available markets. One major consideration is your available internal resources such as cash and personnel. You may have to concentrate on building select markets and then move on to new markets once you have made your current markets profitable.

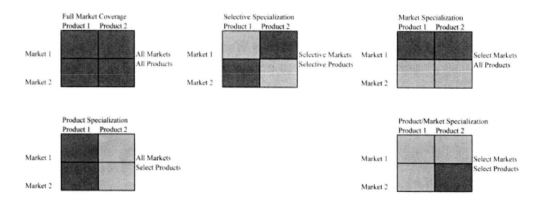

Fig.59 – Market Coverage

Once you have decided which products and markets you will be concentrating on, you need to determine how you are going to be selling selected products into your selected markets.

Intensive Market Coverage
If you are selling a convenience-type product, you will want Intensive

Market Coverage. This way, a purchaser will have it nearby and will need a minimum amount of time searching for the product.

Selective Market Coverage
In Selective Market Coverage, you will place your products at only a select number of outlets. This type of market coverage is used for products that consumers will buy only after comparing quality, price, and product style.

Exclusive Market Coverage
Exclusive Market Coverage is when you give a middleman the sole right to sell your product in a defined geographic territory. Exclusive Market Coverage is the opposite of Intensive Market Coverage in that products are purchased and consumed over a long period of time, and service or information is required to develop a satisfactory sales relationship.

PROMOTION

The last element of the marketing mix that we will discuss is promotion. The primary elements of promotion are advertising, sales promotion, public relations, personal selling, and direct response marketing. You will use a mix of these approaches to market your company and your product. You may not use them all, but it is a good idea to know the basics of each promotional element so if the opportunity arises, you can take advantage of it. As a small business, you cannot compete with the promotional dollar spending of large companies. They have what may appear at times to be unlimited funds to spend on promotion. Although you cannot compete on a dollar-for-dollar basis, you can maximize the benefits of the dollars that you do spend by understanding the basics of promotion and planning carefully.

As you develop your marketing message, as a Christian, your company is founded on Godly principles, thus you will have integrity at all times in your marketing message. Your message should always be true and accurate. Part of that integrity is to avoid "hyping" your product.

Your goals will be to inform, persuade and/or remind your customers and potential customers about your company and products.

Inform

1. Increase consumer awareness of your new product
2. Explain how your new product works
3. Suggest new uses of existing products
4. Build a new company/product image

Persuade

1. Encourage consumers to switch to your brand
2. Change customer perceptions of your company/product
3. Encourage customers to buy now

Remind

1. Remind consumers that your product might be needed later.
2. Remind consumers where to buy your product.
3. Maintain consumer awareness of your company/ product.
4. Manage buyer remorse. Sometimes people will purchase a product and still want it, but will have some buyer remorse. They may have spent more than they think they should have. Of course, you should have a liberal return policy, but you also need to help them manage their after-purchase feelings. On big-ticket items, it's a good idea to send your customer a note soon after they make their purchase. You can congratulate them on their purchase, give them information on additional ways to enjoy their purchase, share current news releases about their product, etc.

Promotion – Advertising

Advertising is the placement of announcements and persuasive messages in time or space purchased in mass media to inform, persuade and/or remind members of a particular target market or audience about your products, services, organization, or ideas. Most people think of television, radio, print, outdoor, and the Internet when they want to place an ad. As we will see in this discussion, there are many more places to place ads than the five just listed. My underlying theme in this book is that Christians should be the most creative people on the planet. The ideas presented in this book and the media discussed below are meant to stimulate your creative thought process.

Use the discussions of various media to stimulate your own ideas. There is a saying "Unless you are the lead dog, the view never changes." Innovate, chart new territory in marketing. This is the way that you can rise above the clutter of all of the other advertising in the world.

Costs: You will pay fees for space and time in various media, and the costs of ad design and production. In buying media, you will be buying reach and frequency of your ads.

Strengths   Efficient means of reaching a large number of potential customers. You will have many advertising outlets (e.g., newspapers, TV, radio) to choose from.

Weaknesses   High absolute costs. It is sometimes hard to break through the clutter of other advertising and get your message to the consumer. It is difficult to measure the effectiveness of advertising. Large companies that continuously purchase advertising space and time are often given preferential treatment over the small, infrequent media purchaser.

Promotion – Personal Selling

Personal selling is any of a number of activities designed to promote customer purchase of a product or service. Sales can be done in person or over the phone, through e-mail, or other communication media. The process generally includes stages such as assessing customer needs, presenting product features and benefits to address those needs, and negotiation on price, delivery, and other elements.

Costs: Salaries and commissions paid to sales staff.

Strengths: Personal selling can be very effective if personnel are effectively trained and given the proper incentives to sell. You can also get immediate feedback from your salespeople. Many customers prefer to be sold to in person. If you have good salespeople, they can be very persuasive and tailor their message "on the fly" to each customer. Salespeople are the best way to communicate complex information directly to your customers. Your salespeople can select their audience rather than using the "shotgun" approach used by other elements of the promotional mix. Salespeople can help your company form a relationship with your customers more effectively than "non-personal" promotional approaches.

Weaknesses: Salespeople can be expensive. Salespeople have the built-in unreliability of being human. It can be difficult for all of your salespeople to communicate a uniform message.

Promotion – Public Relations

Public relations is that form of communication management that seeks to make use of publicity and other nonpaid forms of promotion and information to influence the feelings, opinions, or beliefs about the company, its products or services, or about the value of the product or service, or the activities of the organization to buyers, prospects, or other stakeholders.

Costs: There is no direct media cost for public relations. There may be cost associated with the hiring of a professional public relations person. A good public relations person knows where to find media outlets, and they know what these media outlets are looking for. They will often have existing relationships with key people at media outlets. You will normally pay a public relations person a flat fee per month. They will also often concentrate on either industry PR (e.g., selling you and your products to wholesalers, retail buyers, and distributors) or PR directly to your potential consumers.

Strengths: Your buying public normally considers public relations more reliable than other forms of promotion. When the public reads a story about your company and/or product in the newspaper, they tend to give it more credibility than an ad that may appear in the same newspaper. If you have a good story to tell about your company and products, PR can be a very effective selling tool.

Weaknesses: It is often difficult to get the various media outlets to cooperate with you. Also, it is difficult to plan public relations as the various media outlets may not agree with you as to the importance of your news release or story.

Promotion – Sales Promotion

Sales promotion is externally directed incentives offered to the ultimate consumer. These usually consist of offers, such as free trial offers, coupons, premiums, rebates, designed to gain one or more of product trial, repeat usage of product, more frequent or multiple product purchases; introduce a new/improved product; introduce new packaging or different size packages; neutralize competitive advertising or sales promotions; capitalize on seasonal, geographic, or special events; and encourage consumers to trade up to a larger size, more profitable line, or another product in the line.

Costs: The cost of promotions varies widely based on the various sales promotion campaigns that you have during the year.

Strengths: Effective at changing consumer behavior in the short run. If well thought out, your message can be conveyed over a long period of time for a one-time expenditure.

Weaknesses: This type of promotion is easily abused. It can often lead to sales promotion wars with your competitors. Your competitors can easily duplicate your promotion.

Promotion – Direct Response Marketing

Costs: Cost of your media and the design of your message.
Strengths: With direct response marketing (DRM), you can prepare your messages quickly. One of the real strengths of DRM is that you can easily gauge the effectiveness of your media dollars spent. Another big advantage to DRM is the fact that messages can be tailored to specific groups of consumers.

Weaknesses: When direct response first started being used by marketers, it was substantially more effective than now. As an example, when infomercials first started airing on television, they would return 10 to 20 times the cost of media in sales. In 2006, a good infomercial returned 2 times the cost of media in sales.

Promotion – Media

The purpose of this section is to familiarize you with the various options of media available to you as an advertiser and also to jog your creative thinking process in regard to media options. For many of the media types outlined here, we will also discuss their cost. Because of the extensive variables involved in pricing, we can't give you precise costs. The examples will give you an indication of affordability of the various forms of media. As mentioned earlier, to effectively advertise, you must have an effective message and place it in the appropriate media to reach your target audience. Today's most common media channels are television, radio, print, outdoor, and the Internet.

Media is really any place that you can place an ad. I was at the beach boardwalk in Venice, California when I saw a truly unique use of advertising. The boardwalk in Venice is normally so busy that you have to constantly look where you are going to avoid stepping on someone. I looked down and saw a small dog walking around wearing a cloth coat that simply said, "Hungry?" It had an arrow that pointed to a small pocket with business cards telling you how to find a diner there on the beach boardwalk.

The environment in which media is consumed has a tremendous impact on its effectiveness. If a media consumer is relaxed and is at peace with his surroundings, he will be more favorably disposed to your advertising message. If he is stressed, under pressure for whatever reason, he will react differently to your message than if he was relaxed. Radio is often played as background music for other activities. Newspapers are typically read more quickly than other print media and are most often "scanned" rather than read. Because of this, readers are more easily distracted during their newspaper reading time. Common sense tells us that it is best to place your television ad spots in compelling programs that keep the viewer riveted to the television screen. But this same viewer will use the time your ad is on to make some popcorn or take a nature break.

There are some overall concepts and terms that you should be aware of when you start giving consideration to your advertising media:

Clutter – One of the things that substantially reduce the effectiveness of your advertising media is everyone else's advertising in your chosen media outlet and in other media. One of your challenges in your advertising is to attempt to rise above all of this clutter and be noticed by the viewers and readers. If you don't, you will be just another piece of clutter.

Consistency – It is normally better to have a consistent message over time than a short "burst" of advertising. For instance, it's normally a better strategy to spread your advertising budget over an entire year and keep your name consistently before the public rather than spend it all in one month. This does not mean that you should budget your expenditures evenly throughout the year. You may find that you make 50% of your total year's revenues during the last three months before Christmas. This would be an obvious time period in which to spend the greatest chunk of your marketing dollars.

Conversion – Having a good CPM (cost per thousand) for your advertising message is not very meaningful if you don't have a good conversion of "advertising impressions" to sales. If a million people see your advertising message and you only convert 100 of them to sales transactions, you don't have a good conversion ratio.

Cost of Acquisition – It costs to acquire a new customer. It costs substantially less to keep an existing customer, so when you are analyzing where to put your marketing dollars, don't forget about customer retention. It may be difficult to measure the number of new customers that came from specific media efforts, but if at all possible, you should do this analysis. Even if you can't determine which customers came from specific media, you need to analyze your customer acquisition efforts to make sure that "the juice is worth the squeeze." As an example, let's assume that you are planning to advertise for your new bookkeeping business. You know that the average new client will generate $2,000 revenues per year. You also know that your gross margin (revenue less direct expenses to service this client) is approximately $1,000. You also know that your average client will stay with you for about 4 years, meaning that the average client will generate approximately $4,000 gross margin over their revenue generation life for your company. After deducting your desired profit margin of say $2,000, you estimate that you are actually willing to spend up to $2,000 in advertising to acquire this new client. As mentioned, the cost of keeping your existing clients will be substantially less than this amount.

CPM – Cost per thousand. This is a way to compare the cost of your various media using a common basis.

Effectiveness – If at all possible, you should try to measure the effectiveness of each of the media types used in your ad campaign. Some advertising media effectiveness is easier to measure than others. The effectiveness of direct response media (e.g., infomercials, direct mail) is pretty easy to measure. When you put an infomercial on the air, it either sells product or it does not. Non-direct response media is a little more difficult to measure.

One way to measure the effect of general advertising is to isolate select variables. As an example, you might emphasize one product using a particular type of media and a different product with another type of media, and then compare the results.

Frequency – Average number of times a household or a person views your advertising message over a specific time period.

Message Should Fit the Media – Certain messages just do not fit certain types of media. As an example, if your message requires a lot of explanation, you probably will not use billboards. If your message requires visuals to explain your product, you will not use radio. Support media is often used to increase the effectiveness of primary media. This approach makes it even harder to measure the effectiveness of your advertising media components. Structuring a plan to measure the effectiveness of your media components is as important as structuring your media plan.

Per Inquiry ("P.I.") Advertising – This type of advertising is often used in direct response advertising and for generation of leads. It's based on your results rather than airtime. Here's how it works: let's say that you agree with a local station on a target amount of 100 leads for your new bookkeeping business. You agree to pay $10 for each valid lead. The radio station will run your ad until they get you 100 leads, regardless of how many times they have to run your ad. Once they get your 100 leads, you will pay them $1,000. Media outlets are partial to this type of advertising, because they can run your ad when they have nothing else to run. You will like it because you can get measured responses and you won't be limited to a defined number of minutes of airtime.

Remnant Media – Most media outlets will offer leftover media at substantial discounts to fill up their pages and fill in broadcast schedules. Always ask your media outlets about their excess media.

Reach – The number of different or unduplicated households or persons that are exposed to your advertising message for a specific period of time. Reach and Frequency (below) will be important numbers for all of your advertising media analysis and review.

ROP (Run-of-publication) and ROS (Run-of-Station) – In exchange for an often highly discounted ad rate, the media provider can place your ad anywhere in the issue that suits their needs. You can get a substantial discount in a local newspaper if you advertise on an ROP basis. In some scenarios, it might not make sense to use this form of advertising. Say you have a sporting goods store. You'll probably want your store ad placed in the sporting goods section rather than in the cooking section of the newspaper. ROP would not be your best choice. Most media outlets (print and electronic) have ROP/ ROS programs.

Share the Cost – When possible, try to share the cost of your advertising. This can be done with your supplier, merchant associations, and others.

Size – Rather than eliminating an effective type of media because it costs too much, consider reducing the size of your ad or running it less often.

Print Media

Print Media has been around for hundreds of years and thus has a familiar feel to it for most readers. It includes newspapers, magazines, direct mail, yellow pages, and alternative print media. Alternative print media would include package inserts, card decks, catalogs, co-op mailings, statement stuffers, etc.

Newspapers –

Currently, 40% say they get most of their news about national and international issues from the internet, up from just 24% in September 2007. For the first time in a Pew survey, more people say they rely mostly on the internet for news than cite newspapers (35%). Television continues to be cited most frequently as a main source for national and international news, at 70%.[39]

Additional research by Newspaper National Network[40] reveal the following statistics:

- 82% of adults took action as a result of a print newspaper ad in the last 30 days
- 82% used a preprinted insert in the last 30 days
- 64% prefer to receive coupons in newspapers
- 59% rank newspapers first as the medium used to plan shopping or make purchase decision in the last 7 days
- 41% say newspapers are the medium used most to check out ads, more that all electronic media combined

Most newspapers now have a strong Internet presence. This makes sense, because print newspapers have tremendous news-gathering and advertising infrastructures in place to support their Web sites. When considering newspapers as part of your media mix, keep in mind that studies show that the more advertising contained in a newspaper,

39   *Internet Overtakes Newspapers As News Outlet*, Pew Research Center, Pewresearch.org, 2008.
40   *Statistics Show Consumers Prefer Newspaper Ads*, Newspaper National Network, (http://www. nnnlp.com). 2009.

the lower the readership. Also, keep in mind that the fewer pages in a newspaper, the higher the readership.

Pros of Newspaper Advertising

1. Newspapers are still the principle media used at home, and readers don't have to "log onto it." Readers just pick them up. Readers will normally make their purchase soon after seeing your product in their newspaper.
2. Ads and coupons. It is really easy for readers to clip or tear coupons out of the paper and save them for future use. There is a culture of "coupon clipping" that is still alive and well with newspaper readers.
3. Product descriptions. Newspapers can give the readers as much information about your product as necessary to communicate its features and benefits. It can also include pictures.
4. Newspapers are local. People read newspapers to find out what is happening in their local communities. You can target your local community with your ads.
5. Readers will often shop ads for specific information when they are ready to make a purchase.
6. Newspapers typically have more local than national advertising, a definite advantage for you as a smaller company.
7. Choices. Newspapers offer a wide variety of advertising choices:
    a. Size of ad
    b. Frequency of ad
    c. Section of newspaper
    d. Placement of ad on page
    e. Inserts
    f. Color or black & white
    g. Wide choices in copy and graphics
    h. Classified or display
8. You get to mix shopping with consumers' news. Your ads are as fresh as the news.
9. Typically, a good value based on cost-per-thousand basis. Newspapers are one of your least expensive options for media.
10. High single-day reach opportunity to exploit immediacy on important shopping days.

Cons of Newspaper Advertising

1. Newspapers have a short life. People typically read their newspapers under rushed conditions.
2. Newspapers are typically read only once. Magazines are normally passed around.
3. The clutter factor. When your potential customer sits down to enjoy his daily paper, a multitude of ads, different shapes, sizes, and colors, compete for his attention.
4. It might be hard for you to target a specific demographic group. Most newspapers are distributed to a wide variety of demographics. Although the cost per thousand may be good with newspapers, the cost-per-prime prospect may be high.
5. If you want to advertise nationally, you will have to advertise in a number of different newspapers. Newspaper coverage is normally confined to a specific geographical area.
6. You will be sharing space with competitors.
7. Low-quality reproduction in color and black & white ads.

Magazines – Newspapers, with their mass circulation, offer a cross section of your local consumer marketplace. It will include low-income to high-income consumers. I was sitting in a park with my two young children when I saw a gentleman drop a newspaper in the trashcan and then climb into his Porsche. Immediately after he dropped his newspaper into the trashcan, a seemingly homeless man snatched it from the trashcan and started to read it. People at opposite ends of the economic scale enjoy the same newspapers.

When planning to use magazines as ad media, keep in mind that readership falls off in the summer when more people spend time outdoors.

Pros of Magazine Advertising

1. Pass-around value. A single magazine tends to be read by more than one person and kept longer than a newspaper.
2. Readers of magazines tend to have better educations and incomes than readers of newspapers.
3. There are general interest magazines and "special interest" magazines. These special interest magazines enable you to zero in on a particular target market.

4. Although a magazine may be distributed on a national basis, you can still advertise on a regional basis in them.
5. If your business is a business-to-business company, there are thousands of highly specialized "trade journals" where you can pinpoint your ads to a well-defined target market.
6. Graphics tend to be of much higher quality in magazines than in newspapers.
7. The paper stock used in magazines is normally of a much higher quality. This encourages readers to keep magazines for much longer periods of time.
8. Ads can be studied and reviewed at leisure.
9. High impact can be attained with good graphics and smart copy.

Cons of Magazines Advertising

1. Long lead times for getting your ads into magazines.
2. Readers control ad exposure, can ignore campaigns, especially for new products.
3. Difficult to exploit "timing" aspects of your ad campaigns.
4. High out-of-pocket costs.
5. You don't control the editorial content of the magazine, and the magazine's view of the world may be conferred upon your product.
6. High competitive clutter for select product categories.
7. The typical "pass along" figures given by most magazines are grossly exaggerated.

Yellow Pages –According to Newt Barrett at www.contentmarketingtoday.com yellow page usage is declining substantially.

Outdated or not, it's quite clear that usage of the print Yellow Pages is declining. For example, a 2002 article in the American demographics in 2002 suggested that users in 1996 referred to the Yellow Pages an average of 1.8 times per week. By 2000 that had declined to 1.4. That's a drop of 22% in four years.

In an informal study Mr. Barret came up with the following statistics:

- Average age of the respondents is 44; 84% are 50 years old or younger.
- There is essentially no correlation between age of respondents and Yellow Pages usage.
- *not a single respondent* is using the Yellow Pages *more than one time per week.*

- 24% never use the Yellow Pages.
- The average usage is 5.4 times per year.
- 71% of respondents use the Yellow Pages five times per year or less.
- Only three respondents are using the Yellow Pages more than one time per month.

Of course, this is a small sample and is not statistically projectable.

Pros of Yellow Pages Advertising

1. Reaching the customers when they are ready to buy
2. One of the most established advertising medias
3. Pay-as-you-go, since you pay on a monthly basis

Cons of Yellow Pages Advertising

- You are grouped with your competitors under one classification.
- Your ad is the same for an entire year.
- Quality of graphics is lacking.

Direct Mail – Direct mail is one of the best advertising vehicles to use when you want to target a specific market. According to a recent annual Vertis Customer Focus: direct marketing survey, 76% of adult consumers read direct mail advertising. The study also found that women ages 28 to 48 were more likely to read retail, entertainment, and fund-raising direct mail, while men 28 to 39 were more likely to report reading entertainment or automotive direct mail. You are the one that decides who gets it, where they get it, and when they get it. Your mailing piece can be as simple as a postcard or as elaborate as a catalog. Some direct mail packages will contain a letter, a brochure, and a direct response card. Direct mail usually is more expensive per person than any other advertising medium. In order to have a successful direct mail campaign, you need to effectively execute a number of steps:

1. Secure a good mailing list.
   A. Your internally developed mailing list is best.
   B. If you buy a mailing list, review the quality (age of names on list, reputation of mailing list house).
2. Craft a compelling offer.
   A. Motivate response.
   B. Make the response happen now.

3. Develop engaging copy and graphics
   A. Effective copy is normally more successful than creative design.
4. Physically put together your mailing package.
   A. You can do a lot of this yourself.
   B. Collate.
   C. Stuff.
   D. Label.
   E. Deliver to post office according to their latest requirements.
5. Do a test mailing.
   A. Wouldn't you rather have a test fail instead of the entire mailing fail?
   B. Mail some to yourself to see how it arrives.
6. Tweak the package based on the test.
7. Mail out the packages (e.g., may be as simple as a postcard or as intricate as the three-part mailer mentioned above)
8. Track your results.
   A. You will want to know what works and what doesn't.
9. Follow up on responses.
   A. Most direct mail requires some follow-up response from you to inquiries.
   B. Respond in a timely manner.

If you have developed a mailing list from your existing customers, you can use the RFM theory to predict the likelihood of future sales based on an evaluation of three variables:

Recency of last order	35%
Frequency of orders	50%
Monetary value of orders	15%

Pros of Direct Mail Advertising

1. Your campaign can be highly targeted
2. By testing, you can get a relatively accurate estimate of your results for your campaign.
3. You can scale your direct mail campaign as small as you like or as large as you like.
4. You can achieve extensive coverage for your chosen demographic, zone, market area, etc.

5. You have a high degree of control.
6. You have a relatively high response rate when compared to other marketing approaches.

Cons of Direct Mail Advertising

1. There are number of steps that have to be managed very carefully.
2. The cost of creating the mailing pieces, processing them, mailing them, and responding to the mailing pieces can be prohibitively high.
3. Poor mailing lists (e.g., outdated names, duplicate names)
4. Environmental concerns
5. Negative public perception of unsolicited "junk mail."

Alternative Print Media – There are "alternative print media" sources that you should consider when examining print media. These include:

Posters and Bulletin Boards – This would include bulletin boards at grocery stores, coffee shops, etc. I found my gardener from his business card tacked onto a bulletin board at the corner mini-mart. He has been my gardener for over five years, and I think he now services just about every house in my neighborhood.

Concert/Play/Event Programs – There are city concert programs and theater groups that often accept advertising. This can be an inexpensive place to put your ad. Also, consider little league games, art gallery events, school events, and just about any event that has a program associated with it.

Card Decks – This print advertising vehicle usually consist of 20 or more 3 ½ × 5 ½ business reply cards delivered together in poly packs. These cards will have something in common. It may be that all the cards in the deck are hitting one particular demographic group or regional area. Card decks have been used mostly for business-to-business advertising, but there a number of card decks aimed at consumers that are very effective. Card decks are normally inexpensive, costing anywhere from $10 per thousand to $60 per thousand. The main reason that they cost so little is that the response rate is normally under 1.00%.

Package Inserts – Package inserts are freestanding advertising pieces that are inserted into the package of a product. They can be put into your products, or you can contract with another company to include your advertising piece in their product packaging. Whenever you open a box of computer software, there will normally be a number of related advertising pieces in the box. On lower-priced items, you will normally be happy with a response rate of 0.05% to 4.00%.

Co-op Mailings – From the name, you can tell this is a group of noncompetitive advertisers mailing to a common mailing list. Co-op mailings normally go out to large mailing lists. The typical response rates are as low as card decks. The average cost is $15 per thousand.

Ride-Alongs – Your advertising piece gets to hitch a ride with another company's advertising piece mailed to existing and prospective customers. A variation of this is when newspapers allow advertisers to send their advertisements along with their newspapers. I got a free sample of Pert Shampoo with my Los Angeles Times a couple of weeks ago.

Statement Stuffers – If you have bills mailed to your house (I don't know anyone that doesn't), then you have received statement stuffers. Credit card companies, fitness clubs, retailers, utility companies, cable TV companies, magazine companies, mortgage companies, insurance companies, and others often accept statement stuffers. Statements normally get mailed using first-class postage and thus have a low percentage of undelivered mail pieces. You also know envelopes will be opened – this is half the battle in print media. Responses are much better than experienced by co-op mailings and ride-alongs. An average cost for statement stuffers is $45 per thousand.

Newsletters – Consumers always assume that newsletters are more accurate than other types of print media. This is true even if you are the one publishing the newsletter. With the advent of word processing and layout software, it's pretty easy to periodically publish a professional-looking newsletter.

Goody Bags – This advertising media ranges from bags that hold your groceries from your favorite grocery store to prizes given to attendees at conventions and tradeshows. You can target your message if it's going to be on the side of a bag at a convention or remain somewhat general if your ad is going to appear on the side of a grocery bag. What better place to advertise your appliance store than on the side of a giveaway bag at a bridal show? How about advertising your handheld electronics store on the side of goody bags given to freshmen students registering for classes? If you see a bag that is being used by an entity and it doesn't have any advertisements, see if they would be receptive to your advertising on their bags.

Other Print Ideas – Don't forget magazine blow-in cards (those little annoying cards that fall out when you read your favorite magazine), reader response cards, and freestanding inserts. I am sure that you can come up with a number of print media ideas that I haven't mentioned here. Let your imagination run wild.

Television

Most new small companies feel that television advertising is out of their reach. Broadcast TV advertising is expensive with prime-time 30-second commercials in medium-sized cities costing several thousand dollars each. Broadcast TV ads are out of reach for most small businesses. Cable television has come along and changed the dynamics of advertising on TV for the small business. You might not be able to mount a comprehensive national television campaign, but you can still use television effectively. Even though the Internet is the darling of the media world, television is still king. Almost 99% of all North American homes have at least one television. The average person watches TV seven hours day (which seems like a lot, but that is another story and another book).

Where prime-time spots (30 second ads) in a medium-sized city can cost anywhere from $2,000 to $3,000 each, cable spots can go for as little as $200. In some areas of the country, you can get cable spots for a few dollars each. Most of the commercials on cable TV programs are national spots for major corporations, but normally 3 to 6 commercials per hour are made available to local advertisers. Cable rates are highly negotiable and will vary dramatically between channels and between various day parts.

The costly part of your television ad campaign will be the production of your spot. You probably can't afford a slick 60-second spot with high-paid actors. So use the

K.I.S.S. (keep it simple silly) method and don't even attempt to be slick. In Southern California, there are ads run frequently on cable TV for "Leeds Mattresses." There are currently 14 Leeds Mattress stores. The ads are not slick and they feature the owner of Leeds Mattresses saying, "I won't be beat." Repeat the slogan to anyone in Southern California, and they will tell you it's for Leeds Mattresses. No slick ads, just good service and a good product.

Fig.60 – Leeds Mattress ad

Let's say that you want to advertise in the San Fernando Valley just north of Los Angeles. For about $45 for each 30-second spot, you can advertise with Adelphia Cable directly in the local feed of the "Larry King Live Show." This will give your business ad local access to a national program. This, of course, will not be going to the national audience of the Larry King Live Show. It will be going to one of 60 zones in the Los Angeles area. People in the San Fernando Valley area of Van Nuys who like to watch Larry King will see your ads.

Pros of Television Advertising

1. Intrusive impact, high awareness. TV goes right into your customers' home and becomes the center of attention. It is the only medium that has a room in most American homes set up especially for it. Television is "in your face."
2. Television combines sight, motion, and sound for a multiple-sensory experience. It is high impact.
3. Television is relatively low in cost, considering the gross impressions you can make with it.
4. Television comes close to being face-to-face selling. Put a celebrity spokesperson on the screen, and it can be compelling for your audience. Television advertisers have long known that someone wearing a "white coat" on screen can be perceived as a medical authority.
5. Able to target your potential customers by what they like to watch, and when they like to watch it.
6. Maximum reach.
7. You can present a "big" image of your business by advertising in local feeds to nationally syndicated programs.
8. Television is perceived to be more authoritative than other media.

Cons of Television Advertising

1. Content on television has drifted over the years to be somewhat salacious. As a Christian advertiser, you will want to make sure that your ads do not get placed in or near programs such as *Sex in the City*, *Desperate Housewives*, and other inappropriate programs. Cable is regulated a lot less than broadcast television. Both cable and broadcast television are always trying to push the limits of censorship.
2. Broadcast network television (NBC, CBS, ABC) is dominated by the major national advertisers.
3. Cost of production of spots (30-second, 60-second commercials) can be very expensive.
4. Available time slots greatly are affected by any number of things such as major news events, major sporting events, and seasonal cycles.
5. People watch TV to be entertained. Your 30-second commercial may be the time that viewers get up to go to the kitchen or the bathroom.
6. Television cannot be passed along like magazines.

Radio

Radio advertising is not as effective today as it was years ago. With television, Internet and daily life moving at a much more hurried pace, radio advertising has decreased in effectiveness. But don't count radio out completely. It has a place in your advertising budget. A lot of people will hear advertising on the radio and attribute it to some other advertising medium. Have you ever heard a radio spot that has a phone number given and you could not get a pencil fast enough to write it down? It is impossible to know how many people are tuned into a particular radio station at any point in time. Because of this, it is difficult to truly gauge the effectiveness of radio advertising. Ad rates for radio are all over the board, depending on their audience size, day-parts you are buying, frequency the ad runs, and other factors. A live read from a nationally syndicated radio personality can cost up to $20,000. A 60-second spot on a station in Farmville, VA will cost you $12 per spot.

Pros of Radio Advertising

1. You can easily target a demographic based on radio format (e.g., country and western, classic rock).
2. Low production costs.
3. Can be on the air quickly.
4. It enables you to employ time-of-day or day-of-week scheduling of your advertising. A day-part that a lot of advertisers like is what is called drive time.
5. It is mobile. People take it with them wherever they go.
6. Hearing a voice associated with a product can make a person trust the advertising message.
7. Loyalty. People tend to be loyal to their radio station. People typically do not change radio stations as they do when watching television or surfing the Internet.

Cons of Radio Advertising

1. On a per-unit of advertising basis, radio is relatively inexpensive. But it does require a substantial number of exposures to listeners to be effective, thus making it more expensive.
2. The old saying "A picture is worth a 1,000 words" is true, and there are no pictures with radio.
3. Copy testing is difficult with few statistical guidelines.

4. Not a lot of "staying power" with radio ads.
5. People will often listen to the radio as background "noise" and will not be concentrating on any advertising message being delivered.

Outdoor and Transit Advertising

We love our cars, our mass transit systems, and just being outside. Most of us like to get out of our houses as often as possible. Outdoor media plays an important role of reaching consumers that are not reached by other media. When we think of outdoor and transit advertising, we primarily think of billboards and signs on buses, but there are lot more options for outdoor advertising than billboards. In a study by Arbitron, a well-respected media research company, outdoor reaches a lot of potential customers who aren't reached by other types of advertising:

"The media with the strongest reach excel at out-of-home exposure: vehicle driver/ passengers (96%), radio (86%), and pedestrian traffic (79%)."

"One-third of Americans say they shop most near their work or split their shopping between home and work."

The report goes on to identify three new consumer groups that are perfect for outdoor media:

"Mega-milers" – the 29% of consumers who represent 77% of all miles traveled.

"Power-Pedestrians" the 21% of Americans who generate 83% of all miles walked.

"Super-Commuters" – the 24% of Americans who spend 72% of all time commuting.

Pros of Outdoor Advertising

1. High impact based on the image area of billboards.
2. Broad market coverage of the location of billboards, but also gives potential customer selectivity based on geographical targeting.
3. People love being outside, and this is where outdoor advertising is placed.
4. Constant repetition is the strength and actually the purpose of most outdoor advertising.

Cons of Outdoor Advertising

1. Expensive (some outdoor/transit advertising is not expensive. Billboards tend to be expensive.).

2. Short exposure time – normally only a couple of seconds.
3. Affected by weather more than most other media.
4. Low recall on the part of viewers.
5. Product information potential is limited, since no more than ten words can be used on billboards.
6. Scheduling billboards.

Air signs – Air signs are always attention-getters. You can't ignore them when you see them. As you lie on the beach and see the airplane dragging the air sign behind it, you are compelled to read it. Given the nature of air signs, your message has to be short and direct. Air signs are generally from 20 to 40 feet tall and 50 to 120 feet long. Common sizes range from 1,000 to 3,000 square feet. Depending on the size of the message, they can normally be read from ½ to 2 miles away. Air signs average from $150 to $250 for production. For a "non-event" flight, you will pay an average of $350 per hour from pickup to drop. For a major event, you will pay from $750 to $1,250 per hour.

Fig.61 – Gotajob.com banner

You will probably realize a CPM of $2 to $4 using air signs.

Billboards – There are many configurations available in billboard advertising. Each company has different options and different names for their options:

1. 30-sheet poster – 12' × 24'
2. 8-sheet poster – 12' × 24'

3. Wallscapes – entire sides of buildings covered with your advertisement
4. Smaller sizes

Billboards come in a number of sizes. The size will depend on the company that owns the billboards and local sign ordinances. When you are considering the cost of billboards, you need to consider the monthly fees, design fees, production fees, and fees for putting them up and taking them down. Also, you will often be assessed a fee if you need to have your billboards covered if your messages are time sensitive and cannot be exposed past a specific date.

Although billboards can be expensive, they can be effective as support to your other advertising. One Midwestern billboard company charges $500 a month for one 30-sheet poster billboard and $115 for production of each billboard. Billboards can be effectively used by small companies. Say you have a retail store with a unique product with broad consumer appeal. You are located just off a freeway with easy on- and off-ramp access. You put an ad on a strategically placed billboard before the off-ramp on the freeway. Your ad shows your product and an arrow showing commuters how to get to your store. Assume the billboard costs you $1,000 per month. Your product has a retail price of $300 and a direct cost of $100 for a $200 gross margin. You would only have to generate five sales from the billboard to justify the advertising dollars. Also, a new customer could possibly buy additional products from you later.

Blimps – Blimps serve the same basic function of searchlights, but on a more localized basis. Blimps can also be tailored to your particular establishment. Whereas searchlights are only effective at night, blimps are only effective during the day. I'm not referring to the Goodyear-type blimp, as there are only 20 blimps in the entire world, and Goodyear and Fuji own most of them. I mean the tethered, helium-filled balloons available in various sizes. One company I know sells blimps in just about every shape conceivable. As an example, an 8' apple will cost you $470, a 10' pineapple will cost you $1,650, or a 12' × 30" star will cost you $1,206. With your blimps, you get a 120' tether line with a reel and a repair kit. Most blimps larger than 9' (when inflated) can stand up to 30-mile-per-hour winds.

Bus Ads – Bus ads are like moving billboards. As with taxis and other forms of outdoor advertising, there are many options with bus ads. Here are some of the options with sample prices from a middle-America bus company in a city with approximately 155,000 people:

Exterior – street side	30″ × 144″	$100 per sign per month, 39 buses available
Exterior – curb side	30″ × 108″	$80 per sign per month, 10 buses available
Exterior – rear	17″ × 72″	$75 per sign per month, 19 buses available
Exterior – front	17″ × 72″	$75 per sign per month
Interior – overhead	11″ × 28″	$10 per sign per month (up to 10 signs on each bus, with 50 buses available)
Interior – overhead	11″ × 42″	$15 per sign per month (up to 6 signs on each bus, with 50 buses available)
Pocket Brochures		$150 per month for one pocket on each bus, 8 pockets per bus

In another middle-American city with a population of approximately 266,000, a full bus wrap will cost you about $1,800 per month, and you will have to sign a contract for a year. These rates show you that bus advertising is not beyond the means of small businesses. If you happen to live in a larger city, of course, bus advertising will cost you a little more, but you will be exposed to a greater number of potential customers. As an example, in one middle-American city with a population of approximately 1,160,000 people, an exterior side ad 30″ × 144″ will cost you $250 per month with a one-year contract, and a full bus wrap will cost you about $3,000.

Bus Bench Ads – My youngest son asked me why anyone would advertise on a bus bench, since people are always sitting on them. I had to sit and think for a minute. For one thing, people are not always sitting on them. They have proven effective over decades of use. They are at eye level for the millions of drivers and passengers in cars, and they can't be zapped like a television commercial.

Most bus bench ads can be acquired with substantial savings if you are willing to sign a one-year contract. The national average is in the range of $100 per bench per month. In one Southern U.S. city with a population of approximately 545,000, you will pay about

$105 for each bench for each month as long as you sign up for a one-year contract. On a month-to-month basis, these same benches will cost you about $115 per month. To give you an idea of what a bus bench would cost you in a smaller city, one city of about 62,000 in the Southwestern U.S. charges about $80 per bench per month.

Since this is "quick look" media, your message has to be short and sweet and memorable.

Inflatable Figures – It is sometimes hard to get people's attention while they are driving down the street. But it is difficult to ignore a 20-foot-tall gorilla or a 20-foot-tall Tin Man from *The Wizard of Oz* undulating in front of a retail establishment. A major part of any advertising campaign is to get the attention of your potential customers so that you can tell them about your current sale or other message. A Texas company will rent you a 16' tall gorilla for $495 for the first 3 days and $350 a week thereafter. Or you can get a 30' tall gorilla for $995 for the first 3 days and $630 a week thereafter. You can rent just about any inflatable object for your business.

Lifeguard Towers – This is a specialty type of media. You normally need to have beaches to have a number of lifeguard towers. A point to re-emphasize here is that almost anything can be an advertising media. If you want to advertise on guard towers on the beaches in the Los Angeles area, you will be paying about $800 a panel per month with a 25 panel minimum. The minimum panel number can be calculated as one panel 25 times, five panels for five months, etc.

Searchlights – Have you ever been driving and seen a searchlight in the night air looking as if someone is trying to summon Batman? I have seen people winding and zigzagging around city blocks trying to follow a spotlight to its source. You can rent a spotlight in Southern California for $250 per day and 3 days for $350. Or if you are going to use a searchlight often in your advertising, you can buy one for about $7,000. Get your potential customers to find your place of business, and then tell them your message. People who see searchlights either expect to find a carnival or a car dealership at the source of the light. Surprise them.

Sky Writing – Almost a thing of the past, it is very eye-catching and a most unusual form of advertising. Skywriting is usually done at an altitude of about 10,000 feet where it can be seen for twenty miles in all directions. The letters are very large and stay in the sky for approximately 15 minutes, provided there is little or no wind blowing. And as you might guess, the message has to be pretty short, usually no more than 6 letters or a simple symbol. It will cost you about $1,000 to get your short message in the sky. A few messages that come to mind would be "WWJD" (What Would Jesus Do), "Vote W"

(Vote for President Bush), and "Nike."

Sporting Field Ads – If you want to advertise in a major league sports arena or field, you will need to have a fat advertising budget. Advertising in these venues, when you can get the space, is most often outside of the financial capability of a small business. If you have a product that is a fit for advertising in a sports environment, you should consider localized sporting events such as college games and little league.

Here are some samples of what types of advertising happen at sporting arenas and fields:

1. Plaza-level advertising – the banner going around the second level seats
2. Outfield signage
3. Team field boxes
4. Home plate rotational signage
5. Out-of-town scoreboard signage
6. 1st and 3rd base ads
7. View-level signage
8. Remote secondary scoreboard signage
9. Programs
10. Snack areas
11. Giveaway prizes at intermissions
12. Logos on drinking cups
13. Back-of-ticket ads
14. Merchandise co-branding
15. Jumbotron ads
16. Dasher boards at hockey games
17. Ads on ice resurfacers at hockey games
18. Sponsor a "Night of Sports" at an arena

Sports teams and the venues they play are experts at effectively utilizing their assets for generating revenues. Sports is big business.

There is one major league baseball team that auctioned off the back of their tickets for advertising for the 2006 season with a starting bid of $150,000.

Although major sports team advertising is "pricey" for the small business, you do get a lot for your money. At a major league baseball stadium, here's what I could buy for $250,000:

1. One half inning of 28 ½" × 20" backstop rotation.
2. Guaranteed TC exposure with every at bat
3. One backlit 4' × 20' field-level sign
4. A giveaway of my company product, live during an inning break on each Saturday and Sunday regular game (26 games).
5. Sponsoring of Church Community Day at the station with appropriate recognition.
6. Co-branding with the sports team on 10,000 giveaways.
7. 20 each, 15-second commercials on the sports team radio station
8. One television drop-in during local ad promoting church day.
9. 10 scoreboard announcements promoting the sponsoring of church day.
10. Appearance in multiple newspapers with the sports team announcing the sponsoring of church day.
11. A ceremonial first pitch on the sponsored church day.
12. One 18-seat luxury suite on the sponsored church day.
13. 5,000 game tickets to give away at my discretion.

For the right product and for a company big enough to afford it, major league stadium/arena advertising has tremendous value.

If you are a small business just starting out and you need some local exposure, you can still use sports as an advertising platform. Think Little League. One Northern California Little League team has annual sponsorships for $1,000, which includes a number of benefits. And you can be an outfield sign for the entire season for $600. A few miles away in another Northern California town, you can sponsor a team for three years for $5,000 or become a scoreboard sponsor for $2,500 for a three-year period.

If you have products or services that are suitable for advertising at sporting events, there are advertising opportunities if you look for them. Another example of a lower-cost sports arena advertising opportunity is at the **Sauk Rapids, MN Sports Arena.** You can advertise on one of their ice hockey dasher boards for an entire year for $500 or advertise on their ice resurfacer for a year for $1,500. Sauk Rapids has a total population of just over 10,000. This type of advertising could work well for a local sporting goods or hobby store.

Taxi Ads – Taxi ads have been around for several years, but taxi ads have become much more innovative over the last few years. There is not a surface in or on most taxis that doesn't have some type of advertising. Here are some of the more common ways businesses utilize taxis in advertising:

Backlit taxi-top posters
Interior placards
Non-rotatingrotating taxi wheel covers
Receipt advertising
Two-sided taxi-top signs
Three-sided taxi-top signs
Trunk signs

Here's an approximation of rates you would pay in a city with a population of 1,300,000. The city has about 475 square miles.

Front-Facing Taxi-Top Panel (per taxi) – $175 per month, minimum 10 taxis

Ad caps (hubcaps) (per taxi) – $100 per month, minimum 10 taxis

As with all rates given in this book, there will be major variance from city to city and differences based on your individual ad campaign needs. The rates give you a general idea of the "affordability" of this ad media andand the other ad media discussed.

Telephone Kiosk Ads – Here is another source of advertising that may be within the means of your start-up business. In one of the largest cities in the United States, you can place advertising on the right and left side of a telephone kiosk for $230 to $350 per month. In my review of over 100 of these kiosks, I saw very few for local businesses. Most of them were for really big companies. I would not recommend this as your only type of advertising.

Truck Ads – You can't miss truck ads. When you are in your car and a truck with an ad on the side of its trailer pulls up next you, it's like sitting next to a billboard. They definitely get your attention. On average, you will pay $3,000 to $5,000 to design and produce a truck-side ad and $2,000 to $3,000 to rent the space. The fleet that owns the truck itself will earn anywhere from $300 to $500 per truck or trailer per month.

Vehicle wraps – You have, no doubt, seen the really cool-looking vehicles and buses with the great graphics wrapped around them. These are known as *vehicle wraps*. As with other outdoor advertising, vehicle advertising reaches consumers not exposed to newspapers or television. It's been found that it is more difficult to reach consumers that have long commutes. The same study showed that 96% of North Americans travel in a vehicle each week.

Fig.62 – Vehicle Wrap

A full vehicle wrap can set you back about $3,000 dollars. This includes printing and installation. One proposal included an option of $500 if I wanted to have what is called the "window perf" option, where I could see out, but people could not see in. This is for one vehicle. This only makes financial sense if your vehicles get lots of mileage. A vehicle wrap is not very effective if your vehicle sits in your garage most of the time. In a recent Chicago-based study by Traffic Audit Bureau (TAB), an independent nonprofit organization that authenticates the circulation of out-of-home advertising such as billboards, it found that the cost for fleet advertising is half that of traditional outdoor advertising, or 70 cents per 1,000 impressions, while billboard advertising averaged $1.40 per thousand.

Vehicle wraps can be effective, but at $3,000 a vehicle, I would probably opt for good signage on my vehicles rather than vehicle wraps.

Internet Advertising

A company Web site has moved right up there with the business card as a "must-have" for businesses. There are very few businesses that don't need a Web site. One of the first questions someone will ask you once they find that you are a small business owner is "What is your Web site address?" Most business forms, such as credit applications, bank documents, now have a space for your email address and your company URL (your Web site address).

Whether you are using the Web to build up your brick and mortar business or you are building a Web-based business, you will still, as with any other type of marketing media, have to cut through all of the clutter. *Bust! Media* surveyed more than 3,100 Web users. Their study found that while Web users accept advertisements on Web sites, 60.9% have a low tolerance for more than two ad units per page, 34.2% say they will tolerate one ad per page, and 26.7% will tolerate two ads per page. Men are a little more tolerant of multiple ads (29.3%) compared to women (23.2%).

According to the study, clutter affects a user's perceptions of an advertiser's products and services. 51.2% said that they have a less favorable opinion of an advertiser's product when the ads on their web page appear cluttered. The study also found that 73.4% of the respondents pay less attention to ads on a cluttered Web page. The bottom line is that when it comes to Web pages, "Less Is More."

Here are some compelling reasons to have an Internet presence for your business:

"Legitimize" Your Business – I had a meeting with a client the other day, and they were considering a new vendor. Overall, the client liked the vendor but had reservations because the vendor didn't have a Web site. My church has a Web site where I can contact most of the pastors, see what the sermon is going to be about next Sunday, and stay generally plugged in.

Cost Effective – Web site costs vary. You can build one yourself and the monthly hosting is only a few dollars a month. You don't have to be a "super geek" to have a robust Web site. There are a number of Web site building tools on the market that make building your site a snap. One of the best on the market is Yahoo Site Builder. The Web site development tool was used by Easy Brain Labs, Inc. to build their Web site. It is free when you sign up for hosting with Yahoo. If you want the "premium" business hosting package, you will have to shell out a whopping $39.95 a month. Really, this is the best $40 you will spend for your business. For this, you get the following:

1. Your Web site can have up to 100,000 pages on it.
2. Your Web site can accommodate up to 1,200,000 visitors a month.
3. 1,000 email addresses
4. Free Yahoo Site Builder

I am not promoting Yahoo, but they do make it pretty easy to have an incredible Web site. The work of building your Web site is only the beginning. Once you build it, you have to maintain it. Again, this is relatively easy using Yahoo Site Builder.

Establish a Worldwide Presence – There are over 957 million people who have access to the Internet. That is a big market that is as close as your computer screen.

Dealing with a customer in Europe is almost as easy as dealing with a customer a block away.

To Serve Your Existing Customers – Getting and keeping customers is all about servicing them to a level that meets or exceeds their expectations. If you don't, someone else will. Every piece of documentation coming out of your company should have your Web site address on it. You serve your customers better using the Internet. Here are some ways you can use your Web site to better service your customers:

1. Online user manuals for your products that they can view online or print out.
2. Email vehicle on your Web site so that they can communicate with you and get a written response.
3. Product updates via email and on your Web site.
4. New and exciting updates for using your product.
5. News related to your product.
6. A place for your customers to interact with each other (blog).
7. Lets your customers participate in future enhancements to your product.
8. Easy ordering of your product.
9. Stay in touch with your customers via your company ezine.

To Send Out Time-Sensitive Materials – You can send out material via snail mail and it may get to your intended recipient in a few days, or you can send it out via email and it gets there almost immediately after hitting the Send button. The immediacy of the Internet is one of its strongest attributes.

To Sell Your Product – Most businesses can sell directly from their Web sites. It's relatively easy to add a shopping cart to your Web site. This enables you to sell your products directly from the Web site. It's like having a salesperson standing by 24 hours, 7 days a week. Many people run their entire business off of the Internet without any "brick and mortar" presence.

Carry a Broader Line of Merchandise – You only have so many products you can offer out of your brick and mortar store. With a Web site, you can offer an almost infinite number of products from your online store. You can even offer your "in-store" products online and give your customers the option of picking them up at your physical store.

To Answer Frequently Answered Questions – You will always have questions from your customers before, during, and after purchasing your products. A FAQ (frequently asked questions) page on your Web site can be very useful to your customers.

Stay in Touch with Your Employees – You can set your Web site to enable your employees to keep in contact with you at all times. If you have a Yahoo-driven Web site, you can give your employees an email address (TheirName@yourCompanyName.com), and you can always keep in touch with them via email. The great thing about email is that you don't have missed calls, because they can get the email when it is convenient for them. You also have a really good record of the emails that have gone between you and your employees.

To Make Picture, Sound, and Film Files Available – You can quickly and easily deliver these items to your customers, employees, and others without sending them through the mail. You can email them or make them available on your Web site (password-protected if you desire).

To Even the Playing Field – The Internet does tend to give the "small guy" the opportunity to look just as big as the multinational company. I have seen many "mom and dad" type companies with much better Web sites than many international companies. Big companies have big resources to throw at their Web sites, and sometimes will over-option, over-accessorize, and overkill their Web sites. "Keep it simple silly" is very important for your Web site. Look at how simple Google's Web site is. It's one of the most successful Web sites on the Internet.

To "Keep Your Doors Open 24/7" – As mentioned earlier, you can have your store open 24/7 with a Web site. Your business can make money for you while you sleep.

To Test New Products – You can test a new product on your Web site for next to nothing. You can develop a product overview with artists' pictures and solicit input from anyone that visits your web site.

Because everyone is on the Internet – Here are some amazing facts: 83.4% of males, 75.2% females 18 - 24 have Internet access. These figures do not drop below the 50% mark until the 55 - 64 age group.

To Promote Your "Brick and Mortar" Business – Since so many people are online, it is almost a requirement of business to have an online presence. Even if you don't sell your products online, there are cost-effective ways of promoting your physical business online that we will discuss below.

The Tools of Internet Advertising

The Internet offers you more than just having Web sites as marketing tools. Having a Web site is the foundation of a robust arsenal of online marketing tools.

Web site – So you created a Web site and did nothing else. This is like renting a retail store, filling it with product, and expecting to make sales without letting anyone know the store even exists. You might make some sales as people accidentally stumble across your store. It's even worse with your Web site, since you won't have any potential customers walking by. If you put it up and don't market it, you will be lucky to get any traffic. You have to promote it. Below are some tools to help you increase your Web site traffic and your sales.

You will often hear people use the terms, "hits," "visitors," and "page view" when discussing Web site traffic.

Hit – This is the most basic measurement of Web site traffic. Every time a file is sent by a server, be it text, graphic, or video, it is recorded as a *hit*. This isn't a reliable gauge to use when comparing different sites, because a page with 6 graphic elements will register as 7 hits while a page with no graphics will register as one hit.

Visitor – This word is usually used for a person that visits your Web site. Each time someone visits your Web site, it counts as another visitor. So if a person visits your site, then goes to lunch, and returns to your site later, he would count as 2 visitors. A better measure is "unique visitors." It is often difficult to measure unique visitors, and it normally involves the use of "cookies" that attach to a visitor's session. A lot of people consider cookies to be an invasion of privacy and thus set up their computers to not accept cookies. Without being unique, a visitor is probably best defined as a "visit."

Page View – Many people use "page view" as a measure of the success of their Web site—not a good measurement for most purposes. One visitor may come to your Web site, go directly to your online catalog, and purchase something, while another person might feel the need to visit every single page of your Web site and not buy anything.

To measure the effectiveness of your Web site, you will want to measure the conversion of "visits" into purchase transactions. If you are getting 100,000 visits to your Web site a month and these visits result in 1,000 purchase transactions, then you know that you have to generate 100 visits for every purchase. Another measure that you will want to track is the dollar sales per Internet purchase and the cost of generating the visits to your Web site.

You can also track the amount of time that a visitor spends on your Web site. The general theory is that the longer a visitor spends on your site, the more likely they are to buy something, and the more likely they are to visit it again. In order to properly evaluate your Web site's effectiveness, you will need to capture the appropriate statistics.

There are a number of very good analytical packages available on the Internet that can analyze your Web site server Web logs. I would not try to review the raw data from your Web site's Web log, as it is almost impossible do any meaningful analysis of its raw data. The Web log analytics packages cost only a few dollars. Here are some statistics you can normally get from your Web logs:

- How many visitors came to your site
- Pages requested, including most popular and a ranking of the most popular to the least popular
- Which geographic areas your visitors came from
- Which Internet service provider the visitors came from (e.g., AOL, MSN, Yahoo, etc.)
- Which Web browsers your visitors are using
- Which search engine sent the visitor to your Web site

Don't let your Web site go stale. Keep it fresh by adding new elements every month. This will help bring visitors back, which will keep your search engine placement higher. Search engines like new and fresh content.

One way to add interest to your Web site is to use RSS content. RSS is a format for syndicating news and the content of news-like sites, including major news sites like Wired, news-oriented community sites like Slashdot, and personal Web logs. But it's not just for news. Pretty much anything that can be broken down into discrete items can be syndicated via RSS. Content providers such as news services allow their content to be fed to your Web site. This gives your Web site constantly changing content that you don't have to generate yourself.

Each page of your Web site is viewed by the search engine as a home page. This means that search engines will often send people to pages in your Web site that are not your actual home page. You need to critically examine each of your Web site pages to make sure that they can engage the visitors that get dropped into them. Each page needs to be able to stand alone and satisfy your visitor's need for information. Make it really easy to get from each page of your Web site to other pages on your Web site.

Search Engine Placement – This is the most important thing you can do to drive traffic to your Web site. Visitors to search engines are actively searching for information, products, or services. The great thing about these prospects is that that if they land on your Web site, they have probably keyed in some words that match the keywords on your site. Search engine placement should be the foundation of your Internet marketing efforts. You need to be ready to hook a visitor the instant they land at your site. You only have a few seconds for them to see something related to their search. Recent research shows that 80% of searchers never venture past the top 30 search results.

Many Web site owners spend a fair amount of time working on improving their search engine ranking. They study the current literature on the subject and do lots of experimenting. Others will employ professional search engine optimization firms to achieve higher rankings.

Many of the major search engines feature "sponsored" listings. If you elect to use the sponsored listing approach, you will select the key words and phrases with which you want to improve your ranking. Then you will pay a fee for each time that your ad in the search listing results is clicked on.

If you are short on cash, there is a really useful Web site for doing your own listing with search engines and directories. It is www.selfpromotion.com. It helps you list with hundreds of search engines and Web directories. It takes a little work, but it helps your Web site get listed with a lot of places in a very quick and efficient manner.

Affiliate Marketing – This is a popular way of promoting your Web site and increasing sales. You can earn money by driving traffic from your Web site to your chosen affiliated Web sites and vice versa. A couple of examples of Web sites that pay their affiliates handsome rewards for referring business to them will best illustrate this Internet marketing tool. Stamps.com will pay its affiliates for directing traffic to their stamps.com Web site. They will pay $60 for any new customer that signs up for a trial of their services. Homeloancenter.com will pay $10 for each person that your Web site sends to them that completes their entire application. A couple of things to note here: both Stamps.com and Homeloancenter.com have calculated what they are willing to pay for referrals to their site; they have also defined what constitutes "completed transactions" for the purposes of paying out affiliate fees.

You should probably include an affiliate marketing program in your marketing plans, as you will only pay your affiliates for actual performance. Also, if you can find compatible products and services, you should become an affiliate to other, appropriate Web sites. Be sure to fully explore your affiliate's Web site as well as the Web sites to which you agree to be an affiliate. Make sure that they are appropriate and do not run contrary to your Christian principles.

When initially developing your Web site, you might want to consider using an Affiliate Program Service to help you track and manage your affiliate program. Do the math. With an affiliate program management company, you will not only be paying your affiliates, you will also be paying your affiliate program management company. Some of these companies will also help you attract affiliates. You might consider purchasing your own affiliate program management software.

Banner Advertising (Paid Link Ads) – Banners are those rectangular graphic distractions at the top of Web pages. They are the 30-second commercial, the four-color ad, and the billboard of the Internet. Standard banner ads do not move, shake, flash on and off, or speak. They contain information and usually give the viewer the opportunity to click them and be sent to one of the advertisers' Web pages. This is essentially paying for advertising on other Web sites. You will want to investigate shopping sites, industry specific sites, news sites. There are some really good Christian Web sites that offer good banner advertising opportunities.

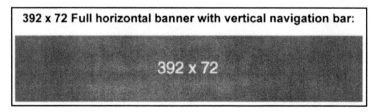

Fig.63 – Banner 468 x 60 (not actual size)

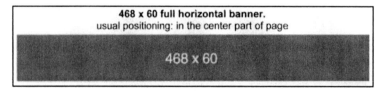

Fig.64 – Banner 460 x 55 (not actual size)

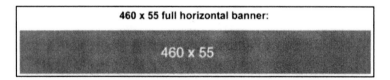

Fig.65 – Banner 392 x 72 (not actual size)

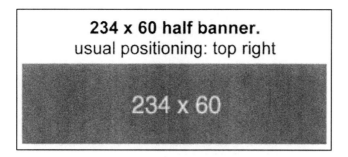

Fig.66 – Banner 234 x 60 (not actual size)

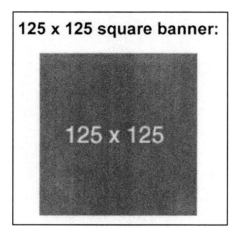

Fig.67 – Banner 125 x 125 (not actual size)

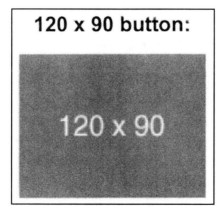

Fig.68 – Banner 120 x 90 (not actual size)

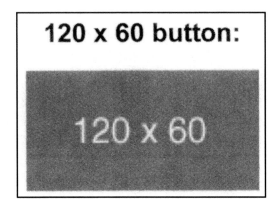

Fig.69 – Banner 120 x 60 (not actual size)

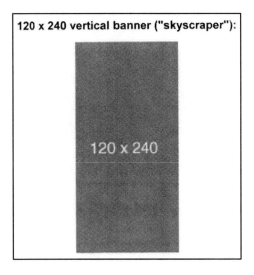

Fig.70 – Banner 120 x 240 (not actual size)

Through a combined effort of the Internet Advertising Bureau (www.iab.net) and the Coalition for Advertising Supported Information and Entertainment, there has been some standardization of banner ad sizes.

Banner ads are usually priced per CPM, or cost per thousand impressions. CPMs can range from $5 to $20 CPMs for RON (run of network) campaigns to $30 to $85 CPMs for highly targeted or popular areas. Some sites allow you to pay by cost per click or by the number of "click-throughs" to your site.

To gauge how effective your banner ads have been, calculate the cost on a click-through basis. For instance, let's say you're buying 100,000 banner impressions for a total of $1,000 at $10 CPM. If 1% of Web users click on the ad, you'll pay $1 per click-through. If only 0.5% click through, you'll end up paying twice that for each click-through. Armed with that info, you can decide whether it was a banner ad or a bust.

We are in a period when banner advertising seems to be on the wane. Average click-through rates have dipped to 0.39% average, and industry magazines regularly carry articles discussing the death of banner ads. But while banner ads aren't as effective as they once were, the truth is that a great many companies, large and small, still use banner ads as part of their advertising mix and will continue to do so. Nevertheless, advertisers are becoming more sophisticated about when and how to use banner ads.

Banner Exchange – This can be a relatively inexpensive way to drive traffic to your Web site. There are some that only require that you cooperatively display other member ads on your site in exchange for their display of your banners on their Web site. There are a number of banner exchange programs available on the Internet. All you need to do is choose the right banner exchange network, place the code on your Web site, upload a banner that displays your logo, and forget about it. Play close attention to the banner exchange ratio, as they will differ tremendously between banner exchange networks. A lot of the traffic you get from banner ads may not be as targeted as other traffic-building approaches.

Blog Marketing – This form of marketing has been around for a long time, but it is not well understood. So what is blog marketing? Let's first wrap our hands around the definition of "blog" and "blogging." According to Wikipedia.com, a blog (a portmanteau made by contracting the phrase "Web log") is a Web site on which items are posted on a regular basis and displayed in reverse chronological order. Like other media, blogs often focus on a particular subject, such as food, politics, or local news. Some blogs function as online diaries. A typical blog combines text, images, and links to other blogs, Web pages, and other media related to its topic. Since its appearance in 1995, blogging has emerged as a popular means of communication, affecting public opinion and mass media around the world.

Blogs can be hosted by dedicated blog hosting services, or they can be run using blog software on regular Web hosting services.

Let's say that you have a business that helps Christians obtain financing for start-up businesses. You have a Web site that explains your services. Your Web site also offers accounting, bookkeeping, and business brokerage services. With all of the clutter on the Internet, you don't get as much traffic to your Web site as you would like. So you start a blog site. You call your blog site "Christian Business Financing" (CBF). On CBF, you write a monthly article. Based on the viral nature of blogs, people come to CBF to comment on your article and post questions and comments. Your first challenge is to get people to your blog site; your second challenge is to then funnel the traffic to your Web site.

It is much easier to generate traffic to your blog site than it is to your Web site. Because the content on your blog site is constantly changing, search engines such as Yahoo and Google will love to list it. With a blog, you can have instant traffic to your blog through the power of syndication of content or RSS. As mentioned above, RSS is where other Web sites include your content on their Web sites with links back to your site. As you update your content, it is automatically updated on the Web sites that have taken your RSS content feed. By submitting your RSS feed to RSS directories, your feed (blog content) can be instantly indexed by major RSS directories in search engines like Yahoo, Technorati, Blogdigger, and others. You will get exposure to tens of thousands of subscribers looking for feeds to which they can subscribe. This will drive traffic to your blog site. To generate business for your Web site, you will, of course, put references to your Web site in your blog articles and in your description of yourself in your blog site. Niche blog sites are an inexpensive and efficient way to drive traffic to your Web site. In addition to placing your Web site with search engines, this is a marketing tool that is incredibly cost effective. Blogs are one of the cheapest and easiest ways to create a presence on the Internet and can substantially increase qualified traffic to your Web site.

Cell Phone Marketing – Cell Phone Marketing is currently referred to as "Mobile Marketing," and it consists of sending text messages or media clips to cell phones in the form of advertisements. There are over 200 million cell phones in the U.S. This type of marketing is used more in Europe and Asia than in the United States. In a 2005 article in *Red Herring* ("Cell Phone Ads Are On the Way"), it was stated that 84% of wireless users are open to the prospect of receiving text message ads on their cell phones. But only 20% of U.S. mobile phone users received an ad test message on their cell phones last year, and the vast majority of them found them annoying. Advertising on cell phones is a developing advertising media that should be approached with great caution. Many cell phone networks will charge a cell phone user for receiving the ad.

Many countries are far more advanced than the U.S. in using cell phones in commerce. In Czechoslovakia, you can walk up to a Coca-Cola machine with your cell phone in hand, press a button on the soda machine, and the Coke will pop out. The amount of your purchase will be debited to your cell phone account. In China, Motorola is selling color Internet-enabled cell phones like hotcakes.

We all hate to get those annoying calls on our home phones during dinnertime. The 1991 Telemarketing Consumer Protection Act (TCPA) makes it illegal for solicitation calls to be made to wireless phone numbers without clear permission from the individual to whom a number has been assigned.

Domain Names – Having the right domain name can be a great marketing tool. Your Web site domain name doesn't necessarily have to be your company name. If you are lucky enough to have a domain name that matches your company name, you can have it point to your Web site of a different name. Sometimes, choosing a generic (common word) domain name help drive traffic to your Web site. People will often type what they are looking for as a Web address. A good example of this is Earl Scheib Auto Painting. You can type in www.earlscheib.com or www.carpainting.com, and either Web site address will take you to the Earl Scheib automobile painting Web site.

E-book Marketing – People love to be informed. If you write some simple e-books and offer them for free download from your Web site, people will visit your site to get the e-books and while there, they just might buy some of your products. There are so many topics you can write about, and it's incredibly easy to produce a downloadable e-book for your Web site. As an example, let's say that you have a small bicycle sales and repair shop. Some examples of possible e-books you could publish are:

1. Bike trails in your area
2. Bicycle maintenance checklist
3. Customizing your bike
4. Bike safety ideas
5. Calendar of biking events in your area.

More reasons why giving away e-books on your Web site makes sense:

1. You will become known for expertise in your area of business.
2. Allow other Web sites to give away your e-books. This will drive traffic to your Web sites, as each e-book will have your Web site address on them.
3. You can sell ad space in your e-books for complementary products.
4. Advertise your products and services in your e-books.
5. You can conduct market research by asking people to complete a few research

questions before they can download your free e-book.

6. Get free advertising by submitting your free e-book to sites that offer free stuff.
7. The word "FREE" is probably one of the most powerful words on the Internet.
8. E-books are easy to write and cost nothing to distribute.

Email Marketing – Almost everyone has an email address, and everyone gets junk email. As a matter of fact, according to the Federal Trade Commission, over 45% of all email is junk mail. On a positive note, in a PricewaterhouseCoopers survey, it was found that 83% of Internet users felt email was their primary reason for using the Internet.

As with direct mail sent through the post office, you need to have a mailing list for an email campaign. Make sure the list is of people who have "opted-in" and want to receive your email. An opt-in email list means the consumer specifically requested information on a particular topic and granted permission to be contacted, via email, about similar offers. A mailing list owner then compiles that data and rents it out to brokers who create lists of viable customers to market to. Since it is purely permission-based, there's little concern about spamming a customer. You can develop your own email list from your customers or buy a list from list brokers.

There are two types of opt-in email lists. One is the single opt-in list, and the other is the double opt-in email list. In the single opt-in email list, a person normally checks a box or puts his email address into a "subscriber" box. In a double opt-in email list, the user takes a second step. After the user signs up for the email, they normally need to verify the request, either by replying to an email confirmation or by clicking a link containing a unique string of characters called a *token*. These actions confirm that the user wants to be on a particular list. I have seen a lot of offers over the years that sound too good to be true such as 1,000,000 email addresses on a CD for $49! Beware. Use these addresses and you will have some real problems:

a. First of all, many of these email addresses will not be real or will be extremely stale.
b. You will probably be labeled a "spammer."
c. You can damage your reputation and lose revenues.
d. Your Internet service provider may shut down your email account.
e. Your Web host may shut down your Web site.
f. Under the new Federal CAN-SPAM Act, you can be fined up to $2 million or go to jail for up to five years.

When you think about it logically, why would you want to waste your time sending emails to people who did not specifically want to receive them anyway?

President George W. Bush signed the CAN-SPAM Act on December 16, 2003, and it became effective January 1, 2004. Here is a brief outline of the activities that are illegal under this new act:

1. Using deceptive subject lines to trick people into opening messages.
2. Creating e-mail or IP addresses specifically to send spam.
3. Sending unsolicited email with sexual content.
4. Sending email to people who have requested to be removed from your list.
5. Falsifying headers (the part of an email that specifies where it came from).
6. "Hijacking" other peoples' email accounts or computers to send spam.

Even if you have a really well-groomed, double opt-in email list, make sure that you always include a working "unsubscribe" link in each email. Never continue sending emails to someone who doesn't want to receive them. You need to make sure that you don't wear out your welcome when it comes to your email recipients.

EZine Marketing – Short for *electronic magazine,* the name for a Web-based electronic magazine that is often modeled after a <u>print</u> magazine. Some ezines are simply <u>electronic</u> versions of existing print magazines, whereas others exist only in their <u>digital</u> format. Most ezines are advertiser-supported, but a few charge a subscription. They are typically delivered via email, viewed on your ezine Web site, or downloaded from your Web site.

You can advertise in other peoples' ezines and distribute your own ezine. If your ezine catches on, you can charge others for advertising in your ezine. Ezines are a low cost, highly targeted medium that gets results.

When you start you own ezine, accept the fact that some or all of your content will be pirated. The lazy pirates (aren't most pirates lazy?) will take your content in large chunks without reprocessing it. This is a good reason to pepper your content with your contact information. Here are some good reasons to start your own ezine:

1. Establish credibility as a leader in your industry
2. Profit through the sale of ad space
3. Educate your target market on your products
4. Encourage repeat Web site visits

5. Increase your number of affiliates
6. Gives you leverage in co-promotion and joint venture opportunities
7. They are relatively inexpensive to publish and distribute
8. A good ezine can actually become a separate stand-alone business.

Here are a few ideas to help you maximize your investment in ezine publishing:

1. If possible, include a "subscribe" box on every page of your Web site.
2. Always make it easy for your subscribers to "Unsubscribe," as you only want qualified people on your subscriber list.
3. Only send your ezine to outside lists if they are "opt-in" lists.
4. Be consistent about your publishing schedule.
5. Have regular topics that you include in every ezine. Here are some ideas:

   1. Hot news about your ezine topic
   2. Reviews of related products
   3. Guest writers
   4. List of useful links
   5. Classified ads
   6. Featured customers
   7. Tips and new uses and variations in using your products
   8. Feedback from readers
   9. Ask the Expert
   10. Giveaways and contests
   11. Relevant scriptures
   12. Integrating the subject of your ezine into your Christian living

6. Encourage your readers to write articles for you.
7. Use (sparingly) free content that is available on the Internet such as RSS (syndication feeds) to supplement your internally developed content. You will have to accept some advertising if you use "free" content, because as we all know, there are very few things on this planet that are free.
8. Build your ezine list
   A. from your Web site visitors

B.   Visitors to your stores (include your Web site address on everything)

C.   Submit your ezine to ezine directories. Type in "ezine directories" into any search engine, and you will be given a long list of options.

9.   Keep it simple so that you can keep it consistent. Since there are so many email programs and browsers, it is better to keep your ezine simple and probably keep it in plain text.

If you see your ezine grow to over a 1,000 readers, you might consider one of a number of ezine distribution companies. They will help you manage distribution, subscriptions, un-subscribers, and list management for a few dollars a month.

If you decide to advertise in other ezines, try to stay away from those that are 90% ads and 10% usable information. You will get lost in the clutter. Do a search on the Internet for ezines that might complement your products. Check out their existing ads. Then check out their ad rates and run times to make sure that you can afford them and that they can possibly help you meet your advertising objectives. You should try replying to a few of the current advertisers. Be up front with them and tell them that you are considering advertising with the ezine, and see what they have to say.

Free Classifieds – There are thousands of places to put your free classified ads on the Internet. First, investigate the "Classified Ad" submitters that are online. Before doing anything in the area of classified ads, go to the classified ad sections for Yahoo and Google (Froogle) and get familiar with them. As with all classified ads, it is somewhat difficult to get noticed. With the major Internet sites like Yahoo, it is easy to set up a classified ad for free, and for very little money, you can enhance it to help it get noticed. Since there are thousands of free classified ad sites on the Internet, you will want to use the services of a classified ad submitter or purchase classified ad submission software. Both of these approaches are relatively inexpensive.

Keywords and Meta Tags – Keywords and meta tags may be the most important reason that people find your Web site. Meta tags are defined by Yahoo as "little bits of HTML code that provide information about a page but are not viewable by the user in a browser." Most search engines examine a page's meta tags, which usually include a page title, description, and keywords to index the page and help determine its ranking in relevant search results. Although not the only way to elevate your site's search engine rankings, adding meta tags to your pages can help." You will have to get into the HTML code of your site to add or modify your keywords. A number of Web site building programs, such as Yahoo Site Builder, enable you to build your Web site without knowing HTML. They also have a menu item that enables you to enter your keywords without getting into the HTML code.

You will want meta tags on all the pages of your Web site; but the most important page for you to have meta tags on is your index page, which is normally your home page.

When you are deciding what keywords to embed into your Web site, think of the words that most accurately describe your products and your business. There are a number of places where you will use your well-thought-out keywords:

1. In the text of your Web site pages
2. When listing your Web site with various directories
3. When registering with search engines

There are the free keywords that you insert into your Web site, and there are paid searches using keywords. It is important to understand the differences to leverage the advantages of each. Paid Placements are predicated on keywords or keyword phrases that have a guaranteed ranking based on the price that is being paid to the search engine. These prices are on a cost-per-click (CPC) basis and are normally determined via a bidding process. As an example, with Yahoo, I wanted to find out what it would cost me for a paid search for the phrase "Christian Business." Yahoo has an automatic calculator that will estimate the cost for top placement of a phrase. The calculator estimated that this phrase would generate 1,944 searches in a month. Yahoo further estimated that of the 1,944 searches for this phrase, I would get 144 click-throughs to my Web site. This is based on Yahoo's experience with searches for this phrase and on the description that I would want to come up about my site in the search listing. My "bid" for this phrase is 74 cents a click, which makes my monthly budget $105.82 a month or approximately $4 a day. I recommend that you consider paid searches to help drive traffic to your site.

Links – You need to get other Web sites to put a link to your Web site on at least one of their pages, and multiple pages if possible. These are called "inbound links," and they provide a couple benefits. These inbound links will bring you more visitors and will help your placement with search engines. Google and other major search engines develop a "popularity index" for Web sites that reflects how many other sites link to yours.

You will want to spend some time each month soliciting links from vendors, partners, and related (but not competitive) Web sites. Also, visit your competitors' Web sites to see who is linking to their sites.

Newsgroups – Newsgroups are similar to Blogs. What is the difference between a blog (see Blogs above) and a newsgroup? A newsgroup is typically focused on a certain subject matter and has many different people posting their comments and questions on that topic. You follow a newsgroup because you are interested in its specific subject matter. A blog is typically focused on a certain author's voice and often covers many different topics of interest to the author. So you follow a blog because you are interested in a particular author's point of view. As with a lot of things in life, there is a grey area in which blogs and newsgroups overlap.

Off-line Marketing – Every piece of literature that comes out of your company should have your Web site (URL) on it.

> Newspaper ads
> Radio commercials
> Sales receipts
> Shopping bags
> TV commercials
> Business cards
> Pens and pencils
> Flyers
> Door hangers

The children's song that says, "Keep it under a bushel—no, I'm going to let it shine" really applies here. Don't hide it, promote it.

Online Auctions – eBay alone boasts over 42 million shoppers. This is a significant number when you consider that most countries have populations smaller than that. According to Forrester Research, online auction sales are expected to reach $50 billion, which represents a quarter of all Internet sales. The major online auction sites are eBay, uBid, Amazon.com, and Yahoo! Auctions.

We can break down online auctions based on the user's roles: business-to-business, consumer-to-consumer, and business-to-consumer. The lines between these models are becoming increasingly blurred, as most major auction sites are becoming a blend of all of these models. People sell everything imaginable on auction sites. I recently saw an entire town for sale on eBay.

Online auctions offer you, the new entrepreneur, a number of marketing opportunities. There are many successful businesses that only sell their products on an online auction site such as eBay. They also offer your brick and mortar businesses additional revenue streams, additional business resources, and solid marketing opportunities. There are a number of ways you can use online auction sites to help build your business:

1. Sell your products.
2. Buy products.
3. Test prices for your products.
4. Test packaging for your products.
5. Determine the demographics that are attracted to your product.
6. There are certain shoppers that just love the excitement of auctions.
7. Develop new customers for your products. IBM sells discontinued and refurbished laptops and other products on online auctions. About 75% of their online shoppers are new customers.
8. Promote your company by selling products with your branding to drive people to your physical or Internet location.
9. Getting rid of excess or obsolete inventory.

It is easy and inexpensive to get your business online, and it is also easy and inexpensive to use online auctions to build your business. There are services that will manage your online product submissions for a small commission. There are also businesses that will help you monitor your competitors' products on online auctions. There has been an entire industry grown around online auctions.

Online Mega Stores (e.g., Amazon, Overstock.com) – In addition to your other efforts online, you can put your products in the online mega stores. Some are easier than others. As an example, your can get your product (and entire catalogue) on Google for free. It will go on their Froogle site, which is listed on their home page. Other mega-store sites (some easier to get your product into than others) are Buy.com, Overstock.com, Yahoo.com, and Amazon.com

Pay-Per-Click Advertising (PPC) – This type of advertising enables you to bid on a keyword in a live auction marketplace. These keywords, along with ad copy, appear in the search engine results page. PPC ads are usually displayed at the top or bottom, or in a special bar at the right-hand side of a results page. PPC ads usually generate rapid results, often as soon as you launch your ad. According to a recent report from Forrester Research, PPC advertising will be the dominant form of advertising on the Internet by 2010.

Podcasting – A podcast is an online audio program that can be downloaded from the Internet. Listeners can find podcasts that fit their needs on the many postcast listings and directories on the Internet. MP3 owners subscribe to podcasts that are either free or very inexpensive. When new shows are published, they will be automatically downloaded first to the subscriber's computer, and then to their MP3 players from their computers.

Because podcasting was designed to work with iPods and other portable devices, many listeners experience podcasts offline; a live connection to the Internet is not required. According to a TDG research study, over 10 million listeners will download and listen to podcasts in 2006. Within five years, the total audience size is expected to reach 56 million; there were over 14 million iPods sold in the fourth quarter of 2005.

As an advertiser, you're reaching a captive audience that has made a choice to download the podcasting content along with your advertisement. All ads are uploaded into the ad server's system where they'll be placed and tracked according to the way you've set up your ad campaign. Kiptronic is an innovator in the area of podcasting; they currently support ad placements at the beginning and end of podcasts. Placement in the middle of a podcast will be supported very soon. Kiptronic charges a cost-per-thousand (CPM) rate for ad placement. The rates vary from podcast to podcast, but are generally between $0.05 and $0.20 per download for a 20–30 second ad placed at the beginning of a podcast. You must purchase ad space in blocks of 1000, but you will only be charged for the number of ads actually downloaded.

Popup Ads – The bottom line with popup ads is: don't use them. The majority of Internet users hate them. Have you ever seen this (see below) on your screen? If you type "popup ads" into any search engine, 99% of the search results will be for software designed to stop popup ads. They are extremely annoying.

Fig.71 – Popup Example

Popup ads are as easy to send to users as emails. But, I have yet to find anyone who wants to receive them.

Writing Articles – Other sites will pick up your article if it is well written. You should encourage this as long as they agree to use your signature block. This will serve as a link back to your Web site. As more Web masters publish your article on their Web pages, you will increase your popularity with search engines like Google.

Social Networks – Twitter, Facebook, MySpace, Friendster, YouTube and Facebook are just a few of the online social networks where you should have a presence. These and other social network sites allow you to get up close and personal with your customers and clients. Bookstore shelves are full of great books on advertising using social media.

Direct Response Marketing

We have already discussed some type of direct response marketing in prior pages. Direct mail and many types of Internet marketing are considered direct response. Before we go any further, let's define what we mean by "direct response." Direct Response Marketing is communicating, selling, and delivering a product or service directly to the consumer. Methods include infomercials, short-form broadcast direct response, seminars, catalogs, e-commerce, and direct mail.

The major difference between general marketing and direct response marketing is the "call to action." Your marketing is requesting the consumer to take action immediately to receive your product or service. This "call to action" can take many forms: "pick up the phone now" as in infomercials, filling out an order form in a catalog or online, and purchasing goods or services at a seminar (often called "back of the room" selling).

In this type of marketing, you normally bypass the retailer and get your products or services directly to the end user. Direct response marketers have gotten smart and realized that they can also target retail. Most infomercial products move into retail once the effectiveness of the infomercial begins to slide. This enables the retailers to benefit from the "impressions" made from the infomercials.

Most media outlets, such as radio and television, have excess media available during off times (times when consumers are not "consuming" their media). They will sell this excess media to direct response companies at substantial discounts. Many media outlets will not sell "non-direct response" media at direct response rates, instead preferring to drive these non-direct response media buyers to the higher price slots where more consumers are viewing or listening to ads. Non-direct response media buyers are looking for impression as opposed to actual product orders, so it makes sense for them to buy media when there are more "eyes and ears." In the early days of cable, when cable was struggling, they relied a lot on direct response marketers to fill their media slots.

The success of direct response marketing relies heavily on the availability of cheap media. During the rest of our discussion of direct response marketing, we will use infomercials as our main example, but all the information applies to other direct response advertising as well.

There are several areas that you have to consider when contemplating a direct response marketing campaign. You will normally concentrate on one or a limited number of products. There is a saying in direct response marketing that "if you give your consumer too many choices, they will not make one." I have found this to be very true in the infomercial world. Here are the areas that are important when you are considering creating an infomercial for your product:

1. Product
2. Creative aspects of your infomercial
3. Media
4. Inbound telemarketing
5. Credit card processing
6. Fulfillment
7. "Backend" management

Infomercial products – Not all products are suitable for infomercial marketing. As I stated earlier, we will be using infomercial marketing as our example of direct response marketing. A product may be suitable for direct mail but not for marketing via infomercials. Here are some questions to answer when considering a product for an infomercial:

1. Does it have a unique selling proposition (USP) to a broad-based audience?
2. Is there widespread public interest in this TYPE of product?
3. Is your product in a product category that has been historically sold via direct response?
4. Are your product's benefits credible, easily proven, and easy to demonstrate/ dramatize in a direct response format?
5. Does the product fulfill a dream, make life easier, provide a magical transformation, or offer immediate gratification?
6. Does your product have a 5:1 markup up or better? This means that if your product retails (on air) for $100, its costs should not be more than $20.
7. Can the consumer be easily persuaded to buy this product on impulse? If not, once the TV channel is switched, he will have forgotten your product.
8. Call all of your product claims be substantiated and pass FTC/ FDA approval?
9. Does your product have a high perceived value?
10. Do you have real and valid testimonials for your product?
11. Do you have real and valid expert testimonials for your product?
12. Has your product been sold elsewhere?
13. Has it been sold on TV?
14. Can your product's developer persuasively and passionately sell your product on TV?
15. Is there a celebrity who can passionately and persuasively endorse your product?
16. Is there a good upsell product available? This is a product that can be sold for more money to the person who calls in to buy the product advertised on air. This must be done with regard to a high standard of ethics. It is okay to make a premium product available or a larger quantity of the product available, but you must keep the upsell product offer within ethical bounds.
17. Can a continuity program be developed off of the core offer? The important concept here is that you have paid for the consumer to pick up the phone, so you want to maximize the sales dollars associated with the call. An ideal product is

one that is consumable or has consumables associated with it. A good example is Proactiv acne medication marketed by the phenomenally success infomercial company Guthy-Renker headquartered in Palm Springs, California. It has been a huge success on TV as an infomercial. Proactiv has annual sales in excess of $250 million. You buy it, it works as promised, and you order more. Another good example is the Omaha Steak infomercial.

18. Can the product be sold within a short format (30-second or 60-second direct response TV spot)?
19. Can the product be sold at retail? The natural sequence of direct response TV is retail.

Infomercials – Creative – To have a successful infomercial campaign, you need to have an infomercial (I know this is a little obvious, but better to make sure). An average infomercial will cost between $150,000 and $500,000 to produce. They are typically 27 ½ minutes in length. They will include 3 to 5 short commercials that will include the call to action (where you ask the consumer to get off the couch, grab the telephone, and place an order). Each infomercial is normally divided up into 3 shorter 9-minute pods.

When you are having an infomercial produced, they will normally also produce 30-second, 60-second, and 120-second direct response commercials. Since these are direct response commercials, you will always have an 800 number to make it easy for consumers to order your products. The infomercial formats most often seen are the documercial, demonstration show, talk show, or a show using a drama/ storytelling format. There have been attempts at producing infomercials with different lengths such as 5 minutes, 10 minutes, and 15 minutes. These attempts have not met with much success. There are a number of reasons these formats did not work, not the least of which is the fact that TV media companies like to sell time in half-hour increments to fit in between their programs.

You have heard the saying "garbage in – garbage out." If you have a bad script for your infomercial, you will have a bad infomercial. There are people trained in the art of infomercial scripting. I would never recommend starting an infomercial project without the services of a proven infomercial scriptwriter (with references).

Infomercials – Media – Infomercials are half hour commercials that include a direct response vehicle (call to action to pick up the phone and order). When media is bought for an infomercial, you would normally work with a media-buying company that specializes in buying infomercial time. They will also buy 30-second, 60-second, and possibly 120-second direct response time slots. These shorter infomercials will support the half-hour commercials by creating more impressions of your product. The heavy lifting (the actual order taking) is normally done by the infomercials. There are studies that indicate that the average viewer has to watch an infomercial 3 times before he will order your product. Your companion shorter TV spots will help reduce this somewhat.

Infomercial media time is usually bought during daytime hours (6:00 am to 11:00 am), late night (11:30 pm to 3:00 am) and on weekends (Friday night through Sunday night). The reason for this is that the media are cheaper at these times. As stated earlier, to make the financial aspects of infomercials work, the media has to be priced correctly. The normal infomercial financial equation is as follows assuming a product selling at $100:

Retail selling price	$100	(few infomercial products are sold below $29.99, and few are sold above $149.00)
Cost of media	$ 50	(a minimum 2:1 media ratio is needed for success)
Cost of product	$ 20	(a 5× product markup is normally needed for success)
Gross margin	$ 30	

Most professional infomercial companies will charge purchasers enough in shipping and handling to cover the cost of product inbound call receiving, shipping and handling, and a small profit. I have seen some infomercials that sold a product at cost and made all of their profit on the shipping and handling. There is a CD product that was on the TV a few years ago that only charged 99 cents for the CD and $4.95 for shipping and handling. The actual average cost of shipping and handling was $3.95, with the seller making $1.00 on each CD sold.

Infomercials – Inbound telemarketing – Telemarketing is a vital part of any infomercial campaign. You can have a tremendous infomercial and have it hit a brick wall if you have not developed a solid inbound telemarketing function. When people see your infomercial on TV and call in, they have to be turned into a purchaser by the telemarketer at the other end of the phone line. Your infomercial has to be put together well also. I once saw a great infomercial about a great product. But there was a big problem, because almost half of the calls to the telemarketing firm were not resulting in sales. The problem was that the price of the product was given after the call to action. So, a large number of the calls were just to find out the price of the product, and after hearing the price from the telemarketer, many people chose to decline the purchase. This doubled the effective cost of the telemarketing inbound call. You want as many calls as possible to result in a sale. Inbound telemarketing companies will charge you by the minute or by the call. An average call should cost you from 50 cents to 95 cents, depending on the complexity of the call.

Many, if not most, infomercial campaigns have the inbound telemarketers also try to upsell the caller to a more expensive product. Research has shown that about 20% of callers can be upsold to higher priced product. You want to make sure that your telemarketing company is not being too aggressive and selling people things they don't want or don't need. Remember that the telemarketing company may be your customer's only contact with you. You want them to project your company values of integrity and Christian-based principles.

You will also have a setup fee to get the ball rolling with your telemarketing company. This setup fee can be anywhere from $3,000 to $20,000.

One last note on inbound telemarketing, your inbound telemarketing company will be supplying the credit card information to your credit card processing company and to your fulfillment company.

Infomercials – credit card processing – You can't sell anything on TV without a merchant account to accept credit cards. And you will want to accept all major credit cards. When you get your merchant card account, manage it closely. Infomercial companies have a really bad reputation when it comes to credit card abuse. Some credit card companies won't even deal with infomercial companies. Your credit card company will charge you a discount fee, which will be a percentage (from 1% to 5% with some third-party processors charging as much as 15%) of each sale and a flat processing fee (25 cents to 50 cents) for each transaction. They will also hold back a certain percentage of each sale for potential bad debts.

However, credit cards aren't processed cheaply, at least not for a start-up. A typical fee schedule for a small-volume account (fewer than 1,000 transactions monthly) would include start-up fees amounting to around $200 and a monthly processing minimum fee of around $20. You will also be charged a "charge back" for each credit card transaction that has to be charged back to your account. To make sure that you get every sale possible from your infomercial, it's a good idea to also accept payments via online checks. Be sure to build the cost of processing credit cards into your product price. As mentioned above, many infomercial companies build the cost of credit card processing into the shipping and handling charged to customers. Remember that you can't process customer credit card orders until your fulfillment house has shipped the product. You really need to keep close control of your merchant credit processing account and reconcile your merchant card statement to your checking account every month. You will normally have the following type of transactions on your merchant account statement:

- Customer collections
- Reserve holdbacks (an agreed upon percentage of each transaction deducted and added to your reserve balance to cover potential bad credit cards. This reserve should be reflected on your balance sheet as an asset because it is funds the credit card company is holding for you.
- Fees and possible interest the credit card company is charging you for the privilege of using your merchant account
- Charge backs. These are transactions where your merchant account is being changed for credit cards transactions from your customers that were not approved.
- Transfers from your merchant account into your company checking account.

Infomercials – fulfillment – This step includes taking your customer's approved order and delivering it to them on a timely basis. A typical infomercial order charge is $2.00 per order plus shipping (UPS, etc.). Fulfillment will normally include the following services (most will require additional fees):

1. Order processing
2. Back-order management
3. Customs clearances
4. Product receiving and storage
5. Product picking and packing
6. Product fulfillment
7. Coupon/literature insertion
8. Inventory management
9. Return processing
10. Inventory movement reporting
11. Managing product shrink
12. Management of product continuity programs

Infomercials – "Backend" management – This is where most companies fail to maximize their investment in their infomercial campaigns. Even if you have a successful infomercial campaign, you will leave a lot of money on the table if you don't properly manage your backend campaign.   The backend includes the following revenue sources:

1. Outbound "aftermarket" calls. Once a person has bought your product, you have a qualified purchaser for additional units of your product or related products. You can't get a more qualified lead. History has shown that 20% of the people who buy from you will buy again if they feel that you have sold them value in the past. First, craft a solid offer, and then hire an outbound telemarketing company to call your list of past customers.

2. List management. If you generated thousands of calls for your product, you have an asset that can be sold to other marketing companies—a list of people who have shown a propensity for buying products from TV. You can sell your list through a list management company. A mailing list management company will normally only be interested if you have at least 1,000 names on your list. Your list will be rented to other marketers, starting at $25 per thousand names. You will typically get 50% of the rental fee. They will typically sell your list for a "one time use" only. The list management company (LMC) will insert "dummy" addresses in your list as a security measure. If the list is used more than once by a purchaser, any contacts made to dummy addresses will go directly back to the list LMC so they can inquire as to why the purchaser used the list more than once.

This discussion on infomercials as an example of direct response marketing was meant to show you the benefits and intricacies of direct response marketing. There are a number of companies that specialize in producing infomercials, buying media time for infomercials, and managing infomercial campaigns. Infomercials typically require a large upfront cash infusion and a lot of detailed management. For these reasons, I recommend presenting infomercial management companies your infomercial oriented products. If accepted, you will be paid a royalty for each unit sold, based on the selling price to consumers and/or to retailers.

Other Advertising Ideas

Listed below are some more ideas for media and marketing to get your advertising message out to potential customers.

ATM Messages

Announcements – read the wedding and birth announcements, and send a "congratulations" newsletter to them

Barter for Services

Bumper Stickers

Business Cards – never give just one at a time out

Business Cards (again) – give to families and friends to hand out

Business license applicants – send out a "starting in business in XYZ town" newsletter

Calendars – Everyone likes a good calendar to put on the front of the refrigerator as long as it's useful

Change machines in arcades

Church function sponsor

Cinema Advertising (surprisingly affordable)

Classified Ads – If done correctly, can be very effective

"Clean the highway" sponsor

Directory Listings

Doctors – ask your doctor if you can leave some brochures in his office

Entertainment Coupon Books

Expos – wedding, car, baby, job fairs, special industries

Free Classified ads

Free Seminars – give a free seminar on your area of expertise

Gift Basket raffles at church bazaars, fish fries, veteran clubs, and school fairs

Grocery Stores

Shopping carts

Bulletin boards

Sales receipts

Shelf talkers

Grocery bags

Coupons

Free samples

Gyms and the YMCA

"Hole-in-the-wall" restaurants are normally very friendly about keeping a supply of your business cards or brochures handy.

Hotel Ads

Libraries (hand out bookmarks after getting permission)

Neighborhood – flyers and door hangers

Networking clubs

News Releases

Owner Operators – If you know an owner/operator, ask them about advertising on their truck(s)

Parking Lot Stripe Ads (ads written on the white parking lot stripes)

Phone Answering Ads – Place ads that sell when your business phone is answered in your absence

Pins and buttons

Postcards

Publish – write articles for magazines – some professionals have a saying "publish or perish"

Research – Do some research and make it available to your local newspapers, TV, radio stations

School Newspapers and Yearbooks

Speaking at community events

Sponsor a community event

Sponsor a school event

Sporting/fitness/leisure facilities

Street Corner Sandwich Boards

T-shirts, hats, tote bags (for you, your staff, your customers, events, etc.)

Town Festival Ads

Truck Mud Flap Advertising

Yacht Sail Advertising

Welcome Wagon baskets

Word of Mouth (friends, family, customers, vendors, suppliers)

PULLING IT ALL TOGETHER – THE MARKETING BUDGET ━━━━━━

Before you started developing your marketing plan and marketing budget, you should have completed your SWOT (strengths, weaknesses, opportunities, and threats) analysis and your PEST (political, economic, social, and technology) review (See the "CREATIVE THINKING IN BUSINESS" chapter). You also need to have your business goals (See "THE BUSINESS PLAN AND OPERATING YOUR BUSINESS" chapter) completely developed and committed to writing. Once you have a good handle on all of the elements of your marketing mix, product, price, place, and promotion and you know how they impact your target market, you are ready to decide how much to spend on marketing. It is not just a question of how much but also a question of when to spend and what to spend on.

Entrepreneurs have many ways of pulling together a marketing budget.

1. Match the competition.
2. By executive decree.
3. The percentage of sales method.
4. By the preferred outcome method.
5. The zero-based budgeting approach.

Match the Competition – This approach is not really efficient. You will never know exactly what your competition is doing. You may see his ad in the newspaper every weekend and you may try to match him ad-for-ad. But, do you know what he is paying for his product? Do you know what he is doing on the Internet? Do you know what he is doing in nontraditional advertising? You probably don't have adequate data to "match the competition." Besides, "me too" in advertising is not effective for the long run.

Executive Decree – You as the "head" of the company look at all of the internal and external information that you can get your hands on, and then decide on an "appropriate" amount to spend. Obviously, this is not a good way to grow a business. As the head of the company, you may have an intuitive feeling about how much you should spend, but you'd better back up your hunch with sound analysis. Even if you come to the same conclusion after your analysis, you at least have a better idea that your "hunch" is correct. As with all analysis, the process of going through your analysis will also spark ideas of how you are going to most efficiently spend your marketing dollars.

The Percentage of Sales Method – This method is used a lot in business because it is easy to understand and easy to implement. There is also a simple elegance to it. You take a sales number and multiply it by a percentage, and voila, you have your marketing budget. Most businesses will take last year's sales and multiply it. What is wrong with this approach? For one thing, it takes a historical sales number and multiplies it by another historical number to establish your future marketing budget. You want to spend based on where you want to go, not where you have been.

Preferred Outcome Method – Knowing where you want to go is the first step to any journey. If you don't know where you want to go, any route will be okay. This is not the way to manage the 3 Ts (Time, Talent, and Treasures) that God has lent to you to manage for him. You should start building your budget for the coming year well before the year arrives. As we discussed in the chapter "THE BUSINESS PLAN AND OPERATING YOUR BUSINESS," under the subsection entitled "The Marketing Plan," there are both financial aspects and nonfinancial aspects of growing your business.

The Preferred Outcome Method of building your marketing budget is based on choosing a target for the coming year. You will estimate what amount of sales you need to cover your operating expenses, make capital purchases, and return a desired net profit back to you. You can use the "Modified Percentage of Sales Method" as an integral part of this budgeting method as long as you are applying your percentages to where you want to be rather than where you have been. Also, temper your percentages with a sound knowledge of what your marketing dollars can generate in sales. Let's walk though the steps of the example below:

This example illustrates only one of many ways to arrive at your marketing budget.

Step #1 – Calculate marketing cost of generating a sale.

This should be a weighted average of all the anticipated ways of marketing your company and products. We will assume for this discussion that you have no customers and you are just starting your business. This involves either doing primary research into the effectiveness of your marketing methods selected and/or secondary research. By primary research, I simply mean testing the methods. As an example, let's assume you pay for a test search on a search engine. Each "click-through" in your paid search costs you 25 cents. For each 10 click-throughs (costing you $2.50), you get one new potential customer. Out of every 10 new potential customers, you get one customer that actually makes a purchase, which means the cost of this customer acquisition is $25.

Through secondary research (published statistics), you know that every new customer will purchase an average of five times during the coming year.

Step #1 - Calculate marketing cost of generating a sale
If it cost $XX to generate XX
new customers

$25 to generate one new customer

Each new customer will buy XX
number of products each year

5 products a customer will by per year

Computed cost to generate one
new sale

$5 Cost to generate one new sale

Step #2 - Calculate average selling price, cost of sales and gross margin

Selling Price of Product	$49	100.00%
Direct Cost of Product	$25	51.02%
Marketing cost associated with generating one sale	$5	10.20%
Total Cost of Sales	$30	61.22%
Gross margin on product	$19	38.78%

Step #3 - Determine sales that are needed to cover your projected sales and operating expenses

			Projected inc. Statement
Computed Sales	100.00%	$548,542	$548,542
Cost of Sales - computed	-61.22%	($335,842)	($279,868)
Add back in marketing cost to generate sales	10.20%	$55,974	
Gross Margin - computed	48.98%	$212,700	$268,674
Projected Rents		$24,000	$24,000
Supplies		$1,800	$1,800
Maintenance		$600	$600
Marketing		$0	$55,974
Insurance		$1,500	$1,500
Staff Salaries		$60,000	$60,000
Staff Exp (ins, employ taxes, etc.)		$4,800	$4,800
Operating Expenses		$92,700	$148,674
Net profit		$120,000	$120,000
Total of operating expenses (without marketing exepnse) and desired net profit		$212,700	

Fig.72 – Marketing Cost to Generate Sales

Step #2 – Calculate average selling price, cost of sales, and gross margin.

These numbers should be easy for you to develop as you know your selling price or average selling price, and you should know your cost of sales. From these two numbers, you can determine your Gross Margin or Average Gross Margin.

Step #3 – Determine sales that are needed to cover your projected operating expenses and desired net income.

The first step within Step #3 is to determine what you anticipate your expenses to be for the year. These will be your fixed expenses, as your cost of sales (variable) are covered in Step #2 above. You can also include any capital expenditures (furniture, equipment, etc.) that you feel you need to make for the year. Also, compute your new target profit. In the example, you want to have a net profit of $120,000 for the year. The Excel spreadsheet projects that to cover your projected expenses of $92,700 and desired net income of $120,000, you will need a marketing budget of $55,974 to generate approximately $548,542 in sales. The proof of this example is in the projected Income Statement.

There are percentages of sales numbers that are considered standards for particular industries. As stated above, these standard percentages should be tempered by your knowledge of what sales your particular marketing expenditures can generate in sales dollars. You can often get these percentages from trade associations. Here are some examples:

A typical retail store   2.5%
New business start-up   7.0%
Consumer goods 10.0%
Pharmaceutical company 20.0%

If you obtain a percentage of sales number from a trade association or other source, use it only as a guideline.

As a final note, here are some guiding principles for setting up your marketing plan and your marketing budget:

1.   Always focus on your existing customers. Once you get new customers, concentrate on keeping them happy. Often, new entrepreneurs will focus solely on getting new

customers. It is much more difficult to get new customers than it is to keep your existing ones happy. Do not forget your existing customers.

2. Test, test, and test some more. Do not be afraid to try new marketing approaches, but test them first. Remember that doing what you have always done will get you what you have always got. New marketing approaches will sometimes get you better results and sometimes get you poorer results. But try them anyway.

3. Make sure you market to your well-defined core demographics unless you have a well-thought-out reason for deviating from your plan.

4. Make sure that you have a consistent marketing plan. All of your marketing efforts, materials, and media should have a consistent flavor so that all of your efforts support each other.

5. Make sure your marketing message is clear and well thought out.

6. If a marketing approach sounds too good to be true, then it probably is. There are no "silver bullets" in marketing.

7. Always get feedback. Although you will test your marketing ideas, continue to get feedback at all times.

Risk Management

So you have worked hard to build your business, accounted for it properly, and all is good—until an unforeseen, unanticipated disaster strikes. Building your business is important, but so is minimizing your risk. You will never eliminate business risk, but you can effectively manage it. Most people think of risk management as the act of buying insurance. This is just one element of risk management. Risk management is the process of analyzing exposure to risk and determining how to best handle such exposure. Risk has two characteristics, uncertainty (probability) and loss, the thought of which can leave a knot in the pit of your stomach. The fear of the unknown can be scary. Creative thinking is important when developing unique products and services for your business. Creative thinking is also a powerful tool in the area of risk management. Be creative in developing ways to manage your risks. Use creative thinking to start your business, build your business, and minimize the risk of losing your business.

Remember the old saying "An ounce of prevention is worth a pound of cure." It is very true in the area of risk management. Taking action before losses occur can save assets, save time in remedial action, and help avoid disruptions to your business.

RISK MANAGEMENT TECHNIQUES ━━━━━━━━━━━━━━━━━━━━━━━━

Common risk management techniques include avoiding risk, diversifying resources to reduce risk, instituting internal controls, sharing risks, transferring risks, and accepting risks. You will probably use all of these risk management techniques to varying degrees.

AVOIDING RISKS

Avoiding risk involves redesigning processes, procedures, and tasks to avoid particular risks, with the plan of reducing overall risk. A man I know had a crafts store that sold unique Plaster-of-Paris-molded figurines. He would take them outside to dry after painting them. He began to notice that some of figurines would systematically disappear every time he put them out to dry. It didn't take a rocket scientist to figure out that if he let them dry in his back room instead, they wouldn't disappear. He avoided the risk of theft by a simple change in his process. Installing locks, security systems, and hiring security guards for the parking lots fall under the "avoiding risks" category.

DIVERSIFYING RISKS

Spread the risk among numerous assets or processes to reduce the overall risk of loss or impairment. Many investors use this technique to minimize their risk in investing. The same approach works well in business. An example here is a company that was buying television airtime for infomercial companies. They were growing like crazy, with three very large accounts. They reached total billings of over forty million dollars. Then one day, their attorney let them know that one of the accounts had just filed for bankruptcy. This client accounted for approximately 50% of the company's total billings. They survived by reducing their staff by 50%, canceling plans for upgrading their computer systems, and a number of other cost-cutting measures. A year later, they were billing thirty million dollars with fifty clients. The average client was only paying approximately two million dollars each. This required more administrative work, but now, if they lost a client, it would only account for 7% of total billings. They substantially reduced their risks by diversification.

On a larger scale, diversification is practiced as a risk management technique by most international corporations. No major oil company has all of its drilling platforms just in the Gulf of Mexico. They have financial and operational interests in Venezuela, Alaska, and the Middle East. Why do they do this? To increase profits, yes, but also to diversify their holdings and minimize their risks. If their drilling platforms in the Gulf of Mexico get damaged by a hurricane, they can rely on their platforms in other parts of the world. Some people refer to this risk management category as "not putting all of your eggs in one basket." As noted above, the administrative cost of diversifying your assets goes up, but the benefits of diversification far outweigh the increased cost.

INTERNAL CONTROLS TO MANAGE RISKS

Internal controls are the design activities to prevent, detect, or contain adverse events or to promote positive outcomes. This is another risk management area that falls under the old saying "an ounce of prevention is worth a pound of cure." If you put the proper controls in place up front, you are going to save yourself a lot of heartache. The small business entrepreneur probably does not have the resources to have extensive internal controls, but they can institute some of the basics. The more you implement, the better. If you cannot implement a full internal control system, you should concentrate first on your more liquid and vulnerable assets like cash, inventory, and accounts receivable. Having internal controls is the fair thing to do for employees. With good internal controls, their honesty is not tested. Having good internal controls is protecting the assets God has lent to you.

The following common challenges facing entrepreneurs and small companies when installing adequate internal controls are:

Lack of an internal audit function. Many large companies have a comprehensive, relatively independent internal audit function. The very fact that a company has an internal audit function is a deterrent to internal fraud, misappropriation, and loss from mismanagement. More important than this is the fact that internal audit functions prevent and/or detect internal fraud and ensure that corrective action is taken. As a small start-up business, you will be the internal auditor (as well as the bookkeeper, salesperson, janitor, president, clerk). You can establish internal control systems, such as monthly bank reconciliations, monthly reconciliation of inventories to accounting records, keeping cash timely deposited to minimize risks.

Lack of segregation of duties. When you only have a few employees, if any, it is hard to segregate duties. If an employee takes in cash from cash sales and makes deposits, it would be relatively easy for him to deposit the cash received in his own bank account. If an employee does some of your bookkeeping and your bank reconciliations, then you could have problems. You could be missing cash and never know it until it is too late.

Lack of relevant, accurate, and timely financial reports. We have discussed elsewhere in this book the importance of what we call R.A.T.

(e.g., relevant, accurate, and timely) financial statements in running and growing your business. R.A.T. reports are also an important part of internal controls. If you periodically reconcile your financial records to your physical assets (e.g., cash, accounts receivable, accounts payable, inventory, fixed assets, intangibles), then you will catch problem areas and be able to take corrective action.

Lack of financial and personnel resources. As a new entrepreneur, you may not be able to afford the financial controls and the personnel resources you need for good internal controls. Financial controls do cost you money and time. When you start a business with just yourself or with you and your spouse, internal controls will not be as much of an issue. The need for internal controls will grow geometrically once you start hiring employees and getting more customers.

Cost-benefit relationship. Early in your business, you will find that the cost-benefit relationship is a little out of balance. As an example, if you are only writing twenty checks a month and you are only generating thirty sales invoices a month for your business, you may think that generating a monthly profit and loss statement is a waste of time. There are a couple of good reasons to view this cost-benefit relationship in a different light. Starting your business off in a disciplined manner will mean that you are organized up front, and it will be easier to stay disciplined as your business grows. Another reason is that it is always easier to install internal controls when there are fewer transactions to deal with. Then, as the volume of transactions starts to grow, you can easily make modifications to your internal controls system as needed. Internal controls have to comply with the saying "The juice has to be worth the squeeze." This simply means that the cost of internal controls should never outweigh the benefits derived from them.

Why Are Internal Controls Important?

Internal controls are designed to provide reasonable assurance regarding the achievement of objectives in the following categories, while at the same time minimizing risks:

Effective, economical, and efficient operations.

I like to refer to effective, economical, and efficient operations as the 3E equation of operations. If you have a 3E approach to operations, you are probably in the profit zone, or at least headed for the profit zone. Solid internal controls can be a powerful tool in trying to achieve your 3E approach to operations. If you don't have good internal controls, you will have a much more difficult time achieving entry into the profit zone.

Reliability of financial and operational reporting.

If you do not have good internal controls, your financial and operational reporting systems will not be reliable. Without proper internal controls, how do you know that all transactions are being recorded? And how do you know that the ones that are recorded are being recorded properly? The answer is, you don't!

Compliance with applicable laws and regulations.

As much as you may not want to think about it, there will always be laws and regulations that you have to comply with if you start your own business. Most of the governmental bodies are totally unforgiving if you do not report to them or you report erroneous information to them. For this reason alone, you should make sure that you have adequate internal controls.

What Are The Components Of Internal Controls?

Internal control consists of five interrelated components. These are derived from the way you, as management, run your business, and are integrated with your management process. Since you will be a small business, your internal controls will most likely be much less structured than those of a mature business, yet you can still have effective internal control.

Control Environment – The control environment sets the overall tone of your new company, influencing the control consciousness of you and your employees. Your control environment factors include the integrity, ethical values, and competence of your staff; your management philosophy and operating style; the way you, as management, assign authority and responsibility, and organize and develop your employees. An organization based on Christian values does not mean one that has no controls and totally trusts everyone that walks in the door. The great thing about good internal controls is that they enable you to have more trust in your employees and customers.

Risk Assessment – Risk assessment is the identification and analysis of relevant risks to achievement of the objectives, forming a basis for determining how the risks should be managed.

Control Activities – Control activities are the policies and procedures that help ensure your directives are carried out. They include a range of activities such as authorizations, approvals, reconciliations (such as bank accounts and physical inventories), analyses, verifications, reviews of operating and financial performance, security of assets, and segregation of duties.

Information and Communication – Pertinent information must be identified, captured, and communicated in a R.A.T. (relevant, accurate, and timely) manner that enables you and your staff to carry out your assigned responsibilities in your new company. Your information systems produce reports containing operational, financial, and compliance-related information that makes it possible to run and control your company. The information generated from your accounting and bookkeeping systems is only useful if it is properly disseminated after it is generated. If the reports generated from your systems are not disseminated, understood, reviewed, and analyzed, then they are useless and of no value from an internal control aspect.

Monitoring – Your internal control system needs to be monitored continuously—a process that assesses the quality of the system's performance over time. This is accomplished through ongoing monitoring activities, separate evaluations, or a combination of the two. Ongoing monitoring occurs in the course of operations. Internal control deficiencies should be corrected as they are discovered. Your business will be constantly changing as it grows, and so will your need for internal controls.

Control Activities Include, But Are Not Limited To, The Following:

Segregation of duties – When duties are divided, or segregated, among different people, there is a reduction of risk of error or inappropriate actions. No one person has control over all aspects of any financial transaction. For example, an accounts payable clerk should not be allowed to order products or services, receive cash, or make deposits. These duties should go to a different employee.

Transaction authorization and approval. Make sure transactions are authorized by a person-delegated approval authority and that the transactions are consistent with your policy and that funds are available. When you start out, you will be the approval authority. With few transactions as a start-up business, you will personally want to authorize most of them. As your business grows, you will delegate certain authority to trusted individuals. Never give total authority to an employee without periodic review, and never give an employee power over an entire transaction from beginning to end.

Review and reconciliation. Ensure records are routinely reviewed and reconciled by someone other than the preparer or transactor to determine that transactions have been properly processed.

Timely recording of transactions. Make sure that all transactions are recorded in a timely manner. When I was an auditor, one of the things I looked for was transactions that were not recorded on a timely basis. All too often, when I looked at the untimely recording of transactions, I found issues of dishonesty or carelessness that resulted in financial loss.

Written policies and procedures. Documenting policies and procedures and making them accessible to employees helps provide day-to-day guidance to staff and will promote continuity of activities in the event of prolonged employee absences or turnover. Your written policies and procedures should include detailed written job descriptions for all of your staff. They need to know what is expected of them, and you will use the written description to evaluate their performance. If you do this, they will be happier, and you will be happier with their performance.

Reconcile physical assets to accounting records. Make certain that equipment, inventories, cash, and other property are secured physically, counted periodically, and compared with item descriptions shown on control records.

Hiring the right people. If you are successful, you will be hiring people. The key is hiring the right people. Hiring Christians only does not make your process any better, as they are people, and you will find that they have the same types of problems as other people. But, they should know up front that they will be working for a company that is based on sound Biblical principles. There are some people who wouldn't want to work for a Bible-based business, and it's better for them to know this before they become part of the team.

Treat your employees fairly. As mentioned elsewhere in this book, as a Christian business owner, you are required to treat your employees well. You will have employees that are not Christians, and your Bible-based business will be a testament to the Lord and you will be witnessing to them with your loving, caring, and no-nonsense management style. You will want to make sure that you hire the right person for the right job. You need to take some simple steps when hiring people. These steps will help increase internal control and help you grow your business through the people whom you hire.

1. Don't hire a person until you have drafted a complete job description that includes their evaluation criteria.

2. Hire people who would be better than you at doing the job. You can't do everything well, so hire people who are the best for the job.

3. Pay at least what the going market is for the position. If you pay more, then it makes it difficult for them to leave. The extra money that they will be getting will let them know that they are appreciated. Money is typically not a motivator, but it can be a

de-motivator if an employee is underpaid. All employees check the marketplace and will always know what they are worth, and so should you. It's always good for them to earn the right, based on time and productivity, to participate in profits in some manner.

4. Check references. This means personal references and job references. For key personnel, I have used employment services and have gotten better results, as they know what questions to ask.

5. Test. If you are hiring a person for a technical job, such as a bookkeeper position, you should test them in the area of their expertise. If you test a bookkeeper candidate who doesn't know the difference between a debit and credit, you should probably not hire that person.

6. Hire people on a probationary basis. The person may have interviewed well, had excellent references, and may have passed your tests with flying colors, and still may prove to be the absolutely wrong person for the job. You might not be able to put your finger directly on the reason, or there may be numerous reasons. But you need a way to unwind the relationship without a complicated process. If you have done your homework, this will rarely happen; but based on Murphy's Law, it will happen.

7. Written employment contract. Your employees need to know what is expected of them. If they do not know, they will fill in the blanks by themselves. They also need to know how they will be evaluated.

Good advisory team members. The very fact that you have a team of advisors is a control factor that helps you guard against risks. Your accountant, attorney, and insurance broker will all work as a team (if they function properly) to help you minimize your risks.

Employee training and guidance. Provide employees with appropriate training and guidance to ensure they have the knowledge necessary to carry out their job duties, are provided with an appropriate level of direction and supervision, and are aware of the proper channels for reporting suspected improprieties. Your employees should be aware of the reasons for internal controls. If you are open and upfront with them, they will become part of the overall risk management function.

Physical controls. If a valuable asset is locked up, it can't be stolen. You have minimized the risk of theft. Physical controls have to be tempered with the realities of access for employees and customers. If your business is a grocery store, you could virtually eliminate all shoplifting if all merchandise were locked up. But who would want to shop at a grocery store with all of its merchandise locked up? You can, however, take reasonable steps to minimize your exposure to loss because of poor physical controls.

In many retail businesses, shrinkage of inventory via theft is a cost of doing business and accepted as a reality. Controls to minimize risk of physical loss include surveillance cameras, locks, one-way mirrors, steel doors, safes, locking filing cabinets, locating your business in a safe location, adequate lighting, security guards, fences, self-locking doors, controlled access, visibility, and lastly, common sense.

Everyone in your company has responsibility for internal control. If everyone adopts a risk reduction/control attitude, risk will be easier to manage. If everyone feels controls are important to the success of the company, reduction of risks will become everyone's responsibility.

Proper control of intangible assets. Intangible assets created by you must be properly documented and protected. If they are not, others can claim ownership of them. If not properly documented, you are at risk of losing ownership of your intangible assets. Intangible assets take the form of reputation, business methods, patents, copyrights, trademarks, brands, and business information.

SHARING RISKS

Another risk management technique is to distribute a portion of the risk through a contract with another party, such as insurance. The insurance industry is complicated at best, and it is good to have a dependable broker help guide you through the insurance maze. Sharing risks is closely related to the technique of transferring risks. With insurance, you are willing to assume some risks, but you want to share a portion of the risk with your insurance company. The trick is to share enough risks with your insurance company so that you are adequately insured but not overinsured. With sharing, you are self-insuring for a portion of your risks. There are other noninsurance ways to share risks. One way is to join a cooperative for buying inventory. You may find other companies similar to yours in different parts of the country that band together to buy everything from products for sale to insurance.

Sometimes, professional organizations have co-op benefits to them. As an example, the accounting profession was having a hard time getting professional liability insurance a few years back. The AICPA (American Institute of Certified Public Accountants) worked together with their member firms to get professional liability that was tolerable from a cost perspective. Sometimes, you can share risks with related, but not competitive businesses. I know of a roofing supply company in Central California that was running out of space to store roofing supplies. They could get better deals if they could bring in truckloads of product. They rented an adjacent industrial yard that was already fenced in with a couple of their professional roofing customers. They shared the cost of the yard, and everyone benefited.

Other risk-sharing techniques are through joint ventures and partnerships. A joint venture is normally for a specific business purpose between two companies. I know of a CPA firm that wanted to bid on the annual audit of their local county. They were considered too small and also did not have all of the areas of expertise required to submit a viable proposal to the county auditor. They formed a joint venture with another local CPA firm that had the expertise they were lacking and submitted the winning proposal. They shared the risk of the proposal. Since it was a joint venture, they were not in business together. They formed the joint venture specifically to bid on the county audit. A partnership between the two firms would have put them in business together and increased their liability for each other's actions.

TRANSFERRING RISKS

Risk transference is transferring all of your risk through a contract with another party, such as outsourcing. There is a popular trend to outsource select staff positions within a company. Doing this increases the cost of the position, as the temporary help company has to make a profit on top of the wages paid to your temporary employee. There are a number of advantages to hiring a temporary employee to transfer risks to an employment company:

1. The employee has been screened by a professional employment counselor.
2. If the employee does not work out, you can request a different staff person.
3. No liability for collecting and paying employment taxes.
4. The act of hiring a temporary employee has converted the cost of the position from a fixed cost to a variable cost. If revenues decrease, just call the temporary employment company and tell them that you will not need the person anymore.

Other risk-transfer techniques are indemnification provisions in contracts, taking goods on consignment, renting equipment instead of buying it, and letting customers buy raw materials.

Most contracts have indemnification clauses. For example, a toy designer licenses a toy design to a major company. The toy designer demands that the contract have an indemnification clause, meaning that once the company takes control of the toy designer's toy, he will no longer be liable for any injuries or other claims that might arise from the consumer's use of the toy. Because the toy designer would no longer have any control over the final development, manufacture, or distribution of the toy, he wanted to transfer liability to the toy company.

Retailers, especially small retailers, can benefit from taking products to sell on consignment. This basically means that you allow the vendor to place the product in your store, but you never actually take ownership of the product. As sales are made, you submit a portion to the supplier and retain your portion. It is never really considered your inventory, since you did not pay for it. You will normally agree to take reasonable steps to make sure that it is not broken or stolen, but the ultimate responsibility is with the supplier.

To minimize the risk of obsolescence, some companies will rent rather than buy equipment. If the equipment being rented is used infrequently, the decision to rent is much easier. But if the equipment is used frequently, you should complete a detailed lease v. buy analysis. Leasing is not always better than buying from a cost standpoint.

ACCEPTING RISKS

Allow minor risks to exist to avoid spending more on managing the risks than the potential harm. This is self-insuring. As mentioned before, the cost of not accepting risk should be less than the potential loss from risk being reviewed.

TYPES OF RISKS

All business risks can be grouped into four categories:

Financial

In the financial category, you can have loss of income, cash, credit, and negotiable instruments. You can also have investment loss. There is a risk that the new big-box store moves next door to you, and now no one comes into your store. There is a risk that you suffer a return rate of 50% because your supplier sent you defective merchandise. You can get business interruption insurance if some unforeseen event gets in the way of your normal process of making money; but other financial risk can effectively be managed by sound business judgment, good internal controls, and daily prayer. When you allow customers to charge their sales and thus have accounts receivable from customers, there is risk of non-collection. The management of risk for accounts receivable is minimized by sound credit management. Don't let customers with shaky credit charge sales.

Physical

Physical loss takes many forms. You can have loss of building, land, equipment, inventory, and supplies. These losses can occur from theft, acts of nature, vendor shortages, accidents, and governmental actions, and just plain carelessness. You can insure against most potential physical losses. The question is, how much risk do you want to assume, and how much risk do you want to transfer to your insurance company?

Human

Human capital is the most important asset of your business. Loss of key business knowledge, loss of skills, loss of key personnel, and loss of the commitment of people are the main areas where you have to manage risk in the area of human capital. Let's discuss the risk of losing the commitment of people. The commitment of people includes family, employees, customers, and vendors. Losing the commitment of any of these people can be fatal to your business. A loving, caring, fair, Christian approach to business is the most important tool in your toolbox when it comes to avoiding the risk of lost commitment from people.

You have seen employees that just go through the motions, never giving more than they have to give. An open, honest approach to business will keep your employees committed to your business. A really good way to keep your employees turned on is to include them in the decision-making process. Make them part of the solution rather than part of the problem.

The place to start having the commitment of good employees is in the hiring process. I don't mean that you employ only Christians. This is not smart on a number of fronts. First, you will find that Christian employees have the same types of problems as non-Christian employees. Second of all, you lose a tremendous opportunity to witness to your non-Christian employees through your Christian approach to business.

Intangible

Reputation, business methods, patents, copyrights, trademarks, brands, and business information are the main areas of potential risks in the area of "intangibles."

As you begin to build your reputation, you will see that it can be a major door opener for you with vendors, employees, and customers. There is a saying "A contract is only as good as the man behind it." I would rather sign a bad contract with a good man than a good contract with a bad man. When you find yourself entering into contracts, their negotiation will go faster and smoother as you develop a reputation as a fair person. It is okay to be a tough negotiator, but always be a fair negotiator and develop a reputation for being tough, but fair. As a final note on the subject of your reputation, it is better to have a good reputation than a big bank account (well, actually it is better to have both), as you will attract the best investors, the best customers, and the best employees with a good reputation.

As you develop your own business methods and generate business information, you will need to protect them as assets of your business. You may find that you have a highly efficient method of delivering your products to customers in less time than your large competitors; you may find that you have a better way to stock inventory than your competitors. Many innovative business methods come from small businesses just starting out. You need to protect these newly developed methods.

You will quickly develop business information that has tremendous value. If it were to fall into the wrong hands, it could destroy your business or seriously damage your competitive edge. The listing of your accounts receivable, your customer profiles, your company Rolodex®, listing of your subcontractors, listing of your suppliers, details on terms you get from suppliers, your balance sheet and profit and loss statements, your tax returns, and your board meeting minutes are a few examples of company information that could be damaging if it were to get into the wrong hands. There are some steps you can take to minimize the risk of your business information getting into the wrong hands:

1. Most accounting systems, including QuickBooks® will block access to business information. You can allow select people to view the reports on screen but not print them. You can also allow people to input data to the system without the

ability to see or print the information.
2. Have employees sign nondisclosure agreements.
3. Have a shredding policy for old reports.
4. Require permission for any employee to print a report.
5. Do not allow employees to take reports home to work on them.
6. Lock all reports up at night.

You will probably have employees that have access to your business methods and business information, so you will probably want to have your employees sign nondisclosure agreements. Sometimes, companies will include nondisclosure provisions directly in their employee agreements. Your unique business methods can be what sets your company apart from the competition.

There are other areas of intellectual property that need to be protected. Inventions and other things that you create sometimes need to be protected by patents, copyrights, and trademarks.

Many people confuse patents, copyrights, and trademarks. Although there are many similarities among these kinds of intellectual property protection, they are different and serve different purposes.

ANALYSIS OF YOUR RISKS

When examining risk, look at it as a matrix. If a particular element of risk has a low probability of happening and the potential loss from the risk situation is very low, causing the risk to fall in the green area of the chart, then you probably will assume the risk without insuring against it.

Probability					
E	Low	Medium	High	High	Very High
D	Low	Medium	Medium	High	High
C	Very Low	Low	Medium	Medium	High
B	Very Low	Very Low	Low	Low	Medium
A	Very Low	Very Low	Very Low	Very Low	Low
	1	2	3	4	5

Potential Loss

Fig. 73 – Risk Matrix

An example of a risk that has a low probability of happening, and if it does happen, the impact will be minimal, is a paint store owner's risks of someone stealing a can of paint. It will happen, but not happen often, and when it does, the impact is not severe.

Let's use the matrix approach to analyze a real problem. You have just started a business. You know that you do not want to take any risk that would cause you to lose $100,000 or more. At the $10,000 risk level, you calculate that if a risk has a 10% chance of occurring, your potential risk is $1,000. If the same risk of $10,000 has a 75% chance of occurring, your potential risk is $7,500. This is still within your comfort range, so you might not insure against it. When you look at a risk that has a possible loss of $50,000, you are willing to assume the potential risk up to a probability of occurrence of 10%. If it has a probability of occurring at the 25% probability level, then you might want to insure against it. Once you go through this type of analysis, you will have to determine what the cost of insuring against the loss is compared to the potential loss. Most people do not go through an analysis this formal when looking at risk. But it does illustrate that the amount of risk you are willing to assume is a function of the probability of its occurrence, the magnitude of its potential loss, and the amount of resources it would take to insure against it.

Probability					
90%	$9,000	$22,500	$45,000	$67,500	$90,000
75%	$7,500	$18,750	$37,500	$56,250	$75,000
50%	$5,000	$12,500	$25,000	$37,500	$50,000
25%	$2,500	$6,250	$12,500	$18,750	$25,000
10%	$1,000	$2,500	$5,000	$7,500	$10,000
	$10,000	$25,000	$50,000	$75,000	$100,000

Potential Loss

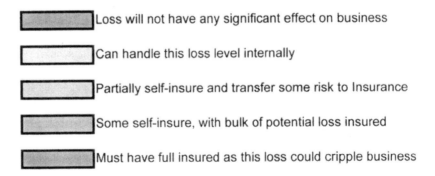

Loss will not have any significant effect on business

Can handle this loss level internally

Partially self-insure and transfer some risk to Insurance

Some self-insure, with bulk of potential loss insured

Must have full insured as this loss could cripple business

Fig.74 – Risk Matrix wiht Numbers

INSURANCE OVERVIEW ━━━━━━━━━━━━━━━━━━

If you are in business, you will require insurance at one time or another as an element of your risk management. Because insurance is invisible, complex, and will differ from business to business, it is hard to know if you have the right coverage without the help of a qualified insurance broker. There are many variables: the industry you are in, your tolerance for accepting risk, your physical location, your employees, your customers, your vendors, and your internal safety and risk reduction programs. All of these factors and more make it impossible to tell what insurance you will need without the help of a trained insurance broker with experience in business risk management. With this being said, ultimately it is your responsibility to make an informed decision and choose the insurance that best fits your business plan. You don't want to find out the hard way, in the middle of a crisis, that you don't have adequate insurance.

Important aspects of business insurance to consider:

> Property Insurance
> Liability Insurance
> Business Owner's Policy
> Umbrella Insurance
> Workers' Compensation
> Auto Insurance
> Employee Health Insurance
> Home Businesses
> Special Areas of Insurance

PROPERTY AND LIABILITY INSURANCE

Property and liability insurance encompasses the most basic insurance that you, as a small businessperson, will need. Property insurance protects your business from such things as fire, theft, and other disasters, while liability insurance protects you from lawsuits due to injury or damage to a third party. You will also probably buy a variety of other special insurance policies, such as earthquake and flood insurance, and if you have employees, you will need workers' compensation insurance. Another insurance that you will need for your small start-up business is automobile insurance.

PROPERTY INSURANCE

If you are in business, you will have property insurance. You will have inventory, a building full of furniture, fixtures, and equipment. You will have computers. One tree falling on your building, crushing your computers and letting the rain ruin your inventory, without insurance, and you could be out of business.

Property insurance basically covers a building and its contents from losses due to most common perils such as fire, theft, and wind damage. Depending on the nature of the business, some companies that qualify choose a Business Owner's Policy (BOP) and then add coverage for other perils as needed.

It's important to know what your policy exclusions are so that you can purchase additional coverage if needed and if it is available. Most property insurance policies can be extended to cover most risks, except those specifically excluded in the policy. Typical exclusions include mechanical breakdowns, nuclear contamination, property wear and tear, water damage, pollution, and losses from floods or earthquakes. Special limitations also apply to outdoor items that are not part of the building, such as detached signs, small detached storage sheds, fences, and trees. Special coverage for these risks is often available under separate policies.

Commercial property insurance will include provisions to determine what valuation method is to be used to calculate any losses you might incur. The most common valuation method in most policies is Actual Cash Value (ACV). Unless otherwise defined in the policy, ACV is normally considered to be Fair Market Value. There are two other methods of valuation that are used in insurance policies: agreed value and replacement costs. Agreed value waives any coinsurance penalty and pays 100% of the stated amount (agreed-upon amount) for any covered loss. Replacement cost covers the amount it takes to replace your property with new property of like kind and quality up to the limits of the stated insurance.

LIABILITY INSURANCE

In the section in this book "Your Team," the statement is made, "The good news is that there are over 1,000,000 lawyers in the United States, and the bad news is that there are over 1,000,000 lawyers in the United States." To be exact, according to the American Bar Association, there are 1,084,504 lawyers in the United States. The issue of liability has become a more important one in recent years as businesses have faced larger and more frequent lawsuits because of something they did—or failed to do, or because we have too many lawyers in the world. Any way you slice it, there are a lot of lawsuits against businesses, and you need to have some defenses against them. Being a Christian and running a Bible-based business will not shield you against lawsuits.

Liability insurance protects a business when it is sued for injury or property damage to third parties. You have no doubt heard of the guy that falls down a flight of stairs while visiting his accountant and has to get a new accountant because when he sued him, the accountant went out of business. Liability insurance generally pays damages related to bodily injury, property damage, personal injury (e.g., libel or slander), or advertising injury. It also pays for the defense and related legal costs for a covered claim or lawsuit.

Many businesses purchase liability coverage with a Business Owner's Policy (BOP) or through a separate policy known as commercial general liability (CGL). The policy always carries certain limits on the maximum amount the insurer will pay during the policy period, and there will normally be a maximum for each occurrence during the policy period.

Depending on your business attributes, you may want to consider purchasing an umbrella insurance policy. Umbrella liability insurance adds extra protection for catastrophic accidents or incidents in which a number of people are injured. It also extends liability limits on the commercial auto policy. Limits are generally purchased in $1 million layers from $1 million to as much as $10 million or more. Nowadays, $1 million dollars is not a lot of insurance.

Large, catastrophic losses, hopefully they never happen, can hit any business at any time. Umbrella coverage provides you with the asset protection needed to survive the devastating financial impact that a loss of this type would have. Your insurance broker can help you determine how much coverage you may need. $1 million should be the minimum purchased nowadays and, depending on what business you are in, you should consider $2 to $3 million. Insurance costs are not based on a straight-line basis, so $2 million of insurance will not cost you twice as much as $1 million in coverage. This is based on the fact that smaller claims are filed a lot more frequently than larger claims.

THE BUSINESS OWNER'S POLICY (BOP)

When reviewing your insurance needs, some of the confusion of what insurance you need is taken care of with a Business Owner's Policy (BOP) for commercial insurance coverage. A BOP is designed to meet a combination of insurance needs for various kinds of low-hazard operations, such as offices, stores, or apartment houses. Some companies, such as trucking companies, may find it difficult to purchase a BOP.

A BOP combines essential insurance coverages in one package that generally costs less than individual policies purchased separately. This makes it easier to manage your insurance program, and it often saves you a substantial amount of money over buying a number of individual insurance policies to cover separate risks. It usually includes property, liability, and crime coverage, as well as a number of specialty coverages, depending on the needs of your business.

Another advantage of the BOP is that the premium is determined upon issuance of the policy. Typically, the premium for non-package liability coverage is adjusted at the end of the year based on an audit of the company's sales. You can also customize your BOP for one low fee to have other coverage, such as coverage of accounts receivable, computer equipment, and valuable papers.

COMMERCIAL UMBRELLA

Your normal business insurance policies will have maximum insurance limits. Once you have hit these limits, your insurance coverage is exhausted. By purchasing a commercial umbrella policy, you can protect your business from being liable for this excess liability. A commercial umbrella policy covers the amount of loss above the limits of a basic liability policy. Commercial umbrella policies can cover commercial automobile, commercial general liability, workers' compensation, or any other liability type policy.

WORKERS' COMPENSATION INSURANCE

If you have employees, you are probably required to carry workers' compensation insurance. Not every employer needs workers' comp. In some states, small companies with fewer than three to five employees are not required to carry workers' compensation insurance. As an example, any business in Alabama that has five (5) or more employees is required by law to have workers' compensation coverage. The term *employee* includes all full-time or part-time employees, officers of a corporation, or members of an LLC. Once the coverage is secured, the employer may choose to exclude the officers or members. A few states, like Texas, do not require an employer to carry workers' compensation insurance.

Normally, when an employer has workers' compensation insurance, the employer is somewhat protected from lawsuits for work-related injuries and illnesses that are job related. Some people think that the way to get around paying employment taxes and workers' compensation is to classify their employees as "independent contractors." The Internal Revenue Service and insurance carriers have dealt with misclassification of employees for many years, so there is no tricking them.

The Internal Revenue Service and insurance carriers use these criteria to determine whether an individual is an employee or an independent contractor. The worker is an employee if...

- You or your representative tells the worker where, when, and how to work.
- You train the worker.
- The business performance depends on the worker.
- The worker has a continuing relationship with the company.
- The worker's services must be personally rendered by him/her.
- You set the worker's work hours.
- The worker works on the employer's premises.
- You are paid by the hour, week, or month.
- You furnish tools and materials.
- You can fire the worker without violating a contract.
- The worker has a right to quit without incurring a liability.
- The worker does not offer the worker's services to the public at large.
- The worker has no opportunity for profit or loss as a result of the worker's service.
- The worker has no significant investment in the business.
- You require the worker to submit oral or written reports.
- The worker is a corporate officer.

When one of your employees suffers a work-related injury or illness, workers' compensation insurance provides benefits based on the type of business or injury sustained. Workers' compensation is based on a "no-fault" system, which means that an injured employee does not need to prove that the injury or illness was someone else's fault in order to receive benefits for an on-the-job injury or illness. The cost of workers' compensation is calculated on salaries covered, job hazards (and their resultant job classification), and the company's experience factor.

COMMERCIAL AUTOMOBILE INSURANCE

Commercial automobile insurance is different than personal automobile insurance coverage. Typically, commercial auto insurance will cover different classes of vehicles and cover different people and property than that covered by personal automobile insurance. If you rarely use your automobile in your business, your personal automobile insurance policy may cover you, but be sure to read your policy and consult your insurance broker. Sometimes, commercial automobile insurance is cheaper than personal coverage. Basically, commercial automobile coverage can protect your company from any liability stemming from automobiles used in your business or any damage caused to the automobiles. Given today's legal environment, you should probably purchase at least $1 million of automobile insurance.

EMPLOYEE INSURANCE

Included in this area of our insurance discussion is insurance on you as the owner of the business. I do this assuming that you are going to be an incorporated new business and thus be its first employee. **Much of this area will change as President Obama has just signed new sweeping nationalized healthcare legislation.**

Group Health Insurance

Once you have employees, one of your biggest expenses will be employee health insurance. As a Christian businessperson, you have the responsibility of taking care of your employees. Part of this care is an adequate health insurance plan. Unfortunately, the United States has the world's most expensive medical system. The various options available to you are Health Maintenance Organization (HMO) plans, Preferred Provider Organization (PPO) plans, Point of Service Plan (POS), and traditional medical plans.

Health Maintenance Organization (HMO)

Typically, the most restrictive in terms of employee choice of services, but this type of plan is the least expensive of the various types of employee health insurance plans. It will generally cover the same areas as other employee insurance plans, but your employees will have to use HMO doctors and hospitals.

Preferred Provider Organization (PPO)

This type of plan is less restrictive on your employees: they can choose to use PPO network doctors and hospitals, or they can use doctors and hospitals outside of the network. If they use doctors and hospitals outside of the network, they normally incur dramatically increased costs.

Point of Service Plan (POS)

This type of plan is a hybrid between a PPO plan and an HMO plan. It uses a primary care doctor as a "gatekeeper." To receive higher benefits, all care must be provided by or referred by the "gatekeeper" doctor.

Option Plans

This type of offering to your employees enables them to choose from a PPO, HMO, POS, or Managed Indemnity Plan (discussed below). The advance to you is that you get a blended rate for the plans. The advantage to your employees is that they get a wider choice of health benefits.

Managed Indemnity Plan

This is the traditional plan that offers standard deductibles, co-payments, and the freedom to use the doctor and hospitals that employees wish to use. These types of plans for your employees will be expensive in today's legal, medical, and economic environment.

Employee Dental and Vision Plans

The great majority of employers do not offer dental and vision care plans to their employees. This type of insurance is comparatively inexpensive when compared to employee health insurance. If you are going to provide medical insurance (and you should) to your employees, strongly consider spending a few extra dollars and provide them with dental and vision care insurance.

HOME BUSINESSES

If you are operating your business from your home, you will still need business insurance. You may be able to purchase an optional business rider on your homeowner's policy to cover your home business. You will want to carry liability insurance for injuries that happen on your property, business property coverage for inventory and equipment, and possibly business auto insurance. As mentioned above, you may be able to cover the automobile used in your business under your personal automobile policy as long as the automobile is used on a limited basis in your business.

SPECIAL AREAS OF INSURANCE

There are several special areas of insurance that are ignored by many small business owners. I am not recommending that you rush out and buy these types of insurance—just making you aware of their existence.

BUSINESS INTERRUPTION INSURANCE

If your business is flooded out and you have flood insurance, you will be covered for the damage caused to your physical assets. But, what about the income that you will lose for the several months your business is closed down during the rebuilding process? The deductible for this type of insurance is typically based on the number of days you have been out of business before it kicks in. You will have to demonstrate the income generated by your business, and you will be reimbursed, after your deductible waiting period, based on some calculated average income.

DISABILITY INSURANCE

You may have life insurance (should you meet your untimely demise), but what if you become disabled or seriously ill, and your income stops? Your health insurance will cover the cost of your medical expenses but not your lost income. Disability coverage provides for your lost income. This type of insurance is closely related to business interruption insurance. Disability insurance normally is offered as long-term and/or short-term insurance. Long-term disability insurance normally has a waiting period of 30 days or more. This waiting period can normally be filled with a short-term disability insurance policy.

EMPLOYMENT PRACTICES LIABILITY INSURANCE

This is an area of growing revenue for attorneys—employees suing their employers because they don't like the way they were being treated for any variety of reasons. Employment Practices Liability Insurance was created to protect employers from lawsuits concerning these employee lawsuits. As a small business owner, you are personally involved in all aspects of managing your business, so this coverage may not be needed. As your business grows and you become dependent on managers to help run your business, you may want to consider this type of insurance.

FLOOD AND EARTHQUAKE INSURANCE

A flood or earthquake can cause huge losses in certain areas of the world. Because this type of threat can be localized, the risk cannot be spread over a large number of clients by the insurance companies. Because of this, the policies for these types of coverage may be relatively high and out of reach for the small business. Flood and earthquake insurance is available through commercial carriers, but premiums and deductibles will probably be high. Flood insurance is also available through the Federal Emergency Management Agency (FEMA).

CRIME INSURANCE

Many insurance policies exclude losses of money and securities. These will often be covered in your Business Owner's Policy (BOP), but if you don't have a BOP, crime insurance can be purchased as part of a policy such as a storekeeper's or office burglary and robbery policy.

FIDELITY BONDS

If your employees deal with cash and other liquid assets, you may want to consider a fidelity bond. This type of insurance coverage is often called dishonesty insurance.

SURETY BONDS

This type of coverage is most often used by construction contractors. It provides monetary compensation in the event a contractor fails to perform as promised or misses a deadline as promised.

KIDNAP AND RANSOM

This type of insurance coverage is critical nowadays if you operate in a foreign country, especially the Middle East. If your company is operated from within the United States, you wouldn't need this type of coverage.

KEY EXECUTIVE LIFE INSURANCE

This type of insurance can reimburse your company for loss of services if a key person dies. This amount would assist you in recruiting and replacing your lost key employee.

PRODUCT LIABILITY INSURANCE

This type of insurance protects your business against claims for damages resulting from the use of your company's products. We hear of cases every day where consumers sue manufacturers, wholesalers, retailers, and service companies for alleged damages. This type of insurance is typically expensive. To help guard against product liability suits, you, as a small business owner, need to set your product standards very high and constantly assess the potential for liability associated with your products and services.

PROFESSIONAL LIABILITY INSURANCE

If you render any type of advice to the public, you should consider professional liability insurance. Doctors, dentists, accountants, and lawyers all have it. Many other services providers should also consider having this type of insurance. Service providers such as bookkeeping services, psychologists, management consultants, and others should consider it as well.

ITEMS TO CONSIDER WITH REVIEWING YOUR PROPERTY INSURANCE NEEDS:

Property (Leased, Rented, Borrowed, Consigned, Stored Off-Site, In Transit, And Owned)

Accounts receivable
Aircraft
Boilers
Bridges
Buildings, outside buildings, attached structures
Business records
Canopies
Carpeting

Cash and cash equivalents, such as stocks and bonds
Computers and other office equipment
Fences
Fixtures
Forklifts
Freezers
Furniture
Gates
Glass
HVAC equipment
Intellectual property such as patents, trademarks, copyrights
Inventory, including raw materials, works in process, and finished goods
Loading/unloading docks
Machinery
Parking structures
Ramps
Security systems
Signs
Telecommunications equipment
Vehicles
Warehouses
Watercraft
Window coverings

Perils to consider when looking at your property and liability insurance needs:
Arson
Burglary
Check fraud by employees
Check fraud by nonemployees
Civil unrest
Civil authority losses caused through the action of governments
Damage caused by aircraft
Earthquake
Embezzlement
Fire

Flood
Firestorm
Foundation collapse
Fungus and mold
Insect damage
Lightning (make sure that your computers and other sensitive equipment are covered)
Mudslide
Rain and hail
Robbery
Roof collapse
Sinkhole
Theft by employees
Theft by nonemployees
Terrorism
Vandalism
Windstorm

Areas of liability to consider when looking at your liability insurance needs:

Bodily injury
Errors and omissions
General liability
Officers and directors
Malpractice insurance
Pollution and contamination
Property damage caused by an employee

Potential employee insurance needs to consider:
Employee dental insurance
Employee health insurance
Employee life insurance
Key-man life insurance
Pension and profit sharing
Vision care

Workers' compensation
Potential auto insurance needs:
Fleet insurance
Uninsured motorists
Public liability and property damage

Special areas of insurance needs to consider:
Business interruption insurance
Kidnap and ransom insurance
Rent insurance

Insurance will be an integral part of your risk management. As a new business, you have limited resources, so you don't want to overspend for insurance, but you will want to minimize your risk. Become familiar with the ins and outs of insurance and you will be able to more effectively work with your insurance broker.

INTELLECTUAL PROPERTY OVERVIEW

As mentioned above, there are various forms of intellectual property that the government will help you protect. Patents, copyrights, and trademarks are designed to let you protect all of the hard work that you put into developing an asset. This is a complicated area of business and requires the services of an attorney. You can help your attorney by preparing a lot of the documentation for your patent yourself. I have increased the net worth of my company with the use of patents. Investors, employees, vendors, and customers are all somewhat in awe of patents. Patents seem to have a magical quality to them. I had a major toy concept that I developed, and the only way that I was able to attract investors was to have a patent for the product.

Documentation is critical to the protection of your intellectual property. It is important to keep all of your notes compiled while developing your invention. All of your notes may someday be called upon to support your patent, copyright, or trademark filings if there is ever a violation of them. You will want to include notes on how you came up with the idea as well as notes on how you built it, tested it, and made continuing improvements to the invention. You should use common sense and always date your notes and include witnesses where appropriate.

There are a few software programs on the market that will assist you in preparing your patents. Although they will actually prepare the patent in the format necessary for filing with the U.S. Patent and Trademark Office, you should still have an attorney review the documents and track them for you. Patents are currently taking 24.6 months to be approved. Once your patent is granted, there will also be periodic maintenance fees and filings that you will have to do to keep your patent current. Again, this is when you will want to have your attorney involved.

If you are going to draft a utility patent or a design patent, you might want to try using PatentEase software from Inventorprise, Inc. (www.inventorprise.com). It currently costs less than $400 and comes with CADPRO for drafting the drawings that are required to accompany your patent application. If you are drafting a provisional patent, you might want to try Patent Wizard from Neustel Law Offices, Ltd. (www.patentwizard.com). You can buy Patent Wizard for about $250. Patents can be very expensive to have drafted. I have one friend who lets her attorney draft her patents, and they typically cost her from $8,000 to $25,000 each. I use PatentEase and Patent Wizard and have my attorney review them. My patents usually cost from $1,000 to $3,000 each to have drafted.

There are basically six types of intellectual property protection: utility patents, provisional patents, design patents, trademarks/service marks, and copyrights.

UTILITY PATENT

This type of patent is granted to anyone who invents or discovers any new and useful process, machine, article of manufacture, or compositions of matters, or any new and useful improvement thereof. A utility patent is granted for 20 years. As of October 2005, the filing and examination fees for a utility patent are $215 if you qualify for small entity status (under 500 employees), and $430 if you do not qualify.

A patent for an invention is the grant of a property right to the inventor, issued by the United States Patent and Trademark Office. The term of a patent is 20 years (utility patent) from the date on which the application for the patent was filed in the United States.

The general right that you get, once a patent is granted to you, is "the right to exclude others from making, offering for sale, or selling" the invention in the United States or "importing" the invention into the United States. You are not granted the right to make, use, offer for sale, sell or import, but rather, the right to exclude others from making, using, offering for sales, selling, or importing the invention. Once you are issued a patent, you must enforce the patent without the aid of the United States Patent and Trademark Office. They will not help you enforce your patent rights. You must enforce your patent rights with the assistance of a patent attorney.

BENEFITS OF FILING PATENTS

There are several benefits to filing patents for your inventions. The major benefit is that it does help you establish ownership to all of the work that you put into developing your invention. It will not protect you against infringement by someone, but it will document your asset when and if you have to go to court to protect your invention. Investors also like to see that you have assets that are important enough to have patents granted. Patents tend to make your inventions seem "real" to outside investors. If you have worked hard to develop something that is patentable, then you will want to protect it. If your patent does attract attention and it does have utility in the marketplace, the patent will fortify your legal rights to it.

PROVISIONAL PATENT

Since June 8, 1995, theUnited States Patent and Trademark Office USPTO has offered inventors the option of filing a provisional application for patent, which was designed to provide a lower-cost first patent filing in the United States and to give U.S. applicants parity with foreign applicants. The main differences between a full utility patent and a provisional patent are:

> Provisional patent is good for one year but must then be perfected with a full utility patent.

> Provisional patents do not require the filing of claims with the patent. The claims for a utility patent are often the most difficult areas of the patent to draft. The claims in your utility patent will establish the boundaries or scope of your invention. They are somewhat like the boundaries in a deed for real estate. They will help you distinguish your invention from what is called *prior art*.

> Prior art is defined as "the state of knowledge existing or publicly available either before the date of an invention or more than one year prior to the patent application date."[41]

> The U. S. Patent and Trademark Office filing and examination fees

---

41   David Pressman and Richard Stim, *Nolo's Patents for Beginners*. Berkeley, CA:Nolo Press, pg. 2/9, 2002.

for a provision patent are only $110 (as of March 31, 2010) if you qualify for small entity or sole inventor status, and $220 if you have 500 or more employees. Check with the U.S. Patent office as fees and definitions change regularly.

Provisional applications provide the means to establish an early effective filing date in a patent application and permit the term "Patent Pending" to be applied in connection with the invention. Provisional Patents may not be filed for design inventions.

You then have up to 12 months to file a non-provisional application for a patent. Provisional patents are NOT examined on their merits. A provisional application will become abandoned by the operation of law 12 months from its filing date. The 12-month pendency for a provisional application is not counted toward the 20-year term of a patent application, which relies on the filing date of the provisional application

DESIGN PATENT

This patent may be granted to anyone who invents a new, original, and ornamental design for an article of manufacture. A design patent is granted for 14 years from the date of patent grant.

There are considerable overlaps for copyright and design patents since aesthetics are the basis for both forms of protection. Design patents are used primarily where the design of the object is inseparable from the object. Copyright can be used for almost any written or artistic creation, whether it is inseparable from the underlying object or not. Basically, copyright can be used for a design that is strictly ornamental in nature. A feature properly covered by a copyright may or may not have a role in the overall function of the underlying object.

PLANT PATENT

This is a special category of patent granted to anyone who invents or discovers and asexually reproduces any distinct and new variety of plants. Although this seems like an odd category for patents, I can't think of any product much more important than plants (think oxygen, food, clothing, beauty, a reminder of God's artistry).

WHAT CAN BE PATENTED?

In the language of the statute, any person who "invents or discovers any new and useful process, machine, manufacture, or composition of matter, or any new and useful improvement thereof, may obtain a patent" subject to the conditions and requirements of the law. The word *process* is defined by law as a process, act, or method and primarily includes industrial or technical processes. The term *machine* used in the same statute needs no explanation. The term *manufacture* refers to articles that are made and includes all manufactured articles. The term *composition of matter* relates to chemical compositions and may include mixtures of ingredients as well as new chemical compounds. These classes of subject matter taken together include practically everything that is made by man and the processes for making the products.

The patent law specifies that the subject matter must be "useful." The term *useful* in this connection refers to the condition that the subject matter has a useful purpose and also includes operativeness; that is, a machine that will not operate to perform the intended purpose would not be called useful, and therefore would not be granted a patent.

Interpretations of the statute by the courts have defined the limits of the field of subject matter that can be patented; thus, it has been held that the laws of nature, physical phenomena, and abstract ideas are not patentable subject matter.

A patent cannot be obtained upon a mere idea or suggestion. The patent is granted upon the new machine, manufacture, etc., as has been said, and not upon the idea or suggestion of the new machine. A complete description of the actual machine or other subject matter for which a patent is sought is required.

NOVELTY AND NON-OBVIOUSNESS CONDITIONS FOR OBTAINING A PATENT

In order for an invention to be patentable, it must be new as defined in the patent law, which provides that an invention cannot be patented if: "(a) the invention was known or used by others in this country, or patented or described in a printed publication in this or a foreign country, before the invention thereof by the applicant for patent" or "(b) the invention was patented or described in a printed publication in this or a foreign country or in public use or on sale in this country more than one year prior to the application for patent in the United States..."

If the invention has been described in a printed publication anywhere in the world, or if it has been in public use or on sale in this country before the date that the applicant made his/her invention, a patent cannot be obtained. If the invention has been described in a printed publication anywhere, or has been in public use or on sale in this country more than one year before the date on which an application for patent is filed in this country, a patent cannot be obtained. In this connection, it is immaterial when the invention was made, or whether the printed publication or public use was by the inventor himself/herself or by someone else. If the inventor describes the invention in a printed publication or uses the invention publicly, or places it on sale, he/she must apply for a patent before one year has gone by, otherwise any right to the patent will be lost. The inventor must file on the date of public use or disclosure, however, in order to preserve patent rights in many foreign countries.

TRADEMARK OR SERVICE MARK

A trademark is a word, name, symbol, or device that is used in trade with goods to indicate the sources of the goods and to distinguish them from the goods of others. A service mark is the same as a trademark except that it identifies and distinguishes the source of a service rather than a product.

There is often confusion as to the difference between TM and the R within the circle, ®. Use of the TM and the SM symbols may be governed by local, state, or foreign laws and the laws of a pertinent jurisdiction to identify the marks that a party claims rights to. The federal registration symbol, the R enclosed within a circle, may be used once the mark is actually registered in the U.S. Patent and Trademark Office. Even though an application is pending, the registration symbol may not be used before the mark has actually become registered.

For a trademark registration to remain valid, an Affidavit of Use must be filed: (1) between the fifth and sixth year following registration and (2) within the year before the end of every ten-year period after the date of registration. Assuming that affidavit of use is timely filed, registrations granted prior to November 16, 1989 have a 20-year term, and registrations granted on or after November 16, 1989 have a 10-year term. This is also true for the renewal periods; renewals granted prior to November 16, 1989 have a 20-year term, and renewals granted on or after November 16, 1989 have a 10-year term.

COPYRIGHT

Copyright is a form of protection provided to the authors of "original works of authorship" including literary, dramatic, musical, artistic, and certain other intellectual works, both published and unpublished. A work that is created (fixed in tangible form for the first time) on or after January 1, 1978 is automatically protected from the moment of its creation and is ordinarily given a term enduring from the author's life plus an additional 70 years after the author's death.

Copyrightable works include the following categories:

1. Literary works
2. Musical works, including any accompanying words
3. Dramatic works, including any accompanying music
4. Pantomimes and choreographic works
5. Pictorial, graphic, and sculptural works
6. Motion pictures and other audiovisual works
7. Sound recordings
8. Architectural works

The Copyright Act of 1976 generally gives the owner of copyright the exclusive right to reproduce the copyrighted work, to prepare derivative works, to distribute copies or phonorecords of the copyrighted work, to perform the copyrighted work publicly, or to display the copyrighted work publicly.

The copyright protects the form of expression rather than the subject matter of the writing. For example, a description of a machine could be copyrighted, but this would only prevent others from copying the description; it would not prevent others from writing a description of their own or from making and using the machine. Copyrights are registered by the Copyright Office of the Library of Congress.

You will work hard to build your business. Don't let a single, unforeseen event take it all away from you. As part of managing the resources that God has put at your disposal, you need to make sure that you manage your risk in a conservative but aggressive manner.

Conclusion

If you have gotten to this point in the book, you are probably pretty serious about starting your own business. Don't let anyone discourage you from moving forward with your plans. There will always be naysayers. When the telephone was first invented, a publication in the telegraph industry, *The Telegrapher*, said in the 1870s, "No direct practical application (for the telephone)." Mr. Albert Einstein summed it up very well with one of his famous one-liners, "Great spirits have always encountered violent opposition from mediocre minds." If you are a Bob Dylan fan, he once said, "Miles Davis (was) booed. Hank Williams was booed. Stravinsky was booed. You're nobody if you don't get booed sometimes." The bottom line is that if you have spent sufficient time in prayer and you have God as your partner, just smile at the naysayers because, who knows, someday they just might work for you.

Darrell Griffin, Sr. is a Certified Public Accountant, (retired/inactive) and received his MBA from California State University, Stanislaus graduating with a 4.00 GPA. He has been consulting to small business for over 30 years. He currently divides his time as a consultant to small businesses and as a writer. He is the author of "Last Journey" (Editors of Barnes and Noble selected it as one of their 10 best non-fiction books for 2009), "Trouble Bound" (Winter 2010). He lives in Southern California where he attends Shepherd of the Hills church in Porter Ranch, CA, with his wife and two children. He has four grown children.

Index